New Frontiers in Regional Science: Asian Perspectives

Volume 13

New Frontiers in Regional Science: Asian Perspectives

This series is a constellation of works by scholars in the field of regional science and in related disciplines specifically focusing on dynamism in Asia.

Asia is the most dynamic part of the world. Japan, Korea, Taiwan, and Singapore experienced rapid and miracle economic growth in the 1970s. Malaysia, Indonesia, and Thailand followed in the 1980s. China, India, and Vietnam are now rising countries in Asia and are even leading the world economy. Due to their rapid economic development and growth, Asian countries continue to face a variety of urgent issues including regional and institutional unbalanced growth, environmental problems, poverty amidst prosperity, an ageing society, the collapse of the bubble economy, and deflation, among others.

Asian countries are diversified as they have their own cultural, historical, and geographical as well as political conditions. Due to this fact, scholars specializing in regional science as an inter- and multidiscipline have taken leading roles in providing mitigating policy proposals based on robust interdisciplinary analysis of multifaceted regional issues and subjects in Asia. This series not only will present unique research results from Asia that are unfamiliar in other parts of the world because of language barriers, but also will publish advanced research results from those regions that have focused on regional and urban issues in Asia from different perspectives.

The series aims to expand the frontiers of regional science through diffusion of intrinsically developed and advanced modern regional science methodologies in Asia and other areas of the world. Readers will be inspired to realize that regional and urban issues in the world are so vast that their established methodologies still have space for development and refinement, and to understand the importance of the interdisciplinary and multidisciplinary approach that is inherent in regional science for analyzing and resolving urgent regional and urban issues in Asia.

Topics under consideration in this series include the theory of social cost and benefit analysis and criteria of public investments, socioeconomic vulnerability against disasters, food security and policy, agro-food systems in China, industrial clustering in Asia, comprehensive management of water environment and resources in a river basin, the international trade bloc and food security, migration and labor market in Asia, land policy and local property tax, information and communication technology planning, consumer "shop-around" movements, and regeneration of downtowns, among others.

More information about this series at http://www.springer.com/series/13039

Tohru Naito
Editor

Sustainable Growth and Development in a Regional Economy

Springer

Editor
Tohru Naito
The University of Tokushima
Tokushima, Tokushima, Japan

ISSN 2199-5974 ISSN 2199-5982 (electronic)
New Frontiers in Regional Science: Asian Perspectives
ISBN 978-4-431-55293-2 ISBN 978-4-431-55294-9 (eBook)
DOI 10.1007/978-4-431-55294-9

Library of Congress Control Number: 2015949141

Springer Tokyo Heidelberg New York Dordrecht London

Printed on acid-free paper

Springer Japan KK is part of Springer Science+Business Media (www.springer.com)

Preface

Recently our society has become more and more complex. Most developing countries are troubled by serious economic differentials or environmental issues. At the same time, it is impossible for developed countries to ignore social security and issues involving the declining birth rate and aging population. So far, most researchers have considered these as issues within a single country. However, recently the economic borders among countries have almost been dissolved by trade agreements, development of transportation, and so on. Consequently, it is now easier for labor and goods to move among countries or regions.

Because the behavior of one country easily affects other countries in the borderless economy, each country has to take account of the economic policies of others and must devise economic policies carefully. For instance, it is not easy to derive optimal policies within environmental economics under such a complex society when we consider a sustainable environmental policy that will not prevent economic growth. This is because most environmental issues are caused by our economic activities. Although social security is required to make economic growth sustainable, adequate prescriptions for this issue depend on the situation of each country. Thus, the economic policy should not be considered only by researchers of public economics.

Although one of a social scientist's missions is to provide a prescription to establish a better society, it is difficult to resolve many kinds of issues in our society and to present appropriate prescriptions for them from a particular point of view. Because economists are also social scientists, we have a duty to achieve this mission. The research presented in this book is a result of collaboration by economists specializing in different fields. For instance, it is not easy to derive optimal policies within environmental economics alone under such complex social conditions when we consider a sustainable environmental policy. In this case, it is necessary to collaborate on a project with those whose specialties are environmental economics, economic growth theory, development economics, and so on.

We understand that it is effective to research these complex issues and to pursue appropriate prescriptions for them in collaboration with researchers in different research fields, and we gradually constructed an academic network through research meetings, workshops, and conferences. Some of the authors of this book belong to the same research project and are continuing it now. Some authors are already working jointly. Thus, our research network is embodied in this book.

We were able to carry out our research smoothly because we were helped by various kinds of support. First of all, we are grateful that the Japan section of RSAI and Springer Japan gave us an opportunity to publish this book. Each chapter of the book is based on studies that each author presented in academic research meetings, conferences, and workshops. The authors received useful comments and suggestions in those venues, and we thank the discussants and participants. Moreover, many people have supported us in the publication of this book. We thank Moriki Hosoe, Keisuke Osumi, Nobuhiro Okuno, Yoshiro Higano, Ki-Dong Lee, Makoto Tawada, Akira Yakita, Dao-Zhi Zeng, Hideo Koide, Gerhard Glomm, Ichiro Daitoh, Isao Miura, Junya Matsunami, Kazutoshi Miyazawa, Makoto Okamura, Ming Hsin Lin, Noriaki Matsushima, Se-il Mun, Tadashi Yagi, Takao Ohkawa, Takatoshi Tabuchi, Tatsuaki Kuroda, Tomoya Mori, Toshihiro Matsumura, Yasunori Fujita, Dan Sasaki, and Daisaku Goto. We are particularly grateful to Hikaru Ogawa, who is the leader of our research project and helped us to complete this book. Without his academic and financial support, this book of research results could not have been published.

Finally we have also received some financial supports from Grants-in-Aid for Scientific Research (KAKENHI) in Japan and the National Research Foundation of Korea as follows: Grant-in-Aid for Scientific Research (A) (25245042), Grant-in-Aid for Scientific Research (B) (25285091, 22330095), Grant-in-Aid for Scientific Research (C) (25516007, 25380303), Grant-in-Aid for Young Scientists (B) (26780148, 22730202), and NRF (2014S1A3A2044643). We are grateful for their financial supports.

Tokushima, Japan
March 2015

Tohru Naito

Contents

Chapter 1
Introduction and Summary

Tohru Naito

1.1 Introduction

Countries or regions playing leading roles worldwide have traded places many times during human history. Countries or regions such as Greece and the Roman Empire, facing the Mediterranean Sea, played leading roles on the front stage of the history in ancient times. Moreover, Spain or Portugal held center stage during the Age of Geographical Discovery. European countries, including Spain and Portugal, made inroads into Asian countries and South America to obtain spices such as pepper and mineral resources such as gold and silver in the fifteenth century. Although the thrust of European countries at the beginning of the Age of Geographical Discovery was trade among non-European countries, European countries colonized those countries. Eventually, Spain and Portugal fell to ruin after that the Spanish Armada was defeated by the large English Royal Navy in 1588. The United Kingdom reigned over the world economy after the rise of the Industrial Revolution in eighteenth century. The U.K. promoted industrialization earlier than other countries and overcame competition with other countries. In fact, the U.K. was the center of the world economy during the eighteenth and nineteenth centuries. Eventually, because its many colonies in Asia and Africa became independent after the two World Wars of the twentieth century, the U.K. lost its capability of sustaining economic growth despite being a victorious country. Moreover, most European countries had been battlefields of World War II. Industries of many kinds were crushed by war and destruction of various kinds. Consequently, their productivity plummeted, requiring time and effort to restore it to pre-war levels.

T. Naito (✉)
Institute of Socio-Arts and Science, Tokushima University, 1-1 Minamijosanjima-cho
Tokushima city, Tokushima 770-8502, Japan
e-mail: naito@tokushima-u.ac.jp

T. Naito (ed.), *Sustainable Growth and Development in a Regional Economy*,
New Frontiers in Regional Science: Asian Perspectives 13,
DOI 10.1007/978-4-431-55294-9_1

As for the United States, the sudden fall of stock prices on the New York exchange signalled the world financial crisis of 1929. The ensuing Great Depression in the United States spread globally. This recession affected the economic policies most countries and exacerbated the origins of World War II. For example, the U.K. and France organized a bloc economy by setting high tariffs or by making trade agreements to save their own economies. Germany and Italy chose fascism because both countries had lost all of their colonies after World War I and had borne a large amount of indemnification through provisions of the Treaty of Versailles. Consequently, their behaviors might be seen as triggers of World War II. As described above, most European countries sustained severe economic damage irrespective of whether they had been victorious or defeated. In stark contrast, the United States was not a main battlefield. Its productivity was not degraded in the least because of World War II. In fact, the United States took its place at the center of the world economy, replacing the U.K. after World War II. Although the United States and capitalist countries competed with socialistic countries such as the Union of Soviet Socialist Republics, most socialistic countries failed to control their respective economies, and ground to a halt by the end of the twentieth century. Nobody can doubt that the United States anchored the world economy after World War II and has pulled the world economy forward consistently through the latter twentieth century. Although the United States has worked through severe trade deficits and budget deficits, it has remained at the top position of the world economy. In fact, GDP in the United States was about 6,724 billion dollars in 2013, which is the highest worldwide. Nevertheless, other countries have been in hot pursuit of the U.S economic dominance through rapid economic growth since the *Bankruptcy of Lehman Brothers* that occurred in 2009.

Recently Asian countries have experienced rapid economic growth. Japan was the only Asian country to have established industrialization before World War II. Although Japan had among the poorest countries in the nineteenth century, Japan succeeded in catching up to other developed countries, such as those in Europe, or the United States, because it had acquired interests in eastern Asia and the Pacific Ocean through victories in the Russo–Japanese War and World War I. However, Japan lost all overseas interests from its defeat during and after World War II. Thereafter, the Japanese economy revived itself through the emergency demands of the Korean War, achieving an economic growth rate higher than 10 % from the 1950s until the oil shock in 1973. Although the progress of the Japanese economy was halted by the oil crisis in 1973 once, stable growth continued after the oil crisis. The glory days of the Japanese economy ended suddenly in 1991. Although the Japanese economy had achieved growth again in the 1980s, the bubble economy in Japan burst in the 1990s. It has taken more than 20 years for the Japanese economy to recover.

As Asian countries aside from Japan gained independence following World War II, they have developed their respective economies. The NIES countries including Korea, Taiwan, Hong Kong, and Singapore attracted worldwide attention during the 1970s. ASEAN countries such as Malaysia, Thailand, Indonesia, and the Philippines achieved rapid economic growth during the 1980s. China introduced market mechanisms to Chinese economy in the 1980s, although political systems in China have been maintained. The Chinese economy emerged even more strongly in 2000s, when its GDP in China overtook that of Japan, making it the second largest economy in the world. Although China has played the role of the world's factory, it has become an extremely important country in the world economy because it has a huge market with more than one billion population. Although each country's economy has undergone a transition through history, it is expected that Asian countries will serve an even more important role in the global economy.

Economic growth has brought wealth to us and has improved human society. However, it has brought not only benefits but also costs to us. Humanity cannot be blind to the negative aspects brought by economic growth to achieve sustainable economic growth. Humanity has made sacrifices in exchange for economic growth. Using fossil fuels has dramatically improved industrial productivity, but has caused severe environmental issues such as air pollution, global warming, and acid rain. For instance, population growth has brought benefits as a population bonus. However, agglomeration of population to a particular region or city has led to the generation of a dualistic economy and has brought differential and urban unemployment. Economically developed countries must show resolve to tackle urgent issues related to aging population and low birth rates to sustain social security systems. In economically developing countries, population growth presents numerous social issues that must be addressed. Asian country populations, which are markedly larger than those in other regions, must achieve economic growth based on the recognition of these disadvantages.

Considering this economic backdrop, we can provide prescriptions for readers to pursue sustainable economic growth in the region. This book comprises two parts. Part I presents a basic model required to analyze the issues of economic growth and regions. Applied economic models in Part II are based on models of this part. We overview basic models to analyze economic growth, spatial economy, social security, transportation network, and the environment. In Part II, we assess prescriptions for a sustainable economy by analyzing the applied model. It is necessary to elucidate the population, urbanization, and other matters in particular countries to consider sustainable economic growth in each countries. We construct an economic model and analyze it with the Asian economy in mind. Therefore, we refer to population, urbanization, agglomeration of Asian countries in the next section.

1.1.1 Population in Asian Countries

This section presents an overview of population, urbanization, agglomeration, and environment in Asian countries. First, we refer to a transition of population in Asian countries. Most Asian countries became independent of their respective suzerains during the 1950s–1970s. After gaining independence, their populations uniformly increased. The populations of Asian countries were about 1,400 million in 1950.

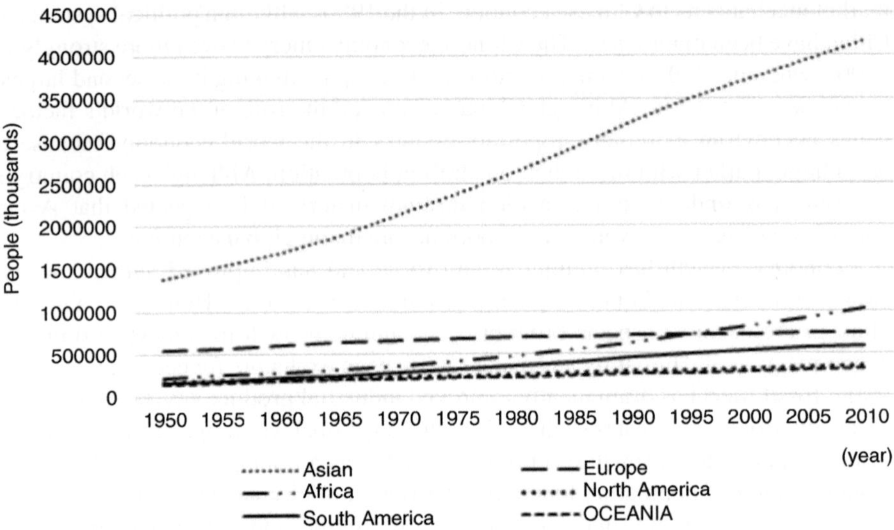

Fig. 1.1 Population in Asia and other areas (Source: **UN** World Urbanization Prospects: 2014 Revision)

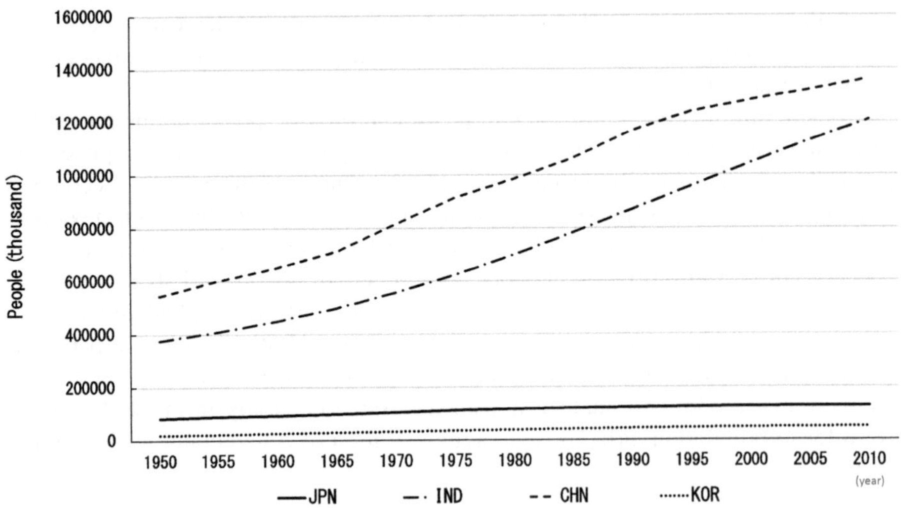

Fig. 1.2 Population growth in major Asian countries (Source: **UN** World Urbanization Prospects: The 2014 Revision)

However, they increased to about 4,165 million in 2010. Figure 1.1 shows the population in each region during 1950–2010. As Fig. 1.1 shows, population growth in Asia is higher than in other areas except for Asia. From Fig. 1.1, it is apparent that the population in Asia is increasing. However, the degree of population growth differs among countries. Figure 1.2 presents the transition of population growth of

China, India, Korea, and Japan. As Fig. 1.2 shows, the populations in Japan and Korea have not increased rapidly, although that in China and India continues to increase. According to Statistics Korea and the Japan Statistics Bureau, the fertility of Korea in 2013 was 1.19. That of Japan was 1.43. Now both countries confront severe issues with the declining birth rate. However, population growth in China and India has increased since 1950. Generally speaking, the rate of population in developing countries is higher than that in developed countries.

1.1.2 Urbanization in Asian Countries

Urbanization often affects human society, economy, environment, and so on, irrespective of whether it occurs in an economically developed country or developing country. In the general population, it tends to produce agglomeration in particular cities or regions as the economy in each country shows growth. Presuming that we define the ratio of urban population to the total population as urbanization rate, the urbanization rates of Asia were 16.8 % in 1950, that rate increases to 41.8 % in 2010. It is about 2.5 times the rate in 1950. Considering that the urbanization rate of each region except for Asia is about 75 %, it is possible that the urbanization rate in Asia will increase this percentage.

Next we consider the transition of urbanization rates in major countries. Figure 1.3 depicts the urbanization rate transition in 1950, 1970, 1990, and 2010. In

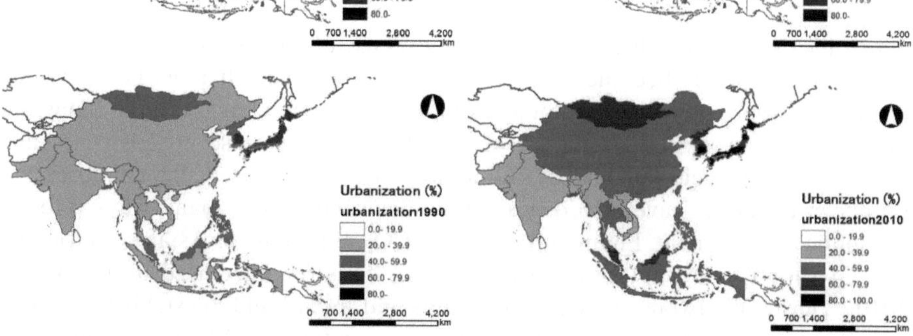

Fig. 1.3 Urbanization trends in Asia during 1950–2010 (Source: UN World Urbanization Prospects: The 2014 Revision)

1950, countries in which urbanization rate was higher than 50 %, are Japan, Korea, and city states such as Hong Kong, and Singapore. However, the urbanization rates of Vietnam, Laos, Cambodia, and Thailand are low. The only countries in eastern Asia and Southeast Asia where urbanization rates were lower than 20 % were Bhutan and Nepal in 2010.

1.1.3 Agglomeration in Asian Countries

In a previous section, we explained how urbanization extends itself in Asian countries. However, we do not show why population agglomerates in particular cities or regions using economic theory. Agglomeration of population in particular cities or regions does not occur randomly. Traditional international economics theory has been based on assumptions of constant returns of scale and no transportation costs of goods or input factors such as labor and capital. Although traditional international economics has addressed trade between countries, spatial factors have been ignored.

Krugman [5] and Fujita, Krugman, and Venables [3] constructed what is known as the new economic theory by combining traditional trade theory with economic geography. They consider the issue of why industries agglomerate in particular places. Spatial economics, on which some models in this book are based, plays an important role in resolving how spatial structures are determined endogenously and how some industry resources and facilities are allocated geographically. Spatial economics take account of product differentiation, increasing returns to scale, and transportation costs, in addition to traditional trade theory.

1.1.4 Environments in Asian Countries

Economic development has occurred at the expense of damage to the environment. Global warming has become a severe problem worldwide. It must be addressed immediately and intensively. Although European countries advanced the Industrial Revolution using fossil fuels, the use of fossil fuels has caused severe environmental problems such as acid rain and air pollution in these countries. Asian countries and European countries have also degraded the environments in many ways through economic development. Figure 1.4 describes CO_2 emissions in Asian countries.As Fig. 1.4 shows, CO_2 emissions in most Asian countries increased during 1980–2010.[1] During the twenty-first century, China and India stand to establish the most remarkable economic development among Asian countries. When we analyze the

[1] CO_2 emissions in Fig. 1.4 are not emissions per capita but gross emissions.

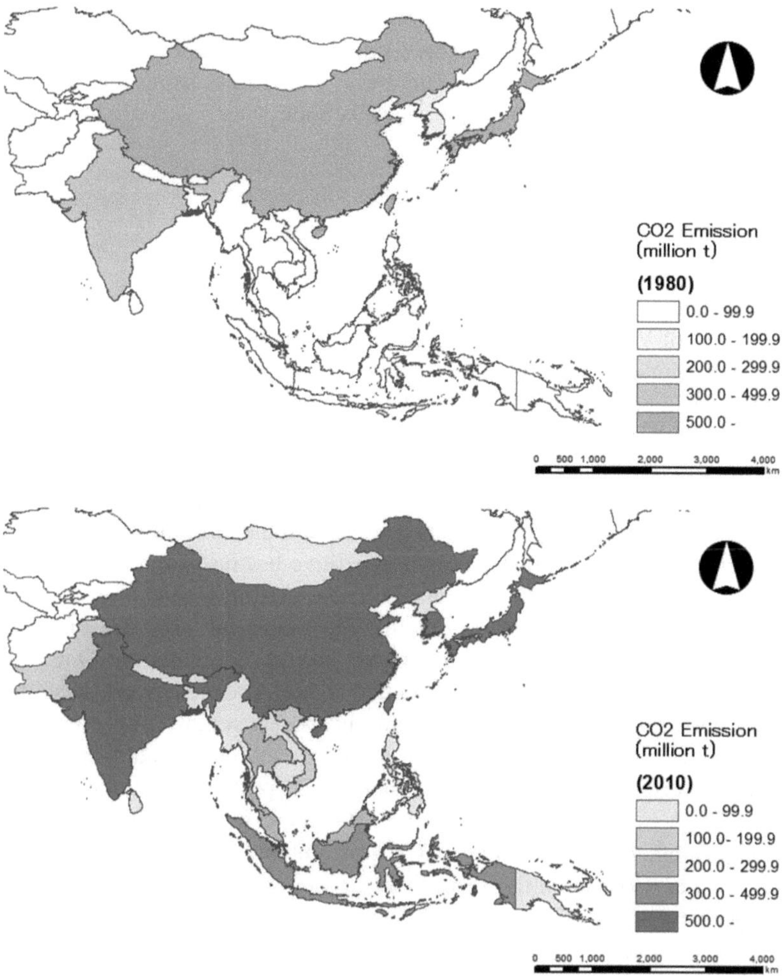

Fig. 1.4 CO_2 emissions in Asian countries (Source: The World Bank 2014)

environment, scrupulous attention must be devoted to analysis of their effects. For instance, recent emphasis on air pollution has shown that the PM2.5 issue has affected not only China domestically, but also eastern Asian countries. The PM2.5 particulates are created by the combustion of fossil fuels. They are harmful to human health. It is difficult to resolve this environmental issue because only environmental policies of a particular country establish an optimal situation. Some environmental regulations might stall economic growth. Therefore, the regulatory authorities must take account of the effects of environmental regulation on economic activities. When analyzing the environment, it is necessary to devote scrupulous attention to its analysis because environmental problems include specific properties in economic analysis, i.e., externality, transboundary pollution, free rider problems, and so on. To achieve a sustainable economy, it is impossible to ignore the attendant environmental problems. Therefore, we address some models including environmental factors in some chapters of this book.

1.1.5 Transportation in Asian Countries

We have already described the urbanization in Asian countries that has progressed since the end of World War II. Although the diversity of goods and economies of scale have had major impacts on regional agglomeration, decreasing transportation costs play an important role in economic development. Decreasing transportation costs facilitate movement of people and goods between regions. In fact, economic borders in Europe have disappeared because of decreasing transportation costs. Recently, the intensity of competition among transportation firms has been rising in Asian countries. That competition has decreased transportation fares. Particularly, airline markets in Asia are extremely competitive because some low-cost carriers (LCCs) have entered airline markets in Asia. Airlines constitute a distinctive industry with the transportation domain. The industrial structure of the airline industry in the United States has changed through deregulation. One reason is mergers. Another is a new network called a hub–spoke network system. Each company performs restructuring of operating routes, setting a specific airport as a hub, with radially organized feeder routes to increase load factors. Airlines in Asian countries have reconstructed their own operating routes by setting hub airports, which include Narita, Singapore, Incheon, Peking, Shanghai, Bangkok, and Hong Kong. Recently, some LCCs have entered international and domestic airline markets. Consequently, incumbent airlines must consider the routing and airfare of these carriers for network operations. Although transportation costs are often given exogenously as a parameter in spatial economics or international economics, transportation costs (fares) are determined endogenously by the transportation industry behavior. Moreover, they depend on relations among regions. Transportation costs are crucially important to determine the strategies of industries in respective countries. Therefore, it is necessary to consider this transportation network carefully. We devote more attention to behaviors of these transport sectors in several chapters of this book.

1.2 Summary in This Book

This book is composed of two parts. On of them is the part of basic theories to analyze sustainable growth of regional economy. Particularly, we show the basic model of some categories, which are spatial economics, development economics, endogenous economic growth theory, environmental economics, and network economics. Part I plays a role to introduce readers the benchmark models of advanced models to be developed in Part II.

1.2.1 Part I

In Chap. 2 , we overview the basic model of spatial economy. Spatial economics is developed by taking account of a distance to be one of most important factors in space, which has been ignored in traditional trade theory. Krugman [5] or Fujita, Krugman, and Venables [3] introduced increasing returns of scale, transportation cost, into love of variety into the models, and explained regional agglomeration endogenously. Moreover, Ottaviano, Tabuchi, and Thisse [8] constructed the model to be solvable analytically. Therefore, we show this model as basic spatial model in this chapter.

In Chap. 3, we overview the basic dualistic economy model. Although a dualistic economy in developing countries have been a serious problem since the end of World War II, Lewis [6] paid his attention to the issues of dualistic economy for the first time. Since Lewis [6] assume that an unlimited labor supply is available at subsistence wage, he does not describe a mechanism to occur urban unemployment. However, Lewis [6] did not describe urban unemployment occurred in the world's developing countries at that time. On the other hand, Harris and Todaro [4] succeed to explain a mechanism by which urban unemployment occurred endogenously in the framework of a dualistic economy. Therefore, we overview Harris and Todaro [4] as the basic dualistic economy model in this chapter. This basic dualistic economy model is applied in Chaps. 9 and 14.

In Chap. 4, we discussed long run growth based on neoclassical growth model. The long-run growth rate is shown the growth rate of population and/or the technological progress. If we assume that productivity increases at an exogenously given rate, say g, the long-run growth rates become positive and we can ward off zero growth. However, we cannot explain how and why technology always improves at the rate, g. Moreover, we discuss the overlapping generations model to examine the intergenerational issues. In the overlapping generations model, introducing individual saving behavior into the model with multiple generations, we can discuss the economic behavior at each period explicitly.

In Chap. 5, we explain the mechanism of productivity improvement endogenously in the model. This model is called as endogenous growth model. We discuss a simple endogenous growth theory based on the Diamond's [2] OLG model. The output of final goods depends on capital, labor and productivity. We assume that knowledge stock accumulates and productivity increases if some resources are devoted to the research sector. That is, we assume that productivity increase is induced by the R&D activities. The economy increases total factor productivity

(TFP) if research activities are carried out appropriately, It is shown that the economy can grow perpetually if the improved TFP can avoid the diminishing returns in the long-run.

In Chap. 6 we consider the timing of emission tax policy. Emission tax timing affects the market outcome and the environment. Chapter 6 examines emission tax policy in the monopoly market in a setting where the regulator has precommitment ability/inability for an emission tax. Furthermore, in the presence (absence) of such precommitment abilities, we explore the effects on monopolist's environmental R&D behavior, emission level, and social welfare. In this chapter, we first explain time-consistent emission tax policy for a monopolist, and also demonstrated that a negative emission tax (i.e., emission subsidy) can be partially justified. Second, these analyzes reveal the existence of the emission-reducing effect in the monopoly market. Furthermore, this chapter investigates whether the government's precommitment to an emission tax promotes the monopolist's environmental R&D and enhances social welfare. The analytical framework in chapter will be extended to a differentiated Cournot duopoly model in Chap. 13.

In Chap. 7, we present the basic model of wastes market. Recently the lack of final wastes incinerators owned by local governments has been afraid due to the increase of wastes in the future in Japan. For achievement of sustainable economic society, it is very important to reform the economic system of mass production, mass consumption and mass disposal, and to establish a resource recycling society. Needless to say, if waste is properly processed, serious environmental problems do not occur. However, there are many illegal processing such as illegal dumping in reality. It is necessary to analyze the behavior of waste disposal logically in order to reduce such an illegal waste disposal. In this chapter, we construct the model to describe waste disposal behavior. Moreover, this model will be applied in Chap. 14 of Part II.

In Chap. 8, we introduce a model to analyze not only the airline network formation problem but also the hub location problem by using a theory of industrial organization. This chapter first derives a carrier's strategies (i.e., related to airfare and flight frequency) to maximize profit and the profit amount. Then, we analyze whether a monopolistic carrier chooses a point-to-point network or a hub–spoke network with one hub airport, and analyze what airport becomes the hub. Additionally, we derive the socially preferable network formation and socially preferable hub location. The main results obtained in this chapter are as follows. When the additional travel time cost for connecting passengers is large (small), the monopolistic carrier adopts the point-to-point (hub–spoke) network. With regard to the hub location problem, the monopolistic carrier does not always choose the hub airport to minimize the potential number of connecting passengers. Additionally, the socially preferable hub airport is not always the airport that minimizes the potential number of connecting passengers. The basic model in this chapter will be applied in Chap. 10.

1.2.2 Part II

Chapter 9 extend the basic dualistic economy by combining it with mixed monopolistic competition model. Recently, most of public firms have privatized regardless of developing countries or developed countries. In fact, governments need pay close attention to public firm's privatization because it affects industrial structure, employment, and so on. Mixed oligopoly is the situation, in which a public firm competes with private firms in the common market. A public firm determines his behavior to maximize the social welfare though private firms pursue their profit under mixed oligopoly. Many studies have been accumulated in Industrial Organization. For instance, De Fraja and Delbono [1] compare a mixed oligopoly in which a public firm is full nationalized, with the pure oligopoly. Moreover, Matsumura [7] considers a model in which the public firm maximizes the weighted average of social welfare and profit as the objective function and shows that the partial privatization of public firm is optimal. However, there are a few studies to associate this mixed oligopoly model with spatial economic or development economics. In this chapter we synthesize this mixed oligopoly and dualistic economy model, and analyze the effect of public firm's privatization on urban unemployment rate or social welfare.

Chapter 10 addresses both the incumbent's and entrant's operating route. We assume that three markets exists and that the potential number of one market is smaller than that of the other market. Considering this situation, Chap. 10 demonstrates following. The subgame perfect Nash equilibrium with regard to the entry route decision is described below. When the difference in the potential number of passengers between two markets is not small, the incumbent carrier (or the major carrier) enters a route that has a smaller potential number of passengers and the entrant carrier (or the regional carrier) enters a route that has a greater potential number of passengers. However, when this difference is small, both the major carrier and the regional carrier enter the route that has a smaller potential number of passengers.

Chapter 11 presents a simple overlapping generations model with political corruption and technological progress to consider problems related to sustainable growth. The dynamic behavior of the economy resembles that of the neoclassical growth model if productivity of the R & D sector is low and political power of capital owners who would like to preserve their own vested interests is strong: long-run growth rate becomes 0. However, the per-capita growth rate becomes positive if productivity of the R & D sector is high and political power of the capital owner is weak. We consider the case in which interest groups make a political donation to prevent a government from introducing taxes that increase the future productivity but sacrifice today's consumption. The government accepts political contributions and sets back the introduction of taxes if the benefit of such contributions is high. The economy might stagnate in the long run even if it has the capability of achieving sustainable growth if so. Therefore, an uncorrupted government becomes an important determinant of sustainable growth.

Chapter 12 considers the fertility. Many developed countries face the fertility declining and governments try to recovery it.To do that, governments give parents the incentive to have more children. Among others, the factors not to have children are the raising cost for children, the education cost, the opportunity cost which parents cannot receive the income during the raising and the saving after retirement. On the first part of this chapter, when governments provide public support for children (In-kind) and public subsidy for children (Cash), the effects of such policies on fertility and social security are examined. Allocation changing from public subsidy to public support at the constant tax rate enhances the fertility but decreases the economic growth rate. Additionally, when the effects of decreasing public subsidy on consumption are equal to that of increasing public support for children on fertility, social welfare is maximized in this model.

On the second part of this chapter, introducing a fertility decision and child care cost into an overlapping generations model with public education and social security, we examine the effects of these public policies on fertility. We show that an increase in income tax, which finances social security benefits and public investment in education, increases fertility. On the other hand, with a constant tax rate, a change in the allocation from social security benefits to public investment in education decreases fertility and, with a constant social security tax, the effect of education tax on fertility is neutral.

Chapter 13 extends a time-consistent emission tax model examined in Chap. 6. This chapter presents examination of a differentiated Cournot duopoly model in a setting in which the government has no precommitment ability for an emissions tax. Furthermore, under the assumption of end-of-pipe technology and no R&D spillover effect, we provide a welfare comparison between two R&D regimes: environmental R&D competition and environmental R&D cartelization. Results show the following facts. First, when environmental damage is slight, and the degree of product differentiation is large enough, environmental R&D cartelization is socially more preferable. In contrast, when environmental damage is severe, and the degree of product differentiation is small enough, environmental R&D competition is socially more preferred. Second, both firms have always some incentives for R&D cartelization. Third, negative emission tax (i.e., emission subsidy) might be partially justified, if environmental damage is slight sufficiently. Moreover, Chap. 13 proves the regulatory environment in which a time-consistent emission subsidy can reduce total emissions more than the case of *laissez-faire*. Finally, policy implications derived from results of theoretical investigations in Chap. 13 are considered. At the same time, weak points of Japanese competition policy are discussed.

Chapter 14 presents the recycling activities and unemployment in economically developing countries by applying the Chaps. 3 and 7. Harris and Todaro [4] reported that fixed wage levels that are higher in urban areas than in rural areas might cause migration from rural areas to urban areas and increase unemployment in urban areas. We consider how a subsidy policy for a recycling sector and informal sectors in urban areas affect disposal and recycling of waste and unemployment in economically developing countries using the Harris and Todaro model, which incorporates recycling activities undertaken by the recycling sector and informal sectors. Results clarified that increasing the subsidy rate for the recycling sector can engender a decrease in the number of unemployed people, increasing the demand for labor in manufacturing and recycling sectors, which set higher wages, increasing the indirect utility levels and improving social welfare if marginal productivity in the agriculture sector is sufficiently high. Results show that increasing supporting funds for the informal sector might worsen social welfare and increase the unemployment rate, although it increases the expected wages of workers in informal sectors. Moreover, we consider the policies of economically developing countries and the support of economically developed countries through a comparison of outcomes obtained when the landfill is located in an urban area and when it is located in a rural area. Results clarified that the labor demand for the final goods sector and the waste collection sector in the case in which a landfill in an urban area is greater than that in the case in which a landfill exists in a rural area, although the labor demand for the intermediate goods sector shows an opposite relation.

References

1. De Fraja, G., & Delbono, F. (1990). Game theoretic models of mixed oligopoly. *Journal of Economic Surveys, 4*(1), 1–17.
2. Diamond, P. A. (1965). National debt in a neoclassical growth model. *American Economic Review, 55*(5), 1126–1150.
3. Fujita, M., Krugman, P. R., & Venables, A. J. (1999). *The spatial economy: Cities, regions, and international trade*. Cambridge: MIT.
4. Harris, J. R., & Todaro, M. P. (1970). Migration, unemployment and development: A two-sector analysis. *American Economic Review, 60*(1), 126–142.
5. Krugman, P. R. (1991). Increasing returns and economic geography. *Journal of Political Economy, 99*(3), 483–499.
6. Lewis, W. A. (1954). Economic development with unlimited supplies of labour. *The Manchester School, 22*(2), 139–191.
7. Matsumura, T. (1998). Partial privatization in mixed duopoly. *Journal of Public Economics, 70*(3), 473–483.
8. Ottaviano, G., Tabuchi, T., & Thisse, J. F. (2002). Agglomeration and trade revisited. *International Economic Review, 43*(2), 409–436.

Part I
The Basic Model of Regional Economy

Chapter 2
Regional Agglomeration and Spatial Economics

Tohru Naito

2.1 Introduction

This chapter presents a basic model to analyze regional or spatial economics. Although most economic theories have devoted some attention to space or distance, those factors should not be omitted from stricter economic analysis. For instance, traditional international economic theories such as the Ricardo model or Heckscher–Ohlin model do not incorporate the concept of distance. However, it is not natural to address the trade of goods among countries without considering their transportation cost. Recently many people have been interested in regional economics, urban economics, and spatial economics because they have realized their importance.

Some researchers have persisted in their interest in both distance and space and have recognized their importance. Particularly, von Thünen [7] introduced a bid rent into the model and explained the patterns of crops. Weber [8] specifically assessed the relation of transportation cost between raw material and products and investigated where to locate plant in a city. Hotelling [3] assumes a linear space in his model and analyzes where each firm locates in that space. This model is useful to analyze differentiated goods. Moreover, Alonso [1] applied von Thünen [7] to urban location and contributed importantly to the development of urban economics.

However, models of two kinds have established the prosperity of the current spatial economics, Dixit and Stiglitz [2] and Krugman [4]. Dixit and Stiglitz [2] contributed greatly to the development of the spatial economics because the monopolistic competition model made it easy to use increasing returns of scale when constructing an economic model. Krugman [4] combined this monopolistic

T. Naito (✉)
Institute of Socio-Arts and Science, Tokushima University, 1-1 Minamijosanjima-cho
Tokushima city, Tokushima 770-8502, Japan
e-mail: naito@tokushima-u.ac.jp

T. Naito (ed.), *Sustainable Growth and Development in a Regional Economy*,
New Frontiers in Regional Science: Asian Perspectives 13,
DOI 10.1007/978-4-431-55294-9_2

competition model with transportation cost and constructed the model to make an explanation of regional agglomeration. Because Krugman [4] strongly influenced many researchers in urban economics and international economics, they extended his model from directions of many kinds. We often call the model constructed in Krugman [4] a "core–periphery model". The key words of the core–periphery model are the following words: monopolistic competition, economies of scale, transportation cost, and computers. However, Krugman [4] includes some complex problems in the process of deriving the solution. Because he adopted a Cobb–Douglas utility function in his model, his model is constructed as a nonlinear general equilibrium system. Consequently, it is impossible to derive the solutions analytically. It is necessary to use computer simulation to solve the system. Moreover, the price of differentiated goods is a constant mark up to marginal cost in Krugman [4]. Some economists have attempted to construct the core–periphery model to enable derivation of the equilibrium analytically. Although Pflüger [6] considered a quasi-linear utility function with logarithmic subutility and derive the solution analytically, the price of differentiated goods is independent of the number of differentiated goods, as noted also by Krugman [4]. Ottaviano, Tabuchi, and Thisse [5] constructed the model to overcome these difficulties that had been included in existing studies. Ottaviano, Tabuchi, and Thisse [5] succeed in constructing the model to derive the equilibrium analytically by adopting not a Cobb–Douglas utility function but a quasi-linear utility function. Moreover, they describe the competition promotion effect although they cannot show an income effect in their model. Because we will show the model to make use of this utility function in Chap. 10 of Part II, we overview Ottaviano, Tabuchi, and Thisse [5] as the basic spatial economics in this chapter.

2.2 The Basic Model

2.2.1 Households

Following Ottaviano, Tabuchi, and Thisse [5], we consider a two-region economy that consists of two sectors called a manufactured goods sector and an agricultural goods sector. We define regions as region H and region F. We define the households employed by the manufactured goods sector as "workers," denoted as L, and those employed by the agriculture sector as "peasant," denoted as A. Although workers are mobile between regions, peasants are immobile and are distributed equally between regions. Although manufactured goods are differentiated and are produced by N-private firms in urban area, the agricultural goods are homogeneous and numeraire. We assume that all households have common preferences. Therefore, they have the following same quasi-linear utility function, as noted also by Ottaviano, Tabuchi, and Thisse [5].

$$U_l = \alpha \int_0^N q_l(i)di - \frac{\beta - \gamma}{2} \int_0^N [q_l(i)]^2 di - \frac{\gamma}{2} \left[\int_0^N q_l(i)di \right]^2 + z_l, \quad (l = H, F) \tag{2.1}$$

Therein, $q_l(i)$, z_l, and N respectively denote the consumption of goods produced by the i-th private firm, agricultural goods, and the number of firms in the manufactured goods sector. Regarding parameters in (2.1), we assume that $\alpha > 0$ and $\beta > \gamma > 0$. Therein, α expresses the intensity of preference for differentiated manufactured goods. $\beta > \gamma$ signifies that consumers are biased toward a dispersed consumption varieties. Presuming that β is equal to γ, the substitutability among manufactured goods is perfect.[1] Moreover, we assume that the budget constraint of each household is given as

$$w_l + z_0 = \int_0^N p(i)q_l(i)di + z_l, \tag{2.2}$$

where z_0 and $p(i)$ respectively denote the initial endowment and the price of i-th firm.[2] Maximizing the utility function (2.1) subject to budget constraint (2.2), the first-order condition of $q_l(i)$ is given as

$$\alpha - (\beta - \gamma)q_l(i) - \gamma \int_0^N q_l(j)dj - p(i) = 0, \quad i \in [0, N] \tag{2.3}$$

Solving (2.3), the optimal consumption of i-th differentiated goods is

$$q_l^*(i) = a - bp_i + c \int_0^N [p(j) - p(i)]dj, \tag{2.4}$$

where a, b, and c respectively denote $\alpha/[\beta + \gamma(N-1)]$, $1/[\beta + \gamma(N-1)]$, and $\gamma/(\beta - \gamma)[\beta + \gamma(N-1)]$. We assume symmetry of manufactured goods produced. Therefore, let $q_l(i)$ represent the consumption of manufactured goods produced by the i-th firm. Moreover, we define P as the price index of the manufactured goods market. Therefore, we can rewrite (2.4) as follows.

$$q_l^*(i) = a - [b + cN]p(i) + cP \tag{2.5}$$

[1] For a detailed explanation of this utility function, see Ottaviano, Tabuchi, and Thisse [5].

[2] Here we assume that the initial endowment is sufficiently large.

Price index P of the manufactured goods market is defined as shown below.

$$P \equiv \int_0^N p(j)dj \tag{2.6}$$

Using (2.1) and (2.5), the indirect utility function of household l is the following.

$$v_l = \frac{a^2}{2b} - a\int_0^N p(i)di + \frac{b+cN}{2}\int_0^N [p(i)]^2 di - \frac{c}{2}\left[\int_0^N p(i)di\right]^2 + w_l + z_0 \tag{2.7}$$

2.2.2 Production

Agricultural Goods

Next we consider the supply side including the manufactured goods sector and the agricultural goods sector. In this section, one unit of labor is required to conduct agricultural goods production, which are homogeneous and numeraire. If one assumes that the agricultural goods are transported between regions without transportation cost, then the wage rate of a peasant in either region is equal to one, as $w_H^A = w_F^A = 1$.

Manufactured Goods

We assume that ϕ units of labor are required to produce any amount of manufactured goods, as did Ottaviano, Tabuchi, and Thisse [5]. The marginal cost of manufactured goods sector is equal to zero because the marginal labor input is not necessary. Because the input factor of manufactured goods is only fixed labor, the manufactured goods sector has economies of scale and has production technology with increasing returns to scale.[3] We define λ as the labor distribution of region H for the economy. Consequently, the labor market clearing condition of manufactured goods sector in each region is shown as follows.

$$\phi n_H = \lambda L \tag{2.8}$$

$$\phi n_F = (1-\lambda)L \tag{2.9}$$

[3] Though Krugman [4] considers both marginal labor input and fixed labor input, this model requires no marginal labor input to produce the manufactured goods. Therefore, we consider this ϕ as the measure of the degree of increasing returns to scale.

From (2.8) and (2.9), the total mass of manufactured goods firms, N, is given as presented below.

$$N = n_H + n_F \tag{2.10}$$

Because the total number of workers in this economy is denoted by L, the total mass of manufactured goods firms is equal to L/ϕ. Regarding the number of varieties, (2.8) and (2.9) show that the increase of workers in the region engenders an increase in the total mass of manufactured goods. However, the decrease of ϕ engenders increase the number of varieties. Consequently, the number of manufactured goods firms in region l depends on the number of workers located there.

Next we refer to the wage rate in equilibrium. Presuming that the entry into and exit from manufactured goods market is free, the profit of each firm is zero. Because no firm earns the excess profit under zero profit condition, the revenue of firm is equal to the production cost. Because we assume that only input factor of manufactured goods is labor, the total revenue of manufactured goods is the wage income of workers in equilibrium. Considering the fact that the only input factor of the manufactured goods sector is labor, no firm receives excess profit because of the zero-profit condition; its revenue reverts to the wage paid to workers employed by the manufactured goods sector. Regarding prices of each variety, we assume that firms can carry out price discrimination for goods sold in regions H and F. When we assume that the production technology of manufactured goods is symmetric and that q_{HH} and q_{HF} denote the demands of variety i in regions H and F, respectively, then q_{HH} and q_{HF} are as follows.

$$q_{HH}(i) = a - (b + cN)p_{HH}(i) + cP_H \tag{2.11}$$

$$q_{HF}(i) = a - (b + cN)p_{HF}(i) + cP_F, \tag{2.12}$$

In those equations, $P_l(l = H, F)$ is the price index of manufactured goods in region l:

$$P_H \equiv \int_0^{n_H} p_{HH}(i)di + \int_0^{n_F} p_{FH}(i)di \tag{2.13}$$

$$P_F \equiv \int_0^{n_H} p_{HF}(i)di + \int_0^{n_F} p_{FF}(i)di. \tag{2.14}$$

Here, we can describe the profit function of the firm to produce variety i in region H as follows.

$$\Pi_H = p_{HH}q_{HH}(p_{HH})(A/2 + \lambda L) + (p_{HF} - \tau)\{A/2 + (1 - \lambda)L\} - \phi w_H, \tag{2.15}$$

Therein, w_H and τ respectively denote the wage rate of manufactured goods sector in region H and transportation cost. Regarding transportation cost in this model, it is necessary to note that transportation cost is not "iceberg type," its cost is proportional to the manufactured goods weight.

2.3 Equilibrium

2.3.1 *Equilibrium in the Short Run*

Setting up the basic model of this paper in the previous section, we derive the equilibrium in the short run, in which workers and peasants are immobile between regions. When we derive equilibrium on this model, it is necessary to distinguish *equilibrium in the short run*" from *equilibrium in the long run*. Because equilibrium is defined based on the immobility of workers between regions as equilibrium in the short run, we derive it by treating λ as given. We define equilibrium under their mobility between regions as equilibrium in the long run. The number of firms is sufficiently large under monopolistic competition. Because this model assumes that a continuum of firms in the manufactured goods sector attributable to (2.1), it is possible to consider that the number of firms in the manufactured goods sector is sufficiently large, as it is in other monopolistic competition models. The behavior of no single firm affects the price index of the manufactured goods market although each firm sets its own price to maximize profit under a monopolistic competition market.

To begin with, each firm of manufactured goods sector in each region deals with the price index of manufactured goods sector in region H and region F as given and sets its price to maximize profit. Maximizing profit maximization with respect to its own price in each region yields the equilibrium prices in each region. Assuming the symmetry of variety, the price set by each variety in the same region is identical in equilibrium. Now, letting p^*_{HH} and p^*_{HF} represent p_{HH} and p_{HF} to maximize (2.15). Because p^*_{HH} and p^*_{HF} are given as the function of P_H and P_F, respectively, we derive the following equation by considering the (2.6).

$$n_H p^*_{HH}(P_H) + n_F p^*_{FH}(P_H) = P_H \tag{2.16}$$

$$n_H p^*_{HF}(P_H) + n_F p^*_{FF}(P_H) = P_F \tag{2.17}$$

Because workers are immobile between regions in the short run, we address the number of varieties in each region given by (2.8) and (2.9) as constant. Therefore, we derive the following equilibrium prices, which are p^*_{HH}, p^*_{FH}, p^*_{HF}, and p^*_{FF}.

$$p^*_{HH} = \frac{1}{2}\frac{2a + \tau c(1-\lambda)N}{2b + cN} \tag{2.18}$$

$$p_{FF}^* = \frac{1}{2}\frac{2a + \tau c\lambda N}{2b + cN} \tag{2.19}$$

$$p_{HF}^* = p_{FF}^* + \frac{\tau}{2} \tag{2.20}$$

$$p_{FH}^* = p_{HH}^* + \frac{\tau}{2} \tag{2.21}$$

Although the price of a variety in equilibrium is independent of the number of varieties in Krugman [4], it is known to depend on the number of varieties under Ottaviano, Tabuchi, and Thisse [5]. Here, we can confirm that the competition progressing effect exists in this model because the equilibrium price decreases with respect to N.[4] In comparison with (2.18), (2.20) was larger than (2.18) because (2.20) includes transportation cost, which is denoted as $\tau/2$. If the transportation cost increases, the equilibrium price of each variety also increases. Moreover, nobody has any incentive to arbitrage because the benefit of arbitrage is less than the transportation cost τ. We assume that p_{HF}^* (p_{FH}^*) is larger than τ for any $\lambda \in [0, 1]$. No firm has any incentive to sell products in the other region if p_{HF}^* (p_{FH}^*) is less than τ. Therefore, we make a following assumption related to transpiration cost.[5]

$$\tau < \bar{\tau} \equiv \frac{2a\phi}{2b\phi + cL} \tag{2.22}$$

We supplement the property of $\bar{\tau}$ using comparative static analysis. We know that $\bar{\tau}$ is the function of ϕ describing the intensity of increasing returns.

$$\frac{\partial \bar{\tau}}{\partial \phi} = \frac{2Lac}{(2b\phi + Lc)^2} > 0 \tag{2.23}$$

When ϕ is sufficiently small, ($\phi \doteq 0$), all manufactured goods are produced in each region, i.e., the economy becomes autarkic. Letting Π_{HH}^* and Π_{HF}^* respectively present the gross equilibrium profit by selling the varieties produced at region H in region H and F. Therefore, we can derive the following: Π_{HH}^* and Π_{HF}^* because of (2.18) and (2.20).

$$\Pi_{HH}^* = (b + cN)(p_{HH}^*)^2\left(\frac{A}{2} + \lambda L\right) \tag{2.24}$$

[4]Equilibrium price p_{HH}^* is a decreasing function of N because $\frac{\partial p_{HH}^*}{\partial N} = -c\frac{a - b\lambda\tau}{(2b+Nc)^2} < 0$ under the circumstances in which a is sufficiently large.

[5]Subsequently, we analyze the model under the (2.22).

and

$$\Pi_{HF}^{*} = (b + cN)(p_{HF}^{*} - \tau)^2 \left(\frac{A}{2} + (1 - \lambda)L \right). \tag{2.25}$$

Finally, we refer to the surplus of households in region H from consumption in (2.18) and (2.20). Here we define $S_H(\lambda)$ as the surplus of households in region H from consumption.[6]

$$\begin{aligned} S_H(\lambda) \equiv & \frac{a^2 L}{2b\phi} - \frac{aL}{\phi} \left[\lambda p_{HH}^{*} + (1 - \lambda) p_{FH}^{*} \right] \\ & + \frac{(b\phi + cL)L}{2\phi^2} [\lambda \left(p_{HH}^{*} \right)^2 + (1 - \lambda)(p_{FH}^{*})^2] \\ & - \frac{cL^2}{2\phi^2} \left[\lambda p_{HH}^{*} + (1 - \lambda) p_{FH}^{*} \right]^2 \end{aligned} \tag{2.26}$$

Similarly to $S_H(\lambda)$, we also define $S_F(\lambda)$ as the surplus of households in region F from consumption because of symmetry.

$$\begin{aligned} S_F(\lambda) \equiv & \frac{a^2 L}{2b\phi} - \frac{aL}{\phi} \left[\lambda p_{HF}^{*} + (1 - \lambda) p_{FF}^{*} \right] \\ & + \frac{(b\phi + cL)L}{2\phi^2} [\lambda \left(p_{HF}^{*} \right)^2 + (1 - \lambda)(p_{FF}^{*})^2] \\ & - \frac{cL^2}{2\phi^2} \left[\lambda p_{HF}^{*} + (1 - \lambda) p_{FF}^{*} \right]^2 \end{aligned} \tag{2.27}$$

Because the production of variety is symmetric, we respectively define Q_H and Q_F as the total manufactured goods produced in region H and F.

$$Q_H = \frac{\lambda L}{\phi}(b + cN) \left(\frac{2a - b\tau}{2b + cN} \right) \tag{2.28}$$

$$Q_F = \frac{(1 - \lambda)L}{\phi}(b + cN) \left(\frac{2a - b\tau}{2b + cN} \right) \tag{2.29}$$

Because the gross revenue of the manufactured goods sector located in region H is equal to the total wage income of workers employed in region H in equilibrium, the equilibrium wage in region H is given as

[6] Differentiating (2.26) with respect to λ, one finds that $\frac{d^2 S_H(\lambda)}{d\lambda^2}$ is negative. Consequently, $S_H(\lambda)$ is concave.

$$w_H^*(\lambda) = \frac{b\phi + cL}{4(2b\phi + cL)^2\phi^2}\left\{[2a\phi + \tau cL(1-\lambda)]^2\left(\frac{A}{2} + \lambda L\right)\right.$$
$$\left. + [2a\phi - 2\tau b\phi - \tau cL(1-\lambda)]^2\left[\frac{A}{2} + (1-\lambda)L\right]\right\} \tag{2.30}$$

Similarly, we can derive w_F^* as follows.

$$w_F^*(\lambda) = \frac{b\phi + cL}{4(2b\phi + cL)^2\phi^2}\left\{[2a\phi + \tau cL\lambda]^2\left(\frac{A}{2} + (1-\lambda)L\right)\right.$$
$$\left. +[2a\phi - 2\tau b\phi - \tau cL\lambda]^2\left(\frac{A}{2} + \lambda L\right)\right\} \tag{2.31}$$

2.3.2 Equilibrium in the Long Run

In the previous section, we determined the endogenous variables in the short run when we treated the distribution of workers between regions as given. Although we assume that workers in each region cannot migrate between regions in the short run, we relax that assumption in this subsection. Therefore, it is possible for workers to migrate to the region which provides higher utility after comparing utility levels in respective regions. When we treat the distribution of workers between regions as given, the indirect utility function in region H and F are as follows.

$$V_H(\lambda) = S_H(\lambda) + w_H^*(\lambda) + z_0 \tag{2.32}$$

$$V_F(\lambda) = S_F(\lambda) + w_F^*(\lambda) + z_0 \tag{2.33}$$

Now we consider the distribution of workers between regions in the long run. No migration exists between regions when the utility in both regions is of the same level. Therefore, the equilibrium distribution of workers is λ to satisfy the following equation.

$$\Delta V(\lambda) \equiv V_H(\lambda) - V_F(\lambda) = 0 \tag{2.34}$$

Presuming that $\Delta V(\lambda)$ is positive within $\lambda \in [0, 1]$, every worker agglomerates in region H. However, presuming that $\Delta V(\lambda)$ is negative within $\lambda \in [0, 1]$, they agglomerate in region F. When λ satisfies $\Delta V(\lambda) = 0$ within $\lambda \in [0, 1]$ the equilibrium distribution of workers is λ to satisfy $\Delta V(\lambda) = 0$ within $\lambda \in [0, 1]$. Substituting (2.32) and (2.33) into (2.34), $\Delta V(\lambda)$ is

$$\Delta V(\lambda) = C\tau(\tau^* - \tau)\left(\lambda - \frac{1}{2}\right), \tag{2.35}$$

where C and τ^* are defined as shown below.

$$C \equiv \left[2b\phi(3b\phi + 3cL + cA) + c^2L(A + L)\right] \frac{L(b\phi + cL)}{2\phi^2(2b\phi + cL)^2} > 0 \tag{2.36}$$

$$\tau^* \equiv \frac{4a\phi(3b\phi + 2cL)}{2b\phi(3b\phi + 3cL + cA) + c^2L(A + L)} \tag{2.37}$$

Although λ is determined by (2.34), that solution is not always stable because the sign of $\Delta V(\lambda)$ depends on transportation cost τ. $\Delta V(\lambda)$ is positive when λ is larger than 0.5. However, the sign of $\Delta V(\lambda)$ is negative when λ is smaller than 0.5. In contrast, if transportation cost τ is greater than τ^*, then $\tau^* - \tau$ is negative. Consequently, the sign of $\Delta V(\lambda)$ is negative when λ is larger than 0.5. However, the sign of $\Delta V(\lambda)$ is positive when λ is smaller than 0.5. As a result, the number of workers in region H is equal to that in region F. Now we define the former solution as agglomeration equilibrium, which is $\lambda = 0, 1$. In contrast we define the latter solution as dispersion equilibrium, which is $\lambda = 0.5$. Figure 2.1 depicts the distribution of workers in the long run. Bold lines show a stable distribution of

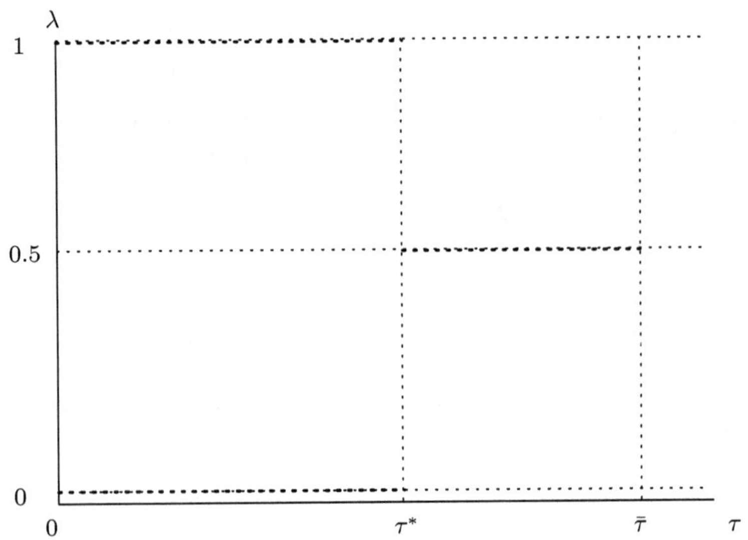

Fig. 2.1 Stable equilibrium and transportation cost

workers. When transportation cost is low ($\tau < \tau^*$), stable distributions of workers are $\lambda = 1, 0$. However, the only stable distribution of workers is $\lambda = 0.5$ when transportation cost is high ($\tau > \tau^*$).

Theorem 2.1 (Ottavian, Tabuchi, and Thisse [5]). *When the transportation cost of manufactured goods between regions is low ($\tau < \tau^*$), all workers agglomerate in one region: (**Agglomeration equilibrium**). In contrast, when the transportation cost of manufactured goods between regions is high ($\tau > \tau^*$), the distribution of workers becomes equal in both regions: (**Dispersion equilibrium**).*

2.4 Welfare

In the previous section, we refer to equilibrium in the short and the long run. We explained that the equilibrium distribution of workers between regions depends on the transportation cost τ. However, we do not refer to the relation between equilibrium and optimum. Now we define the sum of individual indirect utility function as social welfare. Let $W(\lambda)$ represent social welfare. We describe $W(\lambda)$ as follows.

$$W(\lambda) \equiv \lambda L\left[S_H(\lambda) + w_H(\lambda)\right] + \frac{A}{2}\left[S_H(\lambda) + 1\right] + (1-\lambda)L\left[S_F(\lambda) + w_F(\lambda)\right] + \frac{A}{2}\left[S_F(\lambda) + 1\right] \tag{2.38}$$

Here the zero profit condition holds in (2.24) and (2.25), the prices of variety produced in region H are as follows.

$$p^o_{HH} = p^o_{FF} = 0 \tag{2.39}$$

$$p^o_{HF} = p^o_{FH} = \tau \tag{2.40}$$

Consequently, $w^o_H(\lambda)$ and $w^o_F(\lambda)$ are equal to zero for any $\lambda \in [0, 1]$. Substituting (2.39) and (2.40) for (2.26) and (2.27), respectively, then $S_H(\lambda)$ and $S_F(\lambda)$ under social optimum are derived. Now let $S_H(\lambda)^o$ and $S_F(\lambda)^o$ represent $S_H(\lambda)$ and $S_F(\lambda)$ under social optimum. Therefore, $S_H(\lambda)^o$ and $S_F(\lambda)^o$ are given as

$$S^o_H = \frac{a^2L}{2b\phi} - \frac{2aL}{\phi}\left[(1-\lambda)\tau\right] + \frac{(b\phi + cL)L}{2\phi^2}\left[(1-\lambda)\tau^2\right] - \frac{cL^2}{2\phi^2}\left[(1-\lambda)\tau\right]^2 \tag{2.41}$$

and

$$S^o_F = \frac{a^2L}{2b\phi} - \frac{2aL}{\phi}\left[\lambda\tau\right] + \frac{(b\phi + cL)L}{2\phi^2}\left[\lambda\tau^2\right] - \frac{cL^2}{2\phi^2}\left[\lambda\tau\right]^2 \tag{2.42}$$

Fig. 2.2 Case of $\tau > \tau^o$

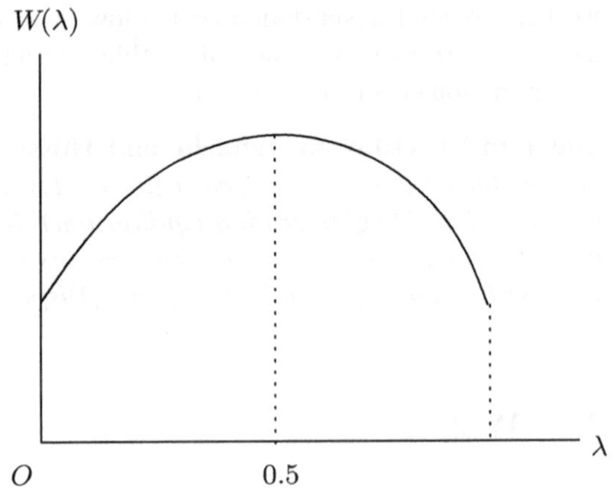

Substituting (2.41) and (2.42) for (2.38), the following social welfare function is given as

$$W(\lambda) = C^o \tau(\tau^o - \tau)\lambda(\lambda - 1)L + \bar{M}. \tag{2.43}$$

Here we define C^o, τ^o, and $\bar{M}$ as follows.

$$C^o \equiv \frac{L(2b\phi + c(A + L))}{2\phi^2}$$

$$\tau^o \equiv \frac{2a\phi}{2b\phi + c(A + L)}$$

$$\bar{M} \equiv 2z_0 + A + \frac{a^2(A + L)L}{2b\phi}$$

Because social welfare is denoted by (2.43), $W(\lambda)$ is the function of τ and λ. The shape of the social welfare function depends on the relation between τ and τ^*.[7] $W''(\lambda)$ is negative if τ is larger than τ^*. Consequently, $W(\lambda)$ is concave with respect to λ. In addition, $W(\lambda)$ becomes maximum when λ is equal to 0.5 because of the first-order condition. Consequently, the dispersion equilibrium is optimal in this case (Fig. 2.2). However, if τ is smaller than τ^*, then $W''(\lambda)$ is positive. Consequently, $W(\lambda)$ is convex with respect to λ. In this case, $W(\lambda)$ is not optimal when λ is equal to 0.5. Presuming that τ is smaller than τ^*, then the distribution of workers is optimal when λ is equal to either 0 or 1. Consequently the agglomeration equilibrium is optimal (Fig. 2.3).

[7] For detailed discussion about these properties, see Ottaviano, Tabuchi, and Thisse [5]. Moreover, both C^o and $\bar{M}$ are positive irrespective of λ.

Fig. 2.3 Case of $\tau < \tau^o$

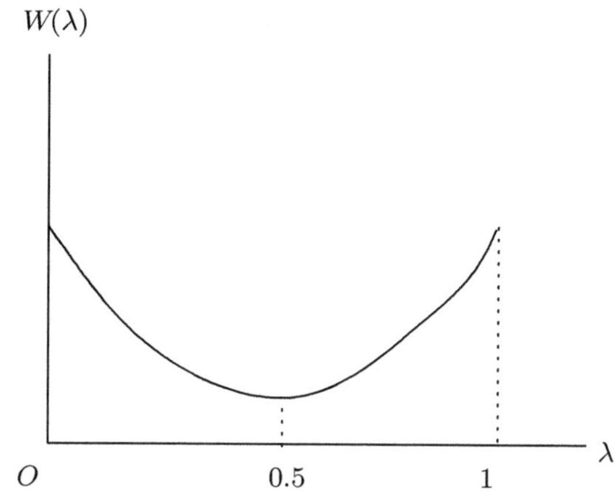

Theorem 2.2 (Ottaviano, Tabuchi, and Thisse [5](2)). *The dispersion equilibrium is optimal when τ is larger than τ^*. The agglomeration equilibrium is optimal when τ is smaller than τ^*.*

2.5 Concluding Remarks

We surveyed Ottaviano, Tabuchi, and Thisse [5] as the basic spatial economics model in this chapter. As stated in the Introduction, Krugman [4] has some problems, although it contributed greatly for spatial economics. One is that it is impossible to solve solutions analytically because of nonlinear general equilibrium. Therefore, it is necessary to use computer resources to derive the equilibrium. Another is that the equilibrium price of variety is the markup of the marginal cost. However, Ottaviano, Tabuchi, and Thisse [5], which is described in this chapter, adopt the quasi-linear utility function to derive the equilibrium of their model analytically. Moreover, they describe the competition progressing effect depending on the number of varieties, although the income effect is eliminated using a quasi-linear utility function. Some key words play an important role about spatial agglomeration and dispersion in this chapter: transportation cost, variety of goods, and economies of scale.

Each variety sets monopolistic price because of goods differentiation under a monopolistic competition model. However, the zero profit condition holds in equilibrium because we assume that entry into or exit from a market is free and that each variety is covered with a fixed cost for production. The increase of variety engenders an increase in household utility attributable to the (2.1). Moreover, transportation costs play an important role in spatial agglomeration and dispersion in the analysis of this chapter. When trade is conducted between regions, a transportation cost is necessary to transport goods from one region to the other region. When trade is conducted between regions, transportation cost is necessary to transport goods from one region to the other region. Presuming that transportation costs are sufficiently large, trade does not occur between regions. Consequently, this case is autarkic. Even if trade were to occur between regions, the distribution of workers is uniform in both regions when the transportation cost is high.

Because the only input of the manufactured goods sector is fixed labor, the increase of production decreases the average cost because of scale economies. Consequently, each firm can decrease the average cost by locating in the region with a large market. Moreover, the mobility of workers between regions is considered in this model. As we explored for labor mobility in Sect. 2.3, workers migrate to the region to enjoy higher utility in the long run because the increase of workers engenders expansion of the scale of market and decreases the average cost. Consequently, the ratio of the manufactured goods sector in the region with a large population to that with a small population is higher than the ratio of workers between regions. This effect, called the "*home market effect*," plays an important role in spatial economics.

References

1. Alonso, W. (1964). *Location and land use*. Cambridge: Harvard University Press.
2. Dixit, A. K., & Stiglitz, J. E. (1977). Monopolistic competition and optimum product diversity. *American Economic Review, 67*(3), 297–308.
3. Hotelling, H. (1929). Stability in competition. *Economic Journal, 39*, 41–57.
4. Krugman, P. R. (1991). Increasing returns and economic geography. *Journal of Political Economy, 99*(3), 483–499.
5. Ottaviano, G., Tabuchi, T., & Thisse, J. F. (2002). Agglomeration and trade revisited. *International Economic Review, 43*(2), 409–436.
6. Pflüger, M. (2004). A simple, analytically solvable, Chamberlinian agglomeration model. *Regional Science and Urban Economics, 34*(5), 565–573.
7. von Thünen, J. H. (1826). *Der isolierte Staat in Beziehung auf Landwirtschaft und Nationalokonomie*. Hamburg. English translation by C.M. Wartenberg, von Thünen's Isolated State. Oxford: Pergramon Press (1966).
8. Weber, A. (1909). *Über den Standort der Industrien*. Tübingen: J.C.B. Mohr. English translation: The theory of the location of industries. Chicago: Chicago University Press (1929).

Chapter 3
Urban Unemployment and Urban–Rural Migration

Tohru Naito

3.1 Introduction

In Chap. 1, we consider the mechanism of regional agglomeration and dispersion with core–periphery model constructed by Ottaviano, Tabuchi, and Thisse [5]. This model is an extremely powerful model to explain how regional agglomeration and dispersion occur endogenously under the influence of economic activities. Because we assumed that full employment was established in Chap.1, we did not take account of unemployment in the model. However, unemployment is an extremely important issue to be resolved in many countries regardless of developing countries or developed countries. Some developing countries experience urban unemployment during economic development.

Recently China has played the role of the "World's Factory" and has also achieved rapid economic growth, becoming a country with economic power. The Chinese government has strictly classified types of households as urban or rural laborer attributable to "domiciliary register registration regulations" established in 1958. The government prohibited rural laborers without domiciliary register to migrate from rural areas to urban areas. In the 1990s, these migrant rural laborers played the role of workers to support China's manufacturing and export industry. Consequently, the Chinese economy experienced rapid economic growth and recorded the second highest GDP in the world. However, in China, regional disparity came to be actualized with economic growth. China also faces some severe social issues, which other developed countries have already experienced, such as environmental issues, unemployment, and social security. As explained in

T. Naito (✉)
Institute of Socio-Arts and Science, Tokushima University, 1-1 Minamijosanjima-cho
Tokushima city, Tokushima 770-8502, Japan
e-mail: naito@tokushima-u.ac.jp

T. Naito (ed.), *Sustainable Growth and Development in a Regional Economy*,
New Frontiers in Regional Science: Asian Perspectives 13,
DOI 10.1007/978-4-431-55294-9_3

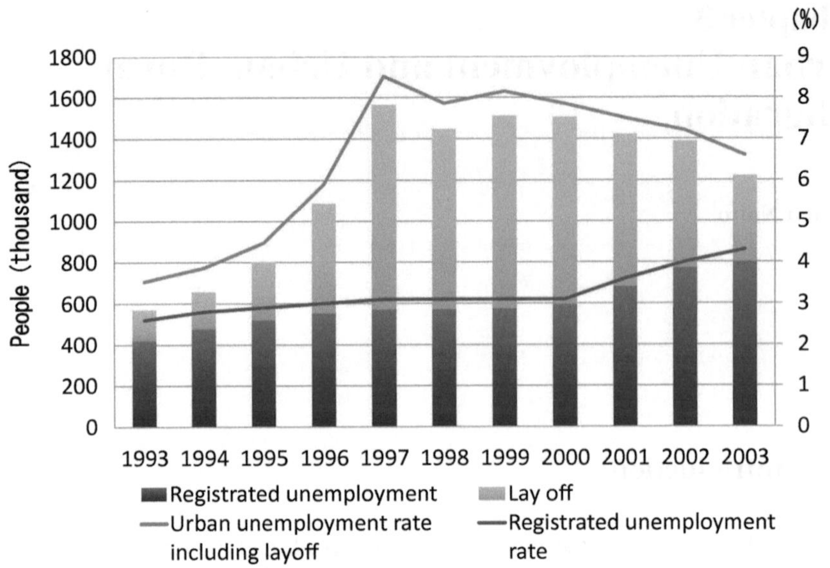

Fig. 3.1 Urban unemployment and the urban unemployment rate in China (Source: http://www.meti.go.jp/report/tsuhaku2005/2005honbun)

Chap. 1, the Chinese government introduced market mechanisms into the Chinese economy in the 1980s. Then, the Chinese economy achieved rapid economic growth. Regarding Chinese economic policies, the central government in China put east coast regions before other regions. Consequently, economic disparity occurred. This differential gave rural people a stark incentive to migrate from rural areas to urban areas. Figure 3.1 describes urban unemployment and the urban unemployment rate during 1993–2003. As one might understand from Fig. 3.1, the urban unemployment rate including layoffs, worsened in the latter half of the 1990s. Particularly, unemployment is a severe issue irrespective of where it occurs. Many economists have been interested in unemployment problems and have sought prescriptions for its improvement. Herein, we present a dualistic economy model in which sectors of two kinds exist attributable to different wage systems in the economy. Lewis [3] conducts pioneering studies of dualistic economy issues. Because Lewis [3] assumes that an unlimited labor supply is available at subsistence wage, he does not describe a mechanism for urban unemployment.

Harris and Todaro [2] conceive a mechanism by which urban unemployment occurred endogenously in the framework of a dualistic economy. The economic model constructed in the study, called the Harris and Todaro model, is as important to studies in this area as that by Lewis [3] is for development economics. Many economists have extended Harris and Todaro model from various viewpoints. For example, although Harris and Todaro [2] regard capital as the fixed specific capital in each sector, Corden and Findlay [1] relax this assumption, and analyze a model with free mobility of capital between the urban area and the rural area. Although

Corden and Findlay [1] are not explicit about the stability of equilibrium, Neary [4] refers to the stability of equilibrium in the Corden and Findlay model.

We overview Harris and Todaro [2] to describe a dualistic economy and to explain urban unemployment endogenously. The model presented in this chapter is applied in the models of Chaps. 10 and 14. In next section, we refer to Harris and Todaro [2] as a basic dualistic economy model. Section 3.3 derives equilibrium of model and analyzes the effects of some parameters on equilibrium using comparative statics. In Sect. 3.4, some policy parameters are introduced into the model; we consider the effects of some economic policies on the urban unemployment rate and other endogenous variables. Finally we conclude the analysis of this chapter.

3.2 The Model

We consider a dualistic economy model constructed by Harris and Todaro [2]. The dualistic economy in this section consists of urban and rural areas.[1] The population in this economy is denoted by L. Although a manufactured goods sector is located in the urban area, an agricultural goods sector is located in the rural area. Now X and Y respectively denote the manufactured goods sector and the agricultural sector. We assume that the urban wage is fixed above the labor market-clearing level, as do Harris and Todaro [2], and that it has downward rigidity attributable to the minimum wage system, and so on. Particularly, let $\bar{w}_X$ represent the minimum wage in the urban area, which is higher than the rural wage.

Here we normalize the price of agricultural goods to one because we deal with the agricultural goods as numeraire. Presuming that this economy is a small open economy, then the price of manufactured goods is given exogenously.[2] Moreover, we consider that both sectors face a competitive market.

3.2.1 Production

Because we assume a small open economy, we define p as the price of manufactured goods. Similarly to Harris and Todaro [2], both sectors require labor and capital as inputs for production. Although labor is mobile between the urban area and rural area, capital is immobile between them. We regard the capital used in each sector as a sector-specific input.

[1] Although we often use "area" and "region" in this chapter, we do not distinguish "area" from "region" strictly. However, we strictly distinguish "urban" from "rural."

[2] We assume a small open economy for simplification in this section though the price of agricultural goods in Harris and Todaro [2] is determined endogenously.

Manufactured Goods Sector

Manufactured goods are produced in the urban area. They require two factors to produce the manufactured goods: labor and capital. Following Harris and Todaro [2], we also deal with capital as fixed input. Consequently, the manufactured goods sector determines only labor input to maximize their profit. Here we define the production function of manufactured goods as follows.

$$X = X(L_X, \bar{K}_X), \tag{3.1}$$

Therein, L_X and $\bar{K}_X$ respectively indicate the amount of labor input and fixed capital input into the manufactured goods production. We assume that the marginal product of labor and capital is positive[3] and that the production function is concave, continuous, and differentiable, i.e.,

$$X_L \equiv \frac{\partial X}{\partial L_X} > 0, \;\; X_K \equiv \frac{\partial X}{\partial \bar{K}_X} > 0, \;\; X_{LL} \equiv \frac{\partial^2 X}{\partial L_X^2} < 0, \;\; X_{KK} \equiv \frac{\partial^2 X}{\partial \bar{K}_X^2} < 0$$

The manufactured goods market is competitive, and the price of manufactured goods is denoted by p. Consequently, the first order condition with respect to labor is given by

$$pX_L - \bar{w}_X = 0 \tag{3.2}$$

Agricultural Goods Sector

Next we consider the behavior of the agricultural goods sector. Whereas the manufactured goods are produced in the urban area, the agricultural goods are produced in the rural area, and also require two kinds of input factors for production as docs the manufactured goods sector. Because the agricultural goods sector also deals with sector-specific capital as fixed input, an agricultural goods sector determines only labor input. Consequently, the production function of agricultural goods sector is given as

$$Y = Y(L_Y, \bar{K}_Y), \tag{3.3}$$

where L_Y and $\bar{K}_Y$ respectively denote labor input and fixed capital input of the agricultural goods sector.

$$Y_L \equiv \frac{\partial Y}{\partial L_Y} > 0, \;\; Y_K \equiv \frac{\partial Y}{\partial \bar{K}_Y} > 0, \;\; Y_{LL} \equiv \frac{\partial^2 Y}{\partial L_Y^2} < 0, Y_{KK} \equiv \frac{\partial^2 Y}{\partial \bar{K}_Y^2} < 0$$

[3] Note that $\bar{K}_X$ is constant because $\bar{K}_X$ denotes fixed capital input.

Because the price of agricultural goods is normalized, the first-order condition to maximize the profit of agricultural goods sector is the following.

$$Y_L - w_Y = 0, \tag{3.4}$$

Therein, w_Y is the wage in the rural area. Finally we assume that the following inequality helds in both production functions.

$$X_{LL}X_{KK} - X_{LK}X_{KL} > 0 \tag{3.5}$$

$$Y_{LL}Y_{KK} - Y_{LK}Y_{KL} > 0 \tag{3.6}$$

3.2.2 *Households*

We refer to the behavior of households in the economy presented in this chapter. Particularly, index X, U, and Y respectively signify households employed in the manufactured goods sector, households unemployed in the urban area, and households employed in the agricultural goods sector. All households have common preferences and the same utility function. Let U_i represent the utility function of household $i(= X, Y, U)$. We define the following quasi-linear utility function of household i.

$$U_i(C_X^i, C_Y^i) = u(C_X^i) + C_Y^i \tag{3.7}$$

Therein, C_X^i and C_Y^i respectively denote consumption of manufactured goods and agricultural goods. Moreover, the property of sub-utility function $u(C_X^i)$ satisfies $u' > 0$, and $u'' < 0$. The budget constraint of each household is given by

$$w_i + I = pC_X^i + C_Y^i, \tag{3.8}$$

where w_i and I respectively represent the wage income of household i and a lump sum redistribution.[4] Maximizing (3.7) subject to (3.8), we derive the indirect utility function $V_i(p, w_i)$. Here, no income effect is attributable to (3.7). Consequently, the difference among households depends on the wage income. The minimum wage

[4] Household U does not earn wage income because household U is not employed by the manufactured goods sector. Consequently, w_U is equal to zero. Moreover, although Harris and Todaro [2] consider no redistribution, we assume that the government redistributes the profits of both sectors for households. Therefore, unemployed households can buy both goods to maintain their lives.

with downward rigidity in the urban area is higher than the rural wage. Here we define λ as the urban unemployment rate.

$$\lambda \equiv \frac{L_U}{L_X + L_U} \tag{3.9}$$

Nobody has incentive to move to the other region because the expected wage in urban area is equal to the wage in rural area in equilibrium. Therefore, the migration equilibrium condition is given as

$$(1-\lambda)\bar{w}_X = w_Y \tag{3.10}$$

Presuming that population in the economy is given by L, the population constraint is the following.

$$L_X + L_U + L_Y = L \tag{3.11}$$

Combining (3.9) with (3.11), we rewrite the population constraint as follows.

$$L_X + (1-\lambda)L_Y = (1-\lambda)L \tag{3.12}$$

3.3 Equilibrium and Comparative Statics

3.3.1 Equilibrium

We explained the behaviors of production sectors and households and derived some equilibrium conditions in the previous section. L_X, L_Y, L_U, and λ are determined by the system comprising (3.2), (3.4), (3.9), and (3.12). Arranging these conditions, the system in our model is described using the following three equations:

$$pX_L = \bar{w}_X \tag{3.13}$$

$$Y_L = (1-\lambda)\bar{w}_X \tag{3.14}$$

$$L_X + (1-\lambda)L_Y = (1-\lambda)L \tag{3.15}$$

We describe the equilibrium of this system in Fig. 3.2. The horizontal axis shows the population in this economy. The vertical axis shows wages in each region. The value of marginal products of manufactured goods sector is the decreasing function with respect to labor. Without the downward rigidity of wage, the equilibrium wage is determined by w^*, in which the value of marginal products of manufactured goods sector is equal to the marginal products of the agricultural goods sector. The

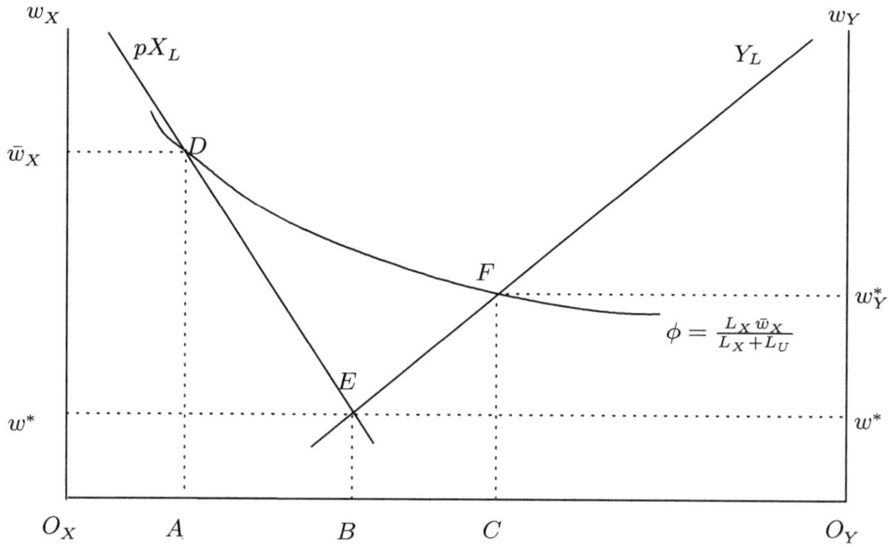

Fig. 3.2 Equilibrium in Harris and Todaro model

employment of the urban area and the rural area are given respectively as $O_X B$ and BO_Y. No urban unemployment exists under these circumstances.

However, urban employment is described by $O_X A$ because we assume that the wage in the urban area has downward rigidity and that it is fixed on $\bar{w}_X$. The marginal products of agricultural goods are also the decreasing function with respect to labor. Next we define the following function ϕ to derive equilibrium under the Harris and Todaro model.

$$\phi \equiv \frac{L_X \bar{w}_X}{L_X + L_U} \tag{3.16}$$

Because L_X is constant because of the downward rigidity of wages, ϕ is the decreasing function with respect to L_U. Migration equilibrium is achieved at point C, in which the expected wage in urban area is equal to the marginal product of the agricultural goods sector. Consequently, w_Y^* becomes an equilibrium wage in rural area. Although labor in urban area is described by $O_X C$ in Fig. 3.2, urban employment is given as $O_X A$. Consequently, urban unemployment is described by AC.

3.3.2 Comparative Statics

Next we consider comparative statics given by the system described above. Differentiating (3.13)–(3.15) completely and expressing them with the matrix, they are as follows.

$$\begin{pmatrix} pX_{LL} & 0 & 0 \\ 0 & Y_{LL} & \bar{w}_X \\ 1 & 1-\lambda & L-L_Y \end{pmatrix} \begin{pmatrix} L_X \\ L_Y \\ \lambda \end{pmatrix} = \begin{pmatrix} -X_L dp \\ 0 \\ (1-\lambda)dL \end{pmatrix} \tag{3.17}$$

If $|\Delta|$ is defined as the determinant of coefficient matrix in (3.17), then $|\Delta|$ is given as

$$|\Delta| = pX_{LL}Y_{LL}(L-L_Y) - pX_{LL}(1-\lambda)\bar{w}_X > 0 \tag{3.18}$$

We analyze the effect of each exogenous variables on endogenous variables, which are L_X, L_Y, and λ. First, we consider the effect of manufactured goods prices on each endogenous variables in equilibrium. Results of comparative statics by consideration of (3.17), (3.18), and by Cramer's formula show the effect of manufactured goods prices on each endogenous variable as

$$\frac{dL_X}{dp} = \frac{-X_L Y_{LL}(L-L_y) + X_L(1-\lambda)\bar{w}_X}{|\Delta|} > 0 \tag{3.19}$$

$$\frac{dL_Y}{dp} = \frac{-X_L \bar{w}_X}{|\Delta|} < 0 \tag{3.20}$$

$$\frac{d\lambda}{dp} = \frac{-X_L Y_{LL}}{|\Delta|} > 0 \tag{3.21}$$

From comparative statics from (3.19)–(3.21), the increase of manufactured goods price is known to aggravate the urban unemployment rate, although it increases employment in the manufactured goods sector. For the urban unemployment rate, we derive the following theorem.

Theorem 3.1. *The increase of manufactured goods price aggravates the urban unemployment rate although it increases urban employment.*

Second, we consider the effect of total population in the economy on endogenous variables, which are L_X, L_Y, and λ. Using Cramer's formula to (3.17) and (3.18), we derive the following results of comparative statics, which show the effects of population L on L_X, L_Y, and λ.

$$\frac{dL_X}{dL} = \frac{0}{|\Delta|} = 0 \tag{3.22}$$

$$\frac{dL_Y}{dL} = \frac{-pX_{LL}\bar{w}_X}{|\Delta|} > 0 \tag{3.23}$$

$$\frac{d\lambda}{dL} = \frac{pX_{LL}Y_{LL}}{|\Delta|} > 0 \tag{3.24}$$

Because the increase of population in the economy does not affect the value of marginal products of manufactured goods sector, the value of marginal products curve is not shifted by it. Moreover, the minimum wage in urban area is unaffected by it. Therefore, urban employment does not change because of the increase of population in the economy. Although the increase of population in the economy does not increase urban employment, it increases rural employment because no downward rigidity occurs in the rural area and full employment is achieved by wage adjustment, in which the equilibrium wage in rural area is equal to the value of marginal products of agricultural goods sector. Because urban employment does not change with increasing population, the agricultural goods sector absorbs part of the surplus labor. Consequently, rural employment increases because of the increase of population in the economy. However, this increase in rural employment causes the equilibrium wage in the rural area to decrease for achievement of full employment in the agricultural goods sector. When the equilibrium wage in the rural area promotes labor to have incentive to migrate from the rural area to the urban area because the difference between the expected wage in the urban area and the wage in the rural area increases. Therefore, the urban unemployment rate also aggravates the urban unemployment rate. Regarding the effect of increasing population in the economy on the urban unemployment rate, we derive the following theorem.

Theorem 3.2. *The increase of labor in the economy aggravates the urban unemployment rate although it engenders increased rural employment.*

This section presents analysis of the effects of exogenous variables, which are p and L, on endogenous variables, which are L_X, L_Y, and λ. However, we have to note that we deal with capital as a fixed input because we consider capital as a sector-specific factor.

3.4 Policy Effects in a Dualistic Economy

We have reviewed the mechanism of simple dualistic economy model constructed by Harris and Todaro [2] and analyzed the properties of equilibrium in the previous section. Although we analyzed the effects of some parameters on equilibrium, this model did not include policy parameters. In this section, we introduce some policies into the model in the previous section to analyze their effects on equilibrium in the dualistic economy. Specifically we introduce subsidy policy of two kinds into a dualistic model: a subsidy for manufactured goods sector, and a subsidy for agricultural goods sector. Similarly to Harris and Todaro [2], we assume that the capital input for each sector is sector-specific input. Therefore, we deal with capital input of both sectors as fixed inputs. Each sector can determine only the labor input because each sector deals with capital input as a fixed input. Let s_X and s_Y represent the subsidy per unit of labor for manufactured goods sector and agricultural goods sector, respectively. Introducing those subsidies into the model, we can revise (3.2) and (3.4) as follows.

$$pX_L - \bar{w}_X + s_X = 0 \tag{3.25}$$

and

$$Y_L - w_Y + s_Y = 0. \tag{3.26}$$

Substituting (3.4) for (3.10), the revised migration equilibrium condition is given as shown below.

$$(1-\lambda)\bar{w}_X = Y_L + s_Y \tag{3.27}$$

Because L_X, L_Y, L_U, and λ are endogenous variables, they are determined by the following system, which consists of (3.9), (3.12), (3.25), (3.26) and (3.27).

$$pX_L = \bar{w} - s_X \tag{3.28}$$

$$Y_L = (1-\lambda)\bar{w} - s_Y \tag{3.29}$$

$$L_X + (1-\lambda)L_Y = (1-\lambda)L \tag{3.30}$$

Completely differentiating (3.28)–(3.30), we describe them with the following matrix.

$$\begin{pmatrix} pX_{LL} & 0 & 0 \\ 0 & Y_{LL} & \bar{w}_X \\ 1 & 1-\lambda & L-L_Y \end{pmatrix} \begin{pmatrix} dL_X \\ dL_Y \\ d\lambda \end{pmatrix} = \begin{pmatrix} -ds_X - X_L dp \\ -ds_Y \\ (1-\lambda)dL \end{pmatrix} \tag{3.31}$$

We define $|\bar{\Delta}|$ as the determinant of the coefficient matrix in (3.31), $|\bar{\Delta}|$ is given as presented below

$$|\bar{\Delta}| \equiv pX_{LL}Y_{LL}(L-L_Y) - (1-\lambda)\bar{w}_X pX_{LL} > 0 \tag{3.32}$$

Applying Cramer's formula to (3.31) and (3.32), the effect of each subsidy on endogenous variables is analyzed. First, we refer to the effect of a subsidy for manufactured goods sector on equilibrium. Results of comparative static analyses are as follows.

$$\frac{dL_X}{ds_X} = \frac{-Y_{LL}(L-L_Y) + (1-\lambda)\bar{w}}{|\bar{\Delta}|} > 0 \tag{3.33}$$

$$\frac{dL_Y}{ds_X} = \frac{-\bar{w}}{|\bar{\Delta}|} < 0 \tag{3.34}$$

$$\frac{d\lambda}{ds_X} = \frac{Y_{LL}}{|\bar{\Delta}|} < 0 \tag{3.35}$$

According to the results of comparative statics from (3.33)–(3.35), we know that a subsidy for manufactured goods sector increases labor demand of manufactured goods sector although it decreases that of agricultural goods sector. Moreover, it is known that a subsidy for manufactured goods sector improves the urban unemployment rate.

Next we analyze the effect of a subsidy for agricultural goods sector on endogenous variables. Similar to above analysis, we apply Cramer's formula to (3.31) and (3.32) and derive the following results of comparative statics.

$$\frac{dL_X}{ds_Y} = 0 \tag{3.36}$$

$$\frac{dL_Y}{ds_Y} = \frac{-(L - L_Y)pX_{LL}}{|\bar{\Delta}|} > 0 \tag{3.37}$$

$$\frac{d\lambda}{ds_Y} = \frac{(1-\lambda)pX_{LL}}{|\bar{\Delta}|} < 0 \tag{3.38}$$

Because a subsidy for agricultural goods sector does not affect the marginal product of labor in the manufactured goods sector, the labor demand of manufactured goods sector is constant in spite of subsidy s_Y. Finally, we refer to the effect of a subsidy for agricultural goods sector on the urban unemployment rate. As a consequence of (3.38), we know that a subsidy for agricultural goods sector as well as that for manufactured goods sector also improves the urban unemployment rate. Therefore, we derive the following theorem based on results of the comparative statics described above.

Theorem 3.3. *A subsidy for sector $i(= X, Y)$ increases the required labor input of sector i and improves urban unemployment rate.*

Moreover, we consider the effect of a subsidy for the manufactured goods sector or the agricultural goods sector on urban unemployed labor. Because we define (3.9) as the urban unemployment rate, urban unemployment labor shown by L_U is given as presented below.

$$L_U = \left(\frac{\lambda}{1-\lambda}\right) L_X \tag{3.39}$$

Differentiating (3.39) with respect to s_X, we derive the effect of s_X on L_U as follows.

$$\begin{aligned} \frac{dL_U}{ds_X} &= \frac{d\lambda}{ds_X} \cdot \frac{dL_U}{d\lambda} \\ &= \frac{d\lambda}{ds_X} \cdot \frac{1}{(1-\lambda)^2} + \left(\frac{\lambda}{1-\lambda}\right) \frac{dL_X}{ds_X} \end{aligned} \tag{3.40}$$

Taking account of (3.33) and (3.35), the sign of (3.40) is known not to be determined uniquely. Although a subsidy for manufactured goods sector improves the urban unemployment rate, it is possible that labor increases more than improvement of the urban employment with a subsidy for urban sector migration from the rural area to the urban area. Consequently, urban unemployed labor increases, although a subsidy for manufactured goods sector improves the urban unemployment rate. Next we consider the effect of a subsidy for agricultural goods sector on urban unemployed labor. Similarly to analyzing the effect of a subsidy for manufactured goods sector on urban employed labor, we differentiate (3.39) with respect to s_Y.

$$
\begin{aligned}
\frac{dL_U}{ds_Y} &= \frac{d\lambda}{ds_Y} \cdot \frac{dL_U}{d\lambda} \\
&= \frac{d\lambda}{ds_Y} \cdot \frac{1}{(1-\lambda)^2} + \left(\frac{\lambda}{1-\lambda}\right) \frac{dL_X}{ds_Y} < 0
\end{aligned} \tag{3.41}
$$

Although a subsidy for agricultural goods sector increases the required labor of the agricultural goods sector, it does not affect the employment of the manufactured goods sector, i.e., $\frac{dL_X}{ds_Y}$ is equal to zero. Consequently, we know that sign of (3.41) is negative because the improvement of employment in rural area with a subsidy for agricultural goods sector engenders an increase in rural employment, although it does not increase the employment of the manufactured goods sector. Therefore, urban unemployment rate are improved because the total urban labor decreases with this subsidy. Therefore, we can derive the following theorem.

Theorem 3.4. *Although a subsidy for agricultural goods sector decreases unemployed labor in the urban area, that for manufactured goods does not necessarily decrease unemployed labor in the urban area.*

3.5 Concluding Remarks

We reviewed a dualistic economy model in this chapter. Particularly, we examined a model constructed by Harris and Todaro [2] to explain a dualistic economy. This model, called the Harris and Todaro model, is extremely useful to analyze a dualistic economy. Many researchers have extended the Harris and Todaro model in many directions after Harris and Todaro [2]. As we stated in Sect. 3.2, although Harris and Todaro [2] consider that each production sector requires labor and capital for production, they assume that the capital in each region is sector-specific and that it is not mobile among regions. However, this assumption lacks authenticity. Corden and Findlay [1] and Neary [4] extend the Harris and Todaro model by relaxing the assumption of immobile capital. They discussed the stability of equilibrium in the model. Although we do not deal with the model, in which capital is mobile between urban and rural areas, in detail, it is important to analyze a dualistic economy model with mobile capital between them.

We analyze the effects of some economic policies on equilibrium using comparative statics. As referred in Sect. 3.3, a subsidy for the manufactured goods sector increases unemployed labor in the urban area, although it improves the urban unemployment rate. These results are always known as the "Todaro Paradox". Even if the government conducted a subsidy policy for manufactured goods sector to increase urban employment, it is possible that it would engender increased unemployed labor in urban areas. Therefore, the government should take account of the effects of any policy on labor migration among regions when it enacts any policy improving urban unemployment rates. However, a subsidy for agricultural goods sector improves the urban unemployment rate and decreases unemployed labor in urban areas. Consequently, a subsidy for agricultural goods sector is more effective than that for the manufactured goods sector. In fact, although Lewis [3] emphasized that development in urban area resolves a dualistic economy, Harris and Todaro [2] emphasized that development in rural areas is more important than in urban areas.

Although Harris and Todaro [2] is an important study in the field of development economics, their model includes some points to be revised. For instance, they do not address how unemployed laborers (households) make their living because they do not receive wage income. Moreover, in fact, they consider other points, which are environment, social security, and so on, although Harris and Todaro [2] assume that households are interested in the difference between expected wages in urban areas and wages in rural areas. Consequently, it is necessary to resolve those issues using the extended model.

References

1. Corden, W. M., & Findlay, R. (1975). Urban unemployment, intersectoral capital mobility and development policy. *Economica, 42*(165), 59–78.
2. Harris, J. R., & Todaro, M. P. (1970). Migration, unemployment and development: A two-sector analysis. *American Economic Review, 60*(1), 126–142.
3. Lewis, W. A. (1954). Economic development with unlimited supplies of labour. *The Manchester School, 22*(2), 139–191.
4. Neary, P. (1988). Stability of the mobile-capital Harris-Todaro model: Some further results. *Economica, 55*(217), 123–127.
5. Ottaviano, G., Tabuchi, T., & Thisse, J. F. (2002). Agglomeration and trade revisited. *International Economic Review, 43*(2), 409–436.

Chapter 4
Neoclassical Economic Growth and Public Policy

Tatsuya Omori

4.1 Introduction

Most of economic agents evaluate the current economic situation with the economic growth rate, especially the growth rate of gross domestic product (GDP).[1] Every countries face the different economic growth rate such that the economic growth rates of G7 countries are shown in Fig. 4.1 from 1980 to 2014. The fluctuation of economic growth rate in each country is not similar. Why are the economic growth rate in each country different?

For the analysis of that, we develop many economic growth theories.[2] Solow [15], Cass [5] and others develop the neoclassical growth model.[3] At the steady state (long-run market equilibrium) on the neoclassical growth model, the economic growth rate is shown by the exogenous parameters such as the growth rate of

[1]If we denote GDP_t the economic growth rate of year t, we can show the economic growth rate at year t, γ_t as

$$\gamma_t(\%) = \frac{GDP_t - GDP_{t-1}}{GGP_{t-1}} \times 100.$$

[2]For the text book on this issue, we have Intriligator [10], Barro and Sala-i-Martin [4], Acemoglu [1], Aghion and Howitt [2] and others.

[3]The representative growth model other than neoclassical growth model is Harrod [8] and Domar [7].

T. Omori (✉)
School of Business and Public Policies, Chukyo University, 101-2 Yagoto Honmachi, Showa-ku, Nagoya city, Aichi 4668666, Japan
e-mail: tomori@mecl.chukyo-u.ac.jp

T. Naito (ed.), *Sustainable Growth and Development in a Regional Economy*, New Frontiers in Regional Science: Asian Perspectives 13,
DOI 10.1007/978-4-431-55294-9_4

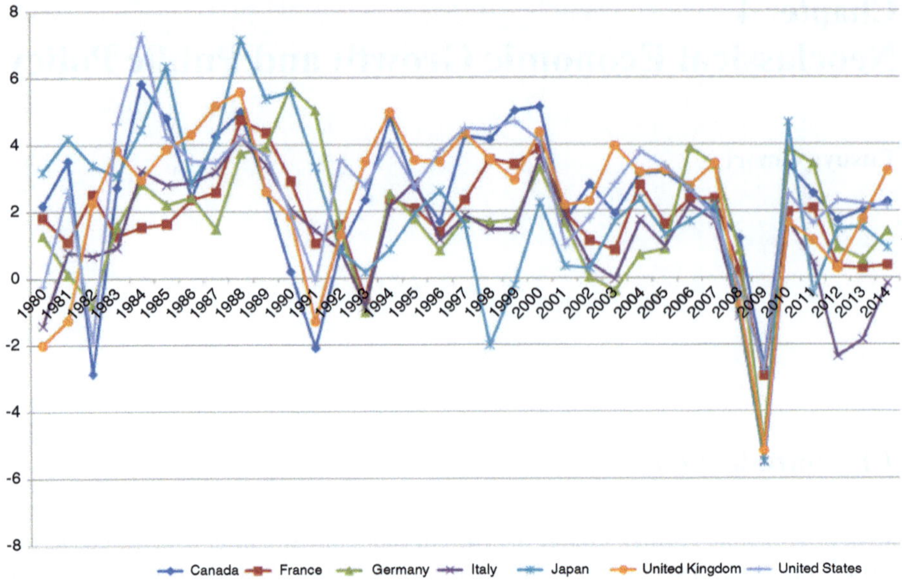

Fig. 4.1 Economic growth rate (Source: www.imf.org/external/pubs/ft/weo/2014/02/weodata/index.aspx)

population and/or the technological growth rate. The growth rates in the steady state are not affected by the economic policy, which affect the economic variables and social welfare. We discuss how economic policy do not influence growth rate. On the other hand, Romer [13], Rebelo [12], and Barro [3] develop the economic model where economic policy affects also economic growth rate in the steady state, as we will discuss this issue next chapter. Based on their models, we can discuss the effects of policy on growth rate. In this chapter, to discuss the policy effects in economic growth model, we show the basic neoclassical growth model.[4] Furthermore, introducing the intergenerational resource allocation into the model, we also show the overlapping generations model developed by Samuelson [14] and Diamond [6].

4.2 Neoclassical Growth Model

In this section, we discuss the neoclassical growth model without consumers' optimal behaviour.[5] In this model, we suppose the closed economy where the aggregative output is produced by the aggregative physical capital and the aggregative

[4] This chapter is based on Omori [11].

[5] You can see the more detail discussion at Intriligator [10].

labour. These inputs are substitutable and the marginal productivity of each input is positive but decreasing. Then, the aggregative production function is shown by

$$Y = F(K, L), \tag{4.1}$$

where Y is the aggregative output, K is the aggregative capital and L is the aggregative labour. In this function, we assume the constant return to scale and the homogeneity of function. When the output per capita is $y = \frac{Y}{L}$ and the capital per capita is $k = \frac{L}{L}$, the production function per capita is given by

$$y = f(k). \tag{4.2}$$

Following Inada [9], the production function is satisfied with the Inada conditions as follows,

$$\lim_{k \to 0} f'(k) = \infty \quad \textit{and} \quad \lim_{k \to \infty} f'(k) = 0.$$

The equilibrium condition of good market is

$$Y = C + I,$$

where C is the aggregative consumption and I is the aggregative investment. As we denote c and i by the consumption per capita and the investment per capita, respectively, the equilibrium condition of good market per capita is

$$y = c + i. \tag{4.3}$$

As the capital accumulation can be differentiated with respect to time, t, the aggregative investment is

$$I = \dot{K} + \mu K. \tag{4.4}$$

where $\dot{K}$ is the variable which is the differentiation with respect to time, t and the μ is the constant positive depreciation rate. When the growth rate of population, $\frac{\dot{L}}{L}$ is shown by n which is the nonnegative parameter and $\dot{k}$ is the per capita variable which is the differentiation with respect to time, the investment per capita is shown by

$$i = \dot{k} + (\mu + n)k = \dot{k} + \lambda k, \tag{4.5}$$

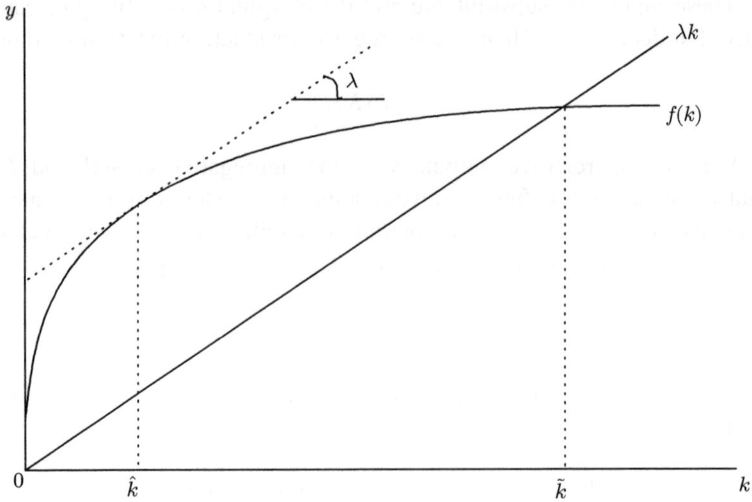

Fig. 4.2 The neoclassical growth equation

where $\lambda = \mu + n$.[6] Using (4.2), (4.3) and (4.5), "The neoclassical growth equation" is derived as

$$f(k) = c + \lambda k + \dot{k}. \tag{4.6}$$

Figure 4.2 shows the relationship between $f(k)$ and λk. The difference between $f(k)$ and λk is $c + \dot{k}$ as shown in Fig. 4.3.

At $\hat{k}$, $c + \dot{k}$ is maximised but, at $\tilde{k}$, $c + \dot{k}$ is zero. We suppose one solution of this differentiation equation, that is $\dot{k} = 0$. At $\hat{k}$, if $\dot{k}$ is zero, the consumption is maximised and the economy is in the "The Golden path". Because the slope of $f(k)$ and λk is the same at $\hat{k}$ as shown in Fig. 4.2, the following condition is satisfied with

$$f'(k) = \lambda = \mu + n. \tag{4.7}$$

[6]Divided (4.4) by L,

$$i = \frac{I}{L} = \frac{\dot{K}}{L} + \mu\frac{K}{L} = \frac{\dot{K}}{L} + \mu k.$$

Furthermore, differentiate the capital per capita, k with respect to time, t,

$$\dot{k} = \frac{d\left(\frac{K}{L}\right)}{dt} = \frac{\dot{K}}{L} - \frac{\dot{L}}{L}\frac{K}{L} = \frac{\dot{K}}{L} - nk.$$

From these equations, we can show (4.5).

Fig. 4.3 $c + \dot{k}$

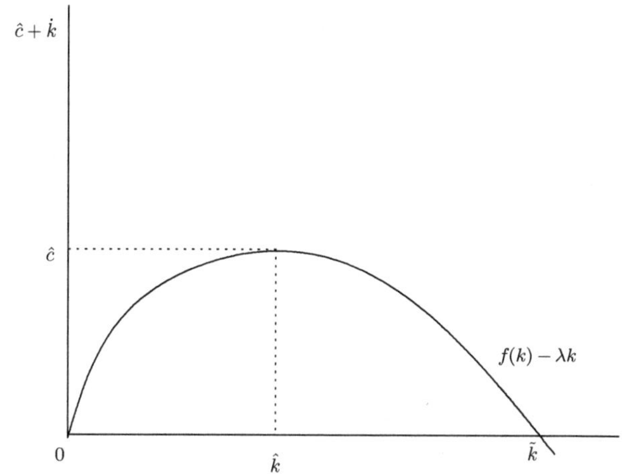

This condition is called the "Golden Rule," because, on this condition, the capital makes consumption maximise. However, this equilibrium is not stable as the capital is decreasing when $\hat{k} > k$.

4.3 Neoclassical Optimal Growth Model

In this section, introducing the consumers' optimal behaviour into the neoclassical growth model, we show the neoclassical optimal growth model. We suppose one representative consumer in the economy. We assume his(her) instantaneous utility as

$$U = U(c), \qquad \frac{dU(c)}{dc} = U'(c) > 0 \quad and \quad \frac{d^2U(c)}{dc^2} = U''(c) < 0.$$

This utility function is assumed to be the following conditions.

$$\lim_{c \to 0} U'(c) = \infty \; and \; \lim_{c \to \infty} U'(x) = 0.$$

The elasticity of marginal utility is assumed by

$$\theta\,(c) = -c\frac{U''(c)}{U'(c)}. \tag{4.8}$$

We note that the marginal utility is positive for the positive consumption.

The representative consumer chooses the sequence of consumption to maximise the lifetime utility subject to the budget constraint. When the positive discount rate is ρ, the optimal behaviour for the representative consumer is formulized as

$$\max_{c} \int_{0}^{\infty} U(c)e^{-\rho t}dt,$$
$$s.t.\ \dot{k} = f(k) - c - \lambda k.$$

The current value Hamiltonian is shown by

$$H = U(c) + q\left(f(k) - c - \lambda k\right), \tag{4.9}$$

where q is the shadow price of capital.[7] Based on the maximum principle, the first order condition for c is

$$\frac{\partial H}{\partial c} = U'(c) - q = 0. \tag{4.10}$$

This condition shows that consumer chooses the sequence of c to equal the marginal utility of consumption with shadow price of capital, q. The time path of q is satisfied with

$$\dot{q} = \rho q - \frac{\partial H}{\partial k} = \left(\rho - f'(k) + \lambda\right) q. \tag{4.11}$$

The transversality condition is

$$\lim_{t \to \infty} qk = 0.$$

Therefore, we can derive the time path of consumption as

$$\dot{c} = \frac{1}{\theta\,(c)} \left[f'\,(k) - \lambda - \rho\right] c.$$

Finally, this economy is summarised with the following dynamical system,

$$\dot{c} = \frac{1}{\theta\,(c)} \left[f'\,(k) - \lambda - \rho\right] c, \tag{4.12}$$

and

$$\dot{k} = f(k) - c - \lambda k. \tag{4.13}$$

[7] See Intriligator [10] for the way to solve the intertemporal decision.

We suppose the one special solution of this dynamical system is $\hat{c} = \hat{k} = 0$. $\dot{c} = \dot{k} = 0$ means that the consumption and the capital per capita is constant in the equilibrium over time. From $\dot{c} = 0$ on (4.12), we can derive the following condition as

$$f'(k^*) = \lambda + \rho. \tag{4.14}$$

and $\dot{k} = 0$ on (4.13) makes us the following equation,

$$c^* = f(k^*) - \lambda k^*. \tag{4.15}$$

In the equilibrium, to satisfy with (4.14) and (4.15), k^* and c^* uniquely exist. These are also satisfied with the following condition,

$$0 < c^* < f(k^*).$$

This equilibrium is in the steady state (steady growth path).

Next, we consider the economic growth rate in the steady state. In the steady state, $\dot{k} = 0$ gives us the following equation,

$$\dot{k} = \frac{d\left(\frac{K}{L}\right)}{dt} = \frac{K}{L}\left(\frac{\dot{K}}{K} - \frac{\dot{L}}{L}\right) = 0.$$

Similarly, $\dot{c} = 0$ gives

$$\dot{c} = \frac{d\left(\frac{C}{L}\right)}{dt} = \frac{C}{L}\left(\frac{\dot{C}}{C} - \frac{\dot{L}}{L}\right) = 0.$$

Therefore,

$$\frac{\dot{K}}{K} = \frac{\dot{C}}{C} = \frac{\dot{L}}{L} = n.$$

The economic growth rate on the steady state in the neoclassical optimal growth model is shown by the exogenous parameter, n, which is the growth rate of population. Because the consumption and capital per capita is constant in the steady state, the aggregative consumption ($C = cL$), the aggregative capital ($K = kL$) and the aggregative output ($Y = yL$) grows at the rate of n.

We discuss the dynamical system (4.12) and (4.13) with the phase diagram on Fig. 4.4.

From (4.12), we can show $f\prime(k) = \lambda + \rho$ in the case of $\dot{c} = 0$ and the following relationships.

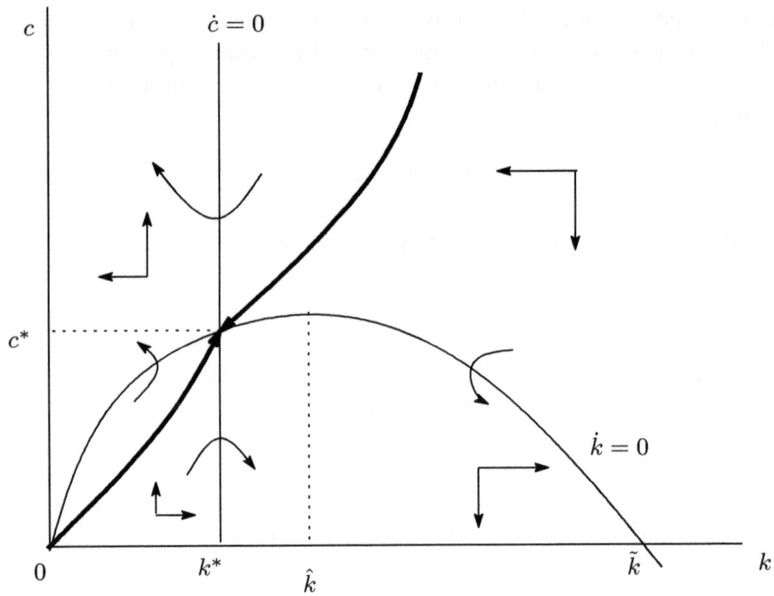

Fig. 4.4 Phase diagram

If

$$f'(k) \begin{bmatrix} > \\ = \\ < \end{bmatrix} \lambda + \rho, \textit{ then } \quad \dot{c} \begin{bmatrix} > \\ = \\ < \end{bmatrix} 0.$$

In other words, if

$$k \begin{bmatrix} < \\ = \\ > \end{bmatrix} k^*, \textit{ then } \quad \dot{c} \begin{bmatrix} > \\ = \\ < \end{bmatrix} 0.$$

When $k < k^*$, c increases but, when $k > k^*$, c decreases.

On the other hand, from (4.13), we can show the following condition. If

$$f(k) - \lambda k \begin{bmatrix} > \\ = \\ < \end{bmatrix} c, \textit{ then } \quad \dot{k} \begin{bmatrix} > \\ = \\ < \end{bmatrix} 0.$$

When c is in the upper area of $\dot{k}$ line, k decreases but, when c is in the lower area of $\dot{k}$ line, k increases.

Therefore, in Fig. 4.4, the two bold lines toward the cross point of (c, k) are on the optimal growth path.

The local stability of solutions to the dynamical system can be determined by the characteristic roots of the coefficients with linearization of system at the neighbourhood of equilibrium. That is,

$$\begin{bmatrix} \dot{c} \\ \dot{k} \end{bmatrix} \cong \begin{bmatrix} 0 & E \\ -1 & \rho \end{bmatrix} \begin{bmatrix} c - c^* \\ k - k^* \end{bmatrix},$$

where $E = \frac{c^* f\prime\prime(k^*)}{\sigma(c^*)}$. As we denote the characteristic root by ϵ, the characteristic equation is

$$\epsilon^2 - \rho\epsilon + E = 0,$$

and the roots are

$$\epsilon = \frac{\rho \pm \sqrt{\rho^2 - 4E}}{2}.$$

Because the roots are real and opposite in sign, the equilibrium of system is a saddle point. Historically given the capital per capita, k_0, the consumers chooses the consumption and the capital for such k_0 and the economy goes to the equilibrium as shown in Fig. 4.4. As the bold path is in the optimal growth path, k and c should kept in the equilibrium over time.

4.4 Technological Progress

Above discussed, the per capita variables are constant in the steady state because the technology is assumed to be constant return to scale and the same production function is assumed over time. However, if we take into consideration the technological progress, the per capita variables would be changed. In this subsection, we examine the neoclassical optimal growth model with the technological progress. We define the technological progress per effective unit labour as

$$M \equiv VL,$$

where V is the technological progress (level). The technological progress is supposed to be the labour augmenting progress, $\nu = \frac{\dot{V}}{V}$. Based on this technological progress, we can rewrite the aggregative production function as

$$Y = F(K, M).$$

Therefore, the dynamical system can be rewritten as

$$\dot{c_M} = \frac{1}{\theta(c)}\left[f'(k_M) - \upsilon - \lambda - \rho\right] c_M, \tag{4.16}$$

and

$$\dot{k_M} = f(k_M) - c_M - (\upsilon + \lambda) k_M, \tag{4.17}$$

where $c_M = \frac{C}{M}$ and $k_M = \frac{K}{M}$.

One special solution of this dynamical system is $\dot{c_M} = \dot{k_M} = 0$. The optimal growth path is the cross point of $\dot{c_M} = 0$ and $\dot{k_M} = 0$. Although c is constant in the steady state without technological progress, c_M is constant in the steady state with technological progress. The aggregative consumption is shown by $C = c_M VL$ and the economic growth rate in steady state is the sum of population growth rate and the technological progress rate.[8] However, these rate are exogenous parameters and economic policy can not affect them in the steady state of neoclassical optimal growth model.

4.5 Neoclassical Economic Growth and Public Policy

The economic policy does not affect the economic growth rate in steady state. To clarify these effects, in this section, introducing public policy into neoclassical optimal growth model, we examine the effects of public policy on economic growth rate in the steady state.

We suppose a government which collects the wage income tax for the productive public goods. Then, we suppose the aggregative production function including

[8] In the steady state, from $\dot{c_M} = 0$,

$$\dot{c_M} = \frac{d\left(\frac{C}{VL}\right)}{dt} = \frac{C}{VL}\left(\frac{\dot{C}}{C} - \frac{\dot{V}}{V} - \frac{\dot{L}}{L}\right) = 0.$$

Similarly from $\dot{k_M} = 0$,

$$\dot{k_M} = \frac{d\left(\frac{K}{VL}\right)}{dt} = \frac{K}{VL}\left(\frac{\dot{K}}{K} - \frac{\dot{V}}{V} - \frac{\dot{L}}{L}\right) = 0.$$

Then,

$$\frac{\dot{K}}{K} = \frac{\dot{C}}{C} = \frac{\dot{V}}{V} + \frac{\dot{L}}{L} = \upsilon + n.$$

.

publicly provided goods as

$$Y = F(K, G, L), \tag{4.18}$$

where G is the aggregative but not accumulated public goods. This production function is also assumed to be homogeneous function. The output per capita is shown by

$$y = f(k, g),$$

where g is the public goods per capita, $g = \frac{G}{L}$. When the wage income tax rate is τ, the budget constraint per capita is

$$\dot{k} = (1 - \tau)f(k, g) - c - \lambda k. \tag{4.19}$$

An instantaneous government budget constrain is given by

$$\tau f(k, g) = g.$$

Therefore, the representative consumer's optimal behaviour is formulized as

$$\max_{c} \quad \int_0^\infty U(c)e^{-\rho t}dt,$$
$$s.t. \quad \dot{k} = (1 - \tau)f(k, g) - c - \lambda k.$$

The current value Hamiltonian is

$$H = U(c) + q\left((1 - \tau)f(k, g) - c - \lambda k\right), \tag{4.20}$$

where q is the shadow price of capital and the first order condition is given by

$$\frac{\partial H}{\partial c} = U'(c) - q = 0. \tag{4.21}$$

The shadow price, q is satisfied with the following condition,

$$\dot{q} = \rho q - \frac{\partial H}{\partial k} = \left(\rho - (1 - \tau)f_k' + \lambda\right) q,$$

where $f_k' = \frac{\partial f(k,g)}{\partial k}$. The transversality condition is

$$\lim_{t \to \infty} qk = 0.$$

Therefore, the consumption per capita is derived from these conditions,

$$\dot{c} = \frac{1}{\theta\left(c\right)}\left[(1-\tau)f_k' - \lambda - \rho\right]c.$$

We can summarised the dynamical system in this model as

$$\dot{c} = \frac{1}{\theta\left(c\right)}\left[(1-\tau)f_k' - \lambda - \rho\right]c, \tag{4.22}$$

and

$$\dot{k} = (1-\tau)f(k,g) - c - \lambda k. \tag{4.23}$$

The special solution of this system is $\dot{c} = \dot{k} = 0$. Without technological progress, the aggregative consumption ($C = cL$), the aggregative capital ($K = kL$) and the aggregative output ($Y = yL$) grows at the rate of n. In the neoclassical optimal growth model, public policy affects the variables per capita and the aggregative variables but does not affect the economic growth rate in steady state.

4.6 Overlapping Generations Model

Until this section, we suppose that time is continuous and the consumer lives infinitely. However, we can not show the intertemporal consumers' behaviour, especially saving behaviour in above models. We can also suppose that time is discrete and the consumer lives for some periods. At one period, the multiple generations of consumer are supposed to exist in the economy. Samuelson [14] and Diamond [6] develop the overlapping generations model which includes these consumers' consideration. In this section, we discuss this model.

In this model, the consumers live for two periods, the working period and the retirement period, in a closed one good economy. The economy grows at the growth rate of population, n. When the population of working generation at period t is assumed to be L_t and that at period $t+1$ is L_{t+1}, the relationship between them is shown by $L_{t+1} = (1+n)L_t$. We assume away the depreciation rate of capital. As shown in Fig. 4.5, at period t, there exists two generations, the working generation and the retirement generation. We call the working generation at period t as generation t.

The utility for the representative consumer of generation t is derived from the consumptions at each period. That is,

$$U^t = U^t\left(c_t^t,\ c_{t+1}^t\right), \tag{4.24}$$

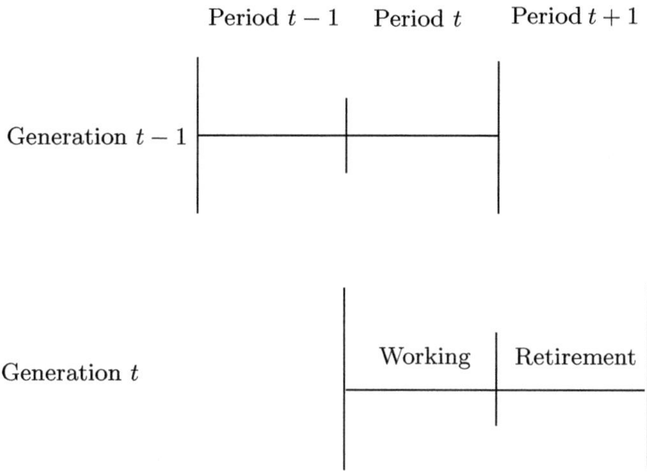

Fig. 4.5 Overlapping generations model

where c_t^t is the consumption of the working period for generation t at period t and c_{t+1}^t is the consumption of the retirement period for generation t at period $t+1$.

The generation t in the first period of their lives, the working generation, supply their labour inelastically to firms. They divide their wage income, w_t, between current consumption, c_t^t and saving for consumption when retirement, s_t. The budget constraint for the working period of representative generation t is

$$w_t = c_t^t + s_t. \tag{4.25}$$

The generation t in the second (final) period of their lives, the retirement, consume their accumulated savings and interest. We assume no bequests. The budget constraint for the retirement period of generation t is given by

$$c_{t+1}^t = (1 + r_{t+1})\, s_t, \tag{4.26}$$

where r_{t+1} is the interest rate at $t+1$.

Given w_t and r_{t+1}, a representative agent of generation t chooses c_t^t and c_{t+1}^t to maximise his utility (4.24) subject to budget constraints (4.25) and (4.26). We can show optimal condition as

$$\frac{U_t^{t\prime}}{U_{t+1}^t} = 1 + r_{t+1},$$

where $U_t^t = \frac{\partial U^t}{\partial c_t^t}$ and $U_{t+1}^t = \frac{\partial U^t}{\partial c_{t+1}^t}$.

Based on this condition, the saving function per capita for generation t is shown as

$$s_t = s_t\left(w_t,\ 1 + r_{t+1}\right). \tag{4.27}$$

Similar to the neoclassical growth model, firms produce output with capital and labour.[9] The aggregate production function is expressed as follows,

$$Y_t = F(K_t, L_t),$$

where Y_t is the aggregate output at period t, K_t the aggregate capital, L_t the aggregate labour at t. The production technology exhibits a constant return to scale, and the marginal productivity of each input is positive and decreasing. We define $y_t \equiv \frac{Y_t}{L_t}$ and $k_t \equiv \frac{K_t}{L_t}$. The output per the working generation can be rewritten:

$$y_t = f(k_t).$$

Firms behave perfect competitively to maximise their profit. From the first-order conditions for profit maximisation, factor prices are derived as follows:

$$w_t = f(k_t) - k_t f\prime(k_t), \tag{4.28}$$

and

$$r_t = f\prime(k_t). \tag{4.29}$$

As the working generation supply their labour inelastically to firms, we consider the capital market for the equilibrium. The equilibrium condition of capital market and Walras' Law makes the goods market be in equilibrium. The equilibrium condition of capital market is

$$(1 + n)\, k_{t+1} = s_t\left(w_t,\ 1 + r_{t+1}\right). \tag{4.30}$$

This economy is summarised to the following dynamic equation,

$$(1 + n)\, k_{t+1} = s_t\left(w_t\left(k_t\right),\ 1 + r_{t+1}\left(k_{t+1}\right)\right). \tag{4.31}$$

When k_t is equal to k_{t+1}, the economy is in the steady state.

Next, we examine the stability of equilibrium. From (4.31), in the neighbourhood of equilibrium, we can show the relationship between k_{t+1} and k_t as

$$\frac{dk_{t+1}}{dk_t} = \frac{-s_w\left(k_t\right) k_t f''\left(k_t\right)}{1 + n - s_r\left(k_{t+1}\right) f''\left(k_{t+1}\right)},$$

where $s_w = \frac{\partial s_t}{\partial w_t}$ and $s_r = \frac{\partial s_t}{\partial r_t}$.

[9] The overlapping generations model is developed based on the neoclassical growth model.

When the following condition is satisfied, the equilibrium is stable. If

$$\left| \frac{-s_w(k^*)\, k^* f''(k^*)}{1 + n - s_r(k^*) f''(k^*)} \right| < 1, \tag{4.32}$$

the equilibrium is stable.

Let the aggregative capital at period $t + 1$ be $K_{t+1} = k_{t+1}L_{t+1}$ and that at period t be $K_t = k_t L_t$. As $k_t = k_{t+1}$ and $L_{t+1} = (1 + n)L_t$ in steady state, the economic growth rate is shown as

$$\frac{K_{t+1}}{K_t} = \frac{k_{t+1}L_{t+1}}{k_t L_t} = (1 + n). \tag{4.33}$$

Even in the overlapping generations model with the neoclassical production function and the explicit saving behaviour, the economic growth rate is shown by the exogenous parameter and the economic policy does not affect the growth rate in steady state.

4.7 Concluding Remarks

Finally, although the economic growth rate fluctuates in each country as in Fig. 4.1, assuming the constant return to scale on aggregative production function in the neoclassical (optimal) economic growth model, the economic growth rate on such model is shown by the exogenous parameters, the growth rate of population and/or technological progress rate. On the model, the economic policy can not affect the economic growth rate. However, as discussed next chapter, if we assume different type of production function, we could examine the effects of economic policy on economic growth rate in steady state.

References

1. Acemoglu, D. (2009). *Introduction to modern economic growth*. Princeton: Princeton University Press.
2. Aghion, P., & Howitt, P. (2009). *The economics of growth*. Cambridge: MIT.
3. Barro, R. J. (1990). Government spending in a simple model of endogenous growth. *Journal of Political Economy, 98*, S103–S125.
4. Barro, R. J., & Sala-i-Martin, X. (2004). *Economic growth* (2nd ed.). London/Cambridge: MIT Press.
5. Cass, S. (1965). Optimum growth in an aggregative model of capital accumulation. *Review of Economic Studies, 32*, 233–240.
6. Diamond, P. A. (1965). National debt in a neoclassical growth model. *American Economic Review, 55*(5), 1126–1150.

7. Domar, E. D. (1946). Capital expansion, rate of growth, and employment. *Econometrica, 14*, 137–147.
8. Harrod, R. F. (1939). An Essay in dynamic theory. *Economic Journal, 49*, 14–33.
9. Inada, K. (1963). On a two-sector model of economic growth: Comments and a generalization. *Review of Economic Studies, 30*(2), 119–127.
10. Intriligator, M. D. (2002). *Mathematical optimization and economic theory*. Philadelphia: Society for Industrial and Applied Mathematics.
11. Omori, T. (2009, in Japanese). Effects of tax and allocation of public expenditure on economic growth. Desertation for Doctor of Economics, Nagoya University.
12. Rebelo, S. (1991). Long-run policy analysis and long-run growth. *Journal of Political Economy, 99*, 500–521.
13. Romer, P. M. (1986). Increasing returns and long-run growth. *Journal of Political Economy, 94*, 1002–1037.
14. Samuelson, P. (1958). An exact consumption-loan model of interest with or without the social contrivance of money. *Journal of Political Economy, 66*, 467–482.
15. Solow, R. M. (1956). A contribution to the theory of economic growth. *Quarterly Journal of Economics, 70*, 65–94.

Chapter 5
Endogenous Growth Model with Public Financed R&D

Daisuke Ikazaki

5.1 Introduction

In Chap. 4, we discussed long run growth based on neoclassical growth models. As shown in Chap. 4, main characteristics of a typical neoclassical production function are as follows. First, the output depends on capital, labor, and productivity. Second, the production function exhibits positive and diminishing marginal products with respect to each input. Third, the marginal product of capital (or labor) approaches 0 as capital (or labor) goes to infinity. We showed in Chap. 4 that the long-run growth rate converges to 0 if the returns to capital are 0 asymptotically. So if we employ a production function in which productivity is constant over time, then growth peters out eventually. However, this result is just not realistic. Economic growth rates of many countries do not seem to converge to 0. To avoid zero growth in the steady state, we must consider alternative production functions in which diminishing returns to capital do not converge to 0 in the long run.

There are some ideas. If we assume that productivity increases at an exogenously given rate, say g, some problems may be solved. This model is called as exogenous growth model and can be considered as an extension of neoclassical growth model that we discuss in Chap. 4. In the steady state, the growth rates of physical capital, output, per capita income become positive. So we can ward off zero growth. The long run growth rates depend on g. However, we cannot explain how and why technology always improves at the rate, g. Another idea is to extend the externalities

---

D. Ikazaki (✉)
Faculty of Human Sciences and Design, Japan Women's University, 2-8-1 Mejirodai, Bunkyo-ku, Tokyo 1128681, Japan
e-mail: ikazaki@fc.jwu.ac.jp

T. Naito (ed.), *Sustainable Growth and Development in a Regional Economy*, New Frontiers in Regional Science: Asian Perspectives 13,
DOI 10.1007/978-4-431-55294-9_5

of capital. If we assume capital used in one firm affect the productivities of the different firms (because there exist positive externalities), it is possible to assume diminishing returns to a capital do not apply.

The other idea is what we will discuss in this chapter. The model that we will discuss in this chapter is called as endogenous growth models. Endogenous growth theory tries to explain the dynamic behavior of productivity. If we compare endogenous growth model with neoclassical growth model, we can reconfirm the importance of productivity improvement. Many papers related to endogenous growth models have stressed the importance of technological progress or productivity growth. Some insist that innovation induced by research and development (R&D) play important roles (Romer [7]; Grossman and Helpman [4, Ch.3, Ch.4]; Aghion and Howitt [2]). Another idea is to extend the bound of capital. If we assume capital in the production function includes not only physical capital but also human capital, it is possible to assume diminishing returns to a broad concept of capital do not apply (Lucas [5]). In endogenous growth models, some resources are devoted research sector or education sector to create innovation, to provide technological progress, and to accumulate human capital or knowledge capital. The long-term growth rates of various variables are determined within the model. Endogenous growth models can explain how and why productivity improvement occurs.

In this chapter, we discuss a simple endogenous growth theory based on the Diamond's [3] overlapping generations model. The output of final goods depends on capital, labor and productivity. We assume that knowledge stock accumulates and productivity increases if a government levies taxes on the output and if tax revenue is devoted to the research sector. That is, we assume that productivity increase is induced by the government policy (R&D policy). However, such tax polices prevent the economy from accumulating physical capital. Therefore, the government must consider the benefit and the cost of tax to seek desirable tax rates.

Then, the dynamic behavior of each variable is analyzed. We show that a government does not impose a tax in the first stage of development. Capital accumulation based strategy becomes optimal if the economy is not developed enough. If an economy develops to a considerable degree, then the government introduces a tax to engage in research activities that increase productivity. As Acemoglu, Aghion, and Zilibotti [1] have reported, innovation-based strategy is important when the economy highly develops. The long-run growth rate becomes positive if certain conditions are met. As in the general endogenous growth model (Romer [7]; Grossman and Helpman [4]; Aghion and Howitt [2]), the sustainability of the economy depends on the productivity of the research sector.

5.2 The Model

First, we analyze the final goods sector. The market for final goods is assumed to be perfectly competitive. Numerous firms manufacture homogeneous final goods subject to the same technology:

$$Y_t = K_t^{\alpha}(A_t L_t)^{1-\alpha}, \tag{5.1}$$

where Y_t is the aggregate output,[1] A_t denotes the productivity (knowledge stock), K_t represents the capital stock, and L_t signifies the labor input. We also assume that $0 < \alpha < 1$. Capital depreciates fully during the production process. It is assumed that firms take the values of A_t as given. As we know later, the dynamic behavior of A_t is determined endogenously in this section. In Sect. 5.4, we assume that A_t is constant or grows exogenously.

The firm profit is given as

$$\pi_t = (1-\tau_t)K_t^{\alpha}(A_t L_t)^{1-\alpha} - (1+r_t)K_t - w_t L_t.$$

Firms maximize their profits at each date, taking the interest rate, r_t, the wage rate w_t, and tax rate τ_t as given. From the firms' profit maximization, we can obtain

$$(1+r_t) = (1-\tau_t)\alpha K_t^{\alpha-1}(A_t L_t)^{1-\alpha}, \tag{5.2}$$

$$w_t = (1-\tau_t)(1-\alpha)K_t^{\alpha}A_t^{1-\alpha}L_t^{-\alpha}, \tag{5.3}$$

We describe consumers next. Generation t is defined as the people who are born in period t. Individuals live for two periods. We assume that the population is constant over time. The population in this economy is assumed to be 2: there is one unit of the younger generation and one unit of the older generation.

Each individual can only work during the first period of their lives. They supply one unit of labor inelastically and earn a wage. Because we assume that the labor market clears at every moment, $L_t = 1$ for all t. During the youth period, individuals do not consume some part of their total income, choosing to save it instead. In old age, they consume those savings. Individuals are non-altruistic in these analyses. Consequently, we obtain the following equation.

$$c_{t+1} = (1+r_{t+1})w_t \tag{5.4}$$

Therein, c_{t+1} represents per-capita consumption. The expected utility of an individual in generation t is

$$U_t = \log c_{t+1}. \tag{5.5}$$

Next, we analyze the government policy. Tax revenue $\tau_t Y_t$ is used for R&D activities that increase productivity. We assume that the dynamic behavior of productivity A_t is specified as

$$A_{t+1} = A_t + \beta\tau_t Y_t, \tag{5.6}$$

[1]Subscript t represents the level in period t throughout this paper.

where $\beta(\beta > 0)$ is the productivity parameter of R&D sector. It is assumed that one unit of input can increase β units of knowledge stock.

5.3 Government Policy

In this section, we consider government policy. A government levy on a tax on firms. Tax revenue is devoted to R&D activities. We assume that the government is short-lived and that its objective is to maximize the utilities of the currently living voters (we relax this assumption in the next section). It does not consider the utility of unborn generations. The objective function of the government is a weighted sum of the utilities of potential voters: the government must set a tax rate to maximize

$$\theta U_{t-1} + U_t,$$

where θ is the relative weight the politicians attach to the utility of elderly people. In addition, U_t is defined in Eq. (5.5). The government in period t looks ahead to the subsequent period because the utility of each young voter depends on c_{t+1} and A_{t+1}. Following Verbon and Verhoeven [8] and Meijdam and Verbon [6], we assume rational expectations and myopic decision-making. Rational expectations means that the short-lived government can estimate the tax rate in the subsequent period accurately. Myopic decision-making implies that the government disregards the impact of current policies on future political decisions. These assumptions imply that the government chooses the tax rate τ_t, taking the tax rate in the next period τ_{t+1} as given.

Next we consider the impact of the tax increases. First, they reduce the interest income and consumption of elderly people, which decreases the utility of each old voter. Second, it drives down wages of young workers. This effect decreases the utility of each young voter. Third, it improves the productivity in period $t + 1$. This effect increases the utility of each young voter. Fourth, the capital stock in period $t + 1$ will decrease because of the decline in wages (note that a market clearing condition for capital is $w_t = s_t = K_{t+1}$), which affects the tax rate in period $t + 1$, and thereby the consumption level of the next period.

Next we derive the lifetime utility of the old in period t. Because $c_t = (1 + r_t)s_{t-1} = (1 - \tau_t)\alpha Y_t$, we can obtain

$$U_{t-1} = \log(1 - \tau_t) + \log(\alpha Y_t). \tag{5.7}$$

Next, we will describe the lifetime utility of the young in period t. Actually, c_{t+1} is rewritten as

$$c_{t+1} = (1 - \tau_{t+1})\alpha[(1 - \tau_t)(1 - \alpha)Y_t]^{\alpha}(A_t + \beta\tau_t Y_t)^{1-\alpha}. \tag{5.8}$$

From Eqs. (5.5), (5.6), and (5.8), we obtain

$$U_t = \alpha \log(1-\tau_t) + (1-\alpha)\log(A_t + \beta\tau_t K_t^{\alpha} A_t^{1-\alpha}) \\ + \log[(1-\tau_{t+1})\alpha\,((1-\alpha)Y_t)^{\alpha}]. \tag{5.9}$$

As shown in Eqs. (5.7) and (5.9), the problem of a government in period t is to choose τ_t to maximize

$$V_t = (\alpha+\theta)\log(1-\tau_t) + (1-\alpha)\log(1+\beta\tau k_t^{\alpha}), \tag{5.10}$$

where $k_t \equiv \frac{K_t}{A_t}$. Actually, $V_t \equiv \theta U_{t-1} + U_t - \Delta_t$, where $\Delta_t \equiv \theta\log(\alpha Y_t) + (1-\alpha)\log A_t + \log[(1-\tau_{t+1})\alpha\,((1-\alpha)Y_t)^{\alpha}]$. The government determines the tax rate τ_t taking the values of Δ_t as given. Therefore, we use V_t instead of $\theta U_{t-1} + U_t$ to simplify the notation. The optimal tax rate is given as

$$\tau_t = \begin{cases} 0 & \text{if } \; k_t \le k_\delta, \\ \frac{(1-\alpha)\beta k_t^{\alpha} - (\alpha+\theta)}{(1+\theta)\beta k_t^{\alpha}} (\equiv \tau_t^*) & \text{if } \; k_t > k_\delta, \end{cases} \tag{5.11}$$

$$k_\delta \equiv \left(\frac{\alpha+\theta}{\beta(1-\alpha)}\right)^{\frac{1}{\alpha}}. \tag{5.12}$$

It is also noteworthy that $\frac{\partial \tau_t^*}{\partial k_t} > 0$, $\frac{\partial^2 \tau_t^*}{\partial k_t^2} < 0$.

If capital stock is scarce compared with knowledge stock (if k_t is small), then the government has no need to devote resources to the research activities. Therefore, the tax rate becomes zero and $Y_t = C_t + K_{t+1}$. Capital accumulation becomes the engine of growth when k_t is small and $\tau_t = 0$. In this situation, the economy uses a capital accumulation based strategy.

Suppose that knowledge stock is scarce compared with capital stock (k_t is large). Then, the government must devote some resources to the research activities. In this situation, the tax rate becomes positive. Innovation becomes the engine of the growth. Under these circumstances, the economy employs an innovation-based strategy. It is also noteworthy that the tax rate is positively related with k_t.

5.4 Dynamic Equilibrium

We consider dynamics in this section. First, we assume that $k_t < k_\delta$. Then, $\tau_t = 0$. Under these circumstances, the following equations must hold:

$$K_{t+1} = w_t = (1-\alpha)K_t^{\alpha} A_t^{1-\alpha}, \tag{5.13}$$

$$A_{t+1} = A_t. \tag{5.14}$$

From Eqs. (5.13) and (5.14), the dynamic behavior of k_t (the relation between k_t and k_{t+1}) is given as

$$k_{t+1} = (1-\alpha)k_t^{\alpha} \equiv f(k_t), \tag{5.15}$$

$f'(k_t) > 0$ and $f''(k_t) < 0$.

Next, we describe the case in which $k_t > k_{\delta}$. In this case, $\tau_t = \tau_t^*$. We obtain

$$k_{t+1} = \frac{\alpha+\theta}{\beta} = f(k_{\delta}) \equiv k^2. \tag{5.16}$$

That is, k_{t+1} is constant for all k_t $(> k_{\delta})$. From (5.15) and (5.16), the dynamic benhavior of k_t is given as

$$k_{t+1} = \begin{cases} (1-\alpha)k_t^{\alpha} \equiv f(k_t) & \text{if} \quad k_t \le k_{\delta}, \\ \frac{\alpha+\theta}{\beta} = f(k_{\delta}) \equiv k^2 & \text{if} \quad k_t > k_{\delta}. \end{cases} \tag{5.17}$$

We assume that the initial value of k_t (which is written as k_0) is low and $k_0 < k_{\delta}$. In period 0, elderly people have K_0 units of assets.

If $k_{\delta} > f(k_{\delta})$, then

$$1-\alpha < \left(\frac{\alpha+\theta}{\beta}\right)^{1-\alpha}$$

In this case, the equilibrium dynamics are as shown in Fig. 5.1. This inequality tends to hold when the productivity of research sector is low (β is small) and the political power of old is high (θ is large). The figure shows that convergence to the unique steady state $k^1 \equiv (1-\alpha)^{\frac{1}{1-\alpha}}$ is monotonic. Furthermore, K_t, A_t, and Y_t grow at the same rate in the steady state because k_t becomes constant in the steady state. Because $k_t < k_{\delta}$ for all t, $\tau_t = 0$ and $A_t = A_0$ for all t. This implies that Y_t and K_t become constant in the steady state. This situation is similar to that of the typical neo-classical growth model. Because productivity or knowledge stock does not change over time and because the marginal product of capital declines over time, the long-run growth rate becomes 0.

If $f(k_{\delta}) > k_{\delta}$ $\left(1-\alpha > \left(\frac{\alpha+\theta}{\beta}\right)^{1-\alpha}\right)$, then we can draw relations between k_t and k_{t+1} as Fig. 5.2. This inequality tends to hold when the productivity of research sector is high (β is large) and the political power of old is low (θ is small). In the first stage of the development, the tax rate is 0 because physical capital is rarely offered in markets and k_t is less than k_{δ}. However, k_t becomes greater than k_{δ} eventually; subsequently, it converges to its steady state level k_2, where $k^2 = f(k_{\delta})$. If we designate the growth rates of Y_t, K_t, and A_t as g, then Eqs. (5.6) and (5.17) imply that

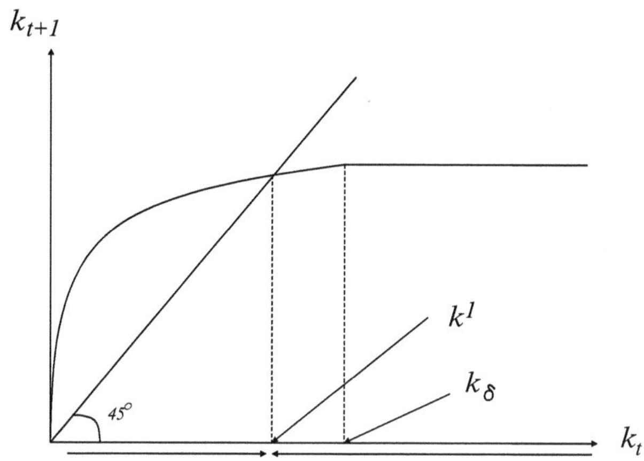

Fig. 5.1 The dynamic behavior of k_t ($k_\delta > f(k_\delta)$)

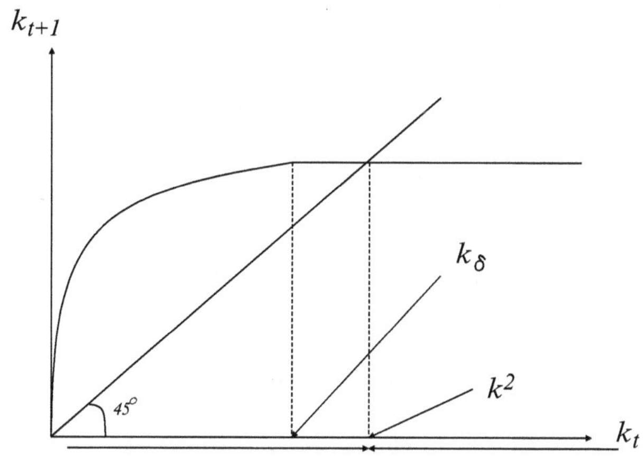

Fig. 5.2 The dynamic behavior of k_t ($k_\delta < f(k_\delta)$)

$$g = \frac{\alpha + \theta}{1 + \theta}\left((1-\alpha)\left(\frac{\beta}{\alpha + \theta}\right)^{1-\alpha} - 1\right) \tag{5.18}$$

in the steady state. Note that $g > 0$ when $f(k_\delta) > k_\delta$: growth rates become positive when $k_\delta < f(k_\delta)$. The growth rate is higher when the productivity of R&D sector is high (higher β); also, the political power of elderly people is weak (lower θ). Then, we obtain the following proposition. Then We can obtain the following proposition.

Theorem 5.1. *(1) If $k_\delta > f(k_\delta)$, then the tax rate is 0 for all t and the economy converges to the unique steady state k^1 $(k^1 < k_\delta)$. In this steady state, the growth rates of Y_t, K_t and A_t become 0.*

(2) *If* $f(k_\delta) > k_\delta$, *then the economy converges to the unique steady state* k^2 $(k^2 > k_\delta)$. *In the steady state, the growth rates of* Y_t, K_t *and* A_t *become* $g = \frac{\alpha+\theta}{1+\theta}\left((1-\alpha)\left(\frac{\beta}{\alpha+\theta}\right)^{1-\alpha} - 1\right) > 0.$

5.5 Concluding Remarks

In this chapter, we construct a simple endogenous growth model and explain how productivity improvement contributes to long run growth. Unlike the previous studies in which intentional R&D promoted by private firms, we assume that the government imposes a tax and devote tax revenue to the research sector. We also assume that the government is short-lived and short-sighted and cares about the utilities of the currently living voters. It does not concern itself with the utility of unborn generations.

In the first stage of development, the government does not impose a tax and employs a capital accumulation based strategy. In this stage, the knowledge stock level is constant because research activity is not conducted. If the research sector is not productive and the elderly citizens' political power is strong, then the tax rate is always zero and the government employs a capital accumulation strategy perpetually. The economy does not move into the second stage of development and the growth rate of capital, productivity, and output become 0.

Presuming that the research sector is productive and that the elderly people's political power is low, then government employs an innovation-based strategy as the economy becomes highly developed. The growth rate in the steady state is positive if and only if strategic change takes place appropriately.

If this strategic change does not take place, our model becomes neoclassical growth model in which each variable becomes constant in the long-run. If the productivity of research sector is high, this strategic change occurs appropriately and the growth rate in the steady state becomes positive. Note that the productivity improvement becomes the determinant of positive growth. Note also that the growth rate depends on the parameters that reflect economic characteristics. So we can explain the mechanism of economic growth within the model.

In the real world, these research activities are conducted not only by the public sector but also by the private firms. We can extend our model to include the role of private sector. However many studies related to endogenous growth have already constructed such model. So we introduce a very simple model in this chapter.

References

1. Acemoglu, D., Aghion, P., & Zilibotti, F. (2006). Distance to frontier, selection, and economic growth. *Journal of the European Economic Association, 4*(1), 37–74.
2. Aghion, P., & Howitt, P. (1992). A model of growth through creative destruction. *Econometrica, 60*(2), 323–351.

3. Diamond, P. A. (1965). National debt in a neoclassical growth model. *American Economic Review, 55*(5), 1126–1150.
4. Grossman G. M., & Helpman, E. (1991). *Innovation and growth in the global economy*. Cambridge: MIT.
5. Lucas, R. E., Jr. (1988). On the mechanics of economic development. *Journal of Monetary Economics, 22*(1), 3–42.
6. Meijdam, L., & Verbon, H. A. A. (1997). Aging and public pensions in an overlapping-generations model. *Oxford Economic Papers, 49*, 29–42. Oxford University Press.
7. Romer, P. (1990). Endogenous technological change. *Journal of Political Economy, 98*(5), S71–S102.
8. Verbon, H. A. A., & Verhoeven, M. J. M. (1992). Decision making on pension schemes under rational expectations. *Journal of Economics, 56*(1), 71–97.

Chapter 6
Emission Tax Timing and a Monopoly Market

Yasunori Ouchida

6.1 Introduction

In many economically developed countries, "voluntary approaches", widely recognized as environmental policy instruments, have been introduced during the last few decades.[1] Attention to "voluntary approaches" has been increasing since the early 2000s. According to the OECD [14, 15], voluntary approaches are classifiable into four types: (i) unilateral commitments made by polluting firms, (ii) private agreements between polluters and pollutees, (iii) environmental agreements negotiated between industry and public authorities, and (iv) voluntary programs developed by public authorities that invite individual firms to participate.

In December 1996, the Japan Business Federation (Nippon Keidanren) started a unilateral action plan designated as the "Keidanren Voluntary Action Plan on the Environment" in Japan.[2] The Japan Business Federation has voluntarily produced some quantitative targets for every industry in that plan. Therefore, at present, the Japanese government must design environmental policies corresponding to voluntary actions (unilateral commitments) from the industrial side. That fact suggests that if the Japanese government adopts an emission tax policy, a time-

[1]For detailed arguments related to voluntary approaches, see Carraro and Lévêque [3] and OECD [14, 15].

[2]For details for Keidanren's voluntary action, see, for example, see the relevant report by Ikkatai et al. [11] among others.

Y. Ouchida (✉)
Department of Economics, Hiroshima University, 1-2-1 Kagamiyama,
Higashi-Hiroshima city, Hiroshima 739-8525, Japan
e-mail: ouchida@hiroshima-u.ac.jp

T. Naito (ed.), *Sustainable Growth and Development in a Regional Economy*,
New Frontiers in Regional Science: Asian Perspectives 13,
DOI 10.1007/978-4-431-55294-9_6

consistent emission tax is introduced. This chapter presents an examination of the regulator's precommitment inability for an emission tax.

Game-theoretic analysis enables us to address the essence of a polluting firm's unilateral investments for emissions reduction in the presence of a strategic interaction between a regulator and oligopolistic firms. Petrakis and Xepapadeas [18], Conrad [6], Poyago-Theotoky and Teerasuwannajak [20], Petrakis and Xepapadeas [19], and Puller [23] describe the timing of an emission tax in the context of imperfect quantity competition. They examine a regulator's ability to precommit to an emission tax rate, and the effects of such a precommitment on pollution abatement, profits, and social welfare. Furthermore, Requate [26] provides an excellent survey of the relevant literature on both environmental R&D and environmental policy instruments. Moreover, Scott [27, 29] presents pioneering studies of environmental R&D from the empirical side.[3]

Policy timing strongly affects the market outcome and the environment. This chapter specifically examines emission tax policy in the monopoly market in a setting where the regulator has precommitment ability/inability for an emission tax. Furthermore, in the presence (absence) of such precommitment abilities, we explore the effects on monopolist's environmental R&D behavior, emission level, and social welfare.

This chapter proceeds in its presentation as follows. Section 6.2 introduces the monopoly model of the time-consistent emission tax policy. Section 6.3 presents a description of the solution procedures of the three-stage game. Section 6.4 describes investigations of the case of *laissez-faire*. In Sect. 6.5, the policy effect of time-consistent emission tax is revealed. Examinations of the scenario of precommitment to an emission tax are provided in Sect. 6.6. The final section summarizes results.

6.2 The Model of a Time-Consistent Emission Tax

This section presents a model of a time-consistent emission tax policy in a monopoly market along with its equilibrium outcomes. We specifically treat the analytical framework developed by Petrakis and Xepapadeas [19].[4]

6.2.1 Market and Technology

The value of q is assumed to represent a firm's output level. The utility of a representative consumer is given as

[3]In addition, Scott [28, 30] considers environmental R&D investment in terms of corporate social responsibility.

[4]For details, see Section 2.1 of Petrakis and Xepapadeas [19].

$$U(q, m) \equiv aq - (1/2)q^2 + m.$$

Therein, $m(> 0)$ signifies the consumption of a numeraire good; $a(> 0)$ is the parameter of market size. Utility maximization yields the following inverse demand function:

$$p(q) = a - q.$$

The value of monopolist's emissions per unit output is assumed to be one. A firm's environmental R&D (emission reduction) effort is denoted as z. The monopolist uses end-of-pipe technology for pollution abatement. Although this abatement technology is insufficient to reduce emissions per unit output (i.e., level of emission/production ratio), it mitigates emissions by eliminating them at the end of the production process.

When the monopolist's production level is q, then environmental R&D expenditures $(\gamma/2)z^2, (\gamma > 0)$ enable the monopolist to abate emissions from a level of q to

$$e(q, z) \equiv q - z.$$

This emission function is end-of-pipe type.[5] A lower value of γ represents higher efficiency of the environmental R&D cost. The analysis in this chapter assumes that no fixed costs for pollution abatement are necessary. In addition, the monopolist's total cost function is additively separable with respect to production costs cq and R&D expenditures $(\gamma/2)z^2$

$$C(q, z) = cq + (\gamma/2)z^2, \tag{6.1}$$

where $a > c > 0$.

6.2.2 *Social Welfare and Environmental Damage*

In this case, net emissions attributable to the monopolist are equal to the total emissions in the market. Total emissions $E = e(q, z)$ depend both on the output and on environmental R&D efforts. Total emissions cause environmental damage

---

[5]The emission function of end-of-pipe type is also used by Ulph [32], Poyago-Theotoky and Teerasuwannajak [20], Straume [31], Poyago-Theotoky [21], Wang and Wang [33], Naito and Ogawa [13], Kato [12], Pal [17], and others. For examples of the emission function of a cleaner production type, see Petrakis and Xepapadeas [18], Chiou and Hu [5], Puller [23], Ben Youssef and Dinar [1], Cato [4], Hattori [9], and others.

$$D(E) \equiv dE^2/2, \tag{6.2}$$

where the value of $d(> \underline{d}_{\text{m}} \equiv -1 + \sqrt{2})$ represents the damage parameter. We assume the case of a quadratic damage function.[6]

Social welfare W is defined as the sum of consumers' surplus and producer's surplus less environmental damage, $D(E)$, and total R&D expenditures, $(\gamma/2)z^2$.[7]

6.2.3 *Timing of the Game*

The government has no precommitment capability for the emission tax rate (t). The emission tax rate is determined to maximize social welfare W after a firm's environmental R&D investment. The timing of the game is the following.

- Stage 1: The monopolist determines z to maximize its own profit (π).
- Stage 2: The regulator determines emission tax rate (t) to maximize social welfare.
- Stage 3: The monopolist determines output level (q) to maximize its own profit.

6.3 Analysis of Time-Consistent Emission Tax

This section presents derivation of the subgame-perfect Nash equilibrium (SPNE) of the described above three-stage game. We use backward induction to obtain the SPNE. In this section, solution procedures are provided.

6.3.1 *Production*

In the third stage, the monopolist chooses its production level to maximize profits:

$$\pi = (a - q)q - cq - t(q - z) - (\gamma/2)z^2. \tag{6.3}$$

The first and the second terms respectively denote revenues and production costs. The third and the fourth terms present tax payments and environmental R&D cost.

The first-order condition for profit-maximization is

[6] Many environmental economics studies employ this type. For an example, see Chiou and Hu [5].

[7] Petrakis and Xepapadeas [19], Wang and Wang [33], and others employ the specialization of $\gamma = 1$.

$$\frac{d\pi}{dq} = a - c - t - 2q = 0. \tag{6.4}$$

Consequently, the optimal output level is derived as

$$q(t) = \frac{A - t}{2}, \tag{6.5}$$

where $A \equiv a - c > 0$.[8] From $dq(t)/dt = -(1/2) < 0$, one can understand that a higher emission tax rate decreases the output level. Profits are expressed as $\pi(t, z) = [(A - t)/2]^2 + tz - (\gamma/2)z^2$.

6.3.2 *Emission Tax*

In the absence of credible commitment to the emission tax rate, the government sets the emission tax rate t to maximize social welfare after a firm's decision-making in environmental R&D. Social welfare at the second stage is calculated as

$$W(t) = \int_0^{q(t)} (A - x)dx - (d/2)(q(t) - z)^2 - (\gamma/2)z^2. \tag{6.6}$$

Therein, the first and the second terms respectively denote total surplus and environmental damage. The third term presents costs for environmental R&D.

The first-order condition for social welfare maximization is given as

$$\frac{dW(t)}{dt} = \Big(A - q(t) - d(q(t) - z)\Big)\frac{dq(t)}{dt} = 0, \tag{6.7}$$

where $dq(t)/dt = -(1/2) < 0$. From this condition, the optimal emission tax rate is derived as follows.[9]

$$t(z) = \frac{(d - 1)A - 2dz}{1 + d}. \tag{6.8}$$

When the government does not have precommitment capability for an emission tax, the monopolist's environmental R&D efforts affect the future emission tax rate. In fact, from (6.11), one obtains

$$\frac{dt(z)}{dz} = \frac{-2d}{(1 + d)} < 0. \tag{6.9}$$

---

[8]The second-order condition is satisfied.

[9]The second-order condition is satisfied.

One can understand that the emission tax rate determined at the second stage decreases with greater R&D efforts in the first stage. In Hepburn [10] and Puller [23], this effect is designated as a "ratchet effect".[10] If $d < 1$, then the value of $t(z)$ is invariably negative irrespective of the value of the environmental R&D effort level (z) determined in the first stage.

After substituting (6.11) into (6.8) and performing some manipulations, we obtain the output, profits, and social welfare as shown below.

$$q(z) = \frac{A + dz}{1 + d}, \tag{6.10}$$

$$\pi(z) = \frac{(A + 2dz + d^2 z)(A - z)}{(1 + d)^2} - \frac{\gamma}{2} z^2, \tag{6.11}$$

$$W(z) = \frac{A^2 + 2Adz - d^2 z}{2(1 + d)} - \frac{\gamma}{2} z^2. \tag{6.12}$$

In addition, net emissions generated by the monopolist are derived as

$$\begin{aligned} e(z) &= q(z) - z \\ &= \frac{A - z}{1 + d}. \end{aligned} \tag{6.13}$$

From $de(z)/dz = -(1/(1 + d)) < 0$, net emissions at the second stage decrease with larger environmental R&D efforts in the first stage.

6.3.3 Emission Reduction

The monopolist determines the environmental R&D effort level, z, to maximize its own profits, $\pi(z)$, in the first stage.

From (6.14), the first-order condition for profit-maximization is

$$\frac{d\pi(z)}{dz} = \frac{A(d^2 + 2d - 1) - 2d(2 + d)z}{(1 + d)^2} - \gamma z = 0. \tag{6.14}$$

From the first-order condition, the monopolist's optimal R&D effort level is found to be the following.[11]

---

[10]For details of arguments about a ratchet effect, see Hepburn [10], Puller [23], and Brunner et al. [2].

[11]The second-order condition is satisfied.

$$z_M = \frac{(d^2 + 2d - 1)A}{\gamma(1 + d)^2 + 2d(2 + d)}. \tag{6.15}$$

Subscript M stands for the case of a monopoly. It is straightforward to verify that $z_M > 0$ under the assumption of $d > \underline{d}_m \equiv -1 + \sqrt{2}$.

After substituting this equilibrium value z_M into (6.11) and performing some manipulation, one can obtain the equilibrium tax rate, output level, emission, profits, and social welfare presented respectively below.

$$t_M = \frac{[\gamma(d + 1)(d - 1) - 2d]A}{\gamma(1 + d)^2 + 2d(2 + d)}, \tag{6.16}$$

$$q_M = \frac{[\gamma(1 + d) + d(3 + d)]A}{\gamma(1 + d)^2 + 2d(2 + d)}, \tag{6.17}$$

$$e_M = \frac{(1 + d)(1 + \gamma)A}{\gamma(1 + d)^2 + 2d(2 + d)}, \tag{6.18}$$

$$\pi_M = \frac{[2\gamma + (1 + d)^2]A^2}{2[\gamma(1 + d)^2 + 2d(2 + d)]}, \tag{6.19}$$

$$W_M = \frac{GA^2}{2[\gamma(1 + d)^2 + 2d(2 + d)]}. \tag{6.20}$$

Therein, $G \equiv (2+\gamma)d^4+(7+4\gamma+\gamma^2)d^3+2(2+2\gamma+\gamma^2)d^2+(-1+4\gamma+\gamma^2)d-\gamma$. The value of equilibrium emission e_M is strictly positive (i.e., $e_M > 0$). However, the sign$\{t_M\}$ is arbitrary. Section 6.5.1 explores the sign of the equilibrium emission tax rate t_M.

6.4 Case of *Laissez-Faire*

This section presents an exploration of the case of *laissez-faire*. Results obtained here are used in the next section. The monopolist does not invest in environmental R&D. Then the profit function is expressed as

$$\pi(q) = (a - q)q - cq. \tag{6.21}$$

The monopolist sets the production level to maximize the profits. The first-order condition for profit-maximization is $a - 2q - c = 0$.[12] Consequently, the optimal production level is obtained as

[12]The second-order condition is satisfied.

$$q_{\rm L} = \frac{A}{2}. \tag{6.22}$$

The subscript L stands for the case of *laissez-faire*.

Because the value of monopolist's emissions per unit output is assumed to be one, emissions generated by the monopolist, $e_{\rm L}$, are equal to $q_{\rm L}$. Therefore, the equilibrium emission level, profits, and social welfare are obtained respectively as follows:

$$e_{\rm L} = q_{\rm L} = \frac{A}{2}, \tag{6.23}$$

$$\pi_{\rm L} = \frac{A^2}{4}, \tag{6.24}$$

$$W_{\rm L} = \frac{(2-d)A^2}{8}. \tag{6.25}$$

6.5 Effect of Time-Consistent Emission Tax

This section presents examination of the sign of the emission tax rate. Furthermore, the policy effect of a time-consistent emission tax is investigated.

6.5.1 Sign of the Emission Tax Rate

First, we specifically examine the sign of the emission tax rate. It is particularly interesting that the equilibrium emission tax rate, $t_{\rm L}$, can be negative. Petrakis and Xepapadeas [19] pointed out that the "optimal ex post emission tax is negative whenever the marginal damage coefficient is sufficiently small".[13] In fact, from (6.19), it is apparent that the sign of $t_{\rm M}$ depends on the numerator of equation (6.19). After some manipulations, the following can be obtained.

$$\begin{aligned} t_{\rm M} &= \frac{[\gamma(d+1)(d-1) - 2d]A}{\gamma(1+d)^2 + 2d(2+d)} > (<) 0 \\ &\iff \gamma > (<)\ \hat{\gamma} \equiv \frac{2d}{(d+1)(d-1)}. \end{aligned}$$

As described in Sect. 6.3.3, sign$\{t_{\rm M}\}$ is arbitrary. Figure 6.1 shows a graphical result related to $t_{\rm M}$. The critical value $\hat{\gamma}$ is presented in Fig. 6.1. Asymptotic line of $\hat{\gamma}$ is

[13] For details, see p. 203 of Petrakis and Xepapadeas [19].

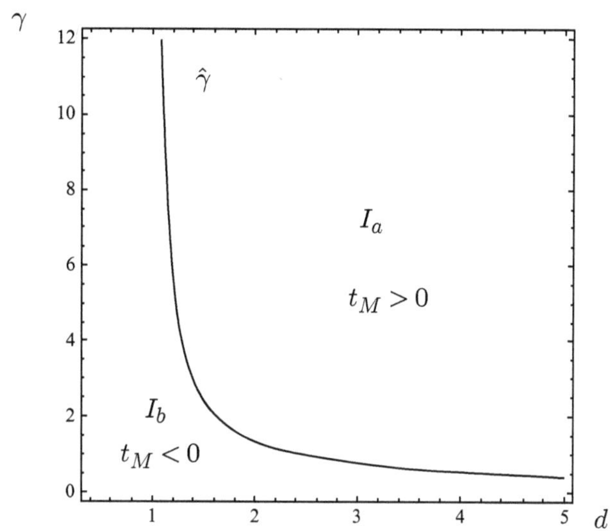

Fig. 6.1 Sign of emission tax rate

$d = 1$. The critical value $\hat{\gamma}$ is a monotonically decreasing function in $d \in (1, +\infty)$. Consequently, in the region above the curve $\hat{\gamma}$ (i.e., Region I_a) in Fig. 6.1, the sign of the equilibrium emission tax rate is positive ($t_M > 0$). In contrast, in the region below the curve $\hat{\gamma}$ (i.e., Region I_b), the sign of the equilibrium emission tax rate is negative ($t_M < 0$). The value of t_M is zero for the parameters set (d, γ) satisfying $\hat{\gamma} = 0$. Negative emission tax denotes an emission subsidy. Theorem 6.1 summarizes these results related to the sign of t_M.

Theorem 6.1. *(i) If $d > 1$ and $\gamma > \hat{\gamma}$, then $t_M > 0$.*
(ii) If $d > 1$ and $\gamma < \hat{\gamma}$, then $t_M < 0$.
(iii) If $d \leq 1$, then $t_M < 0$ for all $\gamma > 0$.

One must consider the reason why emission subsidies are justified. As pointed out by Petrakis and Xepapadeas [19] and Poyago-Theotoky [22], when the environmental damage parameter is sufficiently small, the rate of the time-consistent emission tax might become negative. Such an emission subsidy expands the output level and total emissions. The increase of the output level improves the market inefficiency made by the monopolist, although it generates more environmental damage. The former effect dominates the latter effect if the damage parameter is sufficiently small.[14] David [7] points out that the emission subsidy is unrealistic and unacceptable.[15] Moreover, many people might reject it without rational arguments.

[14]For details, see Requate [24, 25], Petrakis and Xepapadeas [18, 19], Fujiwara [8], Poyago-Theotoky [22], Ben Youssef and Dinar [1], and others.

[15]For details, see p. 518 of David [7].

It is necessary to understand "time-consistent emission subsidy" more exactly. Tax payments are resolved as follows.

$$\begin{aligned} \textit{Tax Payment} &= te \\ &= t(q - z) \\ &= tq - tz. \end{aligned}$$

This equation shows an important result. As described by Ouchida and Goto [16], "time-consistent emission subsidy" is the result of a policy tradeoff of the output subsidy and abatement tax.[16]

6.5.2 Social Welfare and Time-Consistent Emission Tax

Next, we investigate when the time-consistent emission subsidy is socially justified. Time-consistent emission subsidy is socially justified if the value of W_M is greater than W_L.

After some manipulation, the difference between W_M and W_L is obtained as follows.

$$W_M - W_L = \frac{FA^2}{4[\gamma(1+d)^2 + 2d(2+d)]} > (<)0. \tag{6.26}$$

Therein, $F \equiv 4(2+\gamma)d^4 + 4(7+4\gamma+\gamma^2)d^3 + 8(2+2\gamma+\gamma^2)d^2 + 4(-1+4\gamma+\gamma^2)d - 2 + d - 4\gamma$.

Actually, $\text{sign}\{W_M - W_L\}$ is arbitrary. The sign depends on the value of F. The curve γ_W in Fig. 6.2 implies the parameter set of (d, γ) which satisfies $F = 0$. The results of that comparison are shown in Fig. 6.2. In the right region of the curve γ_W (i.e., Region II_a), we have that $W_M > W_L$. Contrary to this, in the left region of the curve γ_W (i.e., Region II_b), we obtain that $W_M < W_L$. Consequently, in Region II_a, policy intervention is justified. The asymptotic line of γ_W is $d = 1$. Figure 6.2 demonstrates that time-consistent emission tax is not always welfare-enhancing. Theorem 6.2 summarizes these results.

Theorem 6.2. *(i) If $d > 1$, then $W_M > W_L$ for all $\gamma > 0$.*
(ii) If $d < 1$ and $\gamma < \gamma_W$, then $W_M > W_L$.
(iii) If $d < 1$ and $\gamma > \gamma_W$, then $W_M < W_L$.

[16]For details, see footnote 13 of Ouchida and Goto [16].

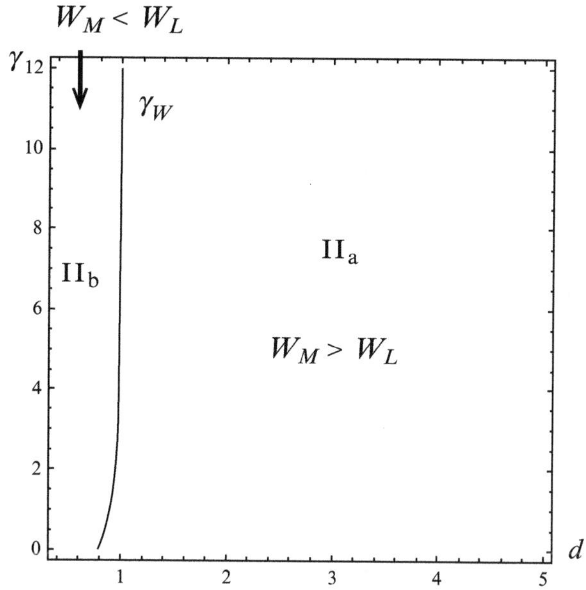

Fig. 6.2 Time-consistent emission tax and social welfare

6.5.3 *Emissions-Reduction Effect of a Time-Consistent Emission Subsidy*

Ouchida and Goto [16] who reexamine the Poyago-Theotoky [21, 22] model, provide an extended examination that was conducted under a corrected damage parameter. They obtained the following. First, social welfare under a time-consistent emission tax (emission subsidy) policy is invariably welfare-enhancing rather than the case of *laissez-faire*. Second, if the environmental damage parameter is sufficiently small, then the equilibrium emission tax rate is always negative. Moreover, total emissions under the emission subsidy scenario become less than those under *laissez-faire* if the environmental damage parameter is sufficiently small, and if the R&D cost is low.[17] Such an emissions-reducing effect of time-consistent emission subsidy was newly reported by Ouchida and Goto [16]. We present the emission-reducing effect of time-consistent emission tax/ subsidy for a polluting monopolist. First, we compare the emissions level under *laissez-faire*, e_{L}, with the equilibrium emissions level, e_{M}, derived in Sect. 6.3.3. Differences between them include the following.

$$e_{\mathrm{L}} - e_{\mathrm{M}} = \frac{[2 - 2d - 2d^2 + (1+d)(1-d)\gamma]A}{2[\gamma(1+d)^2 + 2d(2+d)]} < (>)0$$

[17]For details of emission-reducing effect of time-consistent emission subsidy, see Section 3 of Ouchida and Goto [16].

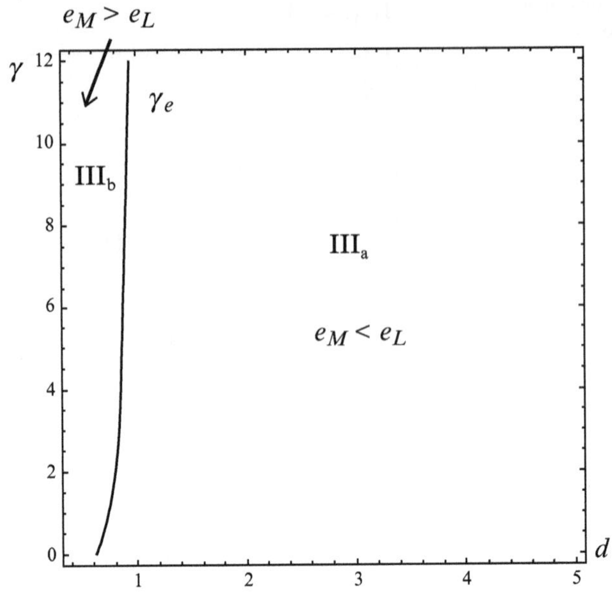

Fig. 6.3 Emissions-reducing effect

$$\Longleftrightarrow \gamma > (<)\gamma_e \equiv \frac{2 - 2d - 2d^2}{(1+d)(1-d)}.$$

Based on this result, the sign of $\{e_{\mathrm{L}} - e_{\mathrm{M}}\}$ is arbitrary. Figure 6.3 expresses the graphical result of the equation above. In the right region of the curve γ_e, $e_{\mathrm{L}} > e_{\mathrm{M}}$ (see, Region $\mathrm{III_a}$). In the right region of curve γ_e, $e_{\mathrm{L}} < e_{\mathrm{M}}$ (see, Region $\mathrm{III_b}$). The asymptotic line of γ_e is $d = 1$.

Based on this comparison, we understand that there might exist the emission-reducing effect in the monopoly market even if a time-consistent emission subsidy is conducted. Theorem 6.3 summarizes these results.

Theorem 6.3. *(i) If $d > 1$, then $e_{\mathrm{M}} < e_{\mathrm{L}}$ for all $\gamma > 0$.*
(ii) If $d < 1$ and $\gamma < \gamma_e$, then $e_{\mathrm{M}} < e_{\mathrm{L}}$.
(iii) If $d < 1$ and $\gamma > \gamma_e$, then $e_{\mathrm{M}} > e_{\mathrm{L}}$.

Figure 6.4 presents a summary of the previously described results. We confirm the following. In the regulatory environment in which a time-consistent emission tax is justified, a monopolist's emissions under a time-consistent emission tax are less than those under *laissez-faire*, irrespective of the sign of the emission tax rate (see Regions $\mathrm{IV_a} + \mathrm{IV_b}$). Furthermore, if the environmental damage parameter is sufficiently large ($d > 1$), then the time-consistent emission tax/subsidy invariably has an emissions-reducing effect and a welfare-enhancing effect. These results are summarized as Theorem 6.4.

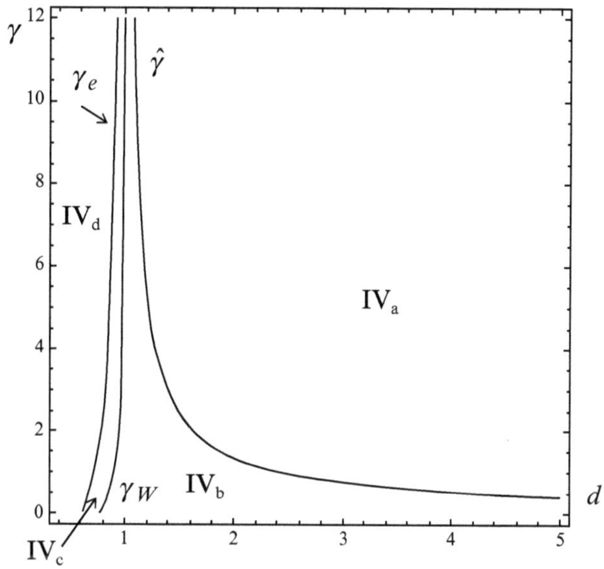

Fig. 6.4 Policy effects of a time-consistent emission tax/subsidy

Theorem 6.4. *Presuming that* $d > 1$*, then the time-consistent emission tax always decreases emissions more than emissions under laissez-faire, even if the equilibrium emission tax rate is negative. Furthermore, a time-consistent emission tax/subsidy is always welfare-enhancing.*

6.6 Precommitment Case of Emissions Tax

We have considered the setting in which the government has no precommitment ability for an emission tax. However, examinations under the precommitment of an emission tax rate are necessary.

Which is socially more preferred: a time-consistent emission tax or a precommitment case of an emission tax? To answer this question, theoretical economic analysis is extremely important and indispensable. The reason is that no report describes the timing of an emission tax policy for the monopolist with end-of-pipe technology, whereas Petrakis and Xepapadeas [18] investigated the case of cleaner production technology.[18] This section presents a solution of the three-stage game of precommitment case of an emission tax, and also provides results related to welfare comparison.

[18]For the case of differentiated Cournot duopoly with end-of-pipe technology, see Poyago-Theotoky and Teerasuwannajak [20].

6.6.1 Timing

An identical model to that introduced in Sect. 6.2 is used, except for several points. Furthermore, this section assumes that $d > 1$ to guarantee that environmental R&D effort level in SPNE is strictly positive.

Assumption $d > 1$.

We investigate the following three-stage game. In the time structure, the different point between two scenarios is that stage 1 and stage 2 are interchanged.

- Stage 1: The regulator determines emission tax rate (t) to maximize social welfare.
- Stage 2: The monopolist determines z to maximize its own profit (π).
- Stage 3: The monopolist determines output level (q) to maximize its own profit.

Hereinafter, we solve this game using backward induction.

6.6.2 Production

In the third stage, the monopolist chooses the output level to maximize the profit (see Eq. (6.6)). The investigations described here are identical to those presented in Sect. 6.3.1. Consequently, the monopolist's output level in subgame equilibrium is obtained as

$$\frac{A-t}{2}. \tag{6.27}$$

Consequently, the firm's profit is calculated as

$$\pi(z) = \left[\frac{A-t}{2}\right]^2 + tz - (\gamma/2)z^2. \tag{6.28}$$

Therein, the first-term represents gross profit from the production market. We find that the first-term does not depend on the environmental R&D effort level z determined in the second stage.

6.6.3 Environmental R&D

In the second stage, the monopolist chooses the environmental R&D effort level z to maximize the profit $\pi(z)$.

The corresponding first-order condition is the following.[19]

$$\frac{d\pi(z)}{dz} = t - \gamma z = 0 \tag{6.29}$$

Therein, the first term t means the revenue generated by the marginal increase of environmental R&D effort. The second term, γz, denotes the marginal environmental R&D cost.

Therefore, from the first-order condition, the optimal environmental R&D effort is determined as

$$z(t) = \frac{t}{\gamma}. \tag{6.30}$$

The sub-game equilibrium output level, emission, profits and social welfare are derived respectively as shown below.

$$q(t) = \frac{A-t}{2}, \tag{6.31}$$

$$\begin{aligned} e(t) &= q(t) - z(t) \\ &= \frac{\gamma A - (2+\gamma)t}{2\gamma}, \end{aligned} \tag{6.32}$$

$$\pi(t) = \left[\frac{A-t}{2}\right]^2 + \frac{t^2}{2\gamma}., \tag{6.33}$$

$$\begin{aligned} W(t) &= Aq(t) - \frac{1}{2}[q(t)]^2 \\ &\quad - \frac{1}{2}(q(t) - z(t))^2 - \frac{\gamma}{2}[z(t)]^2. \end{aligned} \tag{6.34}$$

6.6.4 Emission Tax

The government is a maximizer of social welfare. In the first stage, the government determines the optimal emission tax rate t, to maximize social welfare $W(t)$. Social welfare $W(t)$ has been derived in Sect. 6.6.3.

The first-order condition for maximization is obtained as follows.[20]

$$\frac{dW(t)}{dt} = A\left(\frac{dq(t)}{dt}\right) - q(t)\left(\frac{dq(t)}{dt}\right)$$

---

[19]The second-order condition is satisfied.

[20]The second-order condition is satisfied.

$$-d(q(t)-z(t))\Big(\frac{dq(t)}{dt}-\frac{dz(t)}{dt}\Big)-\gamma z(t)\Big(\frac{dz(t)}{dt}\Big)=0, \qquad (6.35)$$

where $dq(t)/dt=-(1/2)$ and $dz(t)/dt=1/\gamma$.

After performing some manipulations, this first-order condition is rewritten as shown below.

$$\frac{dW(t)}{dt}=0 \iff -\frac{A}{2}+\frac{A-t}{2}+d\Big[\frac{A-t}{2}-\frac{t}{\gamma}\Big]\Big[\frac{1}{2}+\frac{1}{\gamma}\Big]-\frac{t}{\gamma}=0 \qquad (6.36)$$

Therefore, from (6.39), the equilibrium emission tax rate is obtained as follows.

$$t_{\mathrm{CM}}=\frac{A\gamma[2d+\gamma(d-1)]}{d(2+\gamma)^2+\gamma(4+\gamma)}. \qquad (6.37)$$

The subscript CM stands for the precommitment case. In Sect. 6.6.1, we assumed that $d>1$. When $d>1$, we readily find that $t_{\mathrm{CM}}>0$.

Next we seek SPNE outcomes for other variables. Substituting (6.40) into (6.33)–(6.37), one obtains the equilibrium R&D effort level, output, emission, profits, and social welfare as presented below.

$$z_{\mathrm{CM}}=\frac{A[2d+\gamma(d-1)]}{d(2+\gamma)^2+\gamma(4+\gamma)}, \qquad (6.38)$$

$$q_{\mathrm{CM}}=\frac{A(2+\gamma)(d+\gamma)}{d(2+\gamma)^2+\gamma(4+\gamma)}, \qquad (6.39)$$

$$e_{\mathrm{CM}}=\frac{A\gamma(3+\gamma)}{d(2+\gamma)^2+\gamma(4+\gamma)}, \qquad (6.40)$$

$$\pi_{\mathrm{CM}}=\frac{A^2H}{2[d(2+\gamma)^2+\gamma(4+\gamma)]^2}, \qquad (6.41)$$

$$W_{\mathrm{CM}}=\frac{A^2(3+\gamma)(d+\gamma)}{2[d(2+\gamma)^2+\gamma(4+\gamma)]}, \qquad (6.42)$$

Therein, $H\equiv d^3(2+\gamma)^3+2d\gamma(2+\gamma)(4+\gamma)+\gamma^2(8+9\gamma+2\gamma^2)>0$.

It is straightforward to verify that $z_{\mathrm{CM}}>0$ if the value of d is at least greater than one (i.e., $d>1$). Moreover, we readily find that equilibrium emission is strictly positive (i.e., $e_{\mathrm{CM}}>0$).

6.7 Comparison of Tax Regimes

In Sects. 6.3 and 6.6, we derived the SPNE outcome under two tax regimes: time-consistent emission tax and precommitment case. This section compares those results.

6.7.1 Emission Tax Rate

First, we compare the equilibrium emission tax rate under a time-consistent emission tax, t_{M}, with the equilibrium emission level under precommitment case, t_{CM}, derived in Sect. 6.6.4.

After some manipulation, the difference between them is derived as follows.

$$t_{\mathrm{M}} - t_{\mathrm{CM}} = \frac{VA}{[\gamma(1+d)^2 + 2d(2+d)][d(2+\gamma)^2 + \gamma(4+\gamma)]} < 0 \qquad (6.43)$$

Therein, $V \equiv -4[\gamma^2 + \gamma(3+\gamma)d + (2+4\gamma+\gamma^2)d^2] < 0$. The equilibrium emission tax rate under the precommitment case, t_{CM}, is strictly greater than that under the time-consistent emission tax, t_{M}.

Therefore, we have the following theorem.

Theorem 6.5. $t_{\mathrm{M}} < t_{\mathrm{CM}}$ *for all* $d > 1$ *and* $\gamma > 0$.

6.7.2 Environmental R&D Efforts

Second, we compare the equilibrium environmental R&D effort level under the time-consistent emission tax, z_{M}, with equilibrium environmental R&D effort level under the precommitment case, z_{CM}, as derived in Sect. 6.6.4.

After some manipulation, the difference between them is derived as follows.

$$z_{\mathrm{M}} - z_{\mathrm{CM}} = \frac{LA}{[\gamma(1+d)^2 + 2d(2+d)][d(2+\gamma)^2 + \gamma(4+\gamma)]} > (<)0, \qquad (6.44)$$

In that equation, $L \equiv 2[-2(\gamma+d) + d\gamma(1+d)(3+\gamma)]$.

The sign of $z_{\mathrm{M}} - z_{\mathrm{CM}}$ is arbitrary. Figure 6.5 shows a graphical result related to the equation above. The critical value γ_z depicted in Fig. 6.5 is the parameter set (d, γ) that satisfies $z_{\mathrm{M}} - z_{\mathrm{CM}} = 0$. The critical value γ_z is a monotonically decreasing function in $d \in (1, +\infty)$. Consequently, in the region above the curve γ_z (i.e., Region $\mathrm{V_a}$) in Fig. 6.5, the equilibrium environmental R&D effort under the time-consistent emission tax is greater than that under the precommitment case. In contrast, in the region below the curve γ_z (i.e., Region $\mathrm{V_b}$), z_{M} is strictly smaller than z_{CM}. Theorem 6.5 and its corollary show these results.

Theorem 6.6. *(i) If* $\gamma > \gamma_z$, *then* $z_{\mathrm{M}} > z_{\mathrm{CM}}$ *for all* $d > 1$.
(ii) If $\gamma < \gamma_z$, *then* $z_{\mathrm{M}} < z_{\mathrm{CM}}$ *for all* $d > 1$.

Because the critical value γ_z is a monotonically decreasing function in $d \in (1, +\infty)$, the curve γ_z is strictly less than $\gamma_z|_{d=1} = -1 + \sqrt{2}$. The next corollary summarizes this result.

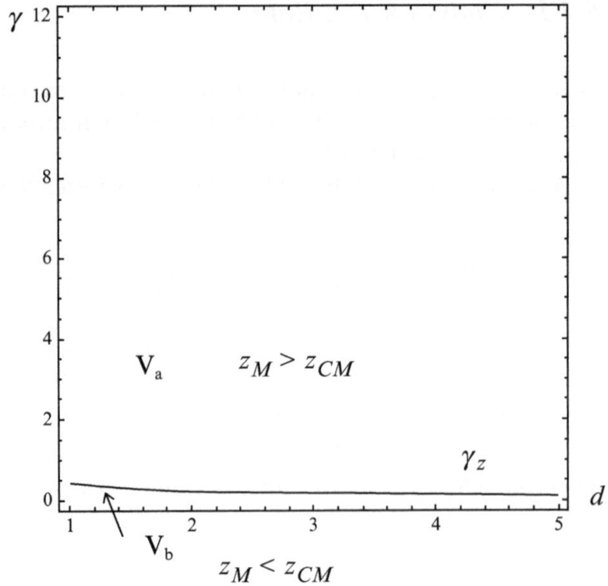

Fig. 6.5 Comparison of environmental R&D effort

Corollary 6.7. $z_{\mathrm{M}} > z_{\mathrm{CM}}$ *for all* $d > 1$ *and* $\gamma > -1 + \sqrt{2}$.

6.7.3 Production Level

Third, we compare the equilibrium output level under a time-consistent emission tax, q_{M}, with the equilibrium output level under a precommitment case, q_{CM}, as derived in Sect. 6.6.4.

After some manipulation, the difference between them is derived as

$$q_{\mathrm{M}} - q_{\mathrm{CM}} = \frac{RA}{[\gamma(1+d)^2 + 2d(2+d)][d(2+\gamma)^2 + \gamma(4+\gamma)]} > 0, \tag{6.45}$$

where $R \equiv 2[\gamma^2 + \gamma(3+\gamma)d + (2+4\gamma+\gamma^2)d^2] > 0$. The equation above shows that the equilibrium production level under a time-consistent emission tax, q_{M}, is strictly greater than that under a precommitment case, q_{CM}, for all $d > 1$ and $\gamma > 0$.

Therefore, the following theorem can be advanced.

Theorem 6.8. $q_{\mathrm{M}} > q_{\mathrm{CM}}$ *for all* $d > 1$ *and* $\gamma > 0$.

6.7.4 Emissions

Here, we compare the equilibrium emission level under a time-consistent emission tax, e_{M}, with the equilibrium emission level under a precommitment case, e_{CM}, as derived in Sect. 6.6.4.

After some manipulations, the difference between them is derived as follows.

$$e_{\mathrm{M}} - e_{\mathrm{CM}} = \frac{YA}{[\gamma(1+d)^2 + 2d(2+d)][d(2+\gamma)^2 + \gamma(4+\gamma)]} > 0. \qquad (6.46)$$

Therein, $Y \equiv 2[\gamma(2+\gamma) + 2d + (2+\gamma)d^2] > 0$. The equation above reveals that the equilibrium emission level under a time-consistent emission tax, e_{M}, is strictly greater than one under a precommitment case, e_{CM}, for all $d > 1$ and $\gamma > 0$.

Therefore, we have the following theorem.

Theorem 6.9. $e_{\mathrm{M}} > e_{\mathrm{CM}}$ *for all* $d > 1$ *and* $\gamma > 0$

6.7.5 Firm Profit

Second, we compare the equilibrium firm's profit under a time-consistent emission tax, π_{M}, with the equilibrium firm's profit under a precommitment case, π_{CM}, derived in Sect. 6.6.4.

After some manipulation, the difference between them is derived as shown below.

$$\pi_{\mathrm{M}} - \pi_{\mathrm{CM}} = \frac{XA^2}{[\gamma(1+d)^2 + 2d(2+d)][d(2+\gamma)^2 + \gamma(4+\gamma)]} > (<)0, \qquad (6.47)$$

where $X \equiv -2\{(2+\gamma)^4 d^5 + (2+\gamma)^4 d^4 - (2+\gamma)^3(4+\gamma)d^3 - [16+\gamma(2+\gamma)(4+\gamma)(8+5\gamma)]d^2 - 8\gamma[4+11\gamma+6\gamma^2+\gamma^3]d - 8\gamma^2(2+4\gamma+\gamma^2)\} > (<)0$. The sign of $\{\pi_{\mathrm{M}} - \pi_{\mathrm{CM}}\}$ depends on the sign of X.

From the equation above, it is apparent that the sign of $\pi_{\mathrm{M}} - \pi_{\mathrm{CM}}$ is arbitrary. In fact, Fig. 6.6 shows a graphical result related to the sign of $\pi_{\mathrm{M}} - \pi_{\mathrm{CM}}$. The critical value γ_π depicted in Fig. 6.6 is parameter set (d, γ) that satisfies $\pi_{\mathrm{M}} - \pi_{\mathrm{CM}} = 0$. The critical value γ_π is a monotonically increasing function in $d \in (d_1, d_2)$. Then, after some manipulations, we obtain that $d_1 \approx 1.24698$ and $d_2 \approx 2.05197$.

Consequently, in the region above the curve γ_π (i.e., Region VI$_{\mathrm{a}}$) in Fig. 6.6, the equilibrium profit under a time-consistent emission tax is greater than that under a precommitment case. In contrast, in the region below the curve γ_π (i.e., Region VI$_{\mathrm{b}}$), π_{M} is strictly smaller than π_{CM}. The asymptotic line of γ_π is the vertical line $d = d_2$.

Theorem 6.10 summarizes these results.

Theorem 6.10. *(i) If* $d \in (1, d_1)$, *then* $\pi_{\mathrm{M}} > \pi_{\mathrm{CM}}$ *for all* $\gamma > 0$.
(ii) If $d \in [d_1, d_2)$ *and* $\gamma > \gamma_\pi$, *then* $\pi_{\mathrm{M}} > \pi_{\mathrm{CM}}$.
(iii) If $d \in [d_1, d_2)$ *and* $\gamma < \gamma_\pi$, *then* $\pi_{\mathrm{M}} < \pi_{\mathrm{CM}}$.
(iv) If $d \in [d_2, +\infty)$, *then* $\pi_{\mathrm{M}} < \pi_{\mathrm{CM}}$ *for all* $\gamma > 0$.

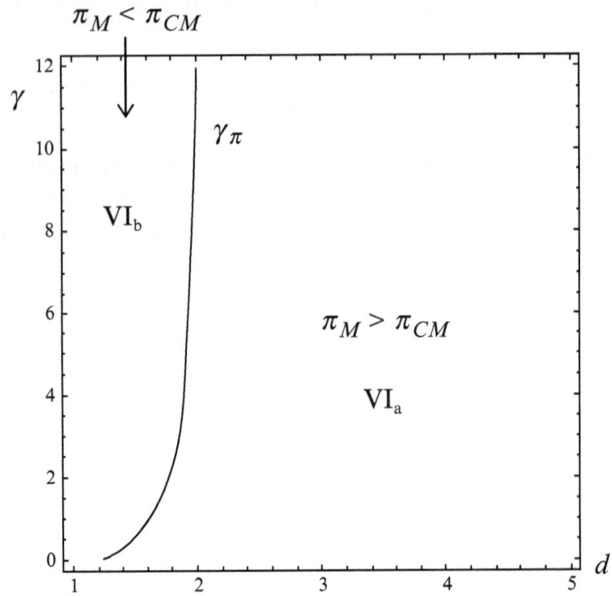

Fig. 6.6 Comparison of profits

6.7.6 Social Welfare

Finally, we compare the equilibrium social welfare under a time-consistent emission tax, W_M, with equilibrium social welfare under a precommitment case, W_{CM}, as derived in Sect. 6.6.4.

After some manipulations, the difference between them is derived as follows.

$$W_M - W_{CM} = \frac{SA^2}{2[\gamma(1+d)^2 + 2d(2+d)][d(2+\gamma)^2 + \gamma(4+\gamma)]}. \tag{6.48}$$

Therein, $S \equiv -(7+2\gamma)\gamma^2 + \gamma(-23+5\gamma^2+\gamma^3)d + (4+\gamma)[-4+\gamma(1+\gamma)(4+3\gamma)]d^2 + (10+55\gamma+50\gamma^2+20\gamma^3+3\gamma^4)d^3 + (2+\gamma)[14+19\gamma+7\gamma^2+\gamma^3]d^4 + (2+\gamma)^3 d^5$.

Next, we seek the sign of S. It is straightforward to verify that $S > 0$ for all $d > 1$ and $\gamma > 0$. Consequently, the sign of $W_M - W_{CM}$ is positive. Therefore, the equilibrium social welfare under a time-consistent emission tax is always greater than that under a precommitment case. Theorem 6.11 presents this result.

Theorem 6.11. $W_M > W_{CM}$ *for all* $d > 1$ *and* $\gamma > 0$.

This theorem suggests that time-consistent emission tax policy has social superiority to the precommitment case when the monopolist uses end-of-pipe technology in emission reduction R&D, and when environmental damage parameter is sufficiently large ($d > 1$).

Petrakis and Xepapadeas [18] investigated whether the government's precommitment to an emission tax promotes the monopolist's environmental R&D and also enhances social welfare. They revealed that social welfare is always lower when the government has no precommitment capability to an emission tax rate.[21] Theorem 6.11 in this chapter sharply contrasts to Result 2 of Petrakis and Xepapadeas [18].

6.8 Conclusion

First, this chapter explained time-consistent emission tax policy for a monopolist, and also demonstrated that a negative emission tax (i.e., emission subsidy) can be partially justified. Second, these analyses examined the existence of the emission-reducing effect in the monopoly market. Furthermore, this chapter investigated whether the government's precommitment to an emission tax promotes the monopolist's environmental R&D and enhances social welfare.

We have obtained several important results. Theorem 6.3 in this chapter proves the regulatory environment in which a time-consistent emission subsidy can reduce emissions more than the case of *laissez-faire*. As one main result, Theorem 6.11 shows that time-consistent emission tax policy invariably has social superiority to the precommitment case if the monopolist uses end-of-pipe technology, and if environmental damage is sufficiently severe.

However, there remains a fundamental question. What mechanism generates (or removes) the regulator's precommitment ability for an emission tax? Few studies have investigated this question.

References

1. Ben Youssef, S., & Dinar, Z. (2011). Regulation of a duopoly and environmental R&D. *Environmental Economics, 2*(3), 47–51.
2. Brunner, S., Flachsland, C., & Marschinski, R. (2012). Credible commitment in carbon policy. *Climate Policy, 12*(2), 255–271.
3. Carraro, C., & Lévêque, F. (1999). *Voluntary approaches in environmental policy*. Dordrecht/Boston: Kluwer Academic.
4. Cato, S. (2011). Environmental policy in a mixed market: Abatement subsidies and emission taxes. *Environmental Economics and Policy Studies, 13*, 283–301.
5. Chiou, J. R., & Hu, J. L. (2001). Environmental research joint ventures under emission taxes. *Environmental and Resource Economics, 20*, 129–146.
6. Conrad, K. (2001). Voluntary environmental agreement vs. emission taxes in strategic trade models. *Environmental and Resource Economics, 19*, 361–381.
7. David, M. (2005). Regulating a polluting oligopoly: Emission tax or voluntary agreement. *Review of Development Economics, 9*(4), 514–529.
8. Fujiwara, K. (2009). Environmental policies in a differentiated oligopoly revisited. *Resource and Energy Economics, 31*, 239–247.

[21] For details, see p. 158 of Petrakis and Xepapadeas [18].

9. Hattori, K. (2013). Environmental innovation and policy harmonization in international oligopoly. *Environment and Development Economics, 18*, 162–183.
10. Hepburn, C. (2006). Regulation by prices, quantities, or both: A review of instrument choice. *Oxford Review of Economic Policy, 22*(2), 226–247.
11. Ikkatai, S., Ishikawa, D., Ohori, S., & Sasaki, K. (2008). Motivation of Japanese companies to take environmental action to reduce their greenhouse gas emissions: An econometric analysis. *Sustainability Science, 3*, 145–154.
12. Kato, K. (2011). Emission quota versus emission tax in a mixed duopoly. *Environmental Economics and Policy Studies, 13*, 43–63.
13. Naito, T., & Ogawa, H. (2009). Direct versus indirect environmental regulation in a partially privatized mixed duopoly. *Environmental Economics and Policy Studies, 10*, 87–100.
14. OECD (1999). *Voluntary approaches for environmental policy: An assessment*. Paris: OECD.
15. OECD (2003). *Voluntary approaches for environmental policy – Effectiveness, efficiency and usage in policy mixes*. Paris: OECD.
16. Ouchida, Y., & Goto, D. (2014). Do emission subsidies reduce emission? in the context of environmental R&D organization. *Economic Modelling, 36*, 511–516.
17. Pal, R. (2012). Delegation and emission tax in a differentiated oligopoly. *The Manchester School, 80*(6), 650–670.
18. Petrakis, E., & Xepapadeas, A. (1999). Does government precommitment promote environmental innovation? In E. Petrakis, E. S. Sartzetakis, & A. Xepapadeas (Eds), *Environmental regulation and market power: Competition, time consistency and international trade* (pp. 145–161). Cheltenham: Edward Elgar.
19. Petrakis, E., & Xepapadeas, A. (2003). Location decisions of a polluting firm and the time consistency of environmental policy. *Resource and Energy Economics, 25*, 197–214.
20. Poyago-Theotoky, J., & Teerasuwannajak, K. (2002). The timing of environmental policy: A note on the role of product differentiation. *Journal of Regulatory Economics, 21*(3), 305–316.
21. Poyago-Theotoky, J. (2007). The organization of R&D and environmental policy. *Journal of Economic Behavior and Organization, 62*(1), 63–75.
22. Poyago-Theotoky, J. (2010). Corrigendum to "The organization of R&D and environmental policy" [Journal of Economic Behavior and Organization 62, 63–75]. *Journal of Economic Behavior and Organization, 76*, 449.
23. Puller, S. (2006). The strategic use of innovation to influence regulatory standard. *Journal of Environmental Economics and Management, 52*, 690–706.
24. Requate, T. (1993). Pollution control under imperfect competition: Asymmetric Bertrand duopoly with linear technologies. *Journal of Institutional and Theoretical Economics, 149*(2), 415–442.
25. Requate, T. (1993). Pollution control in a Cournot duopoly via taxes or permits. *Journal of Economics, 58*(3), 255–291.
26. Requate, T. (2005). Dynamic incentive by environmental policy instruments – A Survey. *Ecological Economics, 54*, 175–195.
27. Scott, J. T. (1996). Environmental research joint Ventures among manufacturers. *Review of Industrial Organization, 11*, 655–679.
28. Scott, J. T. (1997). Schumpeterian competition and environmental R&D. *Managerial and Decision Economics, 18*, 455–469.
29. Scott, J. T. (2003). *Environmental research and development: US industrial research, the clean air act and environmental damage*. Northampton: Edward Elgar.
30. Scott, J. T. (2005). Corporate social responsibility and environmental research and development. *Structural Change and Economic Dynamics, 16*, 313–331.
31. Straume, O. D. (2006). Product market integration and environmental policy coordination in an international duopoly. *Environmental and Resource Economics, 34*, 535–563.
32. Ulph, A. (1996). Environmental policy and international trade when governments and producers act strategically. *Journal of Environmental Economics and Management, 30*(3), 265–281.
33. Wang, L. F. S., & Wang, J. (2009). Environmental taxes in a differentiated mixed duopoly. *Economic Systems, 33*(4), 389–396.

Chapter 7
The Basic Model of Illegal Dumping and Recycling of Wastes

Hirofumi Fukuyama and Daisuke Ikazaki

7.1 Introduction

7.1.1 Extended Producer Responsibility

Recently the lack of final wastes incinerators owned by local governments has been afraid due to the increase of wastes in the future in Japan. The new surface-treating place, which is considered as the final place to disposal the wastes in Tokyo Bay, will overflow 30 years later if the pace of increasing the wastes is maintained.

For achievement of sustainable economic society, it is very important to reform the economic system of mass production, mass consumption and mass disposal, and to establish a resource recycling society. The "Fundamental Law for Establishing a Sound Material-Cycle Society" was enacted in Japan in 2000 to provide a framework for creating a resource recycling society by defining individual responsibilities for the central government, local government, firm, and consumers, respectively. Through the the principle of "Extended Producer Responsibility", the law imposes a post-consumption responsibility of environmental friendly management on a producer. Many firms in various industries are prompted to start activities for more efficient waste management on discharge control, collection, transportation, and recycling.

H. Fukuyama (✉)
Faculty of Law, Economics and the Humanities, Kagoshima University, Korimoto 1-21-24, Kagoshima city, Kagoshima 8908580, Japan
e-mail: fukuyama@leh.kagoshima-u.ac.jp

D. Ikazaki
Faculty of Human Sciences and Design, Japan Women's University, 2-8-1 Mejirodai, Bunkyo-ku, Tokyo 1128681, Japan
e-mail: ikazaki@fc.jwu.ac.jp

T. Naito (ed.), *Sustainable Growth and Development in a Regional Economy*, New Frontiers in Regional Science: Asian Perspectives 13,
DOI 10.1007/978-4-431-55294-9_7

The principle of the extended producer responsibility (EPR) is widespread in Japan and European countries in recent years. The principle has been introduced into "the Containers and Packaging Recycling Law" and "the Home Appliance Recycling Law" in Japan. Thus, the responsibility to firm's environmental problems increases every year, and the firm gets to the society the request of the design of the environmental consideration product. Therefore, it is very important that we consider not only the decision problem at firm's production level but also the decision problem at the environmental consideration level of the product.

According to Ministry of the Environment [7], OECD started the studies of extended producer responsibility as one of the tools on environmental plicies from 1994, and the guidance manual for OECD signatory government as the result was formulated and published in 2001. Table 7.1 shows the guidance manual of the extended producer responsibility.

On the other hand, household waste is made various after high economic growth period of the 1970s in Japan. Recently, the importance of recycling and the necessity of the waste loss in weight for a final disposal dump decrease are recognized. Thus, collecting used papers, plastic such as the food trays, the can and PET bottles in discretion are advanced in Japan. For instance, the collecting and separating of 28 items is being done in the Kagoshima Prefecture Osaki-cho now, and the waste reduction in 1980s has been achieved as a result compared with 1998.

The number of municipalities that deal with the recycling of waste has increased every year. "The Containers and Packaging Recycling Law" that started in 1997 has infiltrated a lot of municipalities. Figure 7.1 shows the result on the implementation of sorted cellection and recycling based on "the Containers and Packaging Recycling Law" in municipalities of Janan. From Fig. 7.1, we can know the number and the proportion of municipalities carrying out the sorted cellection and recycling of glass bottles, paper containers and packaging, PET bottles, and plastic bottles has increased since 1997 "The Containers and Packaging Recycling Law" started.

However, the load of the household grows while the subdivision of the collecting and separating leads to the promotion of recycling and loss in weight of waste. When the collecting and separating becomes complex, the separating of waste might be inadequately done. Therefore, it is interesting to model disutility by the separating waste of the household, and to analyze the separating action of the waste of the household.

Therefore, the first purpose of this chapter is to model the separating action by household and the design action of the environmental consideration product by firm, and to consider the influence that the waste management policy by the local government gives at the level of environmental consideration and virgin resource collection by firm and the level of separating effort of waste by household. Next, the second purpose of this chapter is to derive the condition because of existence of the recycling product market, and to clarify what the optimal waste management policy is.

Table 7.1 The guidance manual of EPR (Source: Ministry of the Environment [7])

(1) Definition	Method in environmental policy of expanding producer's physical or economical responsibility to the following stage after consumer of product at life cycle
	More specifically,
	(1) The producer assumes the responsibility of the product design to minimize the impact to environment at the life cycle of product,
	(2) The producer assumes physical or economical responsibility for the environmental impact with the product that he was not able to exclude by the product design
(2) Main Feature	Transfering all or parts of cost for waste management or a physical responsibility from a local government and general taxpayers to the producer
(3) Major Goals	(1) Reduction in the source
	(2) Waste prevention
	(3) Environment-friendly product design
	(4) Closure of material-use loops to promote sustainable development
(4) Effect	Pressure is given for the upstream side on the material selection and the design of the product. A signal appropriate to internalize the external environment cost with the product for the producer can be sent
(5) Share of Responsibility	Sharing responsibility among parties concerned in the product chain from production to disposal is an inherent key of EPR
(6) Examples of Specific Method on Policy	(1) Take-back of product (2) Deposit and Refund
	(3) Surcharge of product and Tax
	(4) Advance payment of disposal cost
	(5) Criteria for users of recycled products
	(6) Leasing

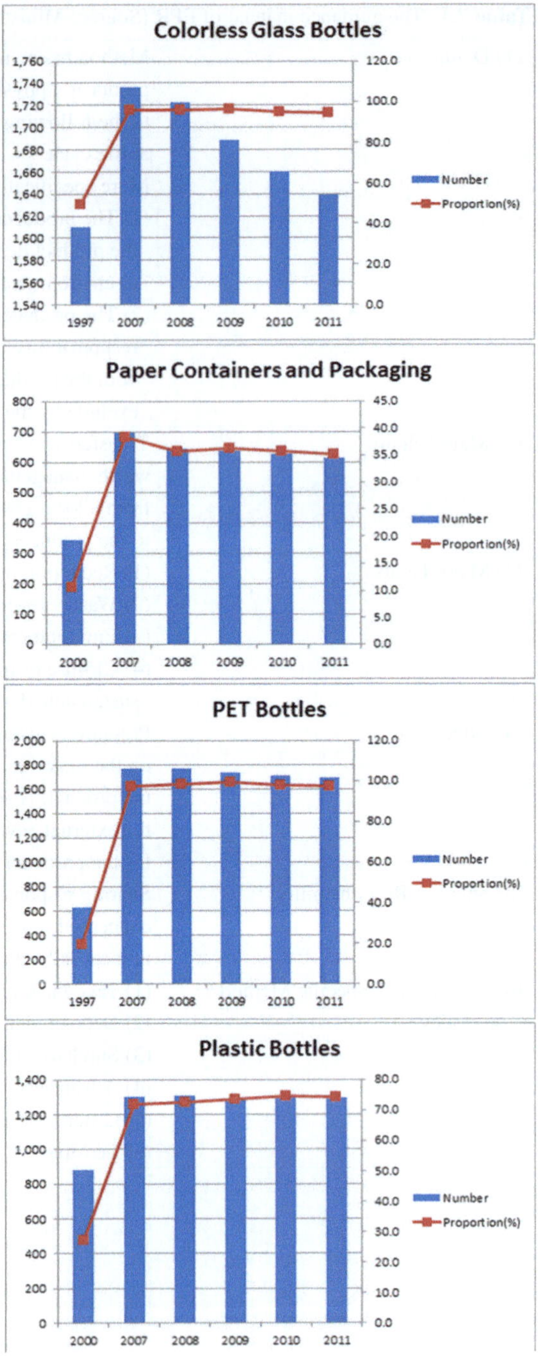

Fig. 7.1 The number and the proportion of municipalities carrying out sorted in Japan (Source: Ministry of the Environment[8])

7.1.2 Related Research

Many studies focus on the topics about the disposal and recycling of wastes. Fullerton and Kinnaman [5] and Fullerton and Wu [6] analyze the general equilibrium model, which include the cycle of goods from consumption to abandonment. Dinan [3] and Walls and Palmer [9] focus on this cycle model taking the disposal and recycling model of consumption goods from the point of view of producer account into. Choe and Fraser [2] take the possibility of illegal disposal as the way to treat it into account. These studies are useful to analyze the disposal and recycling process of wastes in detail by taking account of the material balance between the disposal and recycling of wastes.

This chapter extends Choe and Fraser [2] by introducing the effort to transform "Quality of waste (burnable waste or recyclable waste)" by firm, the effort to separate waste by household, and the recycling market existence condition on recyclable waste. There are already a lot of early researches that analyze the effort to consider environment by firm. Fullerton and Kinnaman [5], Fullerton and Wu [6] and Choe and Fraser [2] analyze the effort to consider environment such as decreasing "Amount of waste" by firm after the product was consumed. Fullerton and Kinnaman [5], Calcott and Walls [1] and Eichner and Pethig [4] analyze the effort to consider environment such as making easiness to recycle waste by firm. We consider the effort to consider environment such as transforming "quality of waste (burnable waste or resource waste)" by firm.

We analyze the effort to separate waste by household unlike Fullerton and Kinnaman [5] and Choe and Fraser [2] that considers the illegal disposal by household. In addition, we pay attention to the existence condition of the market of recycling goods. A current early research was discussed on the assumption that the recycling goods market existed. However, the recycling goods market necessarily does not exist because of a low degree of demand for recycling goods and a high recycling cost. Therefore, it is important to clarify the existence condition of the recycling goods market.

The composition of this chapter is as follows. In the next section, we explain about the model, and derive the market equilibrium conditions first. Next, we derive the social optimum conditions, and compare it with the market equilibrium conditions. And, we show that the optimal solution can be achieved by adding a new policy, and derive the optimal waste management policy. Finally, we refer the summary and the problem in the future.

7.2 The Model

The model of this chapter is composed of household, firm X (firm that produces the goods by using the virgin resource), firm Y (firm that produces the goods by using recycled resource), the virgin resource mining trader and the recycling manufacture.

7.2.1 *Firm X (Firm that Produces the Goods by Using the Virgin Resource)*

When the goods are produced, firm X inputs the virgin resource. We assume the production function of firm X to be $x = f(v)$. v is an amount of using the virgin resource and x is an amount of production. Here, we assume $f' > 0$ and $f'' < 0$.

Moreover, firm X decides the level of environmental design investment that influences the quality of the waste after the goods are consumed at the same time as deciding the amount of using the virgin resource. The amount of the burnable waste is shown with $(1 - \alpha)x$, and the amount the recyclable waste is shown with αx, if we assume the level of environmental design investment to be $\alpha(0 \leq \alpha \leq 1)$. This means the amount of the recyclable waste increases and the amount of the burnable waste decreases when α increases for given value of x. Here, we assume that it costs $\theta(\alpha)$ a unit of the good as an environmental design investment cost. We assume that the investment cost rises when α increases($\theta' > 0$ and $\theta'' > 0$).

When the tax rate to virgin resource is assumed to be τ_v, the price of virgin resource is assumed to be p_v, and the price of goods is assumed to be p_x, the profit of firm X is as follows.

$$\begin{aligned} \Pi_x &= p_x x - (p_v + \tau_v)v - \theta(\alpha)x \\ &= p_x f(v) - (p_v + \tau_v)v - \theta(\alpha)f(v). \end{aligned} \tag{7.1}$$

To maximize the profit of Eq. (7.1), firm X decides an amount v of using the virgin resource and the level α of environmental design investment. Therefore, the first order condition of the profit maximization is as follows.

$$(p_x - \theta(\alpha))f'(v) = p_v + \tau_v, \tag{7.2}$$

$$\frac{dp_x}{d\alpha} = \theta'(\alpha), \tag{7.3}$$

The left side of Eq. (7.3), $dp_x/d\alpha(> 0)$ shows firm X's willingness to accept (WTA) for an increase of one unit in the level α of environmental design investment. When the price p_x is a function at the level α of environmental design investment, such a price p_x is called Hedonic Price.

Next, we consider the behavior of the mining trader of the virgin resource. When the marginal cost of the virgin resource mining is assumed to be c_v, the profit of the mining trader of the virgin resource is shown as follows.

$$\Pi_v = p_v v - c_v v. \tag{7.4}$$

Here, the following equation holds under the perfect competition.

$$p_v = c_v, \tag{7.5}$$

7.2.2 *Firm Y (Firm that Produces the Goods by Using the Recycled Resource)*

Here, firm Y inputs the recycled resource and produces the recycling goods. We assume the production function of firm Y to be $y = h(r)$. r is an amount of using the recycled resource and y is an amount of production. Here, we assume $h^{'} > 0$ and $h^{''} < 0$.

When the subsidy rate to using recyled resource is assumed to be s, the price of recycling goods is assumed to be p_y, and the price of recycled resource is assumed to be p_r, the profit of firm Y is as follows.

$$\begin{aligned} \Pi_y &= p_y y - (p_r - s)r \\ &= p_y h(r) - (p_r - s)r. \end{aligned} \tag{7.6}$$

To maximize the profit of Eq. (7.6), firm Y decides the amount of using the recycled resource r. Therefore, the first order condition of the profit maximization is as follows.

$$p_y h^{'}(r) = p_r - s, \tag{7.7}$$

Next, we condider the behavior of supplier of recycled resource (the recycling manufacture). The recycling manufacture pays the household τ_r and receives the recyclable waste from the household.[1] When the amount of receiving the recyclable waste from the household is assumed to be r and the marginal cost of recycling the recyclable waste is assumed to be c_r, the profit of the recycling manufacture is as follows.

$$\Pi_r = (p_r + \tau_r)r - c_r r. \tag{7.8}$$

Here, the following equation holds under the perfect competition.

$$p_r + \tau_r = c_r, \tag{7.9}$$

7.2.3 *Household*

Here, we consider the action of consuming goods and separating waste by the household. The household is satisfied with consuming three goods. The first is the goods (x) that firm X produces by inputting the virgin resource (it is called goods X at the following). The second is the goods (y) that firm Y produces by inputting

[1]Note that τ_r is positive or negative.

recycled resource (it is called goods Y at the following). The third is numeraire goods (m). We assume that all housholds are homogeneous and utility function is quasi-linear as follows.[2]

$$u(x, y) + m. \tag{7.10}$$

Here, we assume $u_x > 0$ and $u_{xx} < 0$ and $u_y > 0$ and $u_{yy} < 0$. We assume $u_x(t) > u_y(t)$ holds for any t. This means that the marginal utility for the goods X is larger than that of goods Y.

The household emits waste at the same time as consuming goos X and goods Y. We assume that the x unit of waste is generated if the x unit of goods X is consumed, and the y unit of waste is generated if the y unit of goods Y is consumed. The quality of waste generated by the consumption of goods X depends on the level α of environmental design investment of firm X. That is, the change in α influences the amount $(1 - \alpha)x$ of the burnable waste and the amount αx of the recyclable waste. On the other hand, we assume that the waste generated by the consumption of goods Y are all burnable waste for the simplification of the analysis.

Here, the household must separate waste. We assume that when the household separates wastes to the burnable waste and the recyclable waste, he has disutility. For example, it is necessary that the household wash and dry a plastic tray of food and the box lunch in water so that he may separate them to recyclable waste. Moreover, it is necessary that the househld peel off wrapping the PET bottle so that he may separate them to recyclable waste. These actions would bring the household disutility. When we assume the effort level of separating the recyclable waste by household to be $\beta(0 \leq \beta \leq 1)$, then the amount of recyclable waste passed legal to the local government as "recyclable waste" by household is shown by $\alpha\beta x$ and the amount of recyclable waste passed ilegal to the local government as "burnable waste" by household is shown by $(1 - \beta)\alpha x$. Because the total amount of burnable waste is a sum of the amount $(1-\beta)\alpha x$ of recyclable waste passed ilegal to the local government and the amount $(1-\alpha)x$ of the burnable waste, it is shown by $(1-\alpha\beta)x$. Here, housuhold's disutility caused by separating a unit of waste is as follows.

$$\frac{B}{2}\beta^2 \tag{7.11}$$

B is a parameter that shows the size of disutility, and this means disutility grows as the effort level β of separating waste rises. We define the utility function of the household from Eqs. (7.10) and (7.11) as follows.

$$U(x, y, m, \beta) = u(x, y) + m - \frac{B}{2}\beta^2 x. \tag{7.12}$$

[2]Note that quasi-linear utility function is the income effect to be zero.

When the household separates waste and passes it to the local government, he pays the government tax rate τ_g for the burnable waste and pays the recycling manufacture price τ_r for the recyclable waste.[3] Therefore, when we assume the income to be I (parameter), the budget constraint of the household is as follows.

$$I = p_x x + p_y y + m + \tau_g((1-\alpha\beta)x + y) + \tau_r \alpha\beta x, \tag{7.13}$$

The household decides consumption combination (x, y, m), the effort level β of separating waste, and demand α for the environmental design investment of the firm so that he may maximize his utility (Eq. 7.12) under the budget constraint (Eq. 7.13). The first order conditions for maximization of utility of household are as follows.

$$u_x = \frac{B}{2}\beta^2 + p_x + \tau_g(1-\alpha\beta) + \tau_r\alpha\beta, \tag{7.14}$$

$$u_y \leq p_y + \tau_g, \tag{7.15}$$

$$B\beta \geq (\tau_g - \tau_r)\alpha, \tag{7.16}$$

$$\frac{dp_x}{d\alpha} \geq (\tau_g - \tau_r)\beta, \tag{7.17}$$

The left side of Eq. (7.17), $dp_x/d\alpha(>0)$ shows household's willingness to pay (WTP) for an increase of one unit in the level α of environmental design investment.

If $\tau_g - \tau_r < 0$ holds from Eqs. (7.16) and (7.17), the household selects $\alpha = 0$ and $\beta = 0$. This means that the household doesn't buy the goods that α is large and doesn't separate waste, if the price of the recyclable waste is larger than that of the burnable waste. Therefore, we assume $\tau_g - \tau_r > 0$.

Here, We pay attention to Eq. (7.15) to see whether the recycling goods market exists or not. We can understand that there is a possibility that demand for the recycling goods is zero, if the price p_y of recycling goods and the tax rate τ_g for the burnable waste in the right side of Eq. (7.15) are much large. In a word, when the following equation holds, demand for the recycling goods is zero and the recycling goods market does not exist at that time.

$$u_y|_{y=0} < p_y + \tau_g,$$

[3] τ_r is a endogenous variable that depends on relation between demand and supply for the recyclable waste while τ_g is a policy variable by the local government.

7.2.4 Market Equilibrium

Here, we consider market equilibrium. From Eqs. (7.3) and (7.17), the following equation holds because firm's WTA (the left side of Eq. (7.3)) is equal to household's WTP(the left side of Eq. (7.17)) for the level α of environmental design investment under market equilibrium.

$$\theta'(\alpha) = (\tau_g - \tau_r)\beta, \tag{7.18}$$

Therefore, by solving 11 equations that add three equations of $x = f(v)$, $y = h(r)$, and $r = \alpha\beta x$ to (7.2),(7.5),(7.7),(7.9),(7.14)–(7.16) and (7.18), we can obtain $(v, \alpha, \beta, x, y, r, p_x, p_v, p_y, p_r, \tau_r)$ as a market equilibrium solution. These market equilibrium solutions are the functions of (τ_g, τ_v, s) that is the policy variable of the local government.

Here, we bring the equations of 11 on together in three equations. From Eqs. (7.16) and (7.18), the following equation holds:

$$B\beta^2 = \alpha\theta'(\alpha). \tag{7.19}$$

Equation (7.5) is substituted for Eq. (7.2), it transforms into the equation of p_x, and it is substituted for Eq. (7.14). In addition, when Eq. (7.18) is transformed into the equation of τ_r and it is substituted for Eq. (7.14), we obtain the following equation.

$$u_x f' - \frac{B}{2}\beta^2 f' - c_v - \tau_v - \theta(\alpha) f' - \tau_g f' + \alpha\theta'(\alpha) f' = 0. \tag{7.20}$$

Next, Eq. (7.18) is transformed into the equation of τ_r, it substitutes for Eq. (7.9), it transforms into the equation of p_r and it substitutes it for Eq. (7.7). In addition, when Eq. (7.15) is substituted for Eq. (7.7), we obtain the following equation.

$$u_y h'\beta - \theta'(\alpha) - c_r\beta - \tau_g h'\beta + \tau_g\beta + s\beta = 0. \tag{7.21}$$

Therefore, we can request market equilibrium solutions $(\hat{v}, \hat{\alpha}, \hat{\beta})$ by solving three equations of (7.19)–(7.21).

7.3 Social Welfare and First Best

7.3.1 Social Optimum

In this section, we will define the social welfare and consider the appropriate values of v^*, α^*, β^* which maximize the social welfare. Then we will analyze whether or not first best optimum is attained by local government's waste management policies.

The social welfare is defined as follows:

$$SW = u\Big(f(v), h(\alpha\beta f(v))\Big) - \frac{B}{2}\beta^2 f(v) - c_v v - \theta(\alpha)f(v) - c_r\alpha\beta f(v)$$
$$-D(v) - \underline{d}\Big((1-\alpha)f(v) + h(\alpha\beta f(v))\Big) - \overline{d}\alpha(1-\beta)f(v). \qquad (7.22)$$

The first term of Eq. (7.22) is utility from consumption. The second term denotes the disutility of household effort made to separate the waste. The costs to extract virgin resources are shown by the third term. The forth term represents the firms' environmental investment costs. The fifth term is the recycle cost of resources. The sixth term is external cost of extracting virgin resources. We assume that $D' > 0$ and $D'' > 0$. The last two terms are the social damages from disposing the burnable waste and the recyclable waste. $\underline{d}$ and $\overline{d}$ are marginal social costs of disposing each type of waste. Note that the amount of burnable waste is given as $1 - \alpha\beta$. However, some parts of recyclable waste are not separated and disposed as the burnable waste. These amounts are given as $1-\beta f(v)$. This recyclable waste is burned with burnable waste but emit harmful substance. So we assume $\underline{d} < \overline{d}$.

The first order conditions for social optimum are given as follows:

$$\frac{dSW}{dv} = u_x f' + u_y h'\alpha\beta f' - \frac{B}{2}\beta^2 f' - c_v - c_r\alpha\beta f' - \theta(\alpha)f'$$
$$-D'(v) - \underline{d}f'\Big((1-\alpha) + h'\alpha\beta\Big) - \overline{d}\alpha(1-\beta)f' = 0, \qquad (7.23)$$

$$\frac{dSW}{d\alpha} = u_y h'\beta - \theta'(\alpha) - c_r\beta + \underline{d}(1 - h'\beta) - \overline{d}(1-\beta) = 0, \qquad (7.24)$$

$$\frac{dSW}{d\beta} = u_y h'\alpha - B\beta - c_r\alpha - \underline{d}h'\alpha + \overline{d}\alpha = 0. \qquad (7.25)$$

7.3.2 *Is the First Best Optimum Achievable?*

Here we discuss whether or not Eqs. (7.23)–(7.25) can be coincident with (7.19)–(7.21). That is, we will consider government policies which induce social optimum. If there exists combination of policies τ_g, τ_v, and s, which conform $(\hat{v}, \hat{\alpha}, \hat{\beta})$ (the values derived in the market economy) to (v^*, α^*, β^*) (social optimum solutions), these are first-best policies. The problem whether or not these polices exist.[4]

[4]We assume that tax revenues from τ_g and τ_v are incorporated into general revenue and that the local government dips into general revenues to cover the subsidy s. Furthermore, to make the discussion simple, balance of payment of general revenue.

From Eqs. (7.24) and (7.25), we obtain

$$B\beta^2 = \alpha\theta'(\alpha) + \alpha(\overline{d} - \underline{d}). \tag{7.26}$$

If we substitute $(\hat{\alpha}, \hat{\beta})$ in Eq. (7.19) (condition for market equilibrium) for Eq. (7.26) (condition for social optimum), we obtain

$$B\hat{\beta}^2 < \hat{\alpha}\theta'(\hat{\alpha}) + \hat{\alpha}(\overline{d} - \underline{d}).$$

This equation does not hold with equality. This is because Eq. (7.19) does not depend on waste disposal policies (τ_g, τ_v, s). This implies that first best solution cannot be achieved in the market economy even if the local government tries to exercise waste management policies.

Theorem 7.1. *Waste management policies τ_g, τ_v, s can not conform the market equilibrium to social optimum.*

7.4 Optimal Waste Disposal Policies

In Sect. 7.3, we showed that there exist no government policies that induce first best solutions. In this section, we will discuss the reasons of that result and introduce new policies of local government.

7.4.1 Added Policies

First, let us discuss the problems of local government policies analyzed in the previous section. In this chapter, there are three externalities related to virgin resource extraction, burnable waste, and recyclable waste. To internalize first and second externalities, government can impose the tax on the extraction of virgin resources (τ_v) and on burnable waste (τ_g). However, some recyclable waste is disposed as burnable waste because household does not separate recyclable from nonrecyclable trash perfectly. If recyclable waste is burnt, the environmental damage by burning them is higher than that by burning of combustible waste (note that $\overline{d} - \underline{d} > 0$). On the other hand, the tax rate imposed on each house hold is τ_g. So, the tax rate imposed on the recyclable waste disposed as the burnable waste is too low from the social point of view.

From Eq. (7.7), we know that the subsidy rate s affects the demand for recyclable resources r but does not affect the effort level of each household β. So, local government polices discussed in the previous section (τ_g, τ_v, s) does not give the enough incentive to the households to separate their waste.

Next, we will add new policy. The most serious point in the policies discussed in previous section is that some recyclable waste is disposed as burnable waste. Here, we assume that households must pay a fine if they do not separate recyclable from non-recyclable waste and their violating act is found by the authorities. Household must pay τ_p per unit of waste if its illegal behaviors become apparent.

Furthermore we assume that the probability of catching illegal waste is given as $p(\alpha(1-\beta)x),\ p^{'} > 0, p^{''} < 0$ The more the recyclable waste is disposed as burnable waste, the higher the probability of catching illegal waste.

What happens if τ_p is added to the existing policies? First, households will take the probability of catching illegal waste into consideration when they consume the goods x (note that the amount of waste is positively correlated with consumption level of good X). Therefore, Eq. (7.14) should be rewritten as follows:

$$u_x = \frac{B}{2}\beta^2 + p_x + \tau_g(1-\alpha\beta) + \tau_r\alpha\beta + \tau_p p^{'}\alpha(1-\beta). \tag{7.27}$$

Second, households will take the effect of increasing β (the amount of effort to separate waste) on $p(\cdot)$ (probability of catching illegal waste) into consideration when they determine the levels of β. Then Eq. (7.16) becomes

$$B\beta = (\tau_g - \tau_r)\alpha + \tau_p p^{'}\alpha. \tag{7.28}$$

Lastly, households will take the effect of increasing α (the investment level for environmental design) on $p(\cdot)$ (probability of catching illegal waste) into consideration when their demand level for α is determined. Then Eq. (7.17) becomes

$$\frac{dp_x}{d\alpha} = (\tau_g - \tau_r)\beta - \tau_p p^{'}(1-\beta). \tag{7.29}$$

That is, when if τ_p is added to the local government policies, we can obtain the market equilibrium by solving Eqs. (7.2), (7.5), (7.7), (7.9), (7.15) (7.27)–(7.29) and $x = f(v), y = h(r), r = \alpha\beta x$.

7.4.2 Optimal Policies

Here we derive the optimal polices (the combination of $(\tau_g, \tau_v, \tau_p, s)$) that conform market equilibrium to social optimum.

By using Eqs. (7.2), (7.5), (7.7), (7.9), (7.15) (7.27)–(7.29) and $x = f(v), y = h(r), r = \alpha\beta x$, we obtain the following:

$$B\beta^2 = \alpha(\theta^{'}(\alpha) + \tau_p p^{'}), \tag{7.30}$$

$$u_x f' - \frac{B}{2}\beta^2 f' - c_v - \tau_v - \theta(\alpha) f' - \tau_g f' + \alpha\theta'(\alpha) f' = 0, \tag{7.31}$$

$$u_y h'\beta - \theta'(\alpha) - c_r\beta - \tau_g h'\beta + \tau_g\beta + s\beta - \tau_p p'(1-\beta) = 0. \tag{7.32}$$

From these three equations, the market equilibrium values of $(\tau_g, \tau_v, \tau_p, s)$ under new local government policies will be derived.

Let us compare (v^*, α^*, β^*) (these values are obtained by solving Eqs. (7.23)–(7.25)) with $(\tilde{v}, \tilde{\alpha}, \tilde{\beta})$ (these values are obtained by solving Eqs. (7.30)–(7.32)). We will confirm whether or not local government policies can conform $(\tilde{v}, \tilde{\alpha}, \tilde{\beta})$ to (v^*, α^*, β^*).

From Eqs. (7.24) and (7.25), we obtain

$$B\beta^2 = \alpha\theta'(\alpha) + \alpha(\overline{d} - \underline{d}). \tag{7.33}$$

From Eqs. (7.30) and (7.32), the optimal values of fine are given as

$$\tau_p^* = \frac{\overline{d} - \underline{d}}{p'}. \tag{7.34}$$

If we rewrite Eq. (7.24), we must obtain Eq. (7.32). This implies

$$\underline{d}(1 - h'\beta) - \overline{d}(1-\beta) = -\tau_g h'\beta + \tau_g\beta + s\beta - \tau_p^* p'(1-\beta). \tag{7.35}$$

Substituting Eq. (7.34) into Eq. (7.35), we can obtain the relationship between the optimal tax rate for burnable waste τ_g^* and the optimal subsidy rate for using recycle resources s:

$$\tau_g^*(1 - h') + s^* = \underline{d}(1 - h'). \tag{7.36}$$

Equations (7.31) and (7.32) imply

$$\begin{aligned} & u_x f' + u_y h'\alpha\beta f' - \frac{B}{2}\beta^2 f' - c_v - c_r\alpha\beta f' - \theta(\alpha) f' \\ & \quad - \tau_v - \tau_g^* f'(1 + \alpha\beta h' - \alpha\beta) + s^*\alpha\beta f' - \tau_p^* p'\alpha(1-\beta) f' = 0. \end{aligned} \tag{7.37}$$

If Eqs. (7.23) and (7.37) are consistent with each other, the relationship among τ_g^*, s^*, and τ_v^* are as follows:

$$-\tau_g^* f'(1 + \alpha\beta h' - \alpha\beta) + s^*\alpha\beta f' - \tau_v^* = -\underline{d} f'(1 + \alpha\beta h' - \alpha\beta) - D'(v). \tag{7.38}$$

Optimal policies $(\tau_g^*, \tau_v^*, \tau_p^*, s^*)$ are derived by solving three equations, (7.34), (7.36), and (7.37). From Eq. (7.34), we know that τ_p^* is determined uniquely. On the other hand, τ_g^*, τ_v^* and s^* are underspecified. If both Eqs. (7.36) and (7.37) are satisfied, τ_g^*, τ_v^* and s^* yield the first best optimum. So, there are many optimal values of τ_g^*, τ_v^* and s^*.

Theorem 7.2. *If the combination of local government policies satisfies three Eqs. (7.34)–(7.37), then it is the optimal. τ_p^* is determined uniquely but there are many combinations of τ_g^*, τ_v^*, and s^* that achieve social optimum.*

Here, we consider the one combination of policies that satisfies $s^* = 0$ and three Eqs. (7.34), (7.36), and (7.37).

$$\tau_p^* = \frac{\overline{d} - \underline{d}}{p'}, \quad \tau_g^* = \underline{d}, \quad \tau_v^* = D', \quad s^* = 0, \tag{7.39}$$

Even when the local government does not subsidize the firms that use the recycle resources (that is, $s^* = 0$), first best optimum can be achieved. Let us look at Eq. (7.15). The higher the values of $\tilde{p}_y$ and τ_g^* (equilibrium price of recycle goods and tax rate on the burnable waste), the higher the right hand side of Eq. (7.15). If so, it is possible that the demand for recycle goods becomes zero. Note that the higher the values of $\underline{d}$, the higher the optimal tax rate on the burnable waste$\tau_g^* = \underline{d}$ (see Eq. (7.39)). This means that the large values of $\underline{d}$ make it difficult to hold Eq. (7.15). So, the combination like Eq. (7.39) is not an appropriate one.

Equation (7.7) implies that the equilibrium price of recycle goods $\tilde{p}_y$ is a decreasing function with respect to the subsidy rate s^*. This implies that the combination of low subsidy rate for using recycle resources (in the extreme case, $s^* = 0$) and high tax rate on the burnable waste (in the extreme case, $\tau_g^* = \underline{d}$) is not desirable because such combination tends to violate the existence condition of recycle goods market. From the social point of view, high subsidy rate for recycle resources and low rate of burnable waste are more attractive. The we can obtain the following proposition.

Theorem 7.3. *If we consider the existence conditions of recycle goods, the optimal combinations of local government policies (τ_g^*, τ_v^*, τ_p^*, s^*) are limited. Generally speaking, setting τ_g^* lower and s^* higher are more desirable.*

7.5 Concluding Remarks

In this chapter we extend the model discussed in Choe and Fraser [2] by introducing three new elements. First, we assumed that there are two types of waste-burnable waste and recyclable waste-. Second, we discussed the households' behavior when they must separate their trash (Fullerton and Kinnaman [5], Choe and Fraser [2] discuss the problems related to illegal dumping but do not refer to this point). Thirdly, we analyzed the conditions for the functioning recyclable market.

Our main conclusions are as follows. First, first best optimum is not achievable when the government' available policies are imposing tax on burnable waste and on virgin resources, and subsidy to the use of recycle resources (see Theorem 7.1). This is because some recyclable waste is disposed as the burnable waste and this externality is not internalized successfully. So the government introduces the fine policy for that illegal behavior. If such policy is added to the existing local government policies, the market equilibrium becomes first best optimum. We also showed that optimal combination of local government policies is not unique (see Theorem 7.2). On the other hand, if we consider the existing condition of recycle goods, optimal combination of local government is limited (see Theorem 7.3).

The results here suggest several areas for further research. For example, we assumed that households are homogenous. However, they have different preference for environmental characteristics such as the demand for environmental design or recycle goods. So, we should assume the heterogeneous households. Furthermore, our model assumed that the local government can not control the probability of catching illegal waste. Generally speaking, local government uses resources to monitor and find the illegal behavior. So considering the optimal monitoring levels of local government would be also interesting. Lastly, we should consider the second best solution rather than first best solution if first best solution is not attained by some reasons.

References

1. Calcott, K., & Walls, M. (2000). Can downstream waste disposal policies encourage upstream 'design for environment'? *American Economic Review, 90*, 233–237.
2. Choe, C., & Fraser, I. (1999). An economic analysis of household waste management. *Journal of Environmental Economics and Management, 38*, 234–246.
3. Dinan, T. M. (1993). Economic efficiency effects of alternative policies for reducing waste disposal. *Journal of Environmental Economics and Management, 25*, 242–256.
4. Eichner, T., & Pethig, R. (2001). Product design and efficient management of recycling and waste treatment. *Journal of Environmental Economics and Management, 41*, 109–134.
5. Fullerton, D., & Kinnaman, T. (1995). Garbage, recycling, and illicit burning or dumping. *Journal of Environmental Economics and Management, 29*, 78–91.
6. Fullerton, D., & Wu, W. (1998). Policies for green design. *Journal of Environmental Economics and Management, 36*, 131–148.
7. Ministry of the Environment. (2003). Annual report on the environment in Japan 2003. Ministry of the Environment Government of Japan.
8. Ministry of the Environment. (2014). Annual report on the environment, the sound material-cycle society and the biodiversity in Japan 2014. Ministry of the Environment Government of Japan.
9. Walls, M. A., & Palmer, K. (2001). Upsteam pollution, downstream waste disposal, and the design of comprehensive environmental policies. *Journal of Environmental Economics and Management, 41*, 94–108.

Chapter 8
The Basic Model of Airline Network

Akio Kawasaki

8.1 Introduction

From the viewpoint of regional policy, the hub airport is crucial for developing the regional economy. Because various goods, services, and information are gathered in the hub city, many firms aggregate there. As these firms aggregate, many people are also drawn to the region and regional development ensues.

With regard to the hub problem, Konishi [21] is an important and interesting study. According to Konishi [21], which uses the general equilibrium model, if all transportation technology is the same (i.e., in the symmetric transportation technology setting), hub route does not appear in equilibrium; on the contrary, if transportation technology is different between countries (i.e., in the asymmetric transportation technology setting), hub route occurs when the transportation technology of one country is superior.

Given the importance of hubs, this chapter introduces a model to analyze not only the airline network formation problem but also the hub location problem. Much research has considered the airline network formation problem and hub location problem. Previous studies of airline networks and, especially, hub location problems have used operation research (OR). The main purpose of OR analysis is to develop an algorithm minimizing total transportation costs. However, studies using OR analysis have certain shortcomings, notably failing to internalize carriers' strategies (e.g., pricing, flight frequency). In other words, although carriers want to maximize their profit, previous studies have not considered this problem. Rather, minimizing the number of connecting passengers has been thought to be important

A. Kawasaki (✉)
Faculty of Education, Kagoshima University, Korimoto 1-20-6, Kagoshima city, Kagoshima 8900065, Japan
e-mail: kawasaki@edu.kagoshima-u.ac.jp

T. Naito (ed.), *Sustainable Growth and Development in a Regional Economy*, New Frontiers in Regional Science: Asian Perspectives 13,
DOI 10.1007/978-4-431-55294-9_8

for hub airports. However, in the actual airline market, carriers may not choose the hub airport in order to minimize the potential number of connecting passengers. For example, Changi International Airport in Singapore aims to be a hub airport in Asia by attracting more connecting passengers in various ways.[1] Another well-known hub airport in Asia is Hong Kong International Airport; however, the number of passengers coming to Hong Kong is not always large.

Considering these shortcomings in previous research, this chapter first derives a carrier's strategies (i.e., related to airfare and flight frequency) to maximize profit and the profit amount. Then, we analyze whether a monopolistic carrier chooses a point-to-point network or a hub–spoke network with one hub airport (and if the latter, which airport serves as the hub). Additionally, we derive the socially preferable network formation and socially preferable hub location. By considering these problems, this chapter aims to explain the strategies of various actual airline networks including the examples of Changi International Airport and Hong Kong International Airport by using the theory of industrial organization (IO)[2].

The theory of IO has previously addressed only airline network formation by explaining those mechanisms that carriers adopt in a hub–spoke network. For example, economies of density was mainly discussed in the 1990s.[3] Because the hub–spoke network can gather the passengers in two markets onto one route, the carrier's marginal cost decreases compared with the point-to-point network due to economies of density. Consequently, to lower operation cost and increase profit, each carrier adopts the hub–spoke network after the deregulation of the airline market. On the contrary, while studies in the 1990s addressed the network effect with suppliers, many researchers after 2000 started to examine the network effect with passengers. Here, by gathering passengers onto one route, the flight frequency of that route increases, which improves passenger convenience. As a result, the passenger's utility increases and potential demand for carriers rises. According to some studies, in this scenario, each carrier adopts the hub–spoke network to obtain these benefits.

However, while studies have used the theory of IO to examine the airline network formation problem, this theory has rarely been used to consider the hub location problem. One such study is Kawasaki [19]. Therefore, to simplify Kawasaki's [19] analysis, the present chapter introduces a model of IO to analyze the hub location problem.

The main results obtained in this chapter are as follows. When the additional travel time cost for connecting passengers is large (small), the monopolistic carrier adopts the point-to-point (hub–spoke) network. This finding concurs with those of previous studies. On the contrary, with regard to the hub location problem, the monopolistic carrier does not always choose the hub airport to minimize the

[1] For example, it has a games corner, transit hotel, gym, shower room, and swimming pool.

[2] For industrial economic theory, see Tirole [31]. We use the theory of IO to internalize a firm's various strategies.

[3] See Brueckner and Spiller [8], for example.

potential number of connecting passengers. That is, if the potential number of connecting passengers is very large, the monopolistic carrier does not adopt the hub airport to minimize the potential number of connecting passengers. Additionally, the socially preferable hub airport is not always the airport that minimizes the potential number of connecting passengers. Finally, we introduce the per-seat cost to analyze the airline network formation and hub location problems and demonstrate that although the results mentioned above hold when the per-seat cost is small, when this cost is large, the point-to-point network is always adopted.

The remainder of this chapter is organized as follows. In Sect. 8.2, we review previous studies of the airline network problem. Section 8.3 presents the model used in this chapter. In Sect. 8.4, we analyze the model and derive the profit-maximizing flight frequency and airfare. Section 8.5 compares the result of each outcome. In Sect. 8.6, we derive the profit-maximizing network formation and hub location. Section 8.7 derives social welfare and finds the socially preferable hub location. Section 8.8 additionally introduces the per-seat cost and re-analyzes the airline network formation and hub location problems. In Sect. 8.9, the policy implications from this chapter are discussed. Section 8.10 concludes.

8.2 Literature Review

We begin this review of studies of airline networks by discussing those that have used OR analysis. The key aim of studies using OR analysis is to find a location for a hub city such that total transportation costs (e.g., passengers' movement, waiting time) are minimized. A seminal study in this regard is O'Kelly [23]. Thereafter, many researchers developed models that analyze the hub location problem using the OR method. For example, Campbell [10] develops a model to solve a number of hub location problems (see Bryan and O'Kelly [9] for a detailed survey of hub location analyses). Martin and Roman [22] propose a model to solve the hub location problem by considering competition between airlines. Racunica and Wynter [27] formulate a model to solve a hub location problem with intermodal freight, and Rodriguez et al. [28] propose a model with capacity constraints. Similarly, Eiselta and Marianov [13] develop a model to solve the competitive airline market's hub location problem by using gravity-like utility functions for passengers, while De Camargo et al. [11] address the multiple allocation of hub airports under the hub congestion problem.[4]

A representative study of airline network formation using IO is Brueckner and Spiller [8]. By using a quantity competition model with economies of density, they examine whether a monopolistic or competitive market is socially preferable. They find that in the competitive market, although the cost per passenger increases due to the decrease in passengers on one route, airfare decreases. Contrarily, in the

[4]Other examples include Aykin [2] and Alumur and Kara [1].

monopolistic market, airfare increases. Consequently, a competitive market raises social welfare compared with the monopolistic market.

Another important study is that by Hendricks et al. [16], who analyze which network carriers adopted after the deregulation in 1978, demonstrating that both hub–spoke networks and point-to-point networks were used because of economies of density. Hendricks et al. [17] then address the competition between major carriers that adopt hub–spoke networks and regional carriers. They show that adopting a hub–spoke network becomes a dominant strategy, allowing major carriers to continue to operate in spoke markets even when regional carriers exist.[5]

On the demand-side network effects rather than the supplier side, representative studies are Oum et al. [24] and Brueckner [6]. Oum et al. [24] find that incumbent carriers adopt hub–spoke networks as an entry deterrence strategy. Brueckner [6] assumes a monopolistic airline market and discusses why flight frequency increases in modern airline networks by using a model in which the benefit of traveling is introduced, concluding that the reason for this approach is to adopt a hub–spoke network. In addition, Brueckner [6] discusses whether the monopolistic carrier adopts the hub–spoke network or the point-to-point network and concludes that when the marginal operation cost per flight is small, the hub–spoke network is adopted given that its total flight frequency is larger than that for the point-to-point network. Kawasaki [18] points out the shortcomings of Brueckner's [6] study, notably that its results depend on some assumptions and that its model assumes that all passengers use direct services when the point-to-point network is adopted. Kawasaki [18] argues that even when the point-to-point network is adopted, some passengers may use connecting services. To overcome these shortcomings, Kawasaki [18] uses the model of Berechman and Shy [4] and Berechman et al. [3] to analyze whether the hub–spoke network or point-to-point network is adopted by the monopolistic carrier. The important characteristic of Kawasaki's [18] study is that it introduces heterogeneity into the time value (i.e., some passengers use connecting services even when the carrier adopts the point-to-point network). Kawasaki [18] finds that when the difference in the time value between passengers is small (large), the monopolistic carrier has an (no) incentive to adopt the hub–spoke network to discriminate airfares between passengers.

Thereafter, studies of airline competition were published. Brueckner and Flores-Fillol [7] consider the situation in which two carriers in an economy that both adopt hub–spoke networks compete with each other on flight frequency and airfare. They show that by comparing the market equilibrium flight frequency with the socially preferable one, the market equilibrium becomes the socially inadequate flight frequency. Flores-Fillol [7] analyzes airline network formation in a competitive situation, demonstrating that when cost per passenger (or per seat) is sufficiently small, both carriers adopt hub–spoke networks; however, as this cost increases, the equilibrium that at least one carrier adopts the point-to-point network arises.

[5]Other examples include Bittlingmayer [5], who discusses airline pricing under a hub–spoke network by considering economies of scope.

Similarly, Flores-Fillol and Fargeda [15] consider airline network formation with airport congestion and demonstrate that carriers prefer the hub–spoke network even though it may not be preferable from the perspective of social welfare.

Finally, only one study except Kawasaki [19] has addressed the hub location problem. Pels et al. [26] use linear demand and cost functions in a three-city model and assume that one city pair's potential number of passengers is smaller than that of the other city pair. Then, by considering the quantity decisions made by two competitive airlines seeking to maximize profits, they show that the hub city is constructed to minimize the potential number of passengers who travel between spoke cities (i.e., connecting passengers).

As seen from this brief review, although IO addresses the airline network formation problem, the hub location problem has rarely been considered by previous researchers. To address this shortcoming, this chapter introduces a model to analyze both network formation and hub location.

8.3 The Model

Following Brueckner [6] and Kawasaki [18], this chapter uses a model with three cities, termed A, B, and C. In this chapter, we assume for simplicity that the airline market is monopolistic. A carrier chooses either a hub–spoke network with hub city h or a point-to-point network. The carrier flies between city pair $ij(i, j = A, B, C,\ i \neq j)$ f_{ij} times. When the carrier operates its service, it incurs an operation cost, which arises from the flights. We assume that the cost per flight is constant and is denoted by K. The cost per passenger is ignored. Further, we assume for simplicity that the capacity of an aircraft is unlimited.

In each city, there exist potential passengers who plan to travel to their destination. When passengers use airline services to travel to their destination, they gain a benefit. Following Brueckner [6], we assume that this benefit is the sum of the travel benefit and the reduction in schedule delay.[6] This chapter assumes that all passengers have a constant and common time value. The travel benefit is expressed as w. It is assumed that potential passengers evaluate airline services differently. Therefore, this chapter assumes that the travel benefit w is uniformly distributed between $-\underline{W}$ and W. Here, we assume that the absolute value $\underline{W}$ is adequately large. This interpretation is as follows. A passenger for whom $w = -\underline{W}$ has a fear of heights and never travels by air. A passenger for whom $w = W$ prefers to travel by air and often flies. With regard to the density of w, this chapter assumes that the density of w in city pair AC equals 1 and that in city pair AB and BC equals $\beta(\geq 0)$.

[6]The term "schedule delay cost" quantifies the disutility from the difference between passengers' preferred departure or arrival time and the actual departure or arrival time. The schedule delay can be decomposed into the "frequency delay" and the "stochastic delay." Both delays depend on flight frequency. See Douglas and Miller [12] and Panzar [25] for a detailed discussion.

When an airline increases its flight frequency, all passengers enjoy convenience, which subsequently increases passengers' benefit. This means a reduction in schedule delay. For example, in Brueckner [6], when an airline firm increases its flight frequency, the schedule delay cost decreases, thereby increasing passengers' benefit.[7] This chapter uses the Kawasaki-type function [18] for simplicity,[8] that is, $\sqrt{f_{ij}}$.[9] Following Kawasaki [19], we call this reduction in schedule delay (i.e., the increase in convenience) by increasing flight frequency the "scheduling effect."

Further, it is necessary to formulate a benefit function for connecting passengers that differs from that used in previous studies. When connecting passengers travel via a hub city, they need to take two flights on two routes. Consequently, their convenience depends on both routes. Therefore, following Oum et al. [24] Kawasaki [19], and Kawasaki and Lin [20], this chapter assumes that the total reduction in the schedule delay cost depends on the sum of each route's contribution to the reduction in the schedule delay cost. That is, if we express the reduction in the schedule delay cost for the ih route as $g(f_{ih})$, the total reduction in the schedule delay cost for connecting passengers is denoted as $g(f_{ih}) + g(f_{jh})$.

This analysis specifies a benefit function. Therefore, we assume that $g(f_{ih}) = \frac{1}{2}\sqrt{f_{ih}}$. This formula includes the assumption that the marginal scheduling effect of direct passengers is greater than that of connecting passengers. Generally, connecting passengers must wait to change flights at a hub airport. Consequently, even when the frequency of flights on only one route increases, the increase in passengers' convenience is small compared with that of direct passengers.[10]

Moreover, connecting passengers might incur a higher travel time cost T by flying through hub city H than they would if they could take a direct flight (see Brueckner [6]; Kawasaki [18]). Herein, this additional cost is assumed to be sufficiently small, such that at least a passenger with $w = W$ travels using the airline.

From the above discussion, each passenger's utility function is expressed as follows:

$$U_{ij} = \begin{cases} w + \sqrt{f_{ij}} - p_{ij} & \text{if traveling directly} \\ w + \frac{1}{2}\left(\sqrt{f_{ih}} + \sqrt{f_{jh}}\right) - T - p_{ij} & \text{if traveling via hub city } h. \end{cases} \tag{8.1}$$

Without loss of generality, we assume that utility equals zero for passengers not using the airline.

---

[7]There exist similar characteristics in Berechman and Shy [4] and Shy [29].

[8]Although the Brueckner-type utility function [6] has a microfoundation, it is unnecessarily complex for analyzing the model. On the contrary, the Kawasaki-type function [18] is simple. Hence, because the characteristics of the Brueckner-type utility function are similar to those of the Kawasaki-type utility function, we can maintain generality through this analysis.

[9]Even if we use a linear benefit function and a quadratic cost function, we obtain the same result.

[10]Generally, it is more reasonable to assume that a connecting passenger's utility depends on the minimum of the square roots of the spoke frequencies. However, this formulation poses many complex problems for analysis. In fact, Flores-Fillol [14] also uses an average-type utility function.

8.4 Deviation of Each Outcome

By using the above model, this section derives each outcome when the monopolistic carrier adopts the hub–spoke (point-to-point) network.

First, we derive each demand function. Because we assume that a passenger whose utility becomes over zero uses airline services, the demand function for direct airline services is

$$q_{ij}^{d} = n_{ij}\left(W + \sqrt{f_{ij}} - p_{ij}\right), \tag{8.2}$$

and the demand function for connecting airline services is

$$q_{ij}^{h} = n_{ij}\left(W + \frac{1}{2}\left(\sqrt{f_{ih}} + \sqrt{f_{jh}}\right) - T - p_{ij}\right). \tag{8.3}$$

Here, n_{ij} denotes the density of w in city pair ij, while $n_{AB} = n_{BC} = \beta$ and $n_{AC} = 1$.

First, we derive the profit when the monopolistic carrier adopts a hub–spoke network with hub city h. The profit function is as follows:

$$\begin{aligned}\pi_h = {} & n_{ih}\left(W + \sqrt{f_{ih}} - p_{ih}\right)p_{ih} + n_{jh}(W + \sqrt{f_{jh}} - p_{jh})p_{jh} \\ & + n_{ij}\left(W + \frac{1}{2}\left(\sqrt{f_{ih}} + \sqrt{f_{jh}}\right) - T - p_{ij}\right)p_{ij} - (f_{ih} + f_{jh})K. \end{aligned} \tag{8.4}$$

By solving the above profit maximization problem for each airfare and flight frequency, we obtain the following airfares and flight frequencies:

$$p_{ih} = \frac{(8KW - n_{ij}T)(4K - n_{jh})}{\Delta}, \tag{8.5}$$

$$p_{jh} = \frac{(8KW - n_{ij}T)(4K - n_{ih})}{\Delta}, \tag{8.6}$$

$$p_{ij} = \frac{-4K(n_{ih} + n_{jh})(W - 2T) + 32K^2(W - T) - 2n_{ih}n_{jh}T}{\Delta}, \tag{8.7}$$

$$f_{ih} = \left(\frac{8KW(2n_{ih} + n_{ij}) + n_{ih}W(n_{ij} + 4n_{jh}) + n_{ih}n_{jh}(W - 2T) + 8n_{ij}KT}{\Delta}\right)^2, \tag{8.8}$$

$$f_{jh} = \left(\frac{-(n_{ih}n_{jh} + n_{ih}(n_{ij} + 4n_{jh}))W + 8K(2Wn_{jh} + n_{ij}(W - T)) + 2n_{ih}n_{ij}T}{\Delta}\right). \tag{8.9}$$

Here,

$$\Delta \equiv 64K^2 + n_{ih}n_{jh} - 8K(2n_{ih} + n_{ij} + 2n_{jh}) + n_{ih}(n_{ij} + n_{jh}). \tag{8.10}$$

By using the outcomes from Eqs. (8.5) to (8.9), we obtain the following quantity:

$$q_{ih} = \frac{n_{ih}(4K - n_{jh})(8KW - n_{ij}T)}{\Delta}, \tag{8.11}$$

$$q_{jh} = \frac{n_{jh}(4K - n_{ih})(8KW - n_{ij}T)}{\Delta}, \tag{8.12}$$

$$q_{ij} = \frac{2n_{ij}(-2K(n_{ih} + n_{jh})(W - 2T) + 16K^2(W - T) - n_{ih}n_{jh}T)}{\Delta}. \tag{8.13}$$

To satisfy the positive demand of connecting passengers, we assume

$$T \leq \frac{2KW(8K - n_{ih} - n_{jh})}{(4K - n_{ih})(4K - n_{jh})}. \tag{8.14}$$

As a result, the maximized profit when the monopolistic carrier adopts the hub–spoke network with hub h is

$$\begin{aligned}\pi_h^* = \{&2K(-n_{ij}n_{jh} + 8K(n_{ih} + n_{ij} + n_{jh}) - n_{ih}(n_{ij} + 4n_{jh}))W^2 \\ &+4Kn_{ij}(-8K + n_{ih} + n_{jh})WT + (4K - n_{ih})n_{ij}(4K - n_{jh})T^2\}/\Delta.\end{aligned} \tag{8.15}$$

Here, π_h^* represents the maximized profit when the hub–spoke network with hub h is adopted.

In the following, we derive the profit when the monopolistic carrier adopts a point-to-point network. The profit function is as follows:

$$\begin{aligned}\pi_p = &\beta(W + \sqrt{f_{AB}} - p_{AB})p_{AB} + \beta(W + \sqrt{f_{BC}} - p_{BC})p_{BC} \\ &+(W + f_{AC} - p_{AC})p_{AC} - (f_{AB} + f_{BC} + f_{AC})K.\end{aligned} \tag{8.16}$$

By solving the above profit maximization problem for each airfare and flight frequency, we obtain the following airfares and flight frequencies:

$$p_{AB} = p_{AC} = \frac{2KW}{4K - \beta}, \tag{8.17}$$

$$p_{BC} = \frac{2KW}{4K - 1}, \tag{8.18}$$

$$f_{AB} = f_{AC} = \left(\frac{W\beta}{4K - \beta}\right)^2, \tag{8.19}$$

$$f_{BC} = \left(\frac{W}{4K - 1}\right)^2. \tag{8.20}$$

By using the outcomes from Eqs. (8.17) to (8.20), we obtain the following quantity:

$$q_{AB} = q_{AC} = \frac{2KW\beta}{4K - \beta} \tag{8.21}$$

$$q_{BC} = \frac{2KW}{4K - 1}. \tag{8.22}$$

As a result, the maximized profit when the monopolistic carrier adopts the point-to-point network is

$$\pi_p^* = \frac{KW^2\{\beta(3 - 8K) - 4K\}}{(\beta - 4K)(4K - 1)}. \tag{8.23}$$

Here, π_p^* represents the maximized profit when the point-to-point network is adopted.

8.5 Comparison of Each Outcome

In this section, we compare each outcome for the hub–spoke network with hub h case with the point-to-point network case.

8.5.1 *Comparison of Flight Frequency*

In this subsection, we compare flight frequency for the hub–spoke network with hub h with point-to-point network cases. The following Lemma 8.1 shows the comparison result.

Lemma 8.1. *The flight frequency of the hub–spoke network is always larger than that of the point-to-point network.*

This Lemma 8.1 is straightforward. As shown in Brueckner [6], by adopting the hub–spoke network, the monopolistic carrier can aggregate the passengers from two markets onto one route. Consequently, the marginal revenue on its route increases, raising the flight frequency of its route. Additionally, as also shown in Brueckner [6], we verify that flight frequency increases after deregulation because hub–spoke networks are adopted by carriers.

Although it is natural to compare flight frequency when city A is a hub with that when city B is a hub, we omit this comparison because the operating route when city A is the hub is different from that when city B is the hub.[11]

[11] In other words, it is almost meaningless to compare the flight frequencies of the different routes.

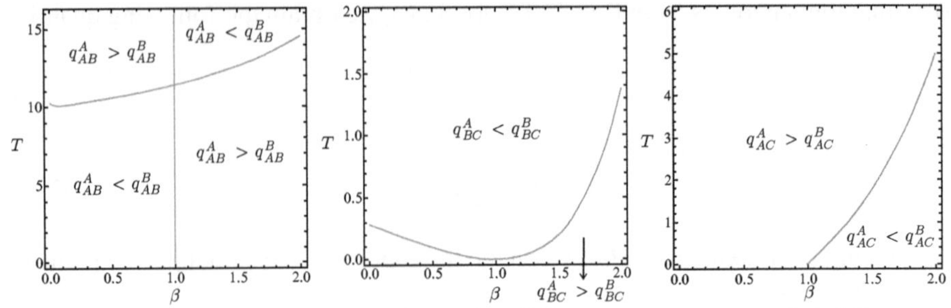

a. market AB b. market BC c. market AC

Fig. 8.1 Comparison result of number of passengers

8.5.2 Comparison of Demand

In the following, we compare each market's number of passengers using airline services for the hub–spoke network with hub h with the point-to-point network. First, we compare market demand when a hub–spoke network and a point-to-point network is adopted, obtaining the following Lemma 8.2.

Lemma 8.2. *In markets ih and jh, the number of passengers using airline services when the hub–spoke network is adopted is always larger than that when the point-to-point network is adopted. In market ij, if T is small (large), this number when the hub–spoke network is adopted is larger (smaller) than that when the point-to-point network is adopted.*

As shown in Lemma 8.1, when the monopolistic carrier adopts the hub–spoke network, flight frequency on one route increases, which increases the scheduling effect for passengers. Therefore, when a carrier adopts a hub–spoke network, the number of passengers in markets ih and jh increases. On the contrary, with regard to the passengers in market ij, although flight frequency increases, which increases a passenger's scheduling effect, he/she incurs an additional travel time cost, which decreases his/her utility. If the additional travel time cost is small, the influence of the larger scheduling effect is greater. Therefore, the number of passengers using airline services increases. However, if the additional travel time cost is large, the influence of the larger scheduling effect becomes smaller. Consequently, the number of passengers decreases.

Finally, we compare the number of passengers in each market when city A is the hub with that when city B is the hub.[12] In Fig. 8.1, we assume $W = 10$ and $K = 1$. Additionally, we express the number of passengers in market ij when city h is the hub as q_{ij}^h.

[12]Here, the number of passengers when city A is the hub and that when city C is the hub is the same. Consequently, we omit the case that city C is the hub.

From Fig. 8.1, we obtain the following Lemma 8.3.

Lemma 8.3. *Comparing the number of passengers using airline services in each market,*

(1) In market AB, given that $\beta \leq 1$, when $T \geq (<) T_A$, q_{AB}^A is larger (smaller) than q_{AB}^B; given that $\beta > 1$, when $T \geq (<) T_A$, q_{AB}^B is larger (smaller) than q_{AB}^A;
(2) In market BC, when $T \geq (<) T_B$, q_{BC}^B is larger (smaller) than q_{BC}^A;
(3) In market AC, when $T \geq (<) T_C$, q_{AC}^A is larger (smaller) than q_{AC}^B.

Here,

$$T_A \equiv \frac{80(\beta(5+\beta) - 8(2+3\beta)K + 64K^2) + 16KW(-7+2\beta)(-1+4K)}{\beta(19-3\beta) + 16(-1+(-5+\beta)\beta)K + 64K^2}, \tag{8.24}$$

$$T_B \equiv \frac{80(\beta(5+\beta) - 8(2+3\beta)K + 64K^2) - 8KW(-7+2\beta)(1+\beta-8K)}{\beta(-23+9\beta) + 8(12+(7-4\beta)\beta)K + 128(-3+\beta)K^2}, \tag{8.25}$$

$$T_C \equiv \frac{-40(\beta(5+\beta) - 8(2+3\beta)K + 64K^2) + 8KW(-7+2\beta)(\beta-4K)}{\beta(-20+3(-2+\beta)\beta) + 4(16+(27-8\beta)\beta)K + 64(-4+\beta)K^2}. \tag{8.26}$$

First, we consider the comparison result of market AB. The number of passengers in market AB is influenced by flight frequency on route AB. When city A becomes the hub, flight frequency on route AB depends on markets AB and BC. When city B becomes the hub, flight frequency depends on markets AB and AC. Here, it is noteworthy that the density of passengers in market AC is 1, while that of passengers in market BC is β. Now, consider the extreme case that the additional travel time cost T is zero. First, we assume that β is smaller than 1. Then, because the density of passengers in market AC is larger than that in market BC, total potential demand on route AB is larger when city B is the hub than when city A is the hub. Here, it is noteworthy that a larger total potential demand brings about larger marginal revenues per flight. Consequently, flight frequency on route AB is larger when city B is the hub than when city A is the hub. As a result, because the scheduling effect when city B is the hub is larger than when city A is the hub, q_{AB}^B is larger than q_{AB}^A. This result holds even when T is small. Given this situation, as T sufficiently increases, the utility of connecting passengers largely decreases, resulting in a fall in the number of connecting passengers. Here, when the density of connecting passengers is large, marginal revenue largely decreases and thus flight frequency largely decreases. Consequently, flight frequency when city A is the hub becomes larger than that when city B is the hub because the influence of the decrease in connecting passengers reduces. As a result, q_{AB}^A becomes larger than q_{AB}^B throughout the scheduling effect.

Contrarily, if we assume that β is larger than 1, the reverse characteristic appears. That is, if T is small (large), an increase in connecting passengers brings more (fewer) number of passengers on route AB, which increases marginal revenues and thus flight frequency. Consequently, q_{AB}^{A} becomes larger (smaller) than q_{AB}^{B} throughout the larger scheduling effect.

In the following, we consider the comparison result of market BC. First, suppose that β is smaller than 1. First, we consider the extreme case, that is, $T = 0$. Then, if city A is the hub, flight frequency on route AB becomes very small and flight frequency on route AC is large, which influences demand in market BC. On the contrary, if city B is the hub, flight frequency on route BC becomes small. Here, in the case that city A is the hub, because flight frequency on route AC is large, the scheduling effect of the passengers in market BC is larger than that in the case that city B is the hub. Consequently, q_{BC}^{A} is larger than q_{BC}^{B}. Given this interpretation, as T increases, it is apparent that the number of connecting passengers decreases. Consequently, when T is large, q_{BC}^{B} becomes larger than q_{BC}^{A}. Suppose that β is larger than 1. Here, we first consider the extreme case $T = 0$. If city A is the hub, flight frequency on route AB becomes very large and that on route AC becomes somewhat large. If city B is the hub, flight frequency on route BC becomes large. Here, in the case that city A is the hub, because flight frequency on route AB is very large, the scheduling effect of the passengers in market BC is larger than that in the case that city B is the hub. Consequently, q_{BC}^{A} is larger than q_{BC}^{B}. Given this interpretation, as T increases, it is apparent that the number of connecting passengers decreases. Consequently, when T is large, q_{BC}^{B} becomes larger than q_{BC}^{A}.

Finally, we consider the comparison result of market AC. Suppose that $T = 0$. When city A is the hub, flight frequency on route AC becomes somewhat large (small) for small (large) β. When city B is the hub, flight frequency on both routes AB and BC, which influences demand for market AC, becomes small (large) for small (large) β. Consequently, for small β, the case that city A is the hub has a larger scheduling effect for passengers than the case that city B is the hub. As a result, q_{AC}^{A} is larger than q_{AC}^{B}. Contrarily, for large β, the case that city B is the hub has a larger scheduling effect for passengers than the case that city A is the hub. As a result, q_{AC}^{B} is larger than q_{AC}^{A}. Given this result, as T increases, if β is small, the result above still holds because the increase in T decreases the number of connecting passengers; if β is large, q_{AC}^{B} is larger (smaller) than q_{AC}^{A} for small (large) T.

8.6 Profit-Maximizing Network Formation and Hub Location

This section analyzes which network is favorable in the monopolistic airline market by comparing each profit. Here, because the profit when the airline adopts the hub–spoke network with hub A and that when it adopts the hub–spoke network with hub C is the same, we assume that in this situation the hub–spoke network with hub

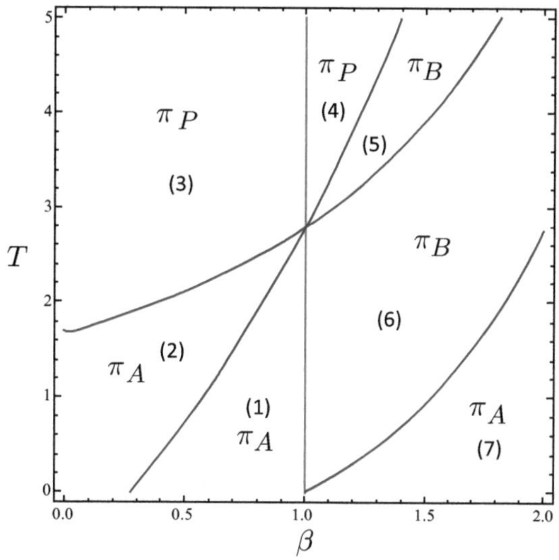

Fig. 8.2 Decision on the choice of network formation and hub city

Table 8.1 The meaning of each range in Fig. 8.2

Range	Comparison of profit	Airline network	City to minimize the potential number of connecting passengers
(1)	$\pi_A > \pi_B, \pi_A > \pi_p, \pi_B > \pi_p$	Hub–spoke with hub *A*	City *A*
(2)	$\pi_A > \pi_B, \pi_A > \pi_p, \pi_B < \pi_p$	Hub–spoke with hub *A*	City *A*
(3)	$\pi_A > \pi_B, \pi_A < \pi_p, \pi_B < \pi_p$	Point-to-point	City *A*
(4)	$\pi_A < \pi_B, \pi_A > \pi_p, \pi_B < \pi_p$	Point-to-point	City *A*
(5)	$\pi_A < \pi_B, \pi_A > \pi_p, \pi_B > \pi_p$	Hub–spoke with hub *B*	City *B*
(6)	$\pi_A < \pi_B, \pi_A > \pi_p, \pi_B > \pi_p$	Hub–spoke with hub *B*	City *B*
(7)	$\pi_A > \pi_B, \pi_A > \pi_p, \pi_B > \pi_p$	Hub–spoke with hub *A*	City *B*

A is adopted. Hereafter, we compare each profit. However, as the calculations are complex, we perform a simulation analysis. In the following, we assume $W = 10$ and $K = 1$ without loss of generality. Figure 8.2 illustrates the comparison results, and Table 8.1 expresses the meaning of each range.

First, Fig. 8.2 and Table 8.1 show that the monopolistic airline adopts the point-to-point network when the additional travel time cost T is large. This characteristic corresponds with Brueckner [6] and Kawasaki [18].

The benefit of adopting the hub–spoke network is to strengthen the scheduling effect and thus to set high airfares. On the contrary, because connecting passengers incur an additional travel time cost (which shifts the demand function downwards), airfares become low, which is a disadvantage of adopting the hub–spoke network. When the additional travel time cost is very large, the utility of connecting passengers largely decreases. Therefore, to let connecting passengers use airline services, the airfare for connecting passengers should become very low. Nonetheless, demand for connecting services also decreases. As a result, although the profits from the other two markets that can use direct services increase throughout the scheduling effect compared with the point-to-point network, total airline profit decreases. Therefore, although the monopolistic carrier cannot obtain a large scheduling effect, the point-to-point network is adopted in order not to lose revenues from connecting passengers.

On the contrary, when the additional travel time cost is small, by adopting the hub–spoke network potential demand in each market increases through the larger scheduling effect, which can increase the airfare in each market. Consequently, the monopolistic carrier adopts the hub–spoke network. Summarizing the above discussion, we obtain Theorem 8.4.

Theorem 8.4. *When the additional travel time cost is large (small), the monopolistic carrier chooses the point-to-point (hub–spoke) network.*

Theorem 8.4 corresponds with various previous studies. According to previous studies, a hub–spoke network has both advantages and disadvantages. If the advantages (i.e., scheduling effect or network effect) are larger (smaller) than the disadvantages (i.e., additional travel time cost), the carrier chooses the hub–spoke (point-to-point) network.

In the following, we discuss which airport becomes a hub. As shown in Table 8.1, in ranges (1), (2), (5), and (6), the hub airport is chosen to minimize the potential number of connecting passengers. On the contrary, in range (7), although city A becomes the hub airport, the city minimizing the potential number of connecting passengers is city B. In other words, in range (7), the hub city is not chosen to minimize the potential number of connecting passengers. This finding shows that the results obtained in previous studies of the hub location problem (i.e., that the hub city is chosen to minimize the potential number of connecting passengers) do not always hold. Indeed, these studies have one important limitation, namely they omit the scheduling effect.

As mentioned earlier, connecting passengers face a decrease in utility by incurring an additional travel time cost. As a result, demand for connecting services becomes small, which causes airfares to fall. If its density (i.e., the potential number of passengers) is large, the monopolistic carrier loses the opportunity to obtain more revenues by letting its passengers use direct services. According to previous studies, because only the disadvantage mentioned above is considered, the monopolistic carrier chooses the hub airport that minimizes the potential number of connecting passengers. However, introducing the scheduling effect allows us to argue that the results of previous studies do not always hold. When demand for one route (not the entire market) increases, the monopolistic carrier increases the flight frequency on that route, which increases the utility of passengers using it. When the density of connecting passengers is large, demand for both routes increases, which raises flight frequency on both routes.

As flight frequency on each route increases, demand for direct services on each route also increases. Furthermore, each airfare increases, and so does the profit of the airline. Consequently, the strategy to minimize the potential number of connecting passengers has a trade-off. This chapter argues that when β (i.e., the density of

BC passengers) is sufficiently large, the advantage of the scheduling effect is larger than the disadvantage of the additional traveling cost. Therefore, the hub airport is not chosen to minimize the potential number of connecting passengers. Contrarily, when β is not sufficiently large, its disadvantage is larger than its advantage; hence, the hub city is chosen to minimize the potential number of connecting services.

Summarizing the above, we obtain Theorem 8.5.

Theorem 8.5. *The monopolistic carrier does not always choose the hub city to minimize the potential number of connecting passengers.*

Next, we discuss the influence of K (i.e., the fixed cost per flight). In the above discussion, we assumed that $K = 1$. When K increases, how do the results obtained here change? As K increases, the monopolistic carrier decreases flight frequency, which reduces the scheduling effect. Therefore, as K increases, the range within which the hub–spoke network is adopted narrows. At the same time, even when the hub–spoke network is adopted, the range within which the potential number of connecting passengers is minimized is also narrow.

8.7 Social Welfare

This section analyzes the socially preferable network formation and socially preferable hub location. Social welfare (W) is defined as the sum of passengers' utility and the carrier's profit. That is,

$$W = \beta U_{AB} + \beta U_{BC} + U_{AC} + \pi_\ell. \tag{8.27}$$

Here, if the hub–spoke network with hub h is adopted, $\pi_\ell = \pi_h$, whereas if the point-to-point network is adopted, $\pi_\ell = \pi_p$. Social welfare when the monopolistic carrier adopts the hub–spoke network with hub city h is expressed as W_h and that when the monopolistic carrier adopts the point-to-point network is expressed as W_p. Because of the complexity of this welfare, we omit the detailed values here.

In the following, we compare social welfare in each case through a simulation analysis. The parameter is the same that used in the previous section. Figure 8.3 shows the result. Here, it is assumed that if social welfare when city A and that when city C is the same, city A is selected as the socially preferable hub. Here, we mainly address the socially preferable hub location. As a result, we obtain Theorem 8.6.

Theorem 8.6. *The socially preferable hub location does not always minimize the potential number of connecting passengers.*

Previous studies using OR have argued that the hub airport should be decided in order to minimize connecting passengers and thus reduce social costs. However, this chapter demonstrates that this argument does not always hold. In other words, when the density of AB and AC passengers is sufficiently large, it is not socially preferable to minimize the potential number of connecting passengers. The mechanism is

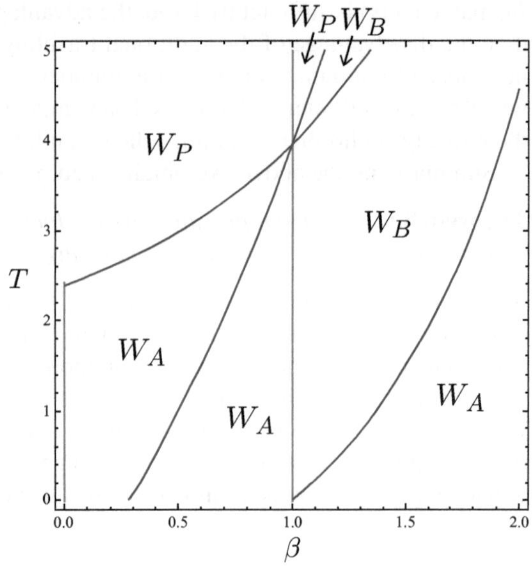

Fig. 8.3 Socially preferable airline network

presented as follows. By increasing the density of connecting passengers on one route, flight frequency increases on that route, which increases passenger utility. Hence, a large scheduling effect arises, which increases not only the number of passengers using airline services but also the utility of those passengers. Although these passengers incur an additional travel time cost, the larger scheduling effect becomes larger than this cost. Consequently, when the density of AB and BC passengers is sufficiently large, social welfare increases by adopting the hub airport with aim of not minimizing the potential number of connecting passengers.

Here, as K increases, the range within which the potential number of connecting passengers is minimized narrows. As mentioned earlier, when K increases, flight frequency decreases, which strengthens the disadvantage of incurring an additional travel time cost. Therefore, it becomes socially preferable to minimize the potential number of connecting passengers.

8.8 Extension

In Sect. 8.6, we assumed that the per-seat cost is zero. Then, if we introduce a positive cost, does the same characteristic appear? Here, we introduce the per-seat cost following Brueckner [6] and re-analyze the airline network formation and hub location problems. Because we mainly address the per-seat cost, it is assumed for simplicity that $T = 0$.

We denote the per-seat cost as τ. The monopolistic carrier uses aircraft which size is s and flies between each city pair f_{ij} times. Here, the load factor is assumed

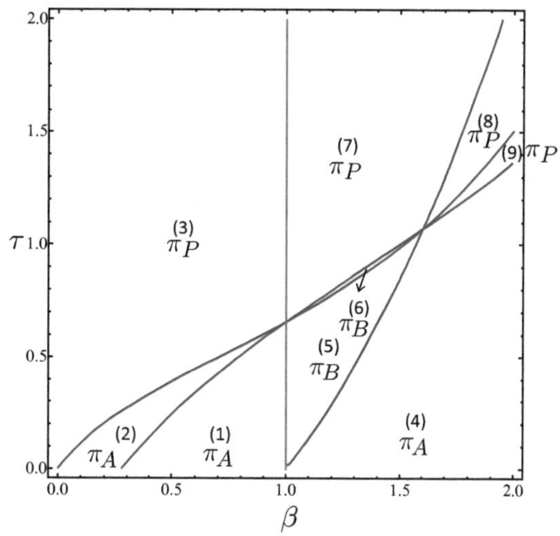

Fig. 8.4 Airline network formation and hub location

to be 100 %. Then, the total number of passengers on one route (Q_{ij}) equals $s \times f_{ij}$. Because we assume that the per-seat cost is τ, total cost becomes $\tau \times s \times f_{ij}$, which equals τQ_{ij}. Consequently, the operating cost per flight is $f_{ij}K + \tau Q_{ij}$.

Instead of showing the detailed profit in each case and discussing the mathematical comparison, we simply show the simulation result in Fig. 8.4.

First, by comparing π_A with π_B, in ranges (1), (2), (3), (4), (8), and (9), π_A is larger than π_B. In ranges (5), (6), and (7), π_B is larger than π_A. Second, by comparing π_A with π_P, in ranges (1), (2), (4), (5), and (9), π_A is larger than π_P. In ranges (3), (6), (7), and (8), π_P is larger than π_A. Finally, by comparing π_B with π_P, in ranges (1), (4), (5), and (6), π_B is larger than π_P. In ranges (2), (3), (7), (8), and (9), π_P is larger than π_B. Consequently, in ranges (1), (2), and (4), the hub–spoke network with hub A is adopted; in ranges (5) and (6), the hub–spoke network with hub B is adopted; and in ranges (3), (7), (8), and (9), the point-to-point network is adopted.

When introducing the per-seat cost, total operating costs increase. In particular, when the monopolistic carrier adopts the hub–spoke network, connecting passengers use airline services twice, thereby doubling the per-seat cost for those passengers. If the per-seat cost is small, an increase in the scheduling effect is larger than the increase in total operating costs. Therefore, the monopolistic carrier adopts the hub–spoke network. Furthermore, it chooses the hub airport in order not to minimize the potential number of connecting passengers. However, as the per-seat cost increases, the incentive to minimize the number of passengers strengthens. At the same time, the incentive to adopt the point-to-point network also strengthens. Therefore, the range within which the hub–spoke network with city A is adopted narrows as τ increases until it finally disappears.

Although we omit the additional travel time cost, we can easily expect that when this is sufficiently small, the same result obtained here holds; however, when the additional travel time cost becomes large, the monopolistic carrier always chooses the point-to-point network.

8.9 Implications

Previous studies of the hub location problem have focused on developing an algorithm to minimize the number of connecting passengers. However, as discussed herein, the airline hub is not always chosen to minimize this number (e.g., Changi International Airport). In this case, Singapore is a small country and the potential number of passengers traveling there is not always large compared with other countries. However, Changi International Airport is still a well-known hub airport in Asia because, as shown in this chapter, total demand for one particular route can rise by increasing the number of connecting passengers, which increases the flight frequencies of airlines. When flight frequency increases, passengers enjoy more convenience by using its route. Therefore, attracting connecting passengers is crucial. Changi International Airport has devised various ways in which to attract connecting passengers. For example, the departure and arrivals gate is the same, while various services (games, theater, shop, hotel, etc.) are provided to entertain connecting passengers. These services add to the successful reputation of Changi International Airport as a hub airport.

In Japan, various ways to become a hub airport have been discussed. However, these discussions mainly address how to entice more passenger visits to Japan. In other words, they consider how to increase the number of direct passengers. However, as shown in this chapter as well as the example of Changi International Airport, attracting more passengers is not always important for a hub airport. Rather, it is more important for connecting passengers to use Japanese airports as a hub. To attract more connecting passengers, increasing airline routes and flight frequencies are important considerations. Furthermore, improving airport services may be necessary.

8.10 Concluding Remarks

This chapter addressed the airline network formation and hub location problems simultaneously by introducing the scheduling effect. With regard to the hub location problem, previous studies using OR have not always addressed the real-life problem. In this chapter, by introducing the scheduling effect, we explained that the airline hub is not always constructed to minimize the potential number of connecting passengers, which adds to the literature in this regard. On the contrary, with regard to airline network formation, this chapter demonstrated that when the additional travel time cost is small (large), the hub–spoke (point-to-point) network is formed, a finding that corresponds with those of previous studies. Additionally, this chapter demonstrated that the socially preferable hub airport is not always one that aims to minimize its potential number of connecting passengers. Furthermore, we found that the same result is obtained when the per-seat cost is small; however, when this cost is large, the point-to-point network is always adopted. Furthermore, based on this chapter's results, we provided policy implications for Japanese airports. To become a hub airport in Asia like Changi International Airport, not only increasing direct passengers but also increasing connecting passengers is important.

Finally, we mention the limitations of this chapter. First, this chapter omitted airport pricing. Recently, Teraji and Morimoto [30] analyzed this important problem for competitive airports. However, future research must introduce an airport pricing strategy and consider the hub location problem. Second, this chapter assumed a monopolistic airline market. However, the actual airline market is highly competitive, implying that how airline competition influences hub location in the real world is unclear. Third, this chapter did not consider congestion, a problem from which hub airports often suffer. If a hub airport's congestion were introduced, what would be the effect on network formation? Additionally, which airports would become hubs, including socially preferable ones? We leave this important and interesting problem to future research.

References

1. Alumur, S., & Kara, B. Y. (2008). Network hub location problems: The state of the art. *European Journal of Operational Research, 190*, 1–21.
2. Aykin, T. (1994). Lagrangian relaxation based approaches to capacitated hub-and-spoke network design problems. *European Journal of Operational Research, 79*, 501–523.
3. Berechman, J., Poddar, S., & Shy, O. (1998). Network structure and entry in the deregulated airline industry. *Keio Economic Studies, 35*, 71–82.
4. Berechman, J., & Shy, O. (1996). The structure of airline equilibrium networks. In J. van den Bergh, P. Nijkamp, & P. Rietveld (Eds.), *Recent advances in spatial equilibrium modeling: Methodology and applications* (pp. 138–155). Berlin/New York: Springer.
5. Bittlingmayer, G. (1990). Efficiency and entry in a simple airline network. *International Journal of Industrial Organization, 8*, 245–257.
6. Brueckner, J. K. (2004). Network structure and airline scheduling. *Journal of Industrial Economics, 52*, 291–312.
7. Brueckner, J. K., & Flores-Fillol, R. (2007). Airline schedule competition. *Review of Industrial Organization, 30*, 161–177.
8. Brueckner, J. K., & Spiller, P. T. (1991). Competition and mergers in airline networks. *International Journal of Industrial Organization, 9*, 323–342.
9. Bryan, D. L., & O'Kelly, M. E. (1999). Hub-and-spoke networks in air transportation: An analytical review. *Journal of Regional Science, 39*, 275–295.
10. Campbell, J. F. (1994). Integer programming formulations of discrete hub location problems. *European Journal of Operational Research, 72*, 387–405.
11. De Camargo, R. S., Miranda, G., Jr., Ferreirab, R. P. M., & Lunac, H. P. (2008). Multiple allocation hub-and-spoke network design under hub congestion. *Computers and Operations Research, 36*, 3097–3106.
12. Douglas, G. W., & Miller, J. C. (1974). Quality competition, industry equilibrium and efficiency in the price-constrained airline market. *American Economic Review, 64*, 657–669.
13. Eiselta, H. A., & Marianov, V. (2008). A conditional p-hub location problem with attraction functions. *Computers and Operations Research, 36*, 3128–3135.
14. Flores-Fillol, R. (2010). Congested hub. *Transportation Research Part B, 44*, 358–370.
15. Flores-Fillol, R., & Fageda, X. (2015). A note on optimal airline networks under airport congestion. *Economics Letters, 128*, 90–94

16. Hendricks, K., Piccione, M., & Tan, G. (1995). The Economics of hubs: The case of monopoly. *Review of Economics Studies, 62*, 83–99.
17. Hendricks, K., Piccione, M., & Tan, G. (1997). Entry and exit in hub-spoke networks. *Rand Journal of Economics, 28*, 291–303.
18. Kawasaki, A. (2008). Network effects, heterogeneous time value, and network formation in the airline market. *Regional Science and Urban Economics, 38*, 388–403.
19. Kawasaki, A. (2012). Hub location with scheduling effects in a monopoly airline market. *Annals of Regional Science, 49*, 805–819.
20. Kawasaki, A., & Lin, M. H. (2013). Airline schedule competition and entry route choices of low-cost carriers. *Australian Economic Review, 52*, 97–114.
21. Konishi, H. (2000). Formation of hub cities: Transportation cost advantage and population agglomeration. *Journal of Urban Economics, 48*, 1–28.
22. Martin, J. C., & Roman, C. (2004). Analyzing competition for hub location in intercontinental aviation markets. *Transportation Research Part E, 40*, 135–150.
23. O'Kelly, M. E. (1987). A quadratic integer program for the location of interacting hub facilities. *European Journal of Operational Research, 32*, 393–404.
24. Oum, T. H., Zhang, A., & Zhang, Y. (1995). Airline network rivalry. *Canadian Journal of Economics, 28*, 836–857.
25. Panzar, J. C. (1979). Equilibrium and welfare in unregulated airline markets. *American Economic Review, 69*, 92–95.
26. Pels, E., Nijkamp, P., & Rietveld, P. (1997). Substitution and complementarity in aviation: Airports vs. airlines. *Transportation Research Part E, 33*, 275–286.
27. Racunica, I., & Wynter, L. (2005). Optimal location of intermodal freight hubs. *Transportation Research Part B, 39*, 435–477.
28. Rodriguez, V., Alvarez, M. J., & Barcos, L. (2007). Hub location under capacity constraints. *Transportation Research Part E, 43*, 495–505.
29. Shy, O. (1995). *Industrial organization: Theory and applications*. Cambridge: MIT.
30. Teraji, Y., & Morimoto, Y. (2014). Price Competition of airports and its effect on the airline network. *Economics of Transportation, 3*, 45–57.
31. Tirole, J. (1998). *The theory of industrial organization*. Cambridge: MIT.

Part II
Sustainable Growth and Development

Chapter 9
Urban Unemployment, Privatization Policy, and a Differentiated Mixed Oligopoly

Tohru Naito

9.1 Introduction

In this chapter, we consider a combination of a traditional dualistic economy model with a differentiated mixed oligopoly model. As shown in Chap. 3, Harris and Todaro [7], who produced a pioneer study in the analysis of dualistic economy, describe a dualistic economy by assuming downward rigidity of wages in an urban area and explain the occurrence of unemployment endogenously. Although the Harris and Todaro model is important for the study of dualistic economy analysis, it is difficult to say that the setting necessarily accords with reality. As we have already referred in Chap. 3, the Harris and Todaro model has been extended from various viewpoints. Corden and Findlay [3] extend the Harris and Todaro model by taking account of mobile capital between regions. Calvo [2] introduces the behavior of labor unions into the Harris and Todaro model and determines the higher fixed wage in an urban area endogenously. Fukuyama and Naito [6] also introduce polluting goods into the Harris and Todaro model and analyze the effect of environmental policy on urban unemployment. Naito [10] combines a mixed duopoly with Fukuyama and Naito [6]. Although he analyzes the effect of public firm privatization on urban unemployment, Naito [10] deals not with differentiated goods but with homogeneous goods. In the real world, it is not natural to assume homogeneous goods produced in an urban area. Although Beladi and Chao [1] consider the mixed ownership of single national firm and show that the privatization can improve social welfare in the long run, they do not deal with a mixed oligopoly market.

T. Naito (✉)
Institute of Socio-Arts and Science, Tokushima University, 1-1 Minamijosanjima-cho
Tokushima city, Tokushima 770-8502, Japan
e-mail: naito@tokushima-u.ac.jp

T. Naito (ed.), *Sustainable Growth and Development in a Regional Economy*,
New Frontiers in Regional Science: Asian Perspectives 13,
DOI 10.1007/978-4-431-55294-9_9

For a mixed oligopoly, De Fraja and Delbono [4] construct a mixed oligopoly market in which private firms compete with public firms in the homogeneous goods market. Although De Fraja and Delbono [4] compare a mixed oligopoly in which a public firm is fully nationalized, with a pure oligopoly, in which a public firm is fully privatized, Matsumura [8] considers a model in which the public firm maximizes the weighted average of social welfare and profit as the objective function. Then Matsumura [8] shows that the partial privatization of public firms is optimal. Matsumura and Kanda [9] take account of free entry of private firms in the mixed oligopoly. Fujiwara [5] considers the quasi-linear utility function constructed by Ottaviano, Tabuchi, and Thisse [11] and introduces product differentiation into a mixed oligopoly model. Although Fujiwara [5] adopts a quasi-linear utility function of Ottaviano, Tabuchi, and Thisse [11] in his paper, he does not account for monopolistic competition.

Regarding the occupancy rate of public firms, areas with shares of less than 10 % increased during 2003–2009 in China, although the trend of differences among regions remains unchanged during that period. Regarding urban employment rate in China, it was 4.09 % in 2010, although the average unemployment rate in China was 2.95 %. Consequently, it is possible that migration has occurred from rural areas to urban areas.

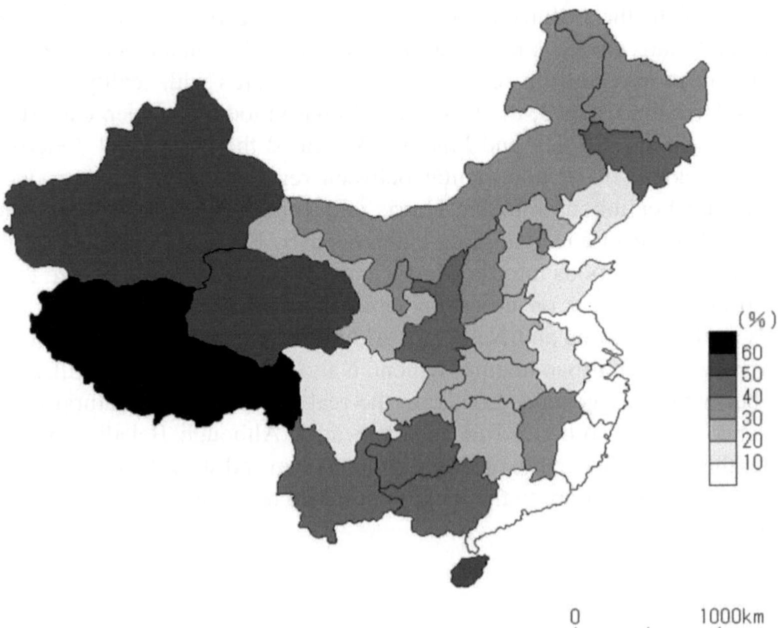

Fig. 9.1 Share of public firms of provinces in China (2003) (Source: China Statistical Yearbook 2004)

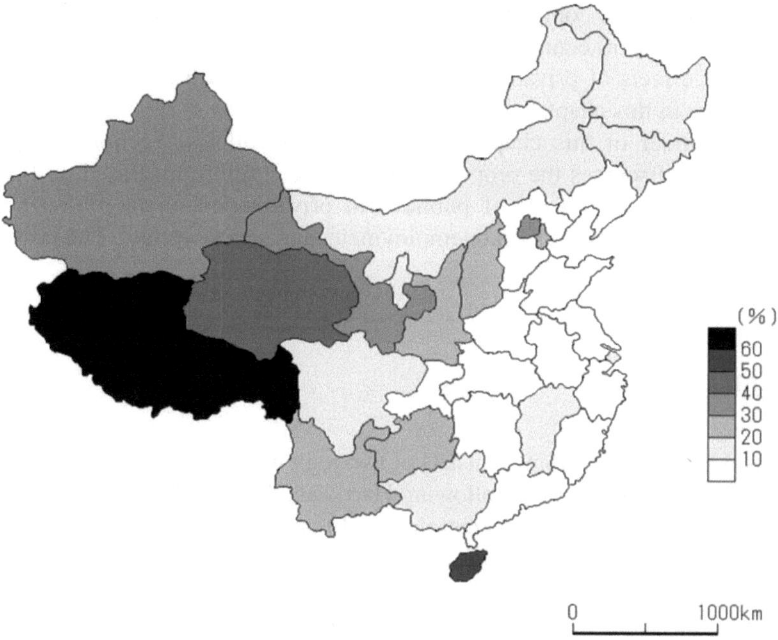

Fig. 9.2 Share of public firms of provinces in China (2009) (Source: China Statistical Yearbook 2010)

The recent economic development of China is remarkable. However, differences exist in the levels of economic development there. Figures 9.1 and 9.2 respectively portray the occupancy rates of public firms of each province in China. Regarding the occupancy rates of public firms, provinces with shares of less than 10 % increased during 2003–2009, although the trend of differences among provinces did not change during that period. Data for the unemployment rate in China do not necessarily reflect reality by the definition. This is because the unemployment rate in China is the unemployment rate for households for which registration was accomplished. Therefore, it is possible that this statistical value is an underestimate. However, as described already in Fig. 3.1 in Chap. 3, urban unemployment rate including layoff increased in the second half of the 1990s because of public firms reform by the central government in China. Privatization of public firms influences labor demand through the privatization of public firms. Therefore, it is necessary for governments to consider the privatization of public firms by taking account of urban unemployment. Therefore, we construct a new economic model by application of the basic models in Chaps. 2 and 3 to this new model. We combine a traditional dualistic economy model with a differentiated mixed monopolistic competition model to construct a model that facilitates analysis of urban unemployment and the privatization of public firms under a differentiated mixed monopolistic competition. We adopt Ottaviano, Tabuchi, and Thisse [11] to describe product differentiation and a mixed monopolistic competition. We also use Harris and Todaro [7] to describe a traditional dualistic economy, which we have already referred in Chap. 3. We consider the effects of privatization of public firms on urban unemployment and social welfare in this chapter.

The remainder of this chapter is organized as follows. Section 9.2 presents the model and discusses the properties of market equilibrium. Based on Sect. 9.2, Sect. 9.3 clarifies the effects of public firm privatization on migration between urban area and rural area, urban unemployment, and social welfare. The last section presents concluding remarks.

9.2 The Model

We consider that the economy consists of two regions in our model. One is an urban area; the other is a rural area. Following Harris and Todaro [7], every household in the economy can migrate between regions with no cost. We consider households of three types in this model. Indexes c, r, and u respectively denote the households employed by the manufactured goods sector in the urban area, those used by agricultural goods sector in rural area, and those not used in either sector, but residing in the urban area.

Now we consider products of two kinds: manufactured goods and agricultural goods. The manufactured goods and agricultural goods are produced respectively in the urban area and rural area. Although the manufactured goods sector requires labor as marginal input and capital as fixed input factor to produce their own products, the agricultural goods sector requires only labor as an input factor. Although manufactured goods are differentiated and are produced by one public firm and n-private firms in an urban area, the agricultural goods are homogeneous.

9.2.1 *Household*

We assume that it has downward rigidity attributable to the minimum wage system and so on, and that the urban wage is fixed above the market-clearing level of labor markets. Particularly, let $\bar{w}(= w_c)$ represent the minimum wage in the urban area, which is higher than the rural wage w_r. That rural wage is determined in the labor market of the agricultural goods sector and is equal to the marginal product of labor in the agricultural goods sector. Here we assume that households residing in the urban area and which are not employed in the manufactured goods sector, do not have a wage income, i.e., w_u is equal to zero. Let L_c, L_r and L_u represent the number of each household type. Moreover, we normalize the total population in the economy as one.

We assume that all households have common preferences. Therefore, they have the following same quasi-linear utility function as reported also by Ottaviano, Tabuchi, and Thisse [11].[1]

$$U_l = \alpha\left(q_{0l} + \sum_{i=1}^{N} q_{il}\right) - \frac{\beta-\gamma}{2}\left([q_{0l}]^2 + \sum_{i=1}^{N}[q_{il}]^2\right) - \frac{\gamma}{2}\left[q_{0l} + \sum_{i=1}^{N} q_{il}\right]^2 + z_l, \quad (l = c, r, u) \tag{9.1}$$

Therein, q_{0l}, q_{il}, z_l, and N respectively denote the consumption of goods produced by a public firm, that of goods produced by the i-th private firm, agricultural goods, and the number of private firms in the manufactured goods sector. Regarding parameters in (9.1), we assume that $\alpha > 0$ and $\beta > \gamma > 0$. Therein, α expresses the intensity of preference for differentiated manufactured goods. $\beta > \gamma$ signifies that consumers are biased toward dispersed consumption varieties. Presuming that β is equal to γ, the substitutability among manufactured goods is perfect.[2] Moreover, we assume that the profits of the agricultural goods sector are redistributed to every household in an economy. Consequently, the budget constraint of each household is given as

$$w_l + R\bar{f} + I = p_0 q_{0l} + \sum_{i=1}^{N} p_i q_{il} + z, \tag{9.2}$$

where p_0, p_i, $R, \bar{f}$ and I respectively represent the price of differentiated goods produced by public firm and i-th private firm, capital rent, the household's endowment of capital and redistribution of profit of the agricultural goods sector. Maximizing the utility function (9.1) subject to budget constraint (9.2), the first-order condition of q_{0l} and q_{il} is

$$\alpha - (\beta-\gamma)q_{l0} - \gamma\left[q_{0l} + \sum_{j=1}^{N} q_{jl}\right] - p_0 = 0 \tag{9.3}$$

and

$$\alpha - (\beta-\gamma)q_{il} - \gamma\left[q_{0l} + \sum_{j=1}^{N} q_{jl}\right] - p_i = 0, \tag{9.4}$$

[1] Although we used a continuous utility function in Chap. 2, here we adopt a discrete utility function in this chapter. However, the discussion presented in this chapter is the same as that in Chap. 2.

[2] For a detailed explanation of this utility function, see Ottaviano, Tabuchi, and Thisse [11].

Solving (9.3) and (9.4), the optimal consumption of each differentiated good is

$$q_{l0}^{*} = a - bp_0 + c\left[\sum_{j=1}^{N}[p_j - p_0]\right] \tag{9.5}$$

and

$$q_{il}^{*} = a - bp_i + c\left[p_0 - p_i + \sum_{j=1}^{N}[p_j - p_j]\right], \tag{9.6}$$

where a, b, and c respectively denote $\alpha/[\beta + \gamma N]$, $1/[\beta + \gamma N]$, and $\gamma/(\beta - \gamma)[\beta + \gamma N]$. We assume symmetry of manufactured goods produced by private firms. Therefore, let q_{il} represent the consumption of manufactured goods produced by ith private firm. Therefore, we can rewrite (9.5) and (9.6) as shown below.

$$q_{0l}^{*} = a - [b + c(N+1)]p_0 + cP \tag{9.7}$$

and

$$q_{il}^{*} = a - [b + c(N+1)]p_i + cP \tag{9.8}$$

Here, the price index P of the manufactured goods market is defined as shown below.

$$P \equiv \left[p_0 + \sum_{i=1}^{N} p_i\right] \tag{9.9}$$

Using (9.7) and (9.8), the indirect utility function of household l is the following.

$$\begin{aligned} v_l = {} & \alpha\left(q_{0l}^{*} + \sum_{i=1}^{N} q_{il}^{*}\right) - \frac{\beta-\gamma}{2}\left([q_{0l}^{*}]^2 + \sum_{i=1}^{N}[q_{il}^{*}]^2\right) \\ & -\frac{\gamma}{2}\left[q_{l0}^{*} + \sum_{i=1}^{N} q_{il}^{*}\right]^2 - p_0 q_{0l}^{*} - \sum_{i=1}^{N} p_i q_{il}^{*} + w_l + R\bar{f} + I \\ = {} & \frac{a^2(N+1)}{2b} - a\left(p_0 + \sum_{i=1}^{N} p_i\right) + \frac{b + c(N+1)}{2}\left([p_0]^2 + \sum_{i=1}^{N}[p_i]^2\right) \\ & -\frac{c}{2}\left[p_0 + \sum_{i=1}^{N} p_i\right]^2 + w_l + R\bar{f} + I \end{aligned} \tag{9.10}$$

Although we assume that all households are mobile between regions, the wage in the manufactured goods sector has downward rigidity because of the minimum wage system. It is higher than the wage in the agricultural goods sector. Consequently, each household compares the expected utility in the urban area with that in the rural area. Now we define λ as the urban unemployment rate in urban area, as shown below.

$$\lambda \equiv \frac{L_u}{L_c + L_u} \tag{9.11}$$

No household has an incentive to migrate between urban area and rural area when the expected utility in the urban area is equal to that in the rural area. Consequently, the migration equilibrium condition is given as the following equation.

$$(1 - \lambda)v_c + \lambda v_u = v_r \quad \Leftrightarrow \quad (1 - \lambda)\bar{w} = w_r \tag{9.12}$$

We assume that the total population in the economy is normalized. Therefore, the population constraint is the following.

$$L_c + L_u + L_r = 1 \tag{9.13}$$

Combining (9.11) with (9.13), the population constraint in the economy is revised as follows.

$$L_c + (1 - \lambda)L_r = 1 - \lambda \tag{9.14}$$

9.2.2 Production

Agricultural Goods Sector

Goods of two kinds are produced in this economy: agricultural goods produced in the rural area, and manufactured goods produced in the urban area. We assume that the agricultural goods market is competitive. The agricultural goods sector has decreasing returns of scale with respect to labor. Particularly, we specify the production function of agricultural goods sector as follows.

$$Z = (L_r)^{\sigma}, \quad \sigma \in (0, 1) \tag{9.15}$$

The agricultural goods market is competitive. The agricultural goods are homogeneous. Moreover, we assume that the wage has no downward rigidity in the rural area. The wage is equal to the marginal product of agricultural goods in the rural area.

$$w_r = \sigma(L_r)^{\sigma-1} \tag{9.16}$$

Manufactured Goods Sector

The manufactured goods sector in the urban area is a mixed monopolistic competitive market. Although Naito [10] also considers mixed duopoly and a *homogeneous* manufactured goods sector, we assume that the manufactured goods sector is *differentiated*. In our model, the public firm competes with private firms in the common market. Here we consider that the manufactured goods market is driven by monopolistic competition as do Ottaviano, Tabuchi, and Thisse [11]. Presumably, the number of private firms is large. The behavior of firms in the urban area, whether public or private, does not affect the price index in the manufactured goods market. First, we derive the total demand of each manufactured good, which is denoted by Q_0, Q_i. Because the demand for each manufactured good is independent of a household's income because of quasi-linear function and because the total number of population is normalized, each demand function is given as shown below:

$$Q_0 = a - [b + c(N+1)]p_0 + cP \tag{9.17}$$

and

$$Q_i = a - [b + c(N+1)]p_i + cP, \quad (i = 1, \cdots, N). \tag{9.18}$$

Referring to the input factors of the manufactured goods explanation given above, we assume that firms producing manufactured goods have homogeneous production technology. The manufactured goods sector requires labor as a marginal input factor and capital as a fixed input factor for production. Presuming that Q_0 and Q_i units of production require l_c^0/m and l_c^i/m units labor and f units as fixed capital input, respectively, the cost functions of public firm and private firm are given as shown below

$$C_0(Q_0) = \bar{w}mQ_0 + Rf \tag{9.19}$$

and

$$C_i(Q_i) = \bar{w}mQ_i + Rf, \tag{9.20}$$

From (9.17), (9.18), (9.19), and (9.20), the profit functions of public and private firm are given as the following π_0 and π_i.

$$\pi_0 = (a - [b + c(N+1)]p_0 + cP)(p_0 - m\bar{w}) - Rf \tag{9.21}$$

$$\pi_i = (a - [b + c(N+1)]p_i + cP)(p_i - m\bar{w}) - Rf \tag{9.22}$$

Although private firms pursue their own profits, public firms choose a level of production that maximizes social welfare. Therefore, it is necessary to define the social welfare function to analyze the behavior of public firms. Let W represent the social welfare in this model as follows.[3]

$$W = \frac{a^2(N+1)}{2b} - a\left(p_0 + \sum_{i=1}^{N} p_i\right) + \frac{b+c(N+1)}{2}\left([p_0]^2 + \sum_{i=1}^{N}[p_1]^2\right)$$
$$-\frac{c}{2}\left[p_0 + \sum_{i=1}^{N} p_i\right]^2 + \pi_0 + \sum_{i=1}^{N}\pi_i + \bar{w}(l_c^0 + \sum_{i=1}^{N} l_c^i)$$
$$+w_r L_r + R\bar{f} + I, \tag{9.23}$$

Because we assume numerous private firms, as do Ottaviano, Tabuchi, and Thisse [11], neither public firms nor private firms affect the price index of the manufactured goods market.[4] Here we consider that the government owns a share of $(1-\theta)$ of public firms as well as Matsumura [8]. The purpose of the public firm (firm 0) is to maximize the weighted average of social welfare and its profit, defined as V (θ). It is possible for us to take account of partial privatization for the optimal privatization level.

$$V(\theta) \equiv \theta\pi_0 + (1-\theta)W$$
$$= (a - [b + c(N+1)]p_0 + cP)(p_0 - m\bar{w}) - Rf$$
$$+(1-\theta)\left[\frac{a^2(N+1)}{2b} - a\left(p_0 + \sum_{i=1}^{N} p_i\right) + \frac{b+c(N+1)}{2}\right.$$
$$\times\left([p_0]^2 + \sum_{i=1}^{N}[p_i]^2\right) - \frac{c}{2}\left[p_0 + \sum_{i=1}^{N} p_i\right]^2 + \sum_{i=1}^{N}\pi_i$$
$$\left. +\bar{w}(l_c^0 + \sum_{i=1}^{N} l_c^i) + R\bar{f} + I + w_r L_r\right], \tag{9.24}$$

---

[3] Because we assume that the profit of the agricultural goods sector in the rural area is redistributed to households in the economy, redistribution I is equal to that of the agricultural goods sector π_r.

[4] Strictly speaking, the manufactured goods market differs from that in Ottaviano, Tabuchi, and Thisse [11] because Ottaviano, Tabuchi, and Thisse [11] do not include analyses of public firms. In our model, the public firm does not determine the product price for profit maximization. However, the public firm behavior does not affect the price index of the manufactured goods market. Regarding private firms, their behavior also affects the price index. Consequently, the market in our model resembles a monopolistic competition market.

Each private firm determines the price to maximize its own profit function (9.22). Therefore, the first-order condition for profit maximization is given as shown below.

$$\frac{\partial \pi_i}{\partial p_i} = a - 2[b + c(N+1)]p_i + cP + [b + c(N+1)]m\bar{w} = 0 \tag{9.25}$$

The public firm determines its price to maximize the weighted average of social welfare and its profit. The first-order condition for the weighted average of social welfare and its profit is the following.[5]

$$\begin{aligned}\frac{\partial V(\theta)}{\partial p_0} &= \frac{\partial \pi_0}{\partial p_0} + (1-\theta)\left\{\frac{\partial CS}{\partial p_0} + \sum_{i=1}^{N}\frac{\partial \pi_i}{\partial p_0} + \bar{w}\frac{\partial L_c^0}{\partial p_0}\right\}\\ &= a - (1+\theta)[b + c(N+1)]p_0 + cP + \theta m\bar{w}[b + c(N+1)]\\ &= 0\end{aligned} \tag{9.26}$$

From (9.25) and (9.26), the price of differentiated goods produced by either a public firm or a private firm is given as the function of the price index. Similar to Ottaviano, Tabuchi, and Thisse [11], the behavior of each firm does not affect this price index, i.e., $\partial P/\partial p_j (j = 0, \cdots, N) = 0$. Taking account of the symmetry of private firms, which is $p = p_1 = \cdots = p_N$. Solving (9.25) and (9.26) with respect to p_0 and p_i, we derive p_0 and p_i as follows.

$$p_0 = \frac{a}{(1+\theta)[b + c(N+1)]} + \frac{c}{(1+\theta)[b + c(N+1)]}P + \left(\frac{\theta}{1+\theta}\right)m\bar{w} \tag{9.27}$$

$$p = \frac{a}{2[b + c(N+1)]} + \frac{c}{2[b + c(N+1)]}P + \frac{m\bar{w}}{2} \tag{9.28}$$

Considering the symmetry of private firms, we write the price index as $P = p_0 + Np$. Substituting (9.27) and (9.28) for (9.9), the following equation is derived.

$$\begin{aligned}P &= p_0 + Np\\ &= \left(\frac{2 + (1+\theta)N}{2(\theta+1)[b + c(N+1)]}\right)a + \left(\frac{2 + (1+\theta)N}{2(\theta+1)[b + c(N+1)]}\right)cP\\ &\quad + \left(\frac{2\theta + (1+\theta)N}{2(1+\theta)}\right)m\bar{w}\end{aligned} \tag{9.29}$$

[5]The objective function of public firms also includes the profit of the agricultural goods sector. Therefore, the objective function of public firms depends on the effect of public firm's behavior on it via migration between urban and rural areas. However, we assume that the public firm does not consider this effect to determine its own level of production. Consequently, the public firm accepts the profit of the agricultural goods sector as given.

Solving (9.29) with respect to price index P, the equilibrium price index P^* is given as

$$P^* = \frac{[2 + (1+\theta)N]\,a + [(2\theta + (1+\theta)N) \times (b + c(N+1))]\,m\bar{w}}{2\,(1+\theta)\,b + (2\theta + (1+\theta)N)\,c} \tag{9.30}$$

Substituting (9.30) for (9.27) and (9.28), we derive the equilibrium price of each firm, which is p_0^* or p^*, as follows.

$$p_0^* = \frac{2a + [2\theta b\,(2\theta + (1+\theta)N)\,c]\,m\bar{w}}{2\,(1+\theta)\,b + (2\theta + (1+\theta)N)\,c} \tag{9.31}$$

$$p^* = \frac{(1+\theta)a + [(1+\theta)\,b + (2\theta + (1+\theta)N)\,c]\,m\bar{w}}{2\,(1+\theta)\,b + (2\theta + (1+\theta)N)\,c} \tag{9.32}$$

Finally we refer to the number of varieties. Because we assume that fixed capital f is necessary to produce each variety, the market clearing condition of capital is given as shown below.

$$(N+1)f = \bar{f} \tag{9.33}$$

Solving (9.33) with respect to N, we derive the number of varieties as follows.[6]

$$N^* = \frac{\bar{f}}{f+1} \tag{9.34}$$

9.3 Urban–Rural Migration

9.3.1 Effect of Public Firm's Privatization on Urban Unemployment

In previous sections, we derived the behavior of households in the economy and production sectors of agricultural goods or manufactured goods sector. We show the migration behavior of households between urban and rural areas in

[6]Strictly speaking, the number of varieties is determined attributable to the zero-profit condition under general monopolistic competition model. In fact, the equilibrium wage is determined endogenously to establish the zero profit condition in Ottaviano, Tabuchi, and Thisse [11], although the number of varieties depends on the number of workers. However, positive profit of manufactured goods sector in equilibrium exists as yet, although the wage has downward rigidity because of minimum wage constraint. Moreover, we assume that $\bar{f}$ is sufficiently large. Consequently, the number of private firms is also efficiently large.

Sect. 9.2.1. Following Harris and Todaro [7], households in our model determine their residential area by comparing the expected utility in the urban area with the utility in the rural area.

First, we derive the number of employed households in the urban area from equilibrium. Letting $\bar{Q}$ and Q respectively represent the total amount of production and each private firm production, then $\bar{Q}$ is given by the sum of public firm production and private firms. Therefore, $\bar{Q}$ is written as presented below.

$$\bar{Q} = Q_0 + N^* Q = (N^* + 1)a - bP^* \tag{9.35}$$

Substituting (9.30) for (9.35), the equilibrium total production of manufactured goods is derived as follows.

$$\begin{aligned}\bar{Q} = &\frac{(2\theta + (1+\theta)N)\,(b + (N+1)c)\,a}{2\,(1+\theta)\,b + (2\theta + (1+\theta)N)\,c} \\ &- \frac{b((2\theta + (1+\theta)N) \times (b + c(N+1)))m\bar{w}}{2\,(1+\theta)\,b + (2\theta + (1+\theta)N)\,c}\end{aligned} \tag{9.36}$$

Differentiating (9.36) with respect to θ, we have

$$\frac{\partial \bar{Q}}{\partial \theta} = \frac{4b\,(a - bm\bar{w})\,(b + (N+1)c)}{(2\,(1+\theta)\,b + (2\theta + (1+\theta)N)\,c)^2} > 0 \tag{9.37}$$

We know that total production of manufactured goods increases according to the progress of public firm privatization. Although a public firm decreases production by progressing privatization, private firms increase production. Consequently, the total production of manufactured goods increases.[7] Next we consider the effects of privatization of public firms on urban unemployment rate. One might recall that Q_0 and Q_i units of production respectively require l_c^0/m and l_c^i/m units labor and f units as fixed capital input. We assume that public and private firms have common production technology. Therefore, the required input to produce manufactured goods is given as $m\bar{Q}$. Therein, $\bar{L}_c$ denotes the number of households employed by public firms and private firms in an urban area. Substituting (9.36) for the production function, we derive total labor demand as follows.

$$\begin{aligned}\bar{L}_c &= m\bar{Q} \\ &= \frac{(2\theta + (1+\theta)N)\,(b + (N+1)c)\,ma}{2\,(1+\theta)\,b + (2\theta + (1+\theta)N)\,c} \\ &\quad - \frac{b((2\theta + (1+\theta)N) \times (b + c(N+1)))m^2\bar{w}}{2\,(1+\theta)\,b + (2\theta + (1+\theta)N)\,c}\end{aligned} \tag{9.38}$$

[7] Here we assume that a is sufficiently large.

Differentiating (9.38) with respect to θ, we have the following.

$$\frac{\partial \bar{L}_c}{\partial \theta} = m\frac{\partial \bar{Q}}{\partial \theta} > 0 \tag{9.39}$$

Therefore, we derive the following lemma by those comparative statics.

Lemma 9.1. *Progress in public firm privatization increases employment in the manufactured goods sector.*

Moreover, we consider the migration equilibrium condition to analyze the effect of public firm privatization on urban employment. Combining (9.12) with (9.16), we can derive the following equation.

$$L_r = (1-\lambda)^{\frac{1}{\sigma-1}} \left(\frac{\bar{w}}{\sigma}\right)^{\frac{1}{\sigma-1}} \tag{9.40}$$

Substituting (9.38) and (9.40) for (9.14), the equilibrium unemployment rate in the urban area is determined using the following equation.

$$\bar{L}_c + (1-\lambda)^{\frac{\sigma}{\sigma-1}} \left(\frac{w}{\sigma}\right)^{\frac{1}{\sigma-1}} + \lambda - 1 = 0 \tag{9.41}$$

Applying the implicit function theorem to (9.41) to analyze the effect of privatization of public firm on urban unemployment rate, $d\lambda/d\theta$ is derived as described below.

$$\frac{d\lambda}{d\theta} = -\frac{m\frac{\partial \bar{Q}}{\partial \theta}}{\left(\frac{\sigma}{1-\sigma}\right)(1-\lambda)^{\frac{1}{\sigma-1}}\left(\frac{w}{\sigma}\right)^{\frac{1}{\sigma-1}} + 1} < 0 \tag{9.42}$$

Although the denominator in (9.42) is positive, the sign of the numerator in it is also positive. Consequently, the sign of (9.42) is determined uniquely. From (9.39), the public firm's privatization increases total amount of production of manufactured goods and required labor input for production. This results of comparative statics hold under the assumption that $a - bm\bar{w}$ is positive. In other words, the urban minimum wage with downward rigidity is small. Summarizing the comparative statics presented above, the following proposition can be derived.

Theorem 9.2. *When the urban minimum wage is low, the progressing privatization of the public firm improves the urban unemployment rate.*

9.3.2 *Effect of Public Firm Privatization on Social Welfare*

Next we consider the effect of public firm privatization on social welfare in equilibrium. The urban unemployment rate in equilibrium is determined endogenously by

(9.41). Next let λ^* represent urban unemployment rate to hold (9.41). Substituting λ^* for (9.40), the equilibrium labor input in agricultural goods sector is given as

$$L_r^* = (1-\lambda^*)^{\frac{1}{\sigma-1}} \left(\frac{\bar{w}}{\sigma}\right)^{\frac{1}{\sigma-1}}. \tag{9.43}$$

Because we define (9.23) as a social welfare function, we substitute (9.30), (9.31), (9.32), and (9.43) into (9.23) to derive the equilibrium social welfare function. Letting W^* represent the equilibrium social welfare function, then the equilibrium social welfare function is the following.

$$\begin{aligned} W^* =& \frac{a(N^*+1)}{2b} - aP^* + \frac{b+c(N^*+1)}{2}\left([p_0^*]^2 + N^*[p^*]^2\right) - \frac{c}{2}\left(P^*\right)^2 \\ &+ p_0^*Q_0^* + N^*p^*Q^* + \left(L_r^*\right)^{\sigma} \end{aligned} \tag{9.44}$$

Differentiating (9.44) with respect to θ, the effect of public firm privatization on social welfare in equilibrium is the following.

$$\begin{aligned} \frac{\partial W^*}{\partial \theta} =& -a\frac{\partial P^*}{\partial \theta} + \left[b + c(N^*+1)\right]\left(p_0^*\frac{\partial p_0^*}{\partial \theta} + N^*p^*\frac{\partial p^*}{\partial \theta}\right) - cP^*\frac{\partial P^*}{\partial \theta} \\ &+ \frac{\partial p_0^*}{\partial \theta}Q_0^* + p_0^*\frac{\partial Q_0^*}{\partial \theta} + N^*\left(\frac{\partial p^*}{\partial \theta}Q^* + p^*\frac{\partial Q^*}{\partial \theta}\right) \\ &+ \sigma\left(L_r^*\right)^{\sigma-1}\frac{\partial L_r^*}{\partial \lambda}\frac{\partial \lambda}{\partial \theta} \\ =& \{2[b+c(N^*+1)]p_0^* + c(P^*-1)\}\frac{\partial p_0^*}{\partial \theta} \\ &+ \{2[b+c(N^*+1)]N^*p^* + cN^*(P^*-1)\}\frac{\partial p^*}{\partial \theta} + p_0^*\frac{\partial Q_0^*}{\partial \theta} + N^*p^*\frac{\partial Q^*}{\partial \theta} \\ &+ \sigma\left(L_r^*\right)^{\sigma-1}\frac{\partial L_r^*}{\partial \lambda}\frac{\partial \lambda}{\partial \theta} \end{aligned} \tag{9.45}$$

From the comparative static analysis presented above, the sign of (9.45) is not determined uniquely in general. When a is sufficiently large, the following inequalities are established.[8]

$$\frac{\partial p_0^*}{\partial \theta} < 0, \quad \frac{\partial p^*}{\partial \theta} < 0, \quad \frac{\partial P^*}{\partial \theta} < 0, \quad \frac{\partial Q_0^*}{\partial \theta} > 0, \quad \frac{\partial Q^*}{\partial \theta} > 0$$

Moreover, the sign of (9.42) is negative. Therefore, we know that the effect of public firm's privatization on social welfare depends on effected of three kinds.

[8] As for these inequalities, see Appendix.

First, we define the first and second term in (9.45) as price effects. Secondly, we define the third and fourth in it as a quantity effect. Moreover, we define the final term in it as a rural employment effect.[9] Presuming that a is sufficiently large, then the price effect and rural employment effect are negative, although the quantity effect is positive. Because public firms and private firms decrease by progressing privatization of public firm, they increase the amount of production. Consequently, households in rural areas migrate from rural areas to urban areas because the progressing privatization of public firm increases urban employment. Therefore, the rural employment effect is negative. Summarizing the discussion presented above, we derive the following proposition.

Theorem 9.3. *Presumed that a is sufficiently large, the progressing privatization of public firms worsens social welfare when the price effect and rural employment effect outstrips quantity effects.*

9.4 Concluding Remarks

Most traditional dualistic economic models incorporate the assumption that both the urban sector (manufactured goods sector) and rural sector (agricultural goods sector) are competitive. However, we consider an economy in which the manufactured goods sector is a mixed monopolistic competition. Although Naito [10] also considers a model including mixed duopoly and dualistic economy models, he does not refer to product differentiation. Although Fujiwara [5] introduces product differentiation into the mixed oligopoly model, his model does not consider the dualistic economy. Moreover, although Fujiwara [5] adopts a quasi-linear utility function used in Ottaviano, Tabuchi, and Thisse [11] to describe product differentiation, that model does not account for the monopolistic competition market of manufactured goods in Ottaviano, Tabuchi, and Thisse [11]. Consequently, our model supplements research gaps of those earlier studies.

We construct a simple model by synthesizing Ottaviano, Tabuchi, and Thisse [11] and Naito [10] and analyze how the privatization of public firms affects urban unemployment or social welfare. Generally, the effect of privatization of public firms on urban unemployment is determined uniquely, i.e., the privatization of public firms can deteriorate urban unemployment. Moreover, we analyze the effects of privatization on social welfare. The effect depends on each parameter and is not determined uniquely. When the price index effect and rural employment effect exceed a price effect, the public firm privatization improves social welfare.

[9]It is necessary to recognize that public firms and private firms ignored the effect of their price setting on price index. Here, however, it is necessary to consider that the change of each firm's price setting affects the social welfare level. Moreover, we assume that the equilibrium price index is greater than one.

Finally, we do not derive the effect of a product differentiation parameter γ on urban employment or social welfare analytically because of solution complexity. It is necessary to make use of numerical analysis with simulation.

9.5 Effect of Public Firm's Privatization on Production

9.5.1 *Effect of θ on Production of Public Firm*

Next we consider the effect of public firm's privatization on production in the manufactured goods sector. Substituting (9.30) and (9.31) for (9.17), the production of public firms in equilibrium is the following.

$$Q_0^* = a - [b + c(N+1)]p_0^* + cP^* \tag{9.46}$$

Differentiating (9.46) with respect to θ, the following equation was derived.

$$\frac{\partial Q_0^*}{\partial p_0^*} = -[b + cN^*]\frac{\partial p_0^*}{\partial \theta} \tag{9.47}$$

When a is sufficiently large, $\frac{\partial p_0^*}{\partial \theta}$ is negative. Consequently, the sign of $\frac{\partial Q_0^*}{\partial \theta}$ is positive.

9.5.2 *Effect of θ on Private Firm Production*

Substituting (9.30) and (9.32) for (9.18), the production of each private firm is given as shown below.

$$Q^* = a - [b + c(N+1)]p^* + cP^* \tag{9.48}$$

Differentiating (9.48) with respect to θ,

$$\frac{\partial Q^*}{\partial \theta} = -(b + c)\frac{\partial p^*}{\partial \theta} \tag{9.49}$$

Similar to (9.46), the sign of (9.49) is also positive when a is sufficiently large.

Appendix

Effect of Public Firm Privatization on Prices of Firms and the Price Index

Effect of θ on the Equilibrium Price of the Private Firm

We consider the effect of public firm privatization on the equilibrium price of private firms. Because the equilibrium price of public firm is given as (9.32), we obtain the following result by differentiating (9.32) with respect to θ.

$$\frac{\partial p^*}{\partial \theta} = \frac{-2c(a - bm\bar{w})}{(2(1+\theta)b + (2\theta + (1+\theta)N)c)^2} \tag{9.50}$$

The sign of (9.50) is not determined uniquely. However, if a is larger than $bm\bar{w}$, then $\frac{\partial p_0^*}{\partial \theta}$ is negative.

Effect of θ on Equilibrium Price of Public Firm

Next we consider the effect of public firm's privatization on the equilibrium price of the public firm. Because the equilibrium price of public firm is given as (9.31), we get the following result by differentiating (9.31) with respect to θ.

$$\begin{aligned}\frac{\partial p_0^*}{\partial \theta} &= \frac{1}{(2(1+\theta)b + (2\theta + (1+\theta)N)c)^2} \\ &\quad \times \left\{\left(\left[2b\,(N+2) + (N+2)^2\,c\right]\theta^2 + 2\left[2b\,(N+2)\right.\right.\right. \\ &\quad + \left.\left. cN\,(N+2)\right]\theta + (cN+2b)\,N\right) bcm\bar{w} - (2b + (2+N)c)a\} \end{aligned} \tag{9.51}$$

Similarly to (9.50), if a is sufficiently large, then the sign of (9.51) is negative.

Equilibrium Price of Price Index

Because the price index is defined by (9.9), we derive the equilibrium price index as follows.[10]

$$P^* = \left[p_0^* + N^* p^*\right] \tag{9.52}$$

[10]Equilibrium price index to be solved explicitly is given as (9.30).

Differentiating (9.52) with respect to θ,

$$\frac{\partial P^*}{\partial \theta} = \left[\frac{\partial p_0^*}{\partial \theta} + N^* \frac{\partial p^*}{\partial \theta} \right] \tag{9.53}$$

Presuming that a is sufficiently large, the sign of (9.49) is negative attributable to (9.46) and (9.47).

References

1. Beladi, H., & Chao, C. (2006). Mixed ownership, unemployment, and welfare for a developing economy. *Review of Development Economics, 10*(4), 604–611.
2. Calvo, G. A. (1978). Urban unemployment and wage determination in LDC's: Trade unions in the Harris–Todaro model. *International Economic Review, 19*(1), 65–81.
3. Corden, W. M., & Findlay, R. (1975). Urban unemployment, intersectoral capital mobility and development policy. *Economica, 42*(165), 59–78.
4. De Fraja, G., & Delbono, F. (1990). Game theoretic models of mixed oligopoly. *Journal of Economic Surveys, 4*(1), 1–17.
5. Fujiwara, K. (2007). Partial privatization in a differentiated mixed oligopoly. *Journal of Economics, 92*(1), 51–65.
6. Fukuyama, H., & Naito, T. (2007). Unemployment, trans-boundary pollution, and environmental policy in a dualistic economy. *Review of Urban and Regional Development Studies, 19*(2), 154–172.
7. Harris, J. R., & Todaro, M. P. (1970). Migration, unemployment and development: A two-sector analysis. *American Economic Review, 60*(1), 126–142.
8. Matsumura, T. (1998). Partial privatization in mixed duopoly. *Journal of Public Economics, 70*(3), 473–483.
9. Matsumura, T., & Kanda, O. (2005). Mixed oligopoly at free entry markets. *Journal of Economics, 84*(1), 27–48.
10. Naito, T. (2012). Urban–rural migration, unemployment, and privatization: A synthesis of Harris–Todaro model and a mixed duopoly. *Letters in Spatial and Resource Sciences, 5*(2), 85–94.
11. Ottaviano, G., Tabuchi, T., & Thisse, J. F. (2002). Agglomeration and trade revisited. *International Economic Review, 43*(2), 409–436.

Chapter 10
The Network Analysis of Transportation

Akio Kawasaki

10.1 Introduction

Since the deregulation of the airline market in 1978, airline networks have rapidly changed. During this time, regional carriers and low-cost carriers (LCCs) have entered or exited airline markets. According to Bamberger and Carlton [1], in 2003, LCCs other than Southwest entered 38 hub routes and 31 non-hub routes (Southwest entered only two non-hub routes). In the same year, major carriers entered 76 own hub routes, 40 other hub routes, and 216 non-hub routes.

In Japan, the airline market was deregulated in 2000, after which new carriers entered. For example, Skymark Airlines entered the market in July 2000, Air-do in October 2000, and Solaseed Air (Skynet-Asia Airline) in May 2002. In this chapter, we examine a number of outstanding questions. Which routes do new carriers enter? How do incumbent carriers change their operating routes? Based on these interests, this chapter assumes that the incumbent carrier chooses the entry route in the first stage and that the new carrier chooses the entry route in the second stage to investigate which route each carrier enters.

Of the scarce literature on the carrier's route problem, Lin and Kawasaki [8] assume that the entry route of the incumbent carrier is given and analyze which route, the hub route of the major carrier or the non-hub route, to enter. They demonstrate that the regional carrier has an incentive to enter the non-hub route in order to avoid competition with the incumbent carrier. Similar to Lin and Kawasaki [8], Kawasaki and Lin [7] assume that the incumbent entry route is given and analyze which route (the hub route or non-hub route of the incumbent carrier) to

---

A. Kawasaki (✉)
Faculty of Education, Kagoshima University, Korimoto 1-20-6, Kagoshima city, Kagoshima 8900065, Japan
e-mail: kawasaki@edu.kagoshima-u.ac.jp

T. Naito (ed.), *Sustainable Growth and Development in a Regional Economy*,
New Frontiers in Regional Science: Asian Perspectives 13,
DOI 10.1007/978-4-431-55294-9_10

enter. However, the later study addresses the cost differential between incumbent carriers and entrants. As this cost differential increases from a small (large) basis, the new carrier strengthens its incentive to enter the incumbent's hub (non-hub) route.

Although these two studies consider the new carrier's entry route problem, they ignore the strategy of the incumbent carrier. To address this shortcoming, the present chapter addresses both the incumbent's operating route and the entrant's entry route. We imagine that if the incumbent expects the new carrier to enter its hub–spoke airline market, the incumbent may change its operating route. We also assume that three markets exist in this model and that the potential number of one market is smaller than that of the other two markets. In addition, the incumbent carrier has already entered one market, which has more potential passengers. Given this situation, each incumbent and entrant chooses only one entry route. That is, the incumbent carrier expects the entry route of the new carrier and chooses the entry route for the first time. Then, realizing the incumbent's entry route, the new carrier chooses the entry route. Considering this situation, which network is formed in equilibrium?

Furthermore, this chapter interprets the selection of the hub airport by the incumbent carrier when it faces potential competition with the entrant carrier. With regard to the hub selection problem in a monopolistic market, Kawasaki [6] demonstrates that a monopolistic carrier does not always choose the hub to minimize the potential number of connecting passengers. Then, by considering the situation in which the incumbent faces competition with the entrant, do the same results as those presented by Kawasaki [6] appear? Finally, by comparing social welfare for each entry pattern, this chapter examines the socially preferable entry pattern.

The main results obtained in this chapter are as follows. The subgame perfect Nash equilibrium with regard to the entry route decision is described below. When the difference in the potential number of passengers between two markets is not small, the incumbent carrier (or the major carrier) enters a route that has a smaller potential number of passengers and the entrant carrier (or the regional carrier) enters a route that has a greater potential number of passengers. However, when this difference is small, both the major carrier and the regional carrier enter the route that has a smaller potential number of passengers.

From the viewpoint of social welfare, the following results are obtained. When the difference in the potential number of passengers between markets is not small, it is socially preferable that both major and regional carriers enter the route that has a smaller potential number of passengers. When this difference is small, it is socially preferable that the regional carrier enters the route that has a smaller potential number of passengers and the major carrier enters the route that has a greater potential number of passengers. Furthermore, by introducing the per-seat cost, this chapter re-analyzes the entry route problem and finds that when this cost is large, the major carrier does not enter the route that has a large potential number of passengers. That is, the major carrier chooses its entry route to decrease the number of connecting passengers.

The remainder of this chapter is organized as follows. In Sect. 10.2, we present the model. Section 10.3 analyzes the flight frequency and quantity of each carrier assuming a restrictive entry pattern. In Sect. 10.4, we compare each carrier's demand with each entry pattern. Section 10.5 analyzes the entry route decision by the entrant carrier given the result obtained in Sect. 10.3. In Sect. 10.6, given the result presented in Sect. 10.5, we analyze the incumbent carrier's entry route and derive the subgame perfect equilibrium. In Sect. 10.7, we derive the socially preferable entry pattern. In Sect. 10.8, we introduce the per-seat cost and discuss its influence. Section 10.9 concludes and discusses further research.

10.2 Model

Following Kawasaki and Lin [7] and Lin and Kawasaki [8], this chapter uses a model with three cities: A, B, and C. The individuals living in each city travel to other cities. All travel is assumed to be in the form of a round trip. There exist two carriers in this economy: a major carrier (or an incumbent carrier) that always uses a hub–spoke network[1] and a regional carrier (or an entrant carrier) that always uses city C's airport and flies only one route. Hereafter, we call the former carrier airline M and the latter airline R.

Each carrier flies between each city pair. We express airline ℓ's ($\ell = M, R$) number of flights between cities $i(= A, B, C)$ and $j(= A, B, C,\ i \neq j)$ as f_{ij}^{ℓ}. Each carrier incurs operating costs when flying between each city pair. In this chapter, following Kawasaki [6] and Kawasaki and Lin [7], we assume for simplicity that the per-seat cost is zero and the constant cost per flight is K.

The two carriers compete by simultaneously choosing the flight frequency and quantity (total traffic) of their market(s). Throughout our analysis, the airfares of airline ℓ ($= 1, 2$) for each city pair ij ($i, j = A, B, C,\ i \neq j$) are represented as p_{ij}^{ℓ}; the flight frequency and quantity of airline ℓ for city pair ij are represented as f_{ij}^{ℓ} and q_{ij}^{ℓ}, respectively.

Before deciding its flight frequency and quantity, each carrier decides its operating routes. We assume that the major carrier always uses a hub–spoke network and operates on route AB, but chooses route BC or AC. On the contrary, we assume that the regional carrier operates on only one route and chooses route AC or BC. Figure 10.1 expresses the network structure used in this chapter.

Finally, following Kawasaki [5], Kawasaki [6], and Kawasaki and Lin [7], we assume that each flight has unlimited capacity.

[1]The economic efficiency relative to a point-to-point network comes from the fact that the incumbent enjoys benefits from higher flight frequencies. The resulting welfare under the adopted hub–spoke network could be superior to that in a point-to-point one. For this argument in a monopoly carrier case, see Brueckner [2] and Kawasaki [5], among others.

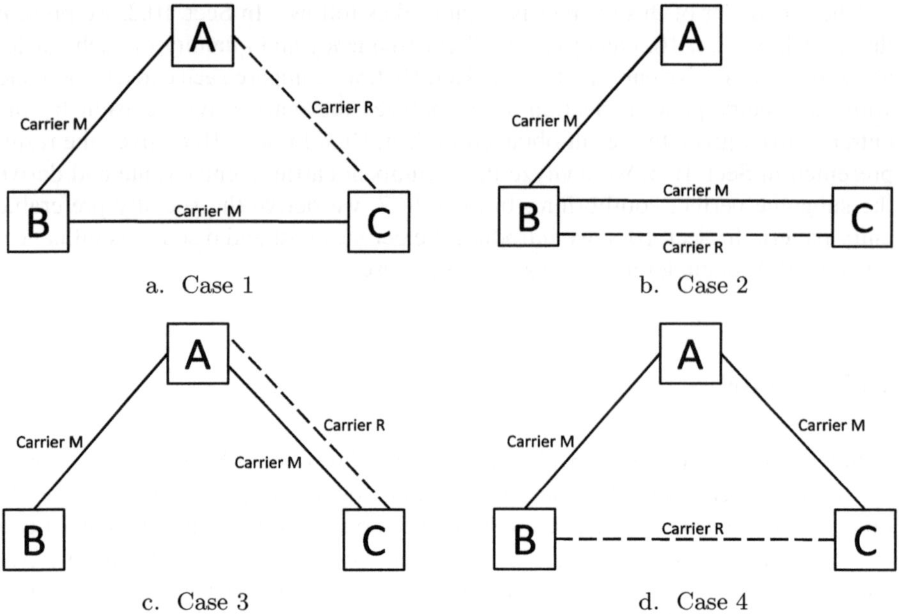

Fig. 10.1 Network structure

10.2.1 Passengers' Utility Function

Each passenger benefits from using airline services. Following Brueckner [2] and Kawasaki [6], we assume that total benefit is composed of the travel benefits and schedule delay cost.

We assume that the travel benefits derived from flight services vary among passengers. Here, a passenger's travel benefit is expressed as w. Following Kawasaki [6], benefit w is assumed to be uniformly distributed between $[-\underline{W}, W]$. We assume that a passenger who has $w = -\underline{W}$ heavily dislikes airline services and never flies on an aircraft. Furthermore, we assume that the density of benefit w is different between each city pair; the density in city pairs AB and AC is 1 and that in city pair BC is $\beta(\leq 1)$.

The waiting time of passengers using a carrier decreases when the carrier increases flight frequency. This additional convenience means that passengers' benefits increase when flight frequency increases.[2] Hereafter, we call this effect the "scheduling effect" and represent the reduction in the schedule delay cost (i.e., the benefit of the increased flight frequency) as $\sqrt{f}$.

[2]This assumption was also made by Oum et al. [9], Brueckner [2], and Brueckner and Flores-Fillol [3].

We separately formulate the benefit function for connecting passengers because flight frequencies differ for each route. When passengers travel via the hub city, they must use two routes. Consequently, their convenience depends on the frequencies of both routes. Following Oum et al. [9], Flores-Fillol [4], and Kawasaki [6], we assume that the benefit of a one-stop service is the average of the two relevant frequencies.

In general, a connecting passenger's travel time cost T when flying through the hub city might be higher than the one incurred if direct flights were available (see Brueckner [2]; Kawasaki [5]). However, when introducing this additional travel time cost, the calculation becomes burdensome. Therefore, this chapter omits this additional travel time cost. By ignoring this cost, the assumption that the major carrier adopts a hub–spoke network becomes rational.[3]

In the following analysis, we assume the following.

Assumption. *Connecting passengers do not change carriers at the hub airport.*

The interpretation of this assumption is as follows. When connecting passengers change carriers at the hub airport, they incur heavy disutility from moving to a different terminal, repeating check-in procedures, or having to wait an excessively long time. Therefore, connecting passengers prefer connecting flights provided by the same carrier or an alliance member; hence, few passengers change carriers.[4]

Here, we assume that the airfare for the connecting flight is lower than the sum of the airfares for the two routes. This assumption ensures that connecting passengers do not purchase tickets for two routes. In the following analysis, this assumption always holds. As a result, the utility function is expressed as follows:

$$U_{ij}= \begin{cases} w + \sqrt{f_{ij}^{\ell}} - p_{ij}^{\ell} & \text{if traveling directly} \\ w + \frac{1}{2}(\sqrt{f_{ih}^{\ell}} + \sqrt{f_{jh}^{\ell}}) - p_{ij}^{\ell} & \text{if traveling via hub city } h. \end{cases} \tag{10.1}$$

The timeline of this game is as follows. In the first stage, the major carrier chooses its entry route. Then, the regional carrier decides its entry route. In the third stage, each carrier decides its flight frequency and quantity simultaneously.

[3] See, for example, Kawasaki [5].

[4] For example, LCCs tend to use point-to-point networks, do not construct flight schedules that consider connecting passengers' transit, and thus have a very low percentage of connecting passengers.

10.3 The Decision on Flight Frequency and Quantity

This section analyzes the flight frequency and quantity decided by each carrier. Because the result depends on the entry route chosen by each carrier, we derive four cases.

10.3.1 Major Carrier Enters Route BC and Regional Carrier Enters Route AC

First, we assume that the major carrier enters route BC and the regional carrier enters route AC. Hereafter, we call this Case 1 (see Fig. 10.1a). In this case, markets AB and BC are monopolized by the major carrier; in market AC, the major carrier competes with the regional carrier. Therefore, each market's demand function becomes as follows:

$$p_{AB}^{M} = W + \sqrt{f_{AB}^{M}} - q_{AB}^{M}, \tag{10.2}$$

$$p_{BC}^{M} = W + \sqrt{f_{BC}^{M}} - q_{BC}^{M}, \tag{10.3}$$

$$p_{AC}^{M} = W + \tfrac{1}{2}\left(\sqrt{f_{AB}^{M}} + \sqrt{f_{BC}^{M}}\right) - (q_{AC}^{M} + q_{AC}^{R}), \tag{10.4}$$

$$p_{AC}^{R} = W + \sqrt{f_{AC}^{R}} - (q_{AC}^{M} + q_{AC}^{R}). \tag{10.5}$$

Consequently, the profit function of each carrier is

$$\pi_M = p_{AB}^{M} q_{AB}^{M} + \beta p_{BC}^{M} q_{BC}^{M} + p_{AC}^{M} q_{AC}^{M} - (f_{AB}^{M} + f_{BC}^{M})K, \tag{10.6}$$

$$\pi_R = p_{AC}^{R} q_{AC}^{R} - f_{AC}^{R} K. \tag{10.7}$$

By solving the profit maximization problem, we obtain the following flight frequency and quantity:

$$f_{AB}^{M} = \left(\frac{W(1 + 4K(-7 + 16K - 3\beta) + 5\beta)}{(1 - 4K)(1 + 48K^2 + 5\beta - 12K(2 + \beta))}\right)^2, \tag{10.8}$$

$$f_{BC}^{M} = \left(\frac{W(1 + 5\beta - 4K(1 + 3\beta))}{1 + 48K^2 + 5\beta - 12K(2 + \beta)}\right)^2, \tag{10.9}$$

$$f_{AC}^{R} = \left(\frac{W(1 + 4K(-5 + 8K - 3\beta) + 5\beta)}{(1 - 4K)(1 + 48K^2 + 5\beta - 12K(2 + \beta))}\right)^2, \tag{10.10}$$

$$q_{AB}^{M} = 2KW\left(\frac{1}{-1+4K} + \frac{1}{1+48K^2+5\beta-12K(2+\beta)}\right), \tag{10.11}$$

$$q_{BC}^{M} = \frac{2KW(-5+12K)}{1+48K^2+5\beta-12K(2+\beta)}, \tag{10.12}$$

$$q_{AC}^{M} = \frac{4KW(-1+4K)}{1+48K^2+5\beta-12K(2+\beta)}, \tag{10.13}$$

$$q_{AC}^{R} = 2KW\left(\frac{1}{-1+4K} - \frac{4K}{1+48K^2+5\beta-12K(2+\beta)}\right). \tag{10.14}$$

Consequently, the maximized profits become as follows:

$$\begin{aligned}\pi_M^1 &= KW^2\{(1+\beta)^2 + 128K^4(13+9\beta) - 2K(1+5\beta)(20+17\beta)\\ &\quad -32K^3(50+9\beta(7+\beta)) + 8K^2(59+\beta(143+48\beta))\}\\ &\quad /(4K-1)(1-24K+48K^2+5\beta-12K\beta)^2,\end{aligned} \tag{10.15}$$

$$\pi_R^1 = \frac{KW^2\{1+4K(-5+8K-3\beta)+5\beta\}^2}{(1+48K^2+5\beta-12K\beta)^2}. \tag{10.16}$$

10.3.2 Major Carrier Enters Route BC and Regional Carrier Enters Route BC

In the following, we assume that both the major carrier and the regional carrier enter route BC. Hereafter, we call this Case 2 (see Fig. 10.1b). In this case, markets AB and AC are monopolized by the major carrier; in market BC, the major carrier competes with the regional carrier. Therefore, each market's demand function becomes as follows[5]:

$$p_{BC}^{M} = W + \sqrt{f_{BC}^{M}} - (q_{BC}^{M} + q_{BC}^{R}), \tag{10.17}$$

$$p_{BC}^{R} = W + \sqrt{f_{BC}^{R}} - (q_{BC}^{M} + q_{BC}^{R}), \tag{10.18}$$

$$p_{AC}^{M} = W + \frac{1}{2}\left(\sqrt{f_{AB}^{M}} + \sqrt{f_{BC}^{M}}\right) - q_{AC}^{M}. \tag{10.19}$$

[5]Because the demand function for market AB is the same as Eq. (10.2), we omit its demand function here. This comment is valid in the following subsections.

Consequently, the profit function of each carrier is

$$\pi_M = p_{AB}^M q_{AB}^M + \beta p_{BC}^M q_{BC}^M + p_{AC}^M q_{AC}^M - (f_{AB}^M + f_{BC}^M)K, \tag{10.20}$$

$$\pi_R = \beta p_{BC}^R q_{BC}^R - f_{BC}^R K. \tag{10.21}$$

By solving the profit maximization problem, we obtain the following flight frequency and quantity:

$$f_{AB}^M = \left(\frac{W(-3K + 72K^2 + \beta - 46K\beta + 5\beta^2)}{192K^3\beta(1+5\beta) - 8K^2(9+16\beta) + K(3+4\beta(11+4\beta))}\right)^2, \tag{10.22}$$

$$f_{BC}^M = \left(\frac{W(\beta + 5\beta^2 + 8K^2(3+4\beta) - K(3+2\beta(9+8\beta))))}{192K^3\beta(1+5\beta) - 8K^2(9+16\beta) + K(3+4\beta(11+4\beta))}\right)^2, \tag{10.23}$$

$$f_{BC}^R = \left(\frac{W\beta(1 + 32K^2 + 5\beta - 16K(1+\beta))}{192K^3\beta(1+5\beta) - 8K^2(9+16\beta) + K(3+4\beta(11+4\beta))}\right)^2, \tag{10.24}$$

$$q_{AB}^M = \frac{KW(96K^2 - 64K\beta + \beta(-1+8\beta))}{192K^3\beta(1+5\beta) - 8K^2(9+16\beta) + K(3+4\beta(11+4\beta))}, \tag{10.25}$$

$$q_{BC}^M = \frac{KW(-1 + 8K(-1 + 8K - 4\beta) + 8\beta)}{192K^3\beta(1+5\beta) - 8K^2(9+16\beta) + K(3+4\beta(11+4\beta))}, \tag{10.26}$$

$$q_{AC}^M = \frac{2KW(-3 + 24K - 2\beta)(2K - \beta)}{192K^3\beta(1+5\beta) - 8K^2(9+16\beta) + K(3+4\beta(11+4\beta))}, \tag{10.27}$$

$$q_{BC}^R = \frac{2KW(1 + 32K^2 + 5\beta - 16K(1+\beta)}{192K^3\beta(1+5\beta) - 8K^2(9+16\beta) + K(3+4\beta(11+4\beta))}. \tag{10.28}$$

Consequently, the maximized profits become as follows:

$$\begin{aligned}\pi_M^2 = {} & KW^2\{2048K^5(9+2\beta) - 2\beta^2(1+5\beta)^2 + K\beta(1+5\beta)(13+48\beta(3+\beta)) \\ & -128K^4(63+40\beta(5+\beta)) + 16K^3(45+4\beta(155+\beta(203+32\beta))) \\ & -2K^2(9+4\beta(88+\beta(533+8\beta(45+4\beta))))\} \\ & /\{192K^3 - \beta(1+5\beta - 8K^2(9+16\beta) + K(3+4\beta(11+4\beta))\}^2, \end{aligned} \tag{10.29}$$

$$\pi_M^2 = \frac{KW^2(4K-\beta)\beta(1+32K^2+5\beta-16K(1+\beta))^2}{\{192K^3 - \beta(1+5\beta) + K(3+4\beta(11+4\beta))\}^2}. \tag{10.30}$$

10.3.3 Major Carrier Enters Route AC and Regional Carrier Enters Route AC

In this subsection, we assume that both the major carrier and the regional carrier enter route AC. Hereafter, we call this Case 3 (see Fig. 10.1c). In this case, markets AB and BC are monopolized by the major carrier; in market AC, the major carrier competes with the regional carrier. Therefore, each market demand function becomes as follows:

$$p_{BC}^{M} = W + \frac{1}{2}\left(\sqrt{f_{AB}^{M}} + \sqrt{f_{AC}^{M}}\right) - q_{BC}^{M}, \tag{10.31}$$

$$p_{AC}^{M} = W + \sqrt{f_{AC}^{M}} - (q_{AC}^{M} + q_{AC}^{R}), \tag{10.32}$$

$$p_{AC}^{R} = W + \sqrt{f_{AC}^{R}} - (q_{AC}^{M} + q_{AC^{R}}). \tag{10.33}$$

Consequently, the profit function of each carrier is

$$\pi_M = p_{AB}^{M} q_{AB}^{M} + \beta p_{BC}^{M} q_{BC}^{M} + p_{AC}^{M} q_{AC}^{M} - (f_{AB}^{M} + f_{AC}^{M})K, \tag{10.34}$$

$$\pi_R = p_{AC}^{R} q_{AC}^{R} - f_{AC}^{R} K. \tag{10.35}$$

By solving the profit maximization problem, we obtain the following flight frequency and quantity:

$$f_{AB}^{M} = \left(\frac{W(2(2+\beta) + K(-32 - 17\beta + 24K(2+\beta)))}{-2(2+\beta) + K(48 + 8K(-22 + 24K - 3\beta) + 15\beta)}\right)^2, \tag{10.36}$$

$$f_{AC}^{M} = \left(\frac{W(2(2+\beta) + K(-24 - 13\beta + 8K(4+3\beta)))}{-2(2+\beta) + K(48 + 8K(-22 + 24K - 3\beta) + 15\beta)}\right)^2, \tag{10.37}$$

$$f_{AC}^{R} = \left(\frac{2W(-1+4K)(-2+4K-\beta)}{-2(2+\beta) + K(48 + 8K(-22 + 24K - 3\beta) + 15\beta)}\right)^2, \tag{10.38}$$

$$q_{AB}^{M} = \frac{KW(8 + 32K(-2+3K) - \beta)}{-2(2+\beta) + K(48 + 8K(-22 + 24K - 3\beta) + 15\beta)}, \tag{10.39}$$

$$q_{BC}^{M} = \frac{KW(5 - 34K + 48K^2)}{-2(2+\beta) + K(48 + 8K(-22 + 24K - 3\beta) + 15\beta)}, \tag{10.40}$$

$$q_{AC}^{M} = \frac{KW(8 - \beta + 8K(-6 + 8K + \beta)))}{-2(2+\beta) + K(48 + 8K(-22 + 24K - 3\beta) + 15\beta)}, \tag{10.41}$$

$$q_{AC}^{R} = \frac{4KW(-1+4K)(-2+4K-\beta)}{-2(2+\beta) + K(48 + 8K(-22 + 24K - 3\beta) + 15\beta)}. \tag{10.42}$$

Consequently, the maximized profits become as follows:

$$\pi_M^3 = 2KW^2\{-4(2+\beta)^2 + 512K^5(13+9\beta) + K(2+\beta)(144+61\beta)$$
$$-64K^4(170+\beta(124+9\beta)) - 8K^3(848+\beta(663+94\beta))$$
$$-K^2(2016+\beta(1712+333\beta))\}$$
$$/\{-2(2+\beta) + K(48+8K(-22+24K-3\beta)+15\beta))\}^2, \quad (10.43)$$

$$\pi_R^3 = \frac{4KW^2(4K-1)^3(2-4K+\beta)^2}{\{-2(2+\beta)+K(48+8K(-22+24K-3\beta)+15\beta))\}^2}. \quad (10.44)$$

10.3.4 Major Carrier Enters Route AC and Regional Carrier Enters Route BC

Finally, we assume that the major carrier enters route AC and the regional carrier enters route BC. Hereafter, we call this Case 4 (see Fig. 10.1d). In this case, markets AB and AC are monopolized by the major carrier; in market BC, the major carrier competes with the regional carrier. Therefore, each demand function becomes as follows:

$$p_{BC}^M = W + \frac{1}{2}\left(\sqrt{f_{AB}^M} + \sqrt{f_{AC}^M}\right) - (q_{BC}^M + q_{BC}^R), \quad (10.45)$$

$$p_{BC}^R = W + \sqrt{f_{BC}^R} - (q_{BC}^M + q_{BC}^R), \quad (10.46)$$

$$p_{AC}^N = W + \sqrt{f_{AC}^M} - q_{AC}^M. \quad (10.47)$$

By solving the profit maximization problem, we obtain the following flight frequency and quantity:

$$f_{AB}^M = \left(\frac{W(-\beta(2+\beta)+2K(3+\beta))}{24K^2+\beta(2+\beta)-6K(1+2\beta)}\right)^2, \quad (10.48)$$

$$f_{AC}^M = \left(\frac{W(-\beta(2+\beta)+2K(3+\beta)))}{24K^2+\beta(2+\beta)-6K(1+2\beta)}\right)^2, \quad (10.49)$$

$$f_{BC}^R = \left(\frac{W\beta(-2+4K-\beta)}{24K^2+\beta(2+\beta)-6K(1+2\beta)}\right)^2, \quad (10.50)$$

$$q_{AB}^M = \frac{KW(12K-5\beta)}{24K^2+\beta(2+\beta)-6K(1+2\beta)}, \quad (10.51)$$

$$q_{BC}^{M} = \frac{2KW(1+4K-2\beta)}{24K^2+\beta(2+\beta)-6K(1+2\beta)}, \tag{10.52}$$

$$q_{AC}^{M} = \frac{KW(12K-5\beta)}{24K^2+\beta(2+\beta)-6K(1+2\beta)}, \tag{10.53}$$

$$q_{BC}^{R} = \frac{2KW(-2+4K-\beta)}{24K^2+\beta(2+\beta)-6K(1+2\beta)}. \tag{10.54}$$

Consequently, each carrier's profit becomes as follows:

$$\begin{aligned}\pi_M^4 &= 2KW^2\{-\beta^2(2+\beta)^2+16K^3(9+2\beta(+K\beta(2+\beta)(13+12\beta)\\ &\quad -4K^2(9+\beta(32+9\beta))\}/\{24K^2+\beta(2+\beta)-6K(1+2\beta)\}^2 \quad (10.55)\end{aligned}$$

$$\pi_R^4 = \frac{KW^2(4K-\beta)\beta(2-4K+\beta)^2}{\{24K^2+\beta(2+\beta)-6K(1+2\beta)\}^2}. \tag{10.56}$$

10.4 Comparison of the Number of Passengers

In this section, we compare the number of passengers by using each carrier in each market. Hereafter, we express case m's number of passengers using airline ℓ in market ij as $q_{ij}^{\ell m}$.

10.4.1 Comparison of Airline M's Number of Passengers

First, we present the comparison result of market AB. The following Lemma 10.1 shows the result.

Lemma 10.1. *When* $\beta \leq 0.838127$, $q_{AB}^{M2} \geq q_{AB}^{M1} \geq q_{AB}^{M3} \geq q_{AB}^{M4}$ *holds. When* $\beta > 0.838127$, $q_{AB}^{M2} \geq q_{AB}^{M3} \geq q_{AB}^{M1} \geq q_{AB}^{M4}$ *holds.*

First, the number of passengers using airline services depends on the flight frequency of the major carrier. In other words, a larger flight frequency increases demand throughout the larger scheduling effect. Therefore, we mainly discuss flight frequency.

In Case 1, route AB, which influences the number of passengers in market AB, has two markets: market AB is a monopoly for the major carrier and market AC is a duopoly for the major carrier. Here, the monopolistic market has larger marginal revenues of flight frequency than the duopolistic market. Furthermore, monopolistic market AB gives full-sized marginal revenues for flight frequency on route AB but duopolistic market AC gives smaller (i.e., half-sized) marginal revenues for it. Therefore, flight frequency becomes large.

In Case 2, route AB has markets AB and AC, which are both monopolies. Therefore, in Case 2, flight frequency depends on the marginal revenues of these two monopolistic markets. Therefore, flight frequency becomes very large.

In Case 3, route AB has markets AB and BC, which are both monopolies. Here, market BC has a smaller potential number of passengers (i.e., the density of market BC is smaller than that of the other markets). In Case 3, flight frequency depends on the marginal revenues of these two monopolistic markets, one of which has a smaller passenger density. Therefore, flight frequency becomes somewhat large.

In Case 4, route AB has market AB, which is a monopoly, and market BC, which is a duopoly. As mentioned above, because market BC has a smaller potential number of passengers, the marginal revenue from market BC becomes smaller than that from the duopoly market. Therefore, flight frequency becomes small.

From the above characteristics of each case, we see that Case 2's scheduling effect is the largest and Case 4's scheduling effect is the smallest among these four cases. Because the larger scheduling effect that arises from the larger flight frequency leads to a larger number of passengers, it is apparent that q_{AB}^{M2} is the largest among the four cases, while q_{AB}^{M4} is the smallest. On the contrary, the comparison result between q_{AB}^{M1} and q_{AB}^{M3} depends on β. When β is large, the marginal revenue from monopolistic market BC is larger than that from duopolistic market AC, which leads to a larger flight frequency on route AB for Case 3 than Case 1. Therefore, Case 3's scheduling effect is larger than that of Case 1's, resulting in q_{AB}^{M3} becoming larger than q_{AB}^{M3}. Contrarily, when β is not large, the marginal revenue from duopolistic market AC is larger than that from monopolistic market BC, which makes Case 1's flight frequency on route AB larger than that of Case 3. Consequently, Case 1's scheduling effect is larger than that of Case 3, and thus q_{AB}^{M1} becomes larger than q_{AB}^{M3}.

In the following, we present the comparison result of market AC. The following Lemma 10.2 shows the result.

Lemma 10.2. *When* $\beta \leq 0.697224$, $q_{AC}^{M4} \geq q_{AC}^{M2} \geq q_{AC}^{M1} \geq q_{AC}^{M3}$ *holds. When* $\beta > 0.697224$, $q_{AC}^{M2} \geq q_{AC}^{M4} \geq q_{AC}^{M1} \geq q_{AC}^{M3}$ *holds.*

To interpret this lemma, we note that the number of passengers in market AC depends on the flight frequency of both routes AB and BC in Case 1 and Case 2.

In Case 1, market AC is a competitive market. At the same time, as mentioned above, the number of passengers depends on flight frequency on routes AB and BC. There are two marginal revenues on both routes; one is a full-sized marginal revenue from the monopolistic market and the other is a half-sized marginal revenue from the duopolistic market. Furthermore, because the potential number of passengers in market BC is small compared with other markets, the marginal revenues from market BC become somewhat small.

In Case 2, market AC is a monopolistic market for the major carrier. In addition, as with Case 1, the number of passengers depends on the flight frequency of both routes AB and BC. On route AB, there exist two monopolistic markets, meaning that the marginal revenue on route AB is large. On the contrary, on route BC, there exist a duopolistic market that has full-sized marginal revenues and a monopolistic market that has half-sized marginal revenues. Additionally, market *BC* has a smaller potential number of passengers than the other markets. Therefore, flight frequency on this route becomes somewhat small.

In Case 3, market *AC* is a competitive market. On the contrary, different from Case 1, the number of passengers depends on only flight frequency on route *AC*. On route *AC*, there exist two marginal revenues: the full-sized marginal revenue from duopolistic market *AC* and the half-sized marginal revenue from monopolistic market *BC*. Additionally, market *BC* has a smaller potential number of passengers. Therefore, flight frequency on route *AC* becomes very small.

In Case 4, market *AC* is a monopolistic market. On the contrary, different from Case 2, the number of passengers depends on only flight frequency on route *AC*. Flight frequency on route *AC* has two marginal revenues. One is from monopolistic market *AC* and is full-sized. The other is from duopolistic market *BC* and is half-sized. Additionally, market *BC* has a smaller potential number of passengers than the other markets.

From the above characteristics of each case, we see that Case 3's scheduling effect is the smallest among the four cases; hence, q_{AC}^{M3} is the smallest. Next, we discuss the other comparison results. First, however, market *AC* in Case 1 is a competitive market but its market in the other cases is a monopolistic market. Consequently, q_{AC}^{M1} becomes the smallest among the three cases (Cases 1, 2, and 4).

Finally, we discuss the comparison result between Cases 2 and 4. First, we consider the extreme case of $\beta = 0$. In Case 4, there are no connecting passengers; therefore, flight frequency on route *AC* depends only on the marginal revenue from market *AC*. Hence, flight frequency on route *AC* becomes very small. On the contrary, in Case 2, although flight frequency on route *BC* is small, that on route *AB* is very large. Therefore, Case 2's scheduling effect becomes larger than that of Case 4. As a result, when $\beta = 0$, q_{AC}^{M2} is larger than q_{AC}^{M4}. This characteristic holds when β is small. However, as β becomes very large, the reverse characteristic occurs. For example, we consider another extreme case that $\beta = 1$. Then, in Case 4, flight frequency on route *AC* is large and thus the scheduling effect for a passenger in market *AC* becomes large. On the contrary, in Case 2, flight frequency on route *BC* is very small; hence, the scheduling effect for a passenger in market *AC* becomes small. Consequently, when $\beta = 1$, q_{AC}^{M4} is larger than q_{AC}^{M2}. This relationship holds when β is large.

In the following, we present the comparison result of market *BC*. The following Lemma 10.3 shows the result.

Lemma 10.3. *When* $\beta \leq 0.982143$, $q_{BC}^{M3} \geq q_{BC}^{M1} \geq q_{BC}^{M4} \geq q_{BC}^{M2}$ *holds. When* $\beta > 0.982143$, $q_{BC}^{M1} \geq q_{BC}^{M3} \geq q_{BC}^{M4} \geq q_{BC}^{M2}$ *holds.*

To interpret this lemma, we note that the number of passengers in market *BC* depends on the flight frequency of both routes *AB* and *AC* in Case 3 and Case 4. Additionally, this lemma's interpretation is similar to that of Lemma 10.2.

In Case 1, market *BC* is a monopolistic market. In addition, the number of passengers depends on flight frequency on route *BC*. Flight frequency on route *BC* has two marginal revenues. One is from monopolistic market *BC*, which has full-sized marginal revenue, and the other is from duopolistic market *AC*, which has half-sized marginal revenue. Furthermore, the potential number of passengers in market *BC* is smaller than that in the other markets.

In Case 2, market *BC* is a competitive market. In addition, the number of passengers depends on flight frequency on route *BC*. Flight frequency on route *BC* has two marginal revenues. One is from duopolistic market *BC*, which has full-sized marginal revenue, and the other is from monopolistic market *AC*, which has half-sized marginal revenue.

In Case 3, market *BC* is a monopolistic market. At the same time, as mentioned earlier, the number of passengers depends on flight frequency on both routes *AB* and *AC*. On route *AB*, there are two monopolistic markets. Therefore, flight frequency on route *AB* becomes very large. On route *AC*, there are two markets. One is duopolistic market *AC*, which has full-sized marginal revenue, and the other is monopolistic market *BC*, which has half-sized marginal revenue. Therefore, flight frequency becomes small.

In Case 4, market *BC* is a competitive market. At the same time, the number of passengers depends on flight frequency on both routes *AB* and *AC*. Here, there are two markets on each route. One is a monopolistic market that has full-sized marginal revenue and the other is a duopolistic market that has half-sized marginal revenue. Therefore, the flight frequency on each route is somewhat large.

From the above characteristics of each case, we see that Case 2's scheduling effect is the smallest among the four cases. Consequently, q_{BC}^{M2} is the smallest. In addition, among the other three cases, market *BC* faces competition in Case 4. Consequently, q_{BC}^{M4} becomes the smallest among the three cases.

Finally, we compare Case 1 with Case 3. First, we consider the extreme case of $\beta = 1$. Then, in Case 3, although flight frequency on route *AC* is not large, flight frequency on route *AB* becomes very large. Consequently, by comparing with Case 1, we see that Case 3's scheduling effect becomes large for a passenger in market *BC*. Therefore, q_{BC}^{M3} is larger than q_{BC}^{M1}. This result holds in the range within which β is sufficiently large. Contrarily, in the range within which β is not sufficiently large, the reverse result occurs. In Case 3, as β decreases, flight frequency on route *AC* decreases; hence, the scheduling effect for a passenger in market *BC* becomes small. Although Case 1's scheduling effect also decreases, this becomes larger than that for Case 3 in the range within which β is not sufficiently large. Therefore, q_{BC}^{M1} becomes larger than q_{BC}^{M3}.

10.4.2 Comparison of Airline R's Number of Passenger

Finally, we show the comparison result for airline *R*'s number of passengers. The following Lemma 10.4 shows the result.

Lemma 10.4. *When* $\beta \leq 0.685546$, $q_{AC}^{R3} \geq q_{AC}^{R1} \geq q_{BC}^{R2} \geq q_{BC}^{R4}$ *holds. When* $\beta > 0.685546$, $q_{AC}^{R3} \geq q_{BC}^{R2} \geq q_{AC}^{R1} \geq q_{BC}^{R4}$ *holds.*

Because airline R always faces competition with airline M, this competition influences the comparison results. Therefore, we first discuss airline M's flight frequency and then airline R's flight frequency and the number of passengers.

In Case 1, airline M and airline R compete with each other in market AC. As mentioned in the above subsection, the major carrier's number of passengers in market AC depends on flight frequency on the two routes, AB and BC. On both routes, the flight frequency of airline M has both a monopolistic market that has full-sized marginal revenue and a duopolistic market that has half-sized marginal revenue. Additionally, the competitive market has a smaller potential number of passengers than the other market. Therefore, the flight frequency of airline M has somewhat large marginal revenues, meaning that the flight frequency of airline M becomes somewhat large. Contrarily, the flight frequency of airline R is somewhat small due to the small marginal revenue.

In Case 2, they compete with each other in market BC. The major carrier's number of passengers in market BC depends on route BC's flight frequency. Its flight frequency has two marginal revenues. One is from duopolistic market BC that has full-sized marginal revenue and the other is from monopolistic market AC that has half-sized marginal revenue. Therefore, the flight frequency of airline M has somewhat small marginal revenue; hence, the flight frequency of airline M becomes somewhat small. Contrarily, the flight frequency of airline R somewhat increases.

In Case 3, they compete with each other in market AC. The major carrier's number of passengers in market AC depends on route AC's flight frequency. Its flight frequency has two marginal revenues. One is from duopolistic market AC that has full-sized marginal revenue and the other is from monopolistic market BC that has half-sized marginal revenue. Therefore, the marginal revenues of airline M become small and thus the flight frequency of airline M becomes small. Contrarily, the flight frequency of airline R increases.

In Case 4, they compete with each other in market BC. As mentioned in the above subsection, the major carrier's number of passengers in market BC depends on the flight frequency of two routes, AB and AC. On both routes, the flight frequency of airline M has both a monopolistic market that has full-sized marginal revenue and a duopolistic market that has half-sized marginal revenue. Additionally, the monopolistic market's potential number of passengers is larger than that of the duopolistic market. Therefore, flight frequency on both routes is very large, meaning that the scheduling effect of airline M becomes very large. On the contrary, because of the larger scheduling effect of airline M, airline R loses more passengers.

From the above characteristics and assumption that market BC has a lower potential number of passengers than markets AB and AC, it is apparent that q_{BC}^{R4} is the smallest among the four cases. Therefore, q_{AC}^{R3} is larger than q_{BC}^{R2}. Additionally, by comparing Case 1 with Case 3, because airline M's scheduling effect in Case 1 is larger than that in Case 3 due to the larger marginal revenues in Case 1, we see that q_{AC}^{R3} becomes larger than q_{AC}^{R1}. Consequently, q_{AC}^{R3} is the largest among the four cases. Finally, we discuss the comparison result of Case 1 and Case 2. First, we consider the extreme case that $\beta = 1$. In this extreme case, the potential number of passengers in each market is the same. By comparing Case 1's scheduling effect of airline M in market AC with Case 2's scheduling effect of airline M in market BC, because airline M has larger marginal revenues in Case 1 than in Case 2, we see that Case 1's scheduling effect in market AC is larger than Case 2's scheduling effect in market BC for airline M. Therefore, q_{AC}^{M1} is larger than q_{BC}^{M2}. Because the number of passengers in the competitive market has a strategic substitution relationship, $q_{AC}^{R1} < q_{BC}^{R2}$ holds. Given this result, as β decreases, because the potential number of passengers decreases, q_{BC}^{R2} largely decreases. Consequently, when β is small, $q_{AC}^{R1} > q_{BC}^{R2}$ holds.

10.5 Entry Route Decision by the Regional Carrier

In this section, we analyze the route that the regional carrier enters. Hereafter, without loss of generality, we assume $K = 1$.

10.5.1 Given that the Major Carrier Enters Route BC

First, we derive the entry route decision by the regional carrier given that the major carrier enters route AC. By comparing π_R^1 and π_R^2, we obtain Lemma 10.5.

Lemma 10.5. *Given that the major carrier enters route BC, if the potential number of passengers in market BC (i.e., the density of w in market BC) is larger than* 0.853, *the regional carrier enters route BC. Otherwise, it enters route AC.*

This mechanism is similar to that presented in Kawasaki and Lin [7]. If the regional carrier enters route AC, the major carrier becomes a monopoly in both AB and BC markets, which strengthens its scheduling effect. Because of the very high scheduling effect of the major carrier, the regional carrier loses passengers in market AC. On the contrary, if the regional carrier enters route BC, although the major carrier becomes a monopoly in both AB and AC markets, the influence of market AB (as a monopoly) disappears on route BC. Therefore, the regional carrier does not suffer from the major carrier's strong scheduling effect compared with the case of entering route AC.

On the contrary, in market BC, the potential number of passengers is smaller than that in market AC. Therefore, if the regional carrier enters route BC, it loses passengers. In other words, the regional carrier has an incentive to enter route AC.

Considering the above trade-off, if β is smaller than 0.853, the latter effect is larger than the former. Consequently, the regional carrier enters route AC. In other words, although the regional carrier suffers from the major carrier's strong scheduling effect, it does not want to lose potential passengers. If β is larger than

0.853, the former effect is larger than the latter. That is, the regional carrier does not want to compete with the major carrier, which has a strong scheduling effect.

10.5.2 Given that the Major Carrier Enters Route AC

In the following, we derive the entry route decision by the regional carrier given that the major carrier enters route AC. By comparing π_R^3 and π_R^4, we obtain Lemma 10.6.

Lemma 10.6. *Given that the major carrier enters route AC, the regional carrier always enters route AC.*

When the major carrier enters route AC, the entry route decision by the regional carrier is different from the case that the major carrier enters route BC. In this case, if the regional carrier enters route BC, it suffers from the major carrier's strong scheduling effect as mentioned earlier. Furthermore, because the potential number of passengers in market BC is smaller than that in market AC, the regional carrier weakens the incentive to enter route BC. Consequently, in this case, the regional carrier always enters route AC.

10.6 Entry Route Decision by the Major Carrier

In the previous section, we analyzed the regional carrier's reaction to the major carrier's decision in the first stage. Given the above results, this section derives which route (AC or BC) the major carrier enters in the first stage.

10.6.1 The Case that $\beta \leq 0.853$

In this case, the regional carrier always enters route AC if the major carrier enters route BC or AC. Therefore, by comparing π_M^1 with π_M^3, we obtain Lemma 10.7.

Lemma 10.7. *The major carrier enters route BC in the range within which β is smaller than* 0.853.

Intuitively, because the potential demand of market BC is small, we expect the major carrier to enter route AC. However, Lemma 10.7 demonstrates that our expectation is violated. In this range, the regional carrier originally has no incentive to enter route BC. Then, if the major carrier enters route BC, it has a large scheduling effect. On the contrary, if it enters route AC, its scheduling effect becomes somewhat weak due to competition in market *AC*.[6] Here, noting that the larger scheduling effect brings about larger profits, the major carrier enters route *BC*. Thus, the major carrier chooses the entry route to seek competitive advantage.

10.6.2 The Case that $\beta \geq 0.853$

In this case, if the major carrier enters route *BC*, the regional carrier also enters route *BC*; if the major carrier enters route *AC*, the regional carrier also enters route *AC*. Therefore, by comparing π_M^1 with π_M^4, we obtain Lemma 10.8.

Lemma 10.8. *The major carrier enters route BC in the range within which β is larger than* 0.853.

In this case, the regional carrier enters the same route as the major carrier. Therefore, the major carrier cannot achieve competitive advantage throughout the larger scheduling effect even when it enters route *AC* or *BC*. In the following, the major carrier is unwilling to compete with the regional carrier in the market that has a large potential number of passengers. In other words, the major carrier does not want to compete in market *AC*. The major carrier realizes that if it enters route *AC*, the regional carrier enters route *AC*; if it enters route *BC*, the regional carrier enters route *BC*. Therefore, to avoid competition in market *AC*, which has a large potential number of passengers, the major carrier enters route *BC*.

By summarizing Lemmas 10.5–10.8, we obtain Theorem 10.9, which is the subgame perfect Nash equilibrium of the entry route decision game.

Theorem 10.9. *The subgame perfect Nash equilibrium with regard to the entry route decision is that the major carrier enters route BC and the regional carrier enters route AC (i.e., Case 1) for $\beta \leq$* 0.853, *while both the major carrier and the regional carrier enter route BC (i.e., Case 2) for $\beta \geq$* 0.853.

Here, we discuss the hub location in the competitive situation. In Kawasaki [6], it was concluded that the monopolistic carrier does not always choose the hub airport to minimize the potential number of connecting passengers. This chapter demonstrated that when the major carrier and entrant carrier compete with each other, the former does not choose the hub airport to minimize the potential number of connecting passengers.

In the monopolistic situation, because the carrier wants to strengthen the scheduling effect, the hub airport is not chosen to minimize the potential number of connecting passengers. On the contrary, in the competitive situation, if the potential number of *BC* passengers is small, to retain competitive advantage, the major carrier does not choose the hub airport to minimize the potential number of connecting

[6]Recall that the regional carrier enters route *AC* to avoid the large scheduling effect of the major carrier when the latter enters route *AC*.

passengers. Moreover, if it is not small, to avoid competition in the market that has a larger potential number of passengers, the major carrier does not choose the hub airport to minimize the potential number of connecting passengers. Summarizing, although the objective is different for the monopolistic and competitive situations, the major carrier's strategy does not change in the competitive situation.

10.7 Social Welfare

In this section, we derive and compare social welfare in each case. Assuming that $K = 1$, the social welfare of each case becomes as follows:

$$SW_1 = \frac{7W^2(997 + 7\beta(-20 + \beta))}{9(25 - 7\beta)^2}, \tag{10.57}$$

$$SW_2 = \frac{W^2(38412 + \beta(-35197 + \beta(4805 + 2224\beta - 294\beta^2)))}{2(123 + \beta(-85 + 11\beta))^2}, \tag{10.58}$$

$$SW_3 = \frac{W^2(4016 + \beta(1038 - 79\beta)}{(60 - 11\beta)^2}, \tag{10.59}$$

$$SW_4 = \frac{W^2(360 - \beta(146 + \beta(85 + 3\beta(-14 + \beta))))}{(18 + \beta(-10 + \beta))^2}. \tag{10.60}$$

We first find that SW_3 is always smaller than SW_1. In the following, we compare the other levels of social welfare. As a result, we can obtain Fig. 10.2. As a result, we obtain Theorem 10.10.

Theorem 10.10. *When β is smaller than 0.9657711, the case that both the major carrier and the regional carrier enter route BC (i.e., Case 2) is socially preferable. When β is larger than 0.9657711, the case that the major carrier enters route AC and the regional carrier enters route BC (i.e., Case 4) is socially preferable.*

Theorem 10.10 argues that the regional carrier should always enter route BC, which has a smaller potential number of passengers, from the viewpoint of social

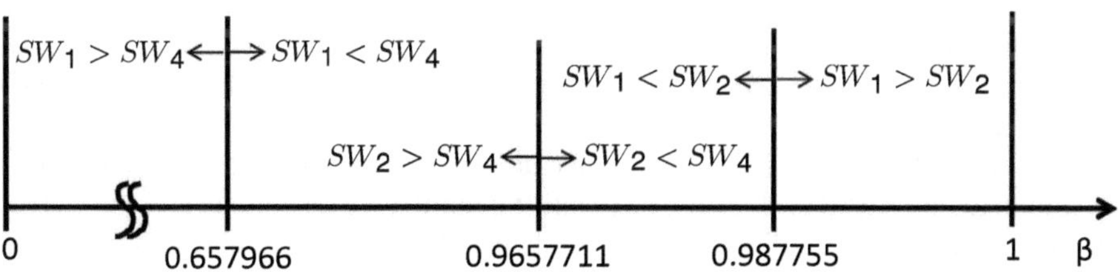

Fig. 10.2 Comparison result of social welfare

welfare. On the contrary, the socially preferable entry route of the major carrier depends on β. First, we discuss the case that β is larger than 0.9657711. In this range, when both carriers enter the same route, the flight frequency of the major carrier on its route becomes small. Consequently, the scheduling effect of the major carrier becomes small. Hence, the larger scheduling effect brings about larger demand and larger utility. Therefore, as the scheduling effect of the major carrier decreases, its demand decreases and the utility of using the major carrier also decreases. Consequently, the case that both carriers enter the same route is not socially preferable in this range.

Furthermore, the case that the major carrier enters route *BC* and the regional carrier enters route *AC* is also not socially preferable. In the market that has a greater potential number of passengers, by allowing the major carrier to operate monopolistically, the flight frequency of the major carrier increases. As a result, more passengers can enjoy the larger scheduling effect. If the major carrier enters route *BC* and the regional carrier enters route *AC*, the flight frequency of the major carrier becomes somewhat small due to the small potential demand of market *BC*, meaning no more passengers enjoy the larger scheduling effect. Consequently, the case that the major carrier enters route *AC* and the regional carrier enters route *BC* is socially preferable in this range.

On the contrary, in the range within which β is smaller than 0.9657711, the socially preferable case differs. In this range, because the potential number of passengers in the *BC* market is small, even when a passenger in market *BC* uses connecting services, the larger scheduling effect hardly occurs. Consequently, to bring about a larger scheduling effect, a passenger in market *AC* should use connecting services. On the contrary, if the major carrier and regional carrier compete with each other in market *AC*, demand for the major carrier decreases; thus, the flight frequency of the major carrier decreases, which decreases the major carrier's scheduling effect. Therefore, to avoid competition in market *AC*, the regional carrier should enter route *BC* from the viewpoint of social welfare.

10.8 Extension

The above analysis assumed that the per-seat cost is zero. However, according to Brueckner [2] and others, this cost is also important for expressing economies of density, which is an important characteristic in the airline industry. Therefore, following Brueckner [2], we introduce the per-seat cost and re-analyze each carrier's entry route problem.

Following Brueckner [2], this chapter denotes the per-seat cost as τ, which is common to both carriers. To satisfy a positive quantity, we assume that $0 \leq \tau \leq 1/3$. Then, when expressing the number of seats per flight as s_ℓ, the carrier's operating cost per flight is $C_\ell = K + \tau s_\ell$. Because airline ℓ flies f_ℓ times on one route, the total cost on one route becomes $f_\ell \times C_\ell = f_\ell K + \tau s_\ell f_\ell$. Here, because it is assumed that the load factor equals 100 %, the total number of passengers on one route always equals the total number of seats ($\equiv s_\ell \times f_\ell$). Therefore, each carrier's cost on one route can be expressed as $f_\ell K + \tau Q_\ell$, where Q_ℓ denotes the total number of passengers on one route.

From the above discussion, each carrier's profit function becomes as follows:

$$\pi_M = \beta_{ih}(p^M_{ih} - \tau)q^M_{ih} + \beta_{jh}(p^M_{jh} - \tau)q^M_{jh} + \beta_{ij}(p^M_{ij} - 2\tau)q^M_{ij} - (f^M_{ih} + f^M_{jh})K, \tag{10.61}$$

$$\pi_R = \beta_{mn}(p^R_{mn} - \tau)q^R_{mn} - f^R_{mn}K. \tag{10.62}$$

Here, $i, h, j \equiv A, B, C$ $(i \neq j \neq h)$, and $m, n \equiv A, B, C$ $(m \neq n)$. Additionally, $\beta_{AB} = \beta_{AC} = 1$ and $\beta_{BC} = \beta$. By solving each profit maximization problem by quantity and flight frequency as in Sect. 10.3, we obtain the profit-maximizing quantity and flight frequency. Here, we omit the detailed values.

Then, by using the profit-maximizing values, we obtain each case's profits. Here, we assume that $K = W = 1$. In the following, we denote Case s's profit of carrier ℓ as π^s_ℓ

$$\begin{aligned}\pi^1_M = &\{14(71 + 8 - 7\beta)\beta) + 4\tau(-866 + \beta(43 + 49\beta))\\ &+\tau^2(3946 + (-1049 + \beta)\beta)\}/3(25 - 7\beta)^2\end{aligned} \tag{10.63}$$

$$\pi^1_R = \frac{((13 - 7\beta) + \tau(11 + \beta))^2}{3(25 - 7\beta)^2}, \tag{10.64}$$

$$\begin{aligned}\pi^2_M = &\{\beta(-12275 + (37510 - 31211\tau)\tau) + \beta^3(-84 + (1058 - 1493\tau)\tau)\\ &+11\beta^4(-6 + \tau(8 + \tau)) + 738(15 + \tau(-44 + 35\tau))\\ &+\beta^2(3815 + \tau(-13152 + 12133\tau))\}/(123 + \beta(-85 + 11\beta))^2,\end{aligned} \tag{10.65}$$

$$\pi^2_R = \frac{\beta(4 - \beta)(17 + 11\beta(-1 + \tau) - 14\tau)^2}{(123 + \beta(-85 + 11\beta))^2}, \tag{10.66}$$

$$\pi^3_M = \frac{\begin{array}{c}1632(-1 + \tau)^2 - +2\beta^2(-2 + 3\tau)(-50 + 119\tau)\\ +4\beta(257 + 31\tau(-35 + 4\tau))\end{array}}{(60 - 11\beta)^2}, \tag{10.67}$$

$$\pi^3_R = \frac{27(4(1 - \tau) + \beta(-2 + 3\tau))^2}{(60 - 11\beta)^2}, \tag{10.68}$$

$$\begin{aligned}\pi^4_M = &\{432 - 4\beta(70 + \beta(3 + (-8 + \beta)\beta) - 864\tau + 4\beta(20 + \beta(104\\ &+\beta(-41 + 4\beta)))\tau + (432 + \beta(488 + \beta(-596 + 3(58 - 5\beta)\beta))\tau^2\}\\ &/((2(18 + (-10 + \beta)\beta)^2),\end{aligned} \tag{10.69}$$

$$\pi^4_R = \frac{\beta(4 - \beta)(2 + \beta(-4 + \tau) + \tau)^2}{(18 + (-10 + \beta)\beta)^2}. \tag{10.70}$$

The comparison results of π^1_R with π^2_R and of π^3_R with π^4_R are shown in Fig. 10.3.

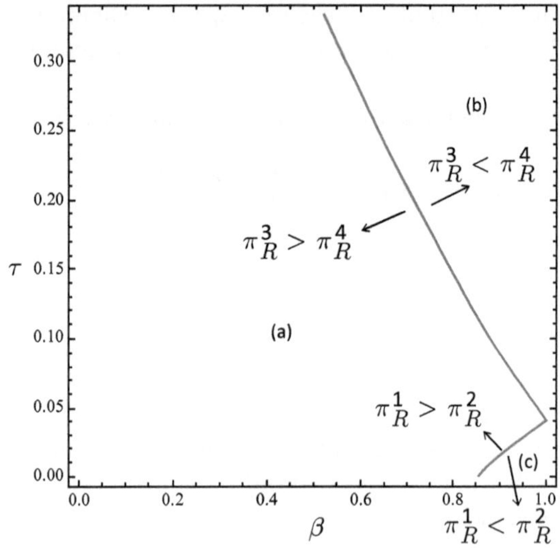

Fig. 10.3 The comparison results of π_R^1 with π_R^2 and of π_R^3 with π_R^4

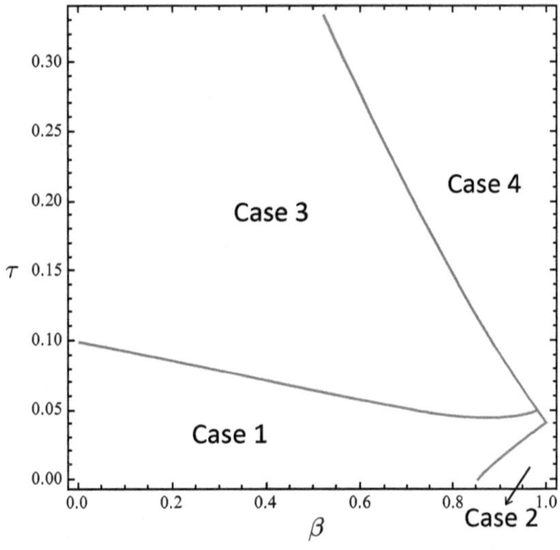

Fig. 10.4 Subgame perfect Nash equilibrium

Given these comparison results, we derive the major carrier's entry route. In range (a), we compare π_M^1 with π_M^3. As a result, we find that when τ is large (small), π_M^3 is larger (smaller) than π_M^1. In range (b), we compare π_M^1 with π_M^1 with π_M^4. As a result, we find that π_M^4 is always larger than π_M^1. In range (c), we compare π_M^2 with π_M^3. As a result, we find that π_M^2 is always larger than π_M^3. Consequently, we obtain Fig. 10.4, which denotes the subgame perfect Nash equilibrium of each range.

When τ is small, the result obtained in Sect. 10.6 now holds. However, as τ becomes large, the equilibrium drastically changes as follows. When introducing the per-seat cost τ, the major carrier does not want to increase the number of connecting passengers because these incur the per-seat cost twice. Actually, in range (a) in

Fig. 10.3, when τ is small, the major carrier enters route BC to increase the number of connecting passengers and the scheduling effect. However, as τ increases, the major carrier does not enter route BC, and alternatively enters route AC to decrease the number of connecting passengers. In range (b), even airline R does not want to increase costs. Consequently, if airline M enters route AC, airline R chooses to enter route BC to decrease costs. At the same time, when airline M enters route BC in this range, more passengers use connecting services. Consequently, to avoid more passengers using connecting services, airline M enters route AC even though the scheduling effect decreases.

10.9 Concluding Remarks

This chapter examined which routes (i.e., those having a large or a small potential number of passengers) major and entrant carriers enter as well as the socially preferable entry pattern. To address these problems, we assumed that three markets exist in this model and that the potential number of one market is smaller than that of the other two markets. Moreover, the incumbent carrier has already entered the market that has a greater potential number of passengers. Given this situation, each incumbent and entrant carrier chooses only one entry route. First, the incumbent carrier expects the entry route of the entrant carrier and chooses the entry route for the first time. Then, realizing the incumbent's entry route, the entrant carrier chooses its entry route. By considering this situation, this chapter derived the subgame perfect Nash equilibrium with regard to the entry route of each carrier.

A number of findings can be drawn. When the potential number of passengers in a market is large, both the major carrier and the entrant carrier enter the same route (i.e., the one that has a small potential number of passengers). When the potential number of passengers in its market is not large, the major carrier enters the route that has the small potential number of passengers and the entrant carrier enters the route that has the large potential number of passengers. This result can be interpreted as that the major carrier does not choose the hub airport to minimize the potential number of connecting passengers in a competitive situation.

From the viewpoint of social welfare, the following results were obtained. When the difference in the potential number of passengers between markets is not small, it is socially preferable for both the major and the regional carrier to enter the route that has a smaller potential number of passengers. When its difference is small, however, it is socially preferable for the regional carrier to enter the route that has a smaller potential number of passengers and the major carrier to enter the route that has a greater potential number of passengers.

Furthermore, by introducing the per-seat cost, we derived the subgame perfect Nash equilibrium. We found that if the per-seat cost is small, the same result as obtained earlier holds; however, if this cost becomes large, different results occur. Thus, to avoid an increase in operating costs, a major carrier does not choose the entry route to increase the number of connecting passengers.

Finally, we discuss the limitations of this chapter. First, it omitted the difference in operating costs between the major carrier and the entrant carrier. Recently, new carriers are mainly LCCs. Therefore, future research should discuss how this cost difference influences the results obtained here. Second, this chapter omitted the additional travel time cost for connecting passengers. Many studies of airline network formation argue that the additional travel time cost is also important for network formation. With regard to this shortcoming, this chapter also ignored the probability of adopting a point-to-point network. Assuming that there is no additional travel time cost meant that omitting the point-to-point network is rational. However, if an additional travel time cost is introduced, the point-to-point network should also be considered. Finally, this chapter assumed that the entrant carrier enters only one route. Future research might consider these important problems.

References

1. Bamberger, G. E., & Carlton, D. W. (2006). Predation and the entry and exit of low-fare carriers. In L. Darin (Ed.), *Advances in airline economics: Competition policy and antitrust* (Vol. 1, pp. 1–23). Boston: Elsevier.
2. Brueckner, J. K. (2004). Network structure and airline scheduling. *Journal of Industrial Economics, 52*, 291–312.
3. Brueckner, J. K., & Flores-Fillol, R. (2007). Airline schedule competition. *Review of Industrial Organization, 30*, 161–177.
4. Flores-Fillol, R. (2010). Congested hub. *Transportation Research Part B, 44*, 358–370.
5. Kawasaki, A. (2008). Network effects, heterogeneous time value, and network formation in the airline market. *Regional Science and Urban Economics, 38*, 388–403.
6. Kawasaki, A. (2012). Hub location with scheduling effects in a monopoly airline market. *Annals of Regional Science, 49*, 805–819.
7. Kawasaki, A., & Lin, M. H. (2013). Airline schedule competition and entry route choices of low-cost carriers. *Australian Economic Review, 52*, 97–114.
8. Lin, M. H., & Kawasaki, A. (2012). Where to enter in hub-spoke airline networks. *Papers in Regional Science, 91*, 419–437.
9. Oum, T. H., Zhang, A., & Zhang, Y. (1995). Airline network rivalry. *Canadian Journal of Economics, 28*, 836–857.

Chapter 11
R&D Policy and Political Corruption in a Growing Economy

Daisuke Ikazaki

11.1 Introduction

Simple growth models were described in Chaps. 4 and 5. The marginal product of capital must not converge to 0 in the long run to attain sustainable growth. Productivity improvement is necessary. Chapter 5 presented analysis of a simple endogenous growth model in which productivity improvement occurs within the model. We consider publicly financed R&D. Therefore, the role of the government is important. As described in Chap. 5, we presume that the government maximizes the social welfare, which is defined as the sum of the utility of households. In practice, many earlier studies of economic growth have assumed that a government maximizes social welfare when market failure occurs (Grossman and Helpman [8], Barro and Sala-i-Martin [4]). However, a government might be selfish or myopic in practice. Governments might carry out policies to please the present generation and leave a huge burden to future generations (e.g., the financial deficit of many countries). Powerful politicians might maximize the welfare of their constituents or major donors rather raising the level of national benefit. Therefore, policies that include sacrifices today to improve future conditions might not be pursued. Resource allocation to research activities or other activities undertaken to improve future conditions tends to be lower than the optimum.

In many countries, adapting industrial structures to changes in the economic environment might be determinants of sustainable growth. Industry structural change produces 'losers'. Therefore, old and cottage industries might shrink by such change. To prevent such industry structural change, some groups (firms or

---

D. Ikazaki (✉)
Faculty of Human Sciences and Design, Japan Women's University, 2-8-1 Mejirodai, Bunkyo-ku, Tokyo 1128681, Japan
e-mail: ikazaki@fc.jwu.ac.jp

T. Naito (ed.), *Sustainable Growth and Development in a Regional Economy*, New Frontiers in Regional Science: Asian Perspectives 13, DOI 10.1007/978-4-431-55294-9_11 industry organizations) might form interest groups and seek to influence government policies. However, the interlocking relations between government and interest groups might cause economic stagnation if such relations rule out the birth of new industries and protect old industries.

However, private sector agents (firms, industry organizations, or interest groups) might argue against instituting policies that reduce their profits. Therefore, they have incentives to make political donations to administrative officials, politicians, and bureaucrats if such donations induce the government to postpone or reject change in the industry structure. Grossman and Helpman [9] provide an important study of the role of interest groups. They construct a model in which interest groups affect trade policies (Grossman and Helpman [10]). Fredriksson [7] and Aidt [3] consider these points from the perspectives of environmental economists. They report that firms are opposed to environmental taxes because the introduction of such taxation tends to decrease their profits.

Productivity and per-capita income might stagnate in the long run. Collusive ties between politicians and businesses can postpone the change of industrial structure.

To elucidate these points, we present a simple overlapping generations model, Diamond's [6] OLG model, which incorporates the R&D sector and political corruption. Many earlier studies of an R&D-based growth model show that productivity in the research sector must be sufficiently high to attain sustainable growth (Grossman and Helpman [8]; Aghion and Howitt [2]). Therefore, our model can be regarded as an extension of the endogenous growth model because technological progress is the main engine for sustainable growth. However, we introduce a corrupt government to elucidate whether or not the collusive relations between government and firm or interest group induce different results. We show that high productivity in the R&D sector might be a necessary condition, but not a sufficient one.

A collusive relation between the public and private sectors might sacrifice future interests to improve conditions today. In that case, necessary resources are not devoted to the R&D sector and the economy piles up in the long run even if the productivity of the R&D sector is sufficiently high. The corruption engenders sluggish economic situations when the government enjoys considerable benefits from the political donations. We argue that even when the economy has the ability to attain sustainable growth, interlocking relations between government and interest groups might cause economic stagnation.

Hall and Jones [11] show that differences in output per worker across countries are fundamentally related to differences in 'social infrastructure' across countries. In their paper, social infrastructure is defined as 'the institutions and government policies that determine the economic environment within which individuals accumulate skills, and within which firms accumulate capital and produce output'. They conclude that countries with long-standing policies that are favorable to productivity produce much more output per worker. Corruption has negative impacts on economic activities if corruption tends to be negatively correlated with desirable social infrastructure. Actually, Lambsdorff [14] and Kurtzman et al. [13] show that per-capita income tends to be low in countries with higher levels of corruption. We attempt to construct a theoretical model that can explain the relation between the growth rate and corruption.

This chapter is organized as follows. Section 11.2 presents a review of the model of Chap. 5. Knowledge stock accumulates and productivity increases if a government levies taxes on the output and if tax revenue is devoted to the research sector. However, such tax policies prevent the economy from accumulating physical capital. Therefore, the government must consider the benefits and costs of a tax to seek desirable tax rates. In Chap. 5, no consideration was given to political donations or problems related to corruption. A government does not impose a tax in the first stage of development. If an economy develops to a considerable degree, then the government introduces a tax to engage in research activities that increase productivity. As Acemoglu, Aghion, and Zilibotti [1] have reported, an innovation-based strategy is important when the economy becomes highly developed. The long-run growth rate becomes positive if certain conditions are met. As in the general endogenous growth model (Grossman and Helpman [8]; Aghion and Howitt [2]), the sustainability of the economy depends on the research sector productivity.

In this chapter, problems related to political corruption are introduced. Interest groups make political donations to the government if such donations can increase their profits to a great extent. Government accepts political donations or bribes if the net benefit of taking political donations is positive. The economy might stagnate if the corrupt government accepts political donations and postpones the introduction of an innovation-based policy. In such a case, growth peters out in the long run even if the economy can achieve sustainable development.

11.2 Basic Endogenous Growth Model (Model of Chapter 5)

In this chapter, we extend the model of Chap. 5 to analyze the relation between political corruption and economic growth. Therefore, at the first part of this chapter, we briefly describe the model of Chap. 5 again.

In Chap. 5, we assumed that the production function of the final good is given as

$$Y_t = K_t^{\alpha}(A_t L_t)^{1-\alpha}, \tag{11.1}$$

where Y_t is the aggregate output,[1] A_t denotes the productivity (knowledge stock), K_t represents the capital stock, and L_t signifies the labor input. It is also assumed that $0 < \alpha < 1$. Capital depreciates fully during the production process. Firms take the values of A_t as given. From the firms' profit maximization, we can obtain $(1 + r_t)K_t = (1 - \tau_t)\alpha Y_t$ and $w_t = (1 - \tau_t)(1 - \alpha)Y_t$. $L_t = 1$ for all t because the labor market clears at every moment and the amount of labor is given as 1.

[1] Subscript t represents the level in period t throughout this chapter.

Each individual can work only during the first period of life. In old age, they consume their savings that they prepared when they are young. The expected utility of each in generation t is given as

$$U_t = \log c_{t+1}, \tag{11.2}$$

where $c_{t+1} = (1 + r_{t+1})w_t$.

Governments use tax revenue $\tau_t Y_t$ for R&D activities that increase productivity. We assume that the dynamic behavior of productivity A_t is specified as

$$A_{t+1} = A_t + \beta \tau_t Y_t, \tag{11.3}$$

where β ($\beta > 0$) is the productivity parameter of R&D sector. It is assumed that one unit of input can increase β units of knowledge stock. The government policies are assumed to determine the dynamic behavior of productivity.

The government must set a tax rate to maximize $\theta U_{t-1} + U_t$, where θ is the relative weight the politicians attach to the utility of elderly people.

We showed in Chap. 5 that the tax rate will be positive if and only if knowledge stock is scarce compared with capital stock. More precisely, the optimal tax rate (τ_t) becomes

$$\tau_t = \frac{(1-\alpha)\beta k_t^{\alpha} - (\alpha + \theta)}{(1+\theta)\beta k_t^{\alpha}} \equiv \tau^* \tag{11.4}$$

if $\frac{K_t}{A_t} \equiv k_t > k_\delta \equiv \left(\frac{\alpha+\theta}{\beta(1-\alpha)}\right)^{\frac{1}{\alpha}}$. Otherwise, the tax rate is 0.

The dynamic behavior of k_t is shown as

$$k_{t+1} = (1-\alpha)k_t^{\alpha} \equiv f(k_t) \tag{11.5}$$

if $k_t < k_\delta$ and $\tau_t = 0$. However, if $k_t > k_\delta$ and $\tau_t = \tau^*$, then

$$k_{t+1} = \frac{\alpha + \theta}{\beta} = f(k_\delta) \equiv k^2. \tag{11.6}$$

For the equations above, k_{t+1} is constant for all k_t $(> k_\delta)$. It is assumed that the initial value of k_t (which is written as k_0) is low and $k_0 < k_\delta$. In period 0, elderly people have K_0 units of assets.

Presuming that $k_\delta > f(k_\delta)$, it is equivalent to

$$1 - \alpha < \left(\frac{\alpha + \theta}{\beta}\right)^{1-\alpha}.$$

Then, the dynamic behavior of k_t is depicted in Fig. 11.1. As the figure shows, convergence to the unique steady state $k^1 \equiv (1-\alpha)^{\frac{1}{1-\alpha}}$ is monotonic. Furthermore,

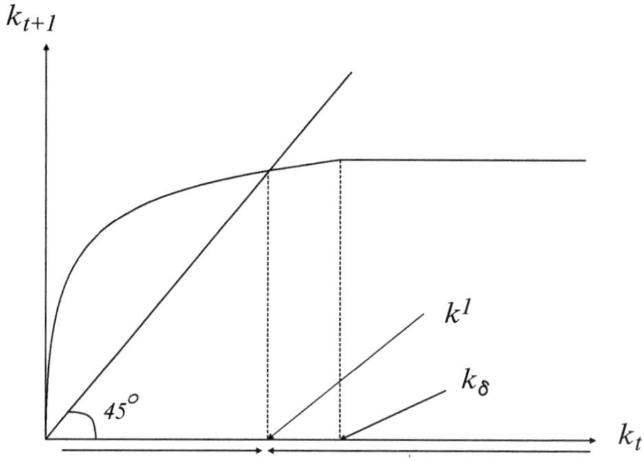

Fig. 11.1 The dynamic behavior of k_t ($k_\delta > f(k_\delta)$)

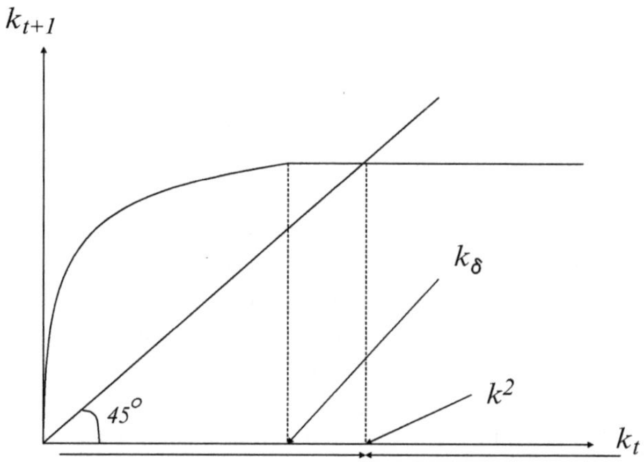

Fig. 11.2 The dynamic behavior of k_t ($k_\delta < f(k_\delta)$)

K_t, A_t, and Y_t grow at the same rate in the steady state because k_t becomes constant in the steady state. Because $k_t < k_\delta$ for all t, $\tau_t = 0$ and $A_t = A_0$ for all t. Then Y_t, K_t and A_t becomes constant in the steady state. This situation is similar to that of the typical neoclassical growth model. Productivity or knowledge stock does not change over time because the marginal product of capital declines over time. Therefore, the long-run growth rate becomes 0.

If $f(k_\delta) > k_\delta$ and $1 - \alpha > \left(\frac{\alpha+\theta}{\beta}\right)^{1-\alpha}$, then we can draw relations between k_t and k_{t+1} as shown in Fig. 11.2. In the first stage of the development, the tax rate is 0 because physical capital is rarely offered in markets and k_t is less than k_δ. However, k_t becomes greater than k_δ eventually. Subsequently, it converges to its steady state level k_2, where $k^2 = f(k_\delta)$.

If we designate the growth rates of Y_t, K_t, and A_t as g, then Eqs. (11.3) and (11.4) imply that

$$g = \frac{\alpha+\theta}{1+\theta}\left((1-\alpha)\left(\frac{\beta}{\alpha+\theta}\right)^{1-\alpha} - 1\right) \tag{11.7}$$

in the steady state. Growth rates become positive ($g > 0$) when $k_\delta < f(k_\delta)$. The growth rate is higher when the productivity of R&D sector is high (higher β); also, the political power of elderly people is weak (lower θ). These are outlines of Chap. 5. From the next section, we will extend the model we introduced into Chap. 5.

11.3 Political Corruption

In this section, we introduce an interest group that makes political donations to head off the introduction of a tax. Here, we assume that those who have financial assets (capital owners) can form an interest group and influence government policies. Consequently, only the elderly generation can donate money to the government.[2] In general, labor unions or younger generations can donate money to the government to increase future productivity. In this case, the long-run growth rate does not change. We specifically examine the case in which only the elderly generation (owners of capital) can give political contributions because we would like to examine specifically whether or not the collusive relations between government and interest groups affect economic performance.

For the analyses presented in this section, we define the utility of the government (V_t^G) as

$$V_t^G = U^G(M_t, Y_t) + (\alpha+\theta)\log(1-\tau_t) + (1-\alpha)\log[1+\beta\tau_t k_t^\alpha], \tag{11.8}$$

where M_t stands for the donation and $U^G(M_t, Y_t)$ signifies the net benefit of such a donation. We assume that $U^G(0, Y_t) = 0$ for all Y_t. In Chap. 5 and the previous part of this chapter, we do not consider political donations (i.e., $M_t = 0$). If $M_t = 0$, then Eq. (11.8) is equivalent to the objective function that we consider in Chap. 5. It is also assumed that a risk of taking a donation to forge a collusive relation exists between interest groups and that such a government might not be supported by voters. We assume that the risk of taking a donation increases with Y_t. Economic development increases the government's risk of taking a donation: we assume that $\frac{\partial U^G}{\partial M} > 0$ and $\frac{\partial U^G}{\partial Y} < 0$. The donation might be regarded as a

[2] Acemoglu, Aghion, Zilibotti et al. [1] consider the case in which older low-skilled managers and capitalists entered into a collusive agreement.

bribe. In many countries, the bribe is illegal, in principle. Bribery scandals might engender a change of government. The government officials might be arrested for corruption. As described in this paper, we assume that the voters tend to claim rectitude in government as the economy develops: a non-corrupt government is a 'superior good'.

Lambsdorff [14] considered the correlation between per-capita GDP and the corruption perceptions index (CPI), which is published by Transparency International, a non-governmental organization that monitors corporate and political corruption in international development. Corruption is defined as the abuse of entrusted power for private gain. A higher score of the index indicates less corruption. The highest (lowest) value is defined as 10 (0). He showed that an improvement in the CPI by one point increases average income by 4 % because appropriate institutions increase capital inflows and raise productivity.[3]

That finding implies that rich countries tend to have cleaner government, fair institutions, and appropriate laws. The risk of taking political donations might increase with per-capita income because citizens in developed countries call for the rectitude of government. To reflect this point, we assume that the net benefit of a political donation increases with M_t and decreases with Y_t. For this chapter, we assume that $U^G(M_t, Y_t) \equiv \gamma \frac{M_t}{Y_t}$.

When $k_t < k_\delta$, the tax rate is 0. Therefore, the interest groups need not make a donation. If $k_t > k_\delta$ and no political corruption exists ($M_t = 0$), then the tax rate is given as $\tau_t = \tau_t^*$. Under these circumstances, the utility of the government (V_t^{G*}) can be written as

$$V_t^{G*} = (\alpha + \theta)\log(1 - \tau_t^*) + (1 - \alpha)\log[1 + \beta\tau_t^* k_t^\alpha]. \tag{11.9}$$

Next, we consider a case in which the interest group makes a donation that prevents the government from introducing the tax. It is assumed that the government postpones the enforcement of tax policies ($\tau_t = 0$) if it takes a donation. If the government takes a donation, then $\tau_t = 0$. Then, Eq. (11.8) implies that its utility (V_t^{GM}) is given as

$$V_t^{GM} = \gamma \frac{M_t}{Y_t}. \tag{11.10}$$

The donation level must be high to satisfy $V_t^{G*} < V_t^{GM}$ because the government will spurn a donation if the donation level is low and $V_t^{G*} > V_t^{GM}$. If $V_t^{G*} < \gamma \frac{M_t}{Y_t}$, then τ_t becomes 0 rather than τ_t^* because of the donation. As described in this paper, we specifically examine two cases in which $\tau_t = \tau_t^*$ and $\tau_t = 0$. Generally speaking, an interior solution of τ_t might be considered, although we will show that interesting

[3] Kurtzman et al. [13] use the opacity index (another index that considers the institutions of the economy) and derive similar results.

conclusions can be derived even in this simplest case. However, this simple case is introduced first because such generalization does not affect any further results.

We can rewrite V_t^{G*} as a function of k_t as

$$V_t^{G*} = h(k_t) = (1+\theta)\log(1+\beta k_t^{\alpha}) - (\alpha+\theta)\log k_t^{\alpha} + \Gamma, \tag{11.11}$$

where $\Gamma \equiv \log \frac{(\alpha+\theta)^{\alpha+\theta}(1-\alpha)^{1-\alpha}}{(1+\theta)^{1+\theta}\beta^{\alpha+\theta}}$. It is possible to show that $h'(k_t) > 0$ if $k_t > k_\delta$ and $h'(k_\delta) = 0$. It is also noteworthy that $\lim_{k_t \to \infty} h(k_t) = \infty$.

The interest group has no incentive to increase the donation if $\tau_t = 0$. Therefore, V_t^{G*} must be equal to V_t^{GM} in equilibrium. Consequently, we obtain

$$M_t^* = \frac{h(k_t)Y_t}{\gamma} \tag{11.12}$$

in equilibrium when political corruption exists. Here, M_t^* denotes the necessary funds for a political donation. From Eq. (11.12), it is known that the necessary funding for a political donation M_t depends on the values of Y_t and k_t. The necessary donation to reduce the tax rate is higher when the capital–knowledge stock ratio is high (higher k_t), the aggregate output in the economy is high (higher Y_t), and the government is less sensitive to donations (lower γ).

Next, we consider the case in which an interest group does not make a donation. The tax rate set by the government is τ_t^*. We can rewrite τ_t^* as a function of k_t.

$$\tau_t^*(k_t) = \frac{(1-\alpha)\beta k_t^{\alpha} - (\alpha+\theta)}{(1+\theta)\beta k_t^{\alpha}}, \tag{11.13}$$

where $\frac{\partial \tau_t^*}{\partial k_t} > 0$, $\frac{\partial^2 \tau_t^*}{\partial k_t^2} < 0$, $\tau_t^*(k_\delta) = 0$, and $\lim_{k_t \to \infty} \tau_t^*(k_t) = \frac{1-\alpha}{1+\theta}$.

The consumption level of elderly people becomes $(1-\tau_t^*)\alpha Y_t$ if no donation exists. If an interest group makes a donation, then the consumption level of elderly people becomes $\alpha Y_t - M_t^*$. Therefore, an interest group makes a donation and the government reduces the tax rate when $\alpha\tau_t^*(k_t) > \frac{h(k_t)}{\gamma} = \frac{M_t}{Y_t}$. From Eq. (11.13) and the definition of $h(k_t)$, we can define a unique k_λ that sat isfies $\alpha\tau_t^*(k_\lambda) = \frac{h(k_\lambda)}{\gamma}$, where $k_\delta < k_\lambda$. k_λ is positively correlated with γ. When $k_\delta < k_t < k_\lambda$, then the tax rate becomes 0 because $\alpha\tau_t^*(k_t) > \frac{h(k_t)}{\gamma}$. When $k_\lambda < k_t$, then the tax rate becomes τ^* because $\alpha\tau_t^*(k_t) < \frac{h(k_t)}{\gamma}$ (see Fig. 11.3).

Therefore, a corrupt system is not supported if the economy is highly developed. Our results derived here are natural because corruption induced by government rent-seeking behavior is apparently more widespread in developing countries than in developed countries (see the dataset of indices of Business International [5]).[4] Then we obtain the following proposition:

[4]Krueger [12] shows that the Indian government recorded more than 7 % of the GNP used for rent seeking behavior in 1964.

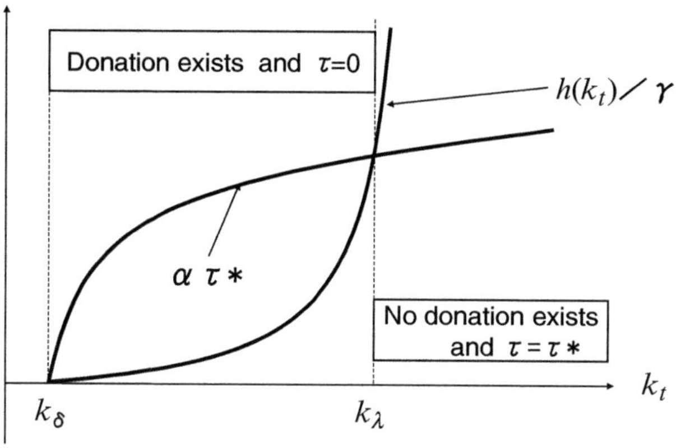

Fig. 11.3 The relationship between $h(k_t)/\gamma$ and $\alpha\tau^*$

Theorem 11.1. *(1) The tax rate becomes* $\tau_t = 0$ *when* $k_t < k_\lambda$*, and* $\tau_t = \tau_t^*$ *when* $k_t > k_\lambda$*. The government accepts (spurns) a political donation if* $k_\delta < k_t < k_\lambda (k_t > k_\lambda)$.
(2) k_λ *is an increasing function of* γ.

Next, we will consider how a political donation affects the dynamics. We are interested in whether or not the economy stagnates because of political corruption. Therefore, we specifically examine the case in which $f(k_\delta) > k_\delta$. In this case, the relation between k_t and k_{t+1} is depicted as Fig. 11.2. Growth is sustainable if the interest group does not make a donation to the government.

If we consider the donation and define $k_{t+1} = \psi(k_t)$, then we can express the function $\psi(k_t)$ as

$$\psi(k_t) = \begin{cases} f(k_t) & \text{if} \quad k_t < k_\lambda, \\ k_2 & \text{if} \quad k_t \geq k_\lambda. \end{cases} \tag{11.14}$$

It is assumed that the government spurns a political donation if $V_t^{G^*} = V_t^{GM}$. Function $\psi(k_t)$ is not continuous at k_λ because $f(k_\lambda) \neq k_2$ (note that $f(k_\lambda) > k_2$).

First, we consider the case in which $k_\delta < k_\lambda < k^2$, which implies $k_\lambda < f(k_\lambda)$. The government introduces the tax to engage in R&D if k_t becomes greater than k_λ. The tax rate remains zero when $k_\delta < k_t < k_\lambda$, although it is expected to be positive (if no donation exists, then the tax rate is given as τ^* when $k_t > k_\delta$). The connections to the government in power induce change in policy when $k_\delta < k_t < k_\lambda$. The value of k_t converges to k^2 in the long run (see Fig. 11.4). The steady state does not change by political corruption, although corruption changes the transitional dynamics to the steady state. Furthermore, Y_t, K_t, and A_t grow at the same rate: g. This case arises when the government is virtuous (smaller γ).

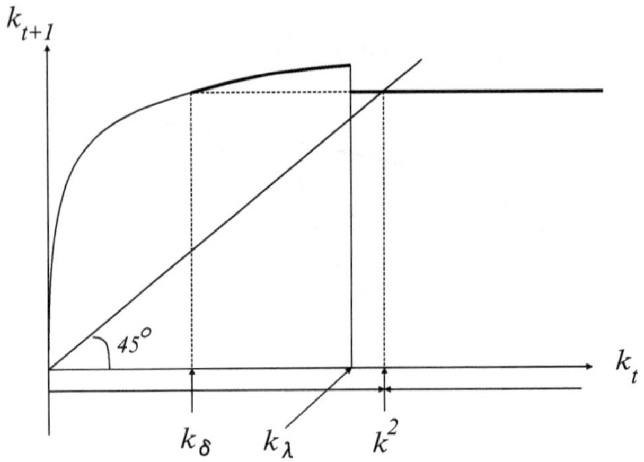

Fig. 11.4 The dynamic behavior of k_t ($k_\delta < k_\lambda < k^2$)

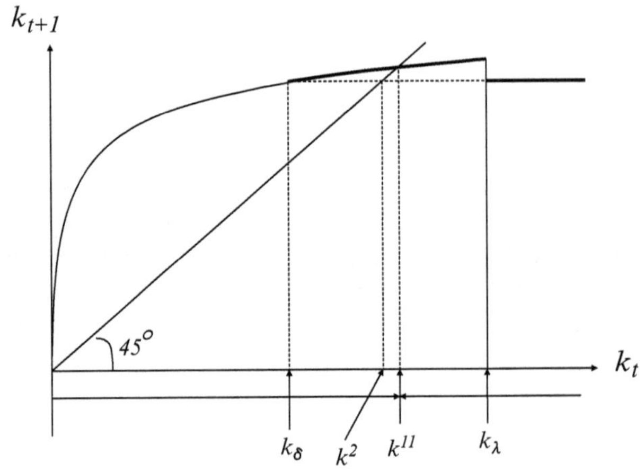

Fig. 11.5 The dynamic behavior of k_t ($k_\delta < k^2 < k_\lambda$ and $k_\lambda > f(k_\lambda)$)

Next, presuming that $k_\delta < k^2 < k_\lambda$ and $k_\lambda > f(k_\lambda)$, then the economy converges to k_2 and the growth rate becomes positive (this rate is given by g) if no political corruption exists. From Fig. 11.5, we know that the economy converges to the steady state k^{11} because of political donations that draw down policy change. In this case, $\tau_t = 0$ for all t. The growth rates of Y_t, K_t, and A_t become 0 for all t if the steady state is given as $k_t = k^{11}$. The powerful combination of money and politics can alter the result dramatically. This case arises when the government is greedy (higher γ).

Finally, we will consider the case in which $k_\delta < k^2 < k_\lambda$ and $k_\lambda < f(k_\lambda)$. This case is depicted in Figs. 11.6 and 11.7. Let T be the first period in which the capital–knowledge stock ratio exceeds k_λ. It follows that $k_t < k_\lambda$ for all $t \leq T$ and $k_T > k_\lambda$ in period T. In this case, it can be shown that $k_{T+1} = k^2$ and $k_{T+2} = f(k^2)$.

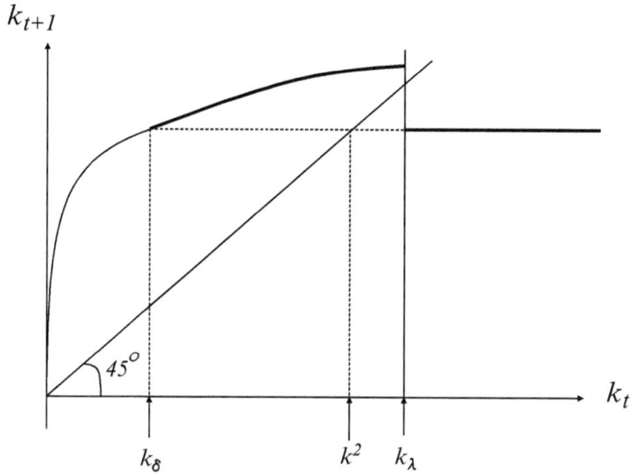

Fig. 11.6 The dynamic behavior of k_t ($k_\delta < k^2 < k_\lambda$ and $k_\lambda < f(k_\lambda)$)

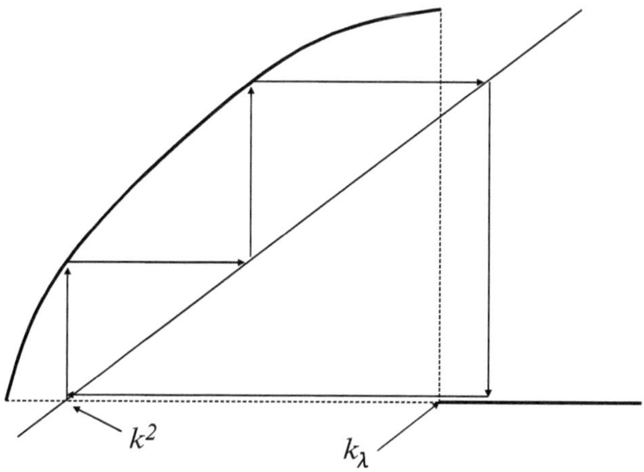

Fig. 11.7 Enlarged view of Fig. 11.6

Then k_t exceeds k_λ again in the near future. We assume that k_{T+n} exceeds k_λ in period $T + n$, which implies $k_{T+n} > k_\lambda$ in period $T + n$ and $k_{t'} < k_\lambda$ in period t' $(T + 2 < t' < T + n)$, where n is a natural number and $n > 2$. Then, we obtain $k_{T+n+1} = k^2$ and $k_{T+n+2} = f(k^2)$. In period $T+2n$, k_t becomes larger than k_λ again, and $k_{T+2n+1} = k^2$ and $k_{T+2n+2} = f(k^2)$ must hold: this system exhibits a cycle of period n. The capital – knowledge stock ratio k_t moves through cycles, perpetually moving back and forth between two phases. One phase is characterized by $k_t < k_\lambda$; the tax rate is zero. The other phase is characterized by $k_t > k_\lambda$; the tax rate is positive. The latter phase appears when $t = T,\ T + n,\ T + 2n \ldots$, where T and n are defined as explained above. Otherwise the former phase appears.

Here, n is positively related with γ because k_λ is an increasing function of γ (From Figs. 11.5 and 11.6, it is readily apparent that n is positively related with k_λ). The possibility of achieving sustainable growth decreases with n because R&D is not conducted when $k_t < k_\lambda$.

Similar discussions are given by Matsuyama [15]. He also presents possibilities of cycles. In that model, one phase is characterized by higher investment and no innovation. The other phase is characterized by lower investment and high innovation. The economy might achieve sustainable growth through cycles, perpetually moving back and forth between two phases. However, Matsuyama did not examine the political problems.

These three cases imply that the economy tends to stagnate if k_λ is large. In fact, k_λ is positively correlated with γ. A high probability exists that the corruption results in sluggish economic situations if the marginal benefit of the donation is high and the government enjoys considerable benefits from the donation. Consequently, we can obtain the following proposition.

Theorem 11.2. *(1) Presuming that $k_\delta < k_\lambda < k^2$, then the donation changes the transitional dynamics. However, the steady state is unaffected by political corruption. The economy converges to the steady state k^2. Per-capita income as well as physical capital and knowledge stock increase in the steady state and the growth rate of each variable is given as g.*

(2) Presuming that $k_\delta < k^2 < k_\lambda$ and $k_\lambda > f(k_\lambda)$, then the economy comes at a steady state before the tax is introduced. The growth rates of per-capita income, physical capital, and knowledge stock are 0 (the economy stagnates in the long run) even if the economy has the ability to attain sustainable growth.

(3) Presuming that $k_\delta < k^2 < k_\lambda$ and $k_\lambda < f(k_\lambda)$, then this system exhibits a cycle of period n where n is a natural number: stable equilibrium loses its stability and a period n cycle appears because of the political corruption.

(4) There exists $\hat{\gamma}$ such that the growth rate in the steady state becomes positive if $\gamma < \hat{\gamma}$. It becomes 0 if $\gamma \geq \hat{\gamma}$.

Presuming that two economies are homogeneous, and that the only difference is that they have different values of γ, we designate the γ of country i ($i = 1, 2$) as γ_i We assume that $\gamma_1 > \hat{\gamma} > \gamma_2$ (the government of country 2 is cleaner than that of country 1). Country 2 might grow unboundedly, although the growth rate of country 1 converges to 0 if so. Uncorrupt government might be crucial for sustainable growth.

11.4 Concluding Remarks

In the first part of this chapter, we review the model of Chap. 5 again. The government is short-lived and short-sighted and cares about the utilities of the currently living voters. It does not concern itself with the utility of unborn generations. In the first stage of development, the government does not impose a tax and employs a capital-accumulation-based strategy. In this stage, the knowledge stock level is constant because research activity is not conducted. If the research sector is not productive and the elderly citizens' political power is strong, then the tax rate is always zero and the government employs a capital accumulation strategy perpetually. The economy does not move into the second stage of development.

Presuming that the research sector is productive and that the elderly people's political power is low, then government employs an innovation-based strategy as the economy becomes highly developed. The growth rate in the steady state is positive if and only if strategic change takes place appropriately.

Next, we extended the model of Chap. 5. Politico-economic problems were integrated into the model because many preceding studies related to endogenous growth theory disregard sufficient consideration of political problems. We analyze the case in which a government accepts political donations and postpones the introduction of a tax to engage in research activities (innovation-based strategy). We assume that capital owners can put together an interest group and can make a political donation to the government. This paper shows that the interlocking relations between the government and interest groups can delay the innovation-based strategy. If the government is more corrupt than some critical level, then the economy does not adopt a desirable policy in the long run. The growth rate declines to zero, even if the economy has the ability to attain sustainable growth. Political corruption engenders economic stagnation. Therefore, preventing politicians' or government officials' unfair meddling in government affairs might be necessary to achieve sustainable growth.

References

1. Acemoglu, D., Aghion, P., & Zilibotti, F. (2006). Distance to frontier, selection, and economic growth. *Journal of the European Economic Association, 4*(1), 37–74.
2. Aghion, P., & Howitt, P. (1992). A model of growth through creative destruction. *Econometrica, 60*(2), 323–351.
3. Aidt, T. S. (1998). Political internalization of economic externalities and environmental policy. *Journal of Public Economics, 69*(1), 1–16.
4. Barro, R. J., & Sala-i-Martin, X. (2003). *Economic growth* (2nd ed.). Cambridge: MIT.
5. Business International Corporation. (1984). *Managing and evaluating country risk assessment*. New York: Business International Corporation.
6. Diamond, P. A. (1965). National debt in a neoclassical growth model. *American Economic Review, 55*(5), 1126–1150.
7. Fredriksson, P. G. (1997). The political economy of pollution taxes in a small open economy. *Journal of Environmental Economics and Management, 33*(1), 44–58.
8. Grossman G. M., & Helpman, E. (1991). *Innovation and growth in the global economy*. Cambridge: MIT.
9. Grossman G. M., & Helpman, E. (1994). Protections for sale. *American Economic Review, 84*(4), 833–850.
10. Grossman G. M., & Helpman, E. (2001). *Special interest politics*. Cambridge: MIT.
11. Hall, R. E., & Jones, C. I. (1999). Why do some countries produce so much more output per worker than others. *Quarterly Journal of Economics, 114*(1), 83–116.

12. Krueger, A. (1990). *Perspectives on trade and development*. Chicago: University of Chicago Press.
13. Kurtzman, J., Yago, G., & Phumiwasana, T. (2004). *The global costs of opacity: Measuring business and investment risk worldwide*. MIT sloan management review.
14. Lambsdorff, J. G. (2007). *The institutional economics of corruption and reform: Theory, evidence and policy*. Cambridge: Cambridge University Press.
15. Matsuyama, K. (1999). Growing through cycles. *Econometrica, 67*(2), 335–348.

Chapter 12
Fertility, Costs for Children and Public Policy

Tatsuya Omori

Population growth is one of factors to affect the economic growth. Such growth affects not only economic growth but also labour supply. Many developed countries face the population declining. For example, Japan is one of the most declining country where the number of population is estimated about 128 million at 2010 and will be estimated around 99 million at 2046. (National Institute of Population and Social Security Research of Japan (2013).)[1] Total fertility rate of Japan had been 3.5 at 1950 but was 1.43 at 2014 (Cabinet office of Japan) as in Fig. 12.1.[2] Both population and total fertility rate will make the demographic change and affect the labour supply, tax revenues and social security systems. Then, these changes indirectly influence economic growth more.

According to Lapan and Enders [21] and Cabinet Office of Japan [6], the reasons to decrease the fertility are summarised as follows. First, the number of people who gets married later in life and not get married increase. Second, there are cost to raise children. Such costs include the opportunity cost for labour supply instead of caring for children.

Whether parents have the children or not depends on not only the utility from having children but also the raising cost including decreasing wage income (opportunity cost) because the raising children makes parents work less. When such decreasing income is one of reason to decrease fertility, government provides public

---

[1]See http://www.ipss.go.jp/site-ad/index_english/esuikei/gh2401e.asp

[2]See http://www8.cao.go.jp/shoushi/shoushika/whitepaper/index.html (in Japanese).

T. Omori (✉)
School of Business and Public Policies, Chukyo University, 101-2 Yagoto Honmachi, Showa-ku, Nagoya city, Aichi 4668666, Japan
e-mail: tomori@mecl.chukyo-u.ac.jp

T. Naito (ed.), *Sustainable Growth and Development in a Regional Economy*, New Frontiers in Regional Science: Asian Perspectives 13,
DOI 10.1007/978-4-431-55294-9_12

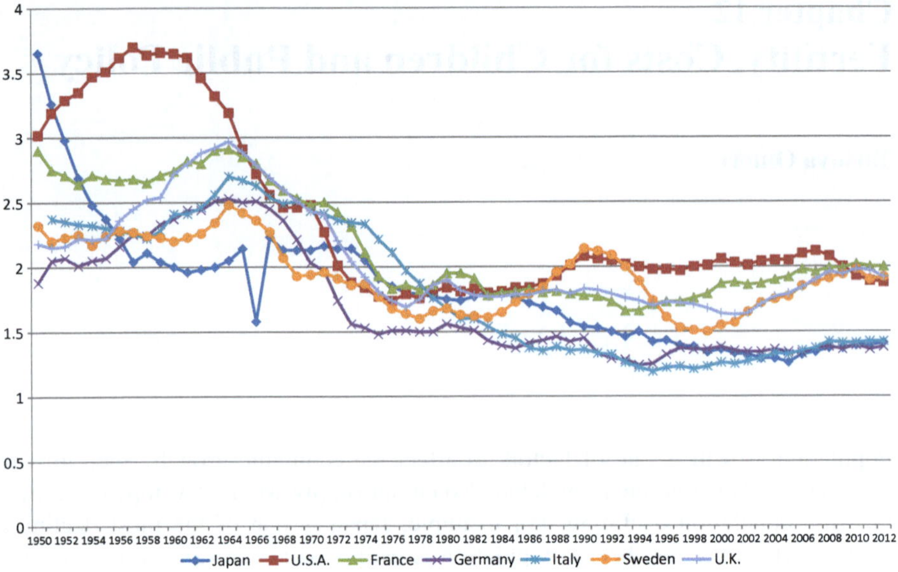

Fig. 12.1 Total fertility rate (Source: Declining birthrate white paper of 2015 Japan (Cabinet office of Japan))

support for children to compensate for such opportunity cost. For example, we have public day care centre which public sector raise children while parents go to work. More public day care centre makes parents work more and gives them the incentive to have more children.

Zhang and Zhang [37], Wigger [34] and others analyse how public policy affects economic growth through fertility change in a model with parents' raising time. Zhang and Zhang [37] examine the relationships between the incentive to have children and social security in the endogenous growth model and reveal that increasing tax for social security worsens economic growth. Similar to Zhang and Zhang [37], Wigger [34] examines public pension and fertility when children give gifts to parents at the retirement. However, in these models, public policy which decreases the opportunity cost to raising children is not discussed.

For such opportunity cost, government can give public subsidy for children to parents. Government compensates parents for the opportunity cost (decreasing wage income due to the raising). Apps and Rees [1] explain how taxation and public child support influence the inverse relationship between female labour supply and fertility. Groezen, Leers and Meijdam [17], Zhang and Zhang [40], and Hirazawa and Yakita [19] examine the relationships between public pension and public subsidy for children in a model with introducing the number of children into the utility function. However, these literatures do not take consideration that public supports compensate for the opportunity cost and do not discuss how such policy affect economic growth and fertility.

The purpose of first half of this chapter is to examine how allocation between public support for children and public subsidy for children affects fertility and economic growth in a model with the decision on having children and opportunity cost for raising children.[3] In the literature, public subsidy is provided by cash and public support is in-kind. There are discussions on cash versus in-kind (Blackorby and Donaldson [5], Munro [23], and Gahvari [12]). However, based on the income redistribution policy, they discussed cash versus in-kind. Blackorby and Donaldson [5] examine the Pareto efficiency between them when government has the imperfect information. Munro [23] and Gahvari [12] examine the effects of them on social security through labour-leisure choice. Furthermore, although these models are static framework and few discussion in the dynamic framework, our model is developed in the dynamic framework.

12.1 Public Support for Children and Public Subsidy for Children

Based on the overlapping generations model developed by Samuelson [30] and Diamond [9], we suppose that identical and perfect foresight consumers, firms and government are in the one good closed economy. For one period, there are three generations; the young generation, the working generation and the retirement generation. The government provides public support for children and public subsidy for children. Population of working generation at the initial period is normalised to one but the growth rate of population is determined endogenously.

12.1.1 Consumers

The consumers live for three period: the young period, the working period and the retirement period. At the young period, consumers are raised by the parents and do not do any decision makings. At the working period, they allocate one unit time between raising children and working. The wage income expends for consumption, saving and the wage income tax.[4] In this model, we assume away the bequest. At the retirement period, they do the consumption financed by saving and that interest.

We call the working generation at period t as generation t. The utility for representative consumer of generation t depends on the consumptions at the working

[3] In the first half of this chapter, our discussion is based on Omori [24, 25].

[4] The consumption include their children consumption.

period and the retirement period and the number of children.[5] We specialise the utility for representative consumer of generation t as

$$U^t = U\left(c_t^t,\ c_{t+1}^t,\ n_{t+1}\right) = \ln c_t^t + \beta \ln c_{t+1}^t + \epsilon \ln\left(1 + n_{t+1}\right), \tag{12.1}$$

where c_t^t and c_{t+1}^t are consumption at the working period and the retirement period of generation t, respectively, and n_{t+1} is the number of children, β is the subjective discount factor, and ϵ is the parameter which shows the preference level to children. For the simplicity, we assume that parents get the utility from not n_{t+1} but $1+n_{t+1}$.[6]

When the population of working generation at period t is shown by N_t, population at period $t+1$ is $N_{t+1} = (1+n_{t+1})N_t$.

We assume that the raising cost is equal to the raising time at period t, h_t and h_t depends on the number of children and public support for children. That is,

$$h_t = h_t(n_{t+1}, G_{p,t}),$$

where $G_{p,t}$ is public support for children per generation t (parents of generation $t+1$) at period t.[7]

The budget constraint for the working period of generation t is

$$c_t^t + S_t = (1-\tau)\left[1 - h_t(n_{t+1}, G_{p,t})\right] W_t + (1+n_{t+1})G_{s,t}, \tag{12.2}$$

and that of the retirement period of generation t is

$$c_{t+1}^t = \left(1 + r_{t+1}\right) S_t, \tag{12.3}$$

where S_t is saving at period t, τ is the wage income tax rate, W_t is the wage rate per time at period t, $G_{s,t}$ is the public subsidy for one child at period t. A representative agent of generation t chooses consumption at the working period, saving and the number of children to maximise his utility (12.1) subject to budget constraints (12.2) and (12.3). For simplicity, we suppose that the perfect foresight consumer knows the amount of public subsidy and he (she) does the decision making based on budget constraints including the amount.[8]

---

[5]Similar to Eckstein and Wolpin [10], parents are interested in the number of children but they are not interested in the utility of their children. Furthermore, in this model, we do not suppose the sexuality.

[6]The technical reason makes us such assumption. If we assume that parents get the utility from n_{t+1}, we cannot analyse our research question.

[7]The increasing raising time decreases the working time and the wage income. Therefore, they generates the opportunity cost. For example, that is public expenditure for day care centre.

[8]Zhang [35, 36] do the similar assumption.

12.1.2 Firms

Firms produce the output with physical capital and the efficiency labour.[9] The production technology is assumed by the constant return to scale and the aggregative production function at period t is shown by

$$Y_t = F(K_t, A_tL_t) = A_tL_tf(k_t), \tag{12.4}$$

where Y_t, K_t, L_t are the aggregative output, the aggregative physical capital and the aggregative labour, respectively at period t.[10] When k_t is the capital per efficiency unit at period t, $k_t \equiv \frac{K_t}{A_tL_t}$.[11]

Following Romer [29] and Grossman and Yanagawa [18], the labour productivity at period t, A_t is

$$A_t = \frac{\frac{K_t}{L_t}}{a}, \tag{12.5}$$

where a is the positive parameter.[12]

The profit maximisation behaviour makes us show the factor prices as

$$r_t = f'(k_t), \tag{12.6}$$

and

$$W_t = A_t\left[f(k_t) - k_tf'(k_t)\right]. \tag{12.7}$$

Therefore, the wage rate per efficiency unit is

$$w_t \equiv \frac{W_t}{A_t}. \tag{12.8}$$

---

[9]For simplicity, we assume no depreciation.

[10]As the consumers are assumed identical, $L_t = (1 - h_t(n_{t+1}, G_{p,t}))N_t$.

[11]The production function per efficiency unit, $f(k_t)$ is $\frac{\partial f(k_t)}{\partial k_t} > 0$ and $\frac{\partial^2 f(k_t)}{\partial k_t^2} < 0$.

[12]The production function (12.4) is specialised to

$$Y_t = (K_t)^{\alpha}(A_tL_t)^{1-\alpha}.$$

Using (12.5), we can rewrite as

$$Y_t = \left(\frac{1}{a}\right)^{1-\alpha} K_t.$$

12.1.3 Government

Government collects the wage income tax to finance public support for children and public subsidy for children. The government budget constraint per capita is

$$\tau\left[1 - h_t(n_{t+1}, G_{p,t})\right] W_t = (1 + n_{t+1})G_{s,t} + G_{p,t}. \tag{12.9}$$

When Δ is the allocation rate to public support for children of total tax revenue at period t, public support for children is shown by

$$G_{p,t} = \Delta\tau\left[1 - h_t(n_{t+1}, G_{p,t})\right] W_t, \tag{12.10}$$

and public subsidy for children is

$$(1 + n_{t+1})G_{s,t} = (1 - \Delta)\tau\left[1 - h_t(n_{t+1}, G_{p,t})\right] W_t. \tag{12.11}$$

Hereinafter, τ and Δ are assumed constant for simplicity.

12.1.4 Economic Growth Rate

Market Equilibrium

In this model, as we suppose that the agents supply labour to firms inelastically, when the capital market is cleared, the markets are in equilibrium. The equilibrium condition of capital market is

$$K_{t+1} = S_t N_t. \tag{12.12}$$

The Number of Children

The technical reason makes us assume that the raising time depends on the number of children and the allocation rate between public support for children and public subsidy for children.[13] $h_t(n_{t+1}, G_{p,t})$ is rewritten by

$$h_t\left(n_{t+1}, \Delta\right) = \eta\Delta^{-(1+\theta)}(1 + n_{t+1}), \quad 0 < \eta < 1, \theta > 0. \tag{12.13}$$

[13]Introducing public subsidy which decreases the raising opportunity cost into the model, Groezen, Leers and Meijdam [17] examine the relationship between public subsidy for children and social security. In the second half of this chapter, we also discuss the effects of social security on fertility.

Based on these assumptions, from (12.13) and (12.11), the lifetime budget constraint for representative agents of generation t is shown by

$$(1-\Delta\tau)\left[1-\eta\Delta^{-(1+\theta)}(1+n_{t+1})\right]W_t = c_t^t + \frac{c_{t+1}^t}{1+r_{t+1}}. \tag{12.14}$$

Therefore, the first order conditions show the number of children for representative consumer of generation t as

$$1+n_{t+1} = \frac{\epsilon}{(1+\beta+\epsilon)\left(\eta\Delta^{-(1+\theta)}\right)}. \tag{12.15}$$

The number of children, (12.15) depends on the allocation rate Δ and the constant parameters. As the identical consumers are supposed, n_{t+1} is the growth rate of population from generation t to generation $t+1$. When the saving rate is s_t, s_t is shown by

$$s_t = \frac{S_t}{(1-\tau)\left[1-\eta\Delta^{-(1+\theta)}(1+n_{t+1})\right]W_t + (1+n_{t+1})G_{s,t}}. \tag{12.16}$$

With (12.11) and the first order conditions of consumer's optimal behaviour, the saving is

$$S_t = \frac{(1-\tau\Delta)\beta W_t}{1+\beta+\epsilon} > 0,$$

and s_t is

$$s_t = \frac{\beta}{1+\beta}. \tag{12.17}$$

Economic Growth Rate

We define the economic growth rate at the steady state as

$$1+\gamma^y \equiv \frac{\frac{Y_{t+1}}{N_{t+1}}}{\frac{Y_t}{N_t}}. \tag{12.18}$$

Using the labour productivity, (12.5), the wage rate per efficiency unit, (12.8), the equilibrium condition of capital market, (12.12) and the definition of saving rate, (12.17), the economic growth rate is rewritten by

$$1+\gamma^y = \frac{s_t(1-\tau\Delta)w_t}{(1+n_{t+1})a}. \tag{12.19}$$

The derivation of this economic growth rate is examined at Appendix 1. Therefore, in this model, the economic growth rate in steady state grows at the constant rate.[14]

12.1.5 Policy Effects

In this subsection, at the constant tax rate, we examine the effects of allocation between public support for children and public subsidy for children on economic growth rate.

From (12.15), at the constant tax rate, the effects of changing allocation from public subsidy for children to public support for children on fertility is

$$\frac{dn_{t+1}}{d\Delta} = \frac{\epsilon(1+\beta+\epsilon)\eta(1+\theta)\Delta^{-(1+\theta)-1}}{[(1+\beta+\epsilon)\eta\Delta^{-(1+\theta)}]^2} > 0. \tag{12.20}$$

Decreasing public subsidy for children and increasing public support for children enhances the fertility. Increasing such support can make consumers supply labour more and get more wage income. Such income gives consumers the incentive to have more children and enhances the fertility rate. This depends on the log utility function, (12.1) and the assumption of raising time because the marginal substitution of consumptions at each period is constant in the log utility function. We note $\frac{dn_{t+1}}{d\tau} = 0$ from (12.15) because we assume the log utility function.

Next, we consider how the allocation change affects the economic growth rate. Differentiation economic growth rate, (12.19) with respect to Δ makes

$$\frac{d(1+\gamma^y)}{d\Delta} = \frac{-s_t w_t \tau(1+n_{t+1})a - (1-\tau\Delta)s_t a w_t \frac{dn_{t+1}}{d\Delta}}{[(1+n_{t+1})a]^2} < 0. \tag{12.21}$$

Changing allocation from public subsidy for children to public support for children decreases public subsidy and saving. Such changing increases public support and saving through wage income and raising cost. The former effect is shown by the first term of right hand side of numerator on (12.21). The latter effect is by the second term of right hand side of numerator on (12.21). In this model, because the negative effect of public subsidy and saving on economic growth rate dominates that of public support and saving, increasing public support for children declines the economic growth rate.[15]

[14]From (12.5) and the definition of physical capital of efficiency unit, $k_t = a$ in the market equilibrium. The wage rate per efficiency unit at steady state, $w_t \left(\equiv \frac{W_t}{A_t}\right)$ is constant.

[15]If the objective for government is to enhance the economic growth rate, we show that this public subsidy can do more allocation than public support.

We note that, from (12.19),

$$\frac{d(1+\gamma^y)}{d\tau} = \frac{-s_t \Delta w_t}{(1+n_{t+1})a} < 0.$$

Increasing wage tax rate decreases the economic growth rate through decreasing disposable income and saving.

12.1.6 Welfare Effect

In this subsection, we examine welfare effects of allocation change at the constant tax rate.

Using (12.11) and (12.13), the optimal plans for representative agent of generation t are

$$c_t^t = \frac{(1-\Delta\tau)\,W_t}{(1+\beta+\epsilon)}, \tag{12.22}$$

and

$$c_{t+1}^t = \frac{(1+r_{t+1})\,\beta\,(1-\Delta\tau)\,W_t}{(1+\beta+\epsilon)}. \tag{12.23}$$

Based on these optimal plans, as a social welfare function, we define the indirect utility function for the representative agent of generation t,

$$V^t = \ln\frac{(1-\Delta\tau)\,W_t}{(1+\beta+\epsilon)} + \beta\ln\frac{(1+f'(a))\,\beta\,(1-\Delta\tau)\,W_t}{(1+\beta+\epsilon)} + \epsilon\ln\frac{\epsilon}{(1+\beta+\epsilon)\,(\eta\Delta^{-(1+\theta)})}. \tag{12.24}$$

At period t, we show the welfare effect of changing allocation from public subsidy for children to public support for children by

$$\frac{dV^t}{d\Delta} = \frac{-\tau\,(1+\beta)}{(1-\Delta\tau)} + (1+\beta)\,\frac{\frac{dW_t}{d\Delta}}{W_t} + \epsilon\,(1+\theta)\,\frac{1}{\Delta}. \tag{12.25}$$

Furthermore, given K_t and L_t, when

$$\frac{\tau\,(1+\beta)}{(1-\Delta\tau)} = \epsilon\,(1+\theta)\,\frac{1}{\Delta} + (1+\beta)\,\frac{\frac{dW_t}{d\Delta}}{W_t}, \tag{12.26}$$

social welfare is maximised at period t. The left hand side of (12.26) shows the negative welfare effect of increasing public support for children and decreasing public subsidy for children and consumption. The first term of right hand side of (12.26) shows the welfare effect of increasing public support for children and the second term of that is the effects of increasing public support for children and wage income through working time.

On the contrary to th effects of these policy on economic growth rate, based on (12.26), allocation change makes social welfare maximise at the constant tax. In the steady state, increasing public support for children decreases the economic growth rate but can enhances the social welfare. Whether these policies are favourable or not depends the objective of government policy.

12.2 Public Education and Social Security

As discussed above, declining fertility affects labour force. Having children enhances parents' utility but generates child care cost and the cost of education for these children. The former cost includes parents' own opportunity cost, which means that in raising children, parents sacrifice working time and income. The latter shows the material sacrifices made by parents. These costs are a disincentive to have children, causing fertility to decline and contributing to the aging of society. For labour force problems, government policies provide public support for children and public subsidy for children and promote human capital accumulation. Public policies should take into consideration the incentives to have children.

Beginning with Becker and Barro [3], it is well known that social security may affect the demand for children. As discussed before, Zhang and Zhang [37] introduce parents' child care time into the model to examine the connection between the disincentive to have children and social security in an endogenous growth model. They show that a higher social security tax rate tends to be detrimental to economic growth and welfare. Groezen, Leers and Meijdam [17], Zhang and Zhang [40] and Hirazawa and Yakita [19] analyse public pensions and child support in a model with endogenous fertility. Cremer, Gahvari and Pestieau [7] discuss the design of pension schemes when fertility is endogenous and parents differ in the ability to raise children. However, they do not take into account educational cost.

Both education and social security can be viewed as mechanisms of intergenerational transfers. Becker and Tomes [4] and Gale and Scholz [13] show that these altruistically motivated transfers have a significant effect on the growth process via their impact on human capital accumulation. Kaganovich and Zilcha [20] examine the effects of the public funding of social security and education on economic growth without assuming population growth. They find that the shifting of tax revenues from social security benefits to education can improve welfare. Similar to Kaganovich and Zilcha [20], Pecchenino and Utendorf [27] assume that working people both educate their dependent children and pay into pay-as-you-go social security. In their view, social security crowds out education and reduces economic growth and social welfare. Pecchenino and Pollard [26] indicate that if the quality of the education system is sufficiently high, increasing the education tax and subsequently lowering the social security tax rate enhance growth and welfare. Glomm and Kaganovich [14] study how the allocation of government expenditures between public education and pay-as-you-go social security affects human capital distribution in an economy with heterogeneous agents. They show that increased spending in public education may lead to higher inequality. In all their models, population growth is assumed to be exogenous and child care time is not considered. Glomm and Kaganovich [15] examine, with the introduction of child care time into a model, how the relationship between economic growth and inequality depends on the levels of funding public education and social security. However, they do not discuss the effects of such public policies on fertility.

In this model, as in Kaganovich and Zilcha [20], parents derive their utility from the human capital of their children, investing in their children's education at considerable material sacrifice. The number of children parents have depends on their investment in education. Glomm and Ravikumar [16] find that public education reduces income inequality more quickly than private education, but private education yields higher per capita income unless the initial income inequality is sufficiently large. In their analysis, any spillovers of these decisions on fertility are abstracted. Introducing child care time into the model without social security, de la Croix and Doepke [8] examine the relationship between private investment in education, public education and parents' fertility decision making. They find that while private schooling leads to higher growth when there is little inequality in human capital endowments across families, public schooling can dominate when inequality is sufficiently high. As social security is abstracted in all their models, it is not well understood how the relationship between incentives to have children and social security impacts individual fertility decisions. Zhang and Zhang [38] examine the effects of unfunded social security with bequests, fertility and human capital by considering a mix of earnings-dependent and universal social security benefits. They show that social security is more likely to promote growth by reducing fertility and increasing human capital investment if its benefits are more dependent on individuals' own earnings. Yew and Zhang [33] discuss the optimal scale of social security in a dynastic family model with human capital externalities, fertility and endogenous growth. In these all models, public education is not introduced.

In the second half of this chapter, we introduce the education cost into the pay-as-you-go social security model to examine the effects of public education and social security on fertility.[16] We suppose that individuals have the disincentive to have children while paying the education cost as a material sacrifice and cutting their working hours while raising children as an opportunity cost. Furthermore, for the compensation of children costs, parents cut their saving for the retirement and they need more social security benefits.

Additionally, to clarify how income tax affects fertility decision, we examine the effects of different types of income taxes on fertility. First, we discuss the effects of capital income tax on fertility. If a capital income tax is available as a source

[16]In the second half of this chapter, our discussion is based on Omori [25].

of revenue to finance education and social security and this makes the old not only beneficiaries but also contributors to the fiscal system, capital income tax might affect the fertility decision.[17] We then examine the effect of capital income tax on fertility. Second, when government budget constraint is decoupled and there are dedicated taxes for both social security and for public investment in education, we can consider the effect of education tax on fertility while keeping the social security tax constant and that of social security tax with a constant education tax. These discussions make it much clearer how parents' decision on children depends on public investment in education and/or social security benefits.

12.2.1 Model

We consider an overlapping generations economy, where is comprised of identical three-period lived agents, perfectly competitive firms, and a government.

Consumers

Agents in the first period of their lives, the young, are raised by their parents and combine inputs provided by their parents and government to develop their human capital. Agents in the second period of their lives, the working, inelastically supply their effective labour to firms. They have children and divide their one unit of time between raising their children and working and their after-tax income among current consumption, saving for consumption when retirement, and private investment in education. Agents in the final period of their lives, the retirement, consume their social security benefits and their accumulated savings. We assume no bequests. The working generation at period t is called generation t. Following Omori [25], the preference of a representative agent of generation t is

$$U\left(c_t^t,\ c_{t+1}^t,\ n_{t+1},\ h_{t+1}\right) = \ln c_t^t\ +\ \beta \ln c_{t+1}^t\ +\ \delta \ln\ n_{t+1} h_{t+1}, \tag{12.27}$$

where c_t^t and c_{t+1}^t are the consumption of generation t during the working period and the retirement period, respectively, n_{t+1} is the number of children for generation t, h_{t+1} is the human capital at $t+1$ and β and δ are the positive parameter.[18]

Let N_t be the total working population at period t, and we have $N_{t+1} = (1+n_{t+1})N_t$. The human capital of each agent in generation $t+1$ is a function of the private investment in education made by parents, e_t, as the material sacrifice,

[17] Razin, Sadka and Swagel [28] point out the same issue.

[18] In this utility function, parents obtain utility from consumption and educating their children. The value of this education is summarised by the child's human capital. This utility is derived from parents' love of or duty to their children.

the public investment in educationmade by the government, E_t, and the parents' child caring time per child, Λ, as the opportunity cost.[19] We note that we can enjoy the economies of scale in education when we privately educate our children. Taking into consideration such insight, we assume the input of private education as

$$\epsilon_t = \frac{e_t}{n_{t+1}^{\psi}}, \tag{12.28}$$

where $\psi \geq 0$. Then, the human capital of each agent in generation $t+1$ is given by

$$h_{t+1} = \epsilon_t^{\eta} E_t^{1-\eta} \Lambda^{\gamma}, \tag{12.29}$$

where $\gamma > 0$ and $0 < \eta < 1$.

The budget constraints of a representative agent of generation t in working and the retirement period are given, respectively, by

$$(1 - \tau_w)\,[1 - n_{t+1}\Lambda]\; w_t h_t = c_t^t + e_t + s_t, \tag{12.30}$$

and

$$(1 + r_{t+1})\, s_t + T_{t+1} = c_{t+1}^t, \tag{12.31}$$

where τ_w is the wage income tax rate , w_t the wage rate at t, s_t his(her)savings, r_{t+1} the interest rate at $t+1$, and T_{t+1} the social security benefits at $t+1$.[20]

Given the wage rate, the interest rate, the human capital, the wage income tax rate, and the child care time per child, a representative agent chooses c_t^t, c_{t+1}^t, n_{t+1}, and e_t to maximise his utility, (12.27), subject to the budget constraints, (12.30) and (12.31).

[19]Communication between parents and their children is helpful for the human capital accumulation of their children. Parents' and public investment in education have a different character as inputs in human capital accumulation. These three inputs are necessary for human capital accumulation.

[20]Originating from Becker and Barro [3] in the literature of fertility choice, when we introduce the cost of raising children into the model, we assume that the parents' child caring time per child is fixed. Barro and Becker [2], Eckstein and Wolpin [10], Morand [22], Yakita [32], Tabata [31], de la Croix and Doepke [8], Groezen, Leers and Meijdam [17], Zhang and Zhang [40], Hirazawa and Yakita [19] and others make the same assumption. However, we can enjoy the economies of scale in raising children. To justify this assumption, we examine it in Omori [25]. Additionally, we assume away the pecuniary fixed cost of child care.

From the first-order conditions, we can show the optimal plans as

$$n_{t+1} = \frac{\delta(1-\eta\psi)}{(1+\beta+\delta(1+\eta(1-\psi)))\Lambda} + \frac{\delta(1-\eta\psi)T_{t+1}}{(1-\tau_w)\Lambda w_t h_t(1+r_{t+1})(1+\beta+\delta(1+\eta(1-\psi)))}, \tag{12.32}$$

$$e_t = \frac{\left((1-\tau_w)w_t h_t + \frac{T_{t+1}}{(1+r_{t+1})}\right)\delta\eta}{(1+\beta+\delta(1+\eta(1-\psi)))}, \tag{12.33}$$

and

$$s_t = \frac{\beta(1-\tau_w)w_t h_t}{(1+\beta+\delta(1+\eta(1-\psi)))} - \frac{(1+\delta(1+\eta(1-\psi)))T_{t+1}}{(1+r_{t+1})(1+\beta+\delta(1+\eta(1-\psi)))}. \tag{12.34}$$

We assume $\beta(1+r_{t+1}) \geq \frac{(1+\delta(1+\eta(1-\psi)))T_{t+1}}{(1-\tau_w)w_t h_t}$ for the non-negative saving.

Firms

Firms behave perfect competitively to maximise their profit and produce output with capital and effective labour. The aggregate production function is expressed as

$$Y_t = AK_t^{\alpha}H_t^{1-\alpha},$$

where Y_t is the aggregate output at period t, A is a time-independent productivity scalar, K_t the aggregate capital at period t, H_t the aggregate effective labour at period t, $H_t = h_t(1-n_{t+1}\Lambda)N_t$, and $0 < \alpha < 1$. The production technology exhibits a constant return to scale, and the marginal productivity of each input is positive and decreasing. We define $y_t \equiv \frac{Y_t}{N_t}$ and $k_t \equiv \frac{K_t}{N_t}$. The output per the generation t can be rewritten by

$$y_t = Ak_t^{\alpha}\left[h_t(1-n_{t+1}\Lambda)\right]^{1-\alpha}. \tag{12.35}$$

From the first-order conditions for profit maximisation, factor prices are derived as follows,

$$w_t = (1-\alpha)Ak_t^{\alpha}\left[h_t(1-n_{t+1}\Lambda)\right]^{-\alpha} = (1-\alpha)\frac{y_t}{\left[h_t(1-n_{t+1}\Lambda)\right]}, \tag{12.36}$$

and

$$1+r_t = \alpha Ak_t^{\alpha-1}\left[h_t(1-n_{t+1}\Lambda)\right]^{1-\alpha} = \alpha\frac{y_t}{k_t}. \tag{12.37}$$

Government

The government is assumed to behave under a balanced budget regime. Tax revenues are collected to finance public investment in education and social security benefits in this period. The government budget constraint in period t is

$$\tau_w \left[1 - n_{t+1}\Lambda\right] w_t h_t N_t = E_t N_t + T_t N_{t-1}.$$

Let us further define a parameter Δ to stand for the fraction of government revenue devoted to public investment in education ($0 < \Delta < 1$). This investment in education in period t is

$$E_t = \Delta \tau_w \left[1 - n_{t+1}\Lambda\right] w_t h_t = \Delta \tau_w (1 - \alpha) y_t, \tag{12.38}$$

and the social security benefits at t are expressed by

$$T_t = (1 + n_t)(1 - \Delta) \tau_w \left[1 - n_{t+1}\Lambda\right] w_t h_t = (1 + n_t)(1 - \Delta) \tau_w (1 - \alpha) y_t. \tag{12.39}$$

In the following discussions, the government predetermines the sequences of τ_w and Δ for simplicity.

12.2.2 Number of Children

The good market clears when the capital market clears. The equilibrium condition of capital market can be written per capita as

$$(1 + n_{t+1}) k_{t+1} = s_t. \tag{12.40}$$

Using (12.34)–(12.39), (12.40) can be rewritten as

$$(1 + n_{t+1})k_{t+1} = \frac{(1 - \alpha)}{(1 + \beta + \delta(1 + \eta(1 - \psi)))} \times \left[\frac{\beta (1 - \tau_w) y_t}{(1 - n_{t+1}\Lambda)} - \alpha^{-1} (1 + \delta(1 + \eta(1 - \psi)))(1 - \Delta) \tau_w (1 + n_{t+1}) k_{t+1}\right]. \tag{12.41}$$

In equilibrium, substituting (12.36), (12.37), (12.39), and (12.41) into the optimal plan for the number of children, (12.32), we can obtain the optimal number of children in the steady state as

$$n_{t+1} = \frac{\delta(1-\eta\psi)}{(1+\beta+\delta(1+\eta(1-\psi)))\Lambda} + \frac{\delta(1-\eta\psi)}{(1+\beta+\delta(1+\eta(1-\psi)))\Lambda} \times \frac{(1-\Delta)\tau_w(1-\alpha)\beta}{[\alpha(1+\beta+\delta(1+\eta(1-\psi))) + (1+\delta(1+\eta(1-\psi)))(1-\alpha)(1-\Delta)\tau_w]}. \tag{12.42}$$

As τ_w and Δ are assumed to be predetermined, n_{t+1} is the time-invariant variable in the equilibrium.[21] The first term on the right-hand side in (12.42) shows the substitute effect of having children and the second term indicates the income effect of social security benefits on the number of children. We note that the first term does not depend on any public policy parameters.

12.2.3 Economic Growth Rate

In this model, the steady state is in the path that the ratio of human capital, (h) and physical capital,(k) is constant. That is,

$$\frac{h_{t+1}}{k_{t+1}} = \frac{h_t}{k_t} = \omega. \tag{12.43}$$

The economic growth rate in the steady state is

$$1+\gamma = \frac{k_{t+1}}{k_t}.$$

Using (12.28)–(12.29) and (12.33)–(12.42), we can show the economic growth rate at the steady state as, in the from of logarithm function,

$$\ln(1+\gamma) = \ln\left(\frac{k_{t+1}}{k_t}\right) = \ln\frac{\dfrac{1}{(1-n_{t+1}\Lambda)}}{\beta(1-\tau_w)(1-\alpha)} + \ln\left[\frac{1}{\alpha}(1+\delta(1+\eta(1-\psi)))(1+n_{t+1})(1-\Delta)\tau_w(1-\alpha) + (1+\beta+\delta(1+\eta(1-\psi)))\right] + \ln(1+\beta+\delta(1+\eta(1-\psi))) + \ln(1-n_{t+1}\Lambda) + (1-\alpha)\ln\omega, \tag{12.44}$$

[21] Hereafter, we assume an internal solution. Omori [25] shows the optimal number of children in the steady state when we can enjoy the economies of scale in rearing children.

where

$$\ln \omega = \ln \left(\frac{h_{t+1}}{k_{t+1}} \right) = \eta \ln \frac{\delta \eta}{(1 + \beta + \delta (1 + \eta (1 - \psi)))}$$

$$+ \eta \ln \left[\frac{1}{\beta (1 - \alpha)} \left[\frac{1}{\alpha} (1 + \delta (1 + \eta (1 - \psi))) (1 - n_{t+1}) (1 - \Delta) \tau_w (1 - \alpha) \right.\right.$$

$$\left.\left. + (1 + \beta + \delta (1 + \eta (1 - \psi))) \right] \right] + (1 - \eta) \ln \Delta \tau_w (1 - \alpha)$$

$$+ \ln \frac{(1 - n_{t+1} \Lambda)}{\beta (1 - \tau_w) (1 - \alpha)} \left[\frac{1}{\alpha} (1 + \delta (1 + \eta (1 - \psi))) (1 - n_{t+1}) (1 - \Delta) \tau_w (1 - \alpha) \right.$$

$$\left. + (1 + \beta + \delta (1 + \eta (1 - \psi))) \right] + \gamma \ln \Lambda - \eta \psi \ln n_{t+1}. \tag{12.45}$$

See the Appendix 2 for the derivation of (12.44). At the steady state, because (12.42) is constant, the right hand side of (12.45) is also constant. Therefore, ω is constant and the economic growth rate, (12.44) is constant. However, as this economic growth rate depends on parameters, it is difficult to discuss the policy effects on economic growth rate. As the purpose of this part is to examine the policy effects on fertility, hereinafter, we discuss that on fertility.

12.2.4 Policy Effect

We examine the effects of wage income tax and allocation between public investment in education and social security benefits on fertility, respectively.

Wage Income Tax

We can show the effect of wage income tax on fertility in the steady state. From (12.42),

$$\frac{dn}{d\tau_w} =$$

$$\frac{\delta (1 - \eta \psi)}{(1 + \beta + \delta (1 + \eta (1 - \psi))) \Lambda}$$

$$\times \left[\frac{\alpha (1 - \Delta) (1 - \alpha) \beta (1 + \beta + \delta (1 + \eta (1 - \psi)))}{[\alpha (1 + \beta + \delta (1 + \eta (1 - \psi))) + (1 + \delta (1 + \eta (1 - \psi))) (1 - \alpha) (1 - \Delta) \tau_w]^2} \right] > 0. \tag{12.46}$$

A higher wage income tax rate always increases fertility. It increases public investment in education and social security benefits. Increasing public investment in education lowers both child care cost as an opportunity cost and the cost of private education as a material sacrifice. Such increases give the incentive to have children. Increasing social security benefits partly compensates for the savings cut. When parents decide to have an additional child, they have to cut their savings to cover the cost of children. To compensate for the savings cut, they need more income and social security benefits. Such tax increases provide the incentive to have children. In this model, the higher wage tax rate encourages the agents to have more children.[22]

Allocation Between Public Investment in Education and Social Security Benefits

Both education and social security can be viewed as mechanisms of intergenerational transfer. To discuss the effects of intergenerational transfers on fertility, we examine the effects on fertility of reallocating public funds from social security benefits to public investment in education. In the steady state, that effect can be shown by, from (12.42),

$$\frac{dn}{d\Delta} = \frac{\delta(1-\eta\psi)}{(1+\beta+\delta(1+\eta(1-\psi)))A} \times \left[\frac{-\alpha\tau_w(1-\alpha)\beta(1+\beta+\delta(1+\eta(1-\psi)))}{[\alpha(1+\beta+\delta(1+\eta(1-\psi)))+(1+\delta(1+\eta(1-\psi)))(1-\alpha)(1-\Delta)\tau_w]^2}\right] < 0. \quad (12.47)$$

With a fixed wage income tax rate, reallocating from social security benefits to public expenditure in education decreases fertility. A reallocation from social security benefits to public investment in education has two effects. One is that increasing public investment in education raises the human capital and generates an income effect in the steady state. As discussed before, this increase serves to decrease both the child care cost and the cost of private education. The other is that such reallocation decreases the income for the retirement generation through the

[22]Using cross-country data, Ehrlich and Zhong [11] find that social security has an adverse effect on fertility. According to Zhang and Zhang [39], empirical evidence suggests that without taking consideration of public education, social security tends to stimulate per capita growth by reducing fertility and increasing human capital investment without affecting savings rate. As they use cross-sectional data, the negative correlation between social security and fertility might be caused by other aspects of public policy such as public support for children (which, in some countries, is paid by lump-sum) or substitutes for child care, which are not discussed here. In this model with public education, as public investment in education is substitutable for the private investment in education, the empirical studies do not explain this theoretical model.

social security benefits. Although having children means costs, from the optimal plans, (12.32)–(12.34), it is clear that decreasing the social security benefits gives the agents the incentives to save more for retirement period consumption and to have fewer children.

Capital Income Tax

As discussed above, both education and social security have mechanisms of intergenerational transfers. We have shown that the reallocation of social security benefits to public investment in education decreases fertility. The capital income tax is considered another way of affecting the fertility decision. In this section, we examine the effect of capital income tax on fertility.

We suppose that government adopts the comprehensive capital tax policy, which is a tax not only on wealth but also on interest income.[23] The budget constraints of a representative agent of generation t in working and the retirement period should be changed, respectively, by

$$[1 - n_{t+1}\Lambda]\ w_t h_t = c_t^t + e_t + s_t, \tag{12.48}$$

and

$$(1 - \tau_i)\,(1 + r_{t+1})\, s_t + T_{t+1} = c_{t+1}^t, \tag{12.49}$$

where τ_i is the capital income tax rate.[24]

The government budget constraint in period t is

$$\tau_i\,(1 + r_t)\, s_{t-1}N_{t-1} = E_t N_t + T_t N_{t-1}.$$

This investment in education in period t is given by

$$E_t = \Delta\tau_i\alpha y_t. \tag{12.50}$$

[23] If we suppose a tax only on interest income, the path may not be essentially different from that including the comprehensive capital tax.

[24] Given w_t, r_{t+1}, h_t, τ_i and Λ, a representative agent chooses c_t^t, c_{t+1}^t, n_{t+1}, and e_t to maximise his utility, (12.27), subject to the budget constraints, (12.48) and (12.49).

The one for social security benefits is given by

$$T_t = (1-\Delta)\tau_i(1+n_t)\alpha y_t. \tag{12.51}$$

Government predetermines the sequences of τ_i and Δ for simplicity.

Using a similar procedure in deriving (12.42), the optimal number of children in the steady state can be given by

$$\begin{aligned} n_{t+1} = & \frac{\delta(1-\eta\psi)}{(1+\beta+\delta(1+\eta(1-\psi)))\Lambda} \\ & + \frac{\delta(1-\eta\psi)}{(1+\beta+\delta(1+\eta(1-\psi)))} \\ \times & \frac{\tau_i(1-\Delta)\beta}{[(1-\tau_i)(1+\beta+\delta(1+\eta(1-\psi)))+(1+\delta(1+\eta(1-\psi)))(1-\Delta)\tau_i]}. \end{aligned} \tag{12.52}$$

The similar explanation in (12.42) applies for the optimal number of children, (12.52).

In the steady state, the effect of capital income tax on fertility is revealed by the differentiation of (12.52) with respect to τ_i. That is,

$$\begin{aligned} \frac{dn}{d\tau_i} = & \\ & \frac{\delta(1-\eta\psi)[(1-\Delta)\beta[(1+\beta+\delta(1+\eta(1-\psi)))-\Delta(1+\delta(1+\eta(1-\psi)))\tau_i]]}{(1+\beta+\delta(1+\eta(1-\psi)))\Lambda[(1+\beta+\delta(1+\eta(1-\psi)))+(1+\delta(1+\eta(1-\psi)))\tau_i]^2} \\ & > 0. \end{aligned} \tag{12.53}$$

A higher capital income tax increases fertility. Increasing capital income tax generates the substitutable effect on the cost of having children because of increasing public investment in education and social security benefits. The higher capital tax rate encourages the agents to have more children.

Contrary to above discussions, (12.53) shows a positive effect on fertility. A capital income tax is only available as a source of revenue to finance public education and social security and this makes the retirement not only beneficiaries but also contributors to the fiscal system. The working are not taxed and they only enjoy the benefits of public investment in education financed by the capital income tax. We show that the intergenerational income redistribution from the retirement to the working through such income tax can positively influence fertility.

Education Tax and Social Security Tax

When the government budget constraint is decoupled and there are dedicated taxes both for public investment in education and for social security, we can consider the effect of education tax on fertility while maintaining a constant social security tax and that of social security tax with a constant education tax. This discussion makes it much clearer to show how parents' decision on children depends on public investment in education and/or social security benefits.[25]

The budget constraints of a representative agent of generation t in working and the retirement period should be changed, respectively, by

$$(1-\tau_E-\tau_T)\,[1-n_{t+1}\Lambda]\;w_t h_t = c_t^t + e_t + s_t, \tag{12.54}$$

and

$$(1+r_{t+1})\,s_t + T_{t+1} = c_{t+1}^t, \tag{12.55}$$

where τ_E is the wage income tax rate for public expenditure on education (education tax) and τ_T is the wage income tax rate for social security benefits (social security tax).[26]

The government budget constraint for public education per capita in period t is given by

$$E_t = \tau_E\,(1-\alpha)\,y_t. \tag{12.56}$$

That for social security benefits is given by

$$T_t = (1+n_t)\,\tau_T\,(1-\alpha)\,y_t. \tag{12.57}$$

For simplicity, τ_E and τ_t are predetermined.

Using a similar procedure to (12.42), the optimal number of children in the steady state can be given by

$$\begin{aligned} n_{t+1} = & \frac{\delta\,(1-\eta\psi)}{(1+\beta+\delta\,(1+\eta\,(1-\psi)))\,\Lambda} \\ & + \frac{\delta\,(1-\eta\psi)}{(1+\beta+\delta\,(1+\eta\,(1-\psi)))\,\Lambda} \\ & \times \frac{\tau_T\,(1-\alpha)\,\beta}{[\alpha\,(1+\beta+\delta\,(1+\eta\,(1-\psi)))+(1+\delta\,(1+\eta\,(1-\psi)))\,(1-\alpha)\,\tau_T]}. \end{aligned} \tag{12.58}$$

[25] Pecchenino and Pollard [26] show how raising the education tax and subsequently lowering the social security tax rate enhances growth and welfare. However, they do not discuss the effects of these two taxes on fertility.

[26] Given w_t, r_{t+1}, h_t, τ_E, τ_T and Λ, a representative agent chooses c_t^t, c_{t+1}^t, n_{t+1}, and e_t to maximise his utility, (12.27), subject to the budget constraints, (12.54) and (12.55).

A similar explanation in (12.42) applies for the optimal number of children (12.58).

The effect of education tax on fertility while holding the social security tax constant is shown by, from (12.58),

$$\frac{dn}{d\tau_E} = 0. \tag{12.59}$$

With a fixed wage income tax rate for social security benefits, the effect of increasing the wage income tax rate for public investment in education on fertility is neutral. As shown in (12.58), the parameter on wage income tax rate for public investment in education does not affect the number of children in the steady state. For the working, although increasing the education tax decreases their disposable labour income, such an increase does not affect parents' decision on children. This result depends on the assumption of the logarithm utility function. There are no effects of the education tax on the marginal rate of substitution in this form.[27] The change in education tax rate affects the amount of saving, but does not influence the savings rate.

On the other hand, in the steady state, the effect of social security tax with constant education tax on fertility is shown by, from (12.58),

$$\frac{dn}{d\tau_T} = \frac{\delta\left(1-\eta\psi\right)}{\left(1+\beta+\delta\left(1+\eta\left(1-\psi\right)\right)\right)\Lambda} \times \left[\frac{\left(1-\alpha\right)\beta\alpha\left(1+\beta+\delta\left(1+\eta\left(1-\psi\right)\right)\right)}{\left[\alpha\left(1+\beta+\delta\left(1+\eta\left(1-\psi\right)\right)\right)+\left(1+\delta\left(1+\eta\left(1-\psi\right)\right)\right)\left(1-\alpha\right)\tau_T\right]^2}\right] > 0. \tag{12.60}$$

With a fixed wage income tax rate for public investment in education, the effect of increasing the wage income tax rate for social security benefits on fertility is positive. As shown in the optimal number of children, (12.58), in the steady state, the optimal number of children does depend not on the wage income tax rate for public investment in education but on the wage income tax rate for social security benefits. In this case, taking into consideration individual behaviours in the retirement period, parents' decision on having children depends on social security. When parents decide to have an additional child, they have to cut their savings to cover the cost of children. To compensate for the savings cut, they need more social security benefits. In this model, we suppose a pay-as-you-go social security system. Having more

[27] From the first-order conditions, the marginal rate of substitution between c_t^t and c_{t+1}^t is

$$\frac{c_{t+1}^t}{c_t^t} = \frac{\beta}{\left(1+r_{t+1}\right)}.$$

children increases the social security benefits for the retirement. Increasing the wage income tax rate for social security benefits encourages the agents to have more children.[28]

The neutrality of education tax with constant social security tax depends on the assumption on utility function. However, even in this model, there exists the positive effect of social security tax with a constant education tax. Social security might have the replacement effect on private saving but education does not have an intertemporal replacement effect. This intertemporal replacement effect changes the individual savings rate and causes the difference between education tax and social security tax.

Finally, in this part, because the model is too complex to examine the welfare effects in this model, this examination is left for the future research.

12.3 Concluding Remarks

The fertility affect the economic activities in the country. How many parents have children depends on the expenditures to their children including the opportunity cost, the raising cost and the education cost.

In the first half of this chapter, we examined the effects of public subsidy for children and public support for children on economic growth and social welfare. Decreasing public subsidy for children but increasing public support for children enhances fertility. Public support for children increases labour supply and more wage income. Such income gives parents the incentive to have children more. However, at the constant wage income tax rate, such support deceases the economic growth rate. In the steady state, increasing public support for children decreases the economic growth rate but can enhances the social welfare. Whether these policies are favourable or not depends the objective of government policy.

In the second half of this chapter, we have examined the effects of public education and social security on fertility by introducing the fertility decision and the child care cost into the overlapping generations model. Both education and social security can be viewed as mechanisms of intergenerational transfers. The intergenerational transfer from the retirement to the young affects the individual's fertility decision. We have shown that an increase in income tax which finances public education and social security benefits raises fertility. Especially, the increases of wage income tax, capital income tax, and social security tax with constant education tax raise fertility. On the other hand, a change in allocation from the

[28]Zhang and Zhang [40] show that in a dynastic model without human capital formation, the positive effects of social security tax on fertility depend on parameters on the taste for utility derived from the consumption of the retirement parent, the taste for utility from the young age consumption and the taste for utility from the number of children relative to that from young-age consumption. Hirazawa and Yakita [19] also discuss such effects in a small open economy populated by overlapping generations who live three periods but do not invest human capital.

social security benefits to public investment in education decreases fertility and, with a constant social security tax, the effect of education tax on fertility is neutral.

To have an additional child, parents must cut their savings to cover the cost of children. Public policy, which lowers child care cost and increases social security benefits, partly compensates for the savings cut and gives parents the incentive to have children. In a fertility declining society, when government creates a policy to enhance fertility, government should take into consideration the parental disincentives to have children and the cost of children. Such public policy can help stimulate fertility.

Appendix 1

We rewrite the definition of economic growth rate (12.18) as,

$$1+\gamma^y = \frac{\frac{Y_{t+1}}{N_{t+1}}}{\frac{Y_t}{N_t}} = \frac{Y_{t+1}}{Y_t}\frac{N_t}{N_{t+1}} = \frac{K_{t+1}}{K_t}\frac{N_t}{N_{t+1}}.$$

From the equilibrium market of capital market, (12.12), the economic growth rate is shown by,

$$1+\gamma^y = \frac{S_t N_t}{K_t}\frac{N_t}{N_{t+1}}.$$

Furthermore, the definition of saving rate, (12.16) and $N_{t+1} = (1+n_{t+1})N_t$ makes it rewrite as,

$$1+\gamma^y = \frac{s_t(1-\tau\Delta)(1-\eta\Delta^{-(1+\theta)}(1+n_{t+1}))W_t N_t}{K_t}\frac{1}{(1+n_{t+1})}.$$

As we denote the aggregative labour at period t $L_t = (1-\eta\Delta^{-(1+\theta)}(1+n_{t+1}))N_t$,

$$1+\gamma^y = \frac{(1-\tau\Delta)s_t L_t W_t}{K_t}\frac{1}{(1+n_{t+1})}.$$

Substituting (12.8) and (12.5) into this,

$$1+\gamma^y = \frac{(1-\tau\Delta)s_t w_t}{(1+n_{t+1})a}.$$

Therefore, we derive the economic growth rate, (12.19).

Appendix 2

Substituting (12.34), (12.36), (12.37), and (12.39) into (12.40), we can get

$$y_t = \frac{(1 - n_{t+1}\Lambda)}{\beta(1-\tau_w)(1-\alpha)}\Big[\frac{1}{\alpha}(1+\delta(1+\eta(1-\psi)))(1-n_{t+1})(1-\Delta)\tau_w(1-\alpha) \\ + (1+\beta+\delta(1+\eta(1-\psi)))\Big]k_{t+1}. \tag{12.61}$$

Next, focusing on the numerator of right hand side of (12.33), the income, I_t is

$$I_t = \left((1-\tau_w)w_t h_t + \frac{T_{t+1}}{(1+r_{t+1})}\right),$$

and based on (12.36), (12.37) and (12.39),

$$I_t = \left[\frac{1}{\beta(1-\alpha)}\Big[\frac{1}{\alpha}(1+\delta(1+\eta(1-\psi)))(1-n_{t+1})(1-\Delta)\tau_w(1-\alpha) \\ + (1+\beta+\delta(1+\eta(1-\psi)))\Big]\right]k_{t+1}. \tag{12.62}$$

From (12.62), (12.33) is rewritten as

$$e_t = \frac{\delta\eta}{(1+\beta+\delta(1+\eta(1-\psi)))} \\ \times\left[\frac{1}{\beta(1-\alpha)}\Big[\frac{1}{\alpha}(1+\delta(1+\eta(1-\psi)))(1-n_{t+1})(1-\Delta)\tau_w(1-\alpha) \\ + (1+\beta+\delta(1+\eta(1-\psi)))\Big]\right]k_{t+1}. \tag{12.63}$$

Furthermore, human capital is shown in the form of logarithm by

$$\ln h_{t+1} = \eta \ln \epsilon_t + (1-\eta)\ln E_t + \gamma \ln \Lambda.$$

Substituting (12.38), (12.61) and (12.63), we can derive (12.45) of the logarithm function of ω. Finally, from (12.43), the production function per the working generation, (12.35) is also shown by

$$y_t = A\omega^{1-\alpha}(1-n_{t+1}\Lambda)^{1-\alpha}k_t. \tag{12.64}$$

Substituting (12.61) into (12.64), the steady state economic growth rate, (12.44) can be derived in the logarithm function.

References

1. Apps, P., & Rees, R. (2004). Fertility, taxation and family policy. *Scandinavian Journal of Economics, 106*, 745–763.
2. Barro, R. J., & Becker, G. S. (1989). Fertility choice in a model of economic growth. *Econometrica, 57*, 481–501.
3. Becker, G. S., & Barro, R. J. (1988). A reformulation of the economic theory of fertility. *Quarterly Journal of Economics, 103*, 1–26.
4. Becker, G. S., & Tomes, N. (1986). Human capital and the rise and fall of families. *Journal of Labor Economics, 4*, S1–S39.
5. Blackorby, C., & Donaldson, D. (1988). Cash versus in-kind, self-selection, and efficient transfers. *American Economic Review, 78*, 691–700.
6. Cabinet Office of Japan. (2004). Declining Birthrate White Paper.
7. Cremer, H., Gahvari, F., & Pestieau, P. (2008). Pensions with heterogeneous individuals and endogenous fertility. *Journal of Population Economics, 21*, 961–981.
8. de la Croix, D., & Doepke, M. (2004). Public versus private education when differential fertility matters. *Journal of Development Economics, 73*, 607–629.
9. Diamond, P. A. (1965). National debt in a neoclassical growth model. *American Economic Review, 55*(5), 1126–1150.
10. Eckstein, Z., & Wolpin, K. I. (1985). Endogenous fertility and optimal population size. *Journal of Public Economics, 27*, 93–106.
11. Ehrlich, I., & Zhong, J. G. (1998). Social security and the real economy: An inquiry into some neglected issues. *American Economic Review, 88*, 151–157.
12. Gahvari, F. (1994). In-kind transfers, cash grants and labor supply. *Journal of Public Economics, 55*, 495–504.
13. Gale, W. G., & Scholz, J. K. (1994). Intergenerational transfers and the accumulation of wealth. *Journal of Economic Perspectives, 8*, 145–160.
14. Glomm, G., & Kaganovich, M. (2003) . Distribution effects of public education in an economy with public pensions. *International Economic Review, 44*, 917–937.
15. Glomm, G., & Kaganovich, M. (2008). Social security, public education and the growth-inequality relationship. *European Economic Review, 52*, 1009–1034.
16. Glomm, G., & Ravikumar, B. (1992). Public versus private investment in human capital endogenous growth and income inequality. *Journal of Political Economy, 100*, 813–834.
17. Groezen, B. V., Leers, B., & Meijdam, L. (2003). Social security and endogenous fertility: Pensions and child allowances as Siamese twins. *Journal of Public Economics, 87*, 233–251.
18. Grossman, G. M., & Yanagawa, N. (1993). Asset bubbles and endogenous growth. *Journal of Monetary Economics, 31*, 3–19.
19. Hirazawa, M., & Yakita, A. (2009). Fertility, child care outside the home, and pay-as-you-go social security. *Journal of Population Economics, 22*, 565–583.
20. Kaganovich, M., & Zilcha, I. (1999). Education, social security, and growth. *Journal of Public Economics, 71*, 289–309.
21. Lapan, H. E., & Enders, W. (1990). Endogenous fertility, Ricardian equivalence, and debt management policy. *Journal of Monetary Economics, 22*, 3–42.
22. Morand, O. F. (1999). Endogenous fertility, income distribution, and growth. *Journal of Economic Growth, 4*, 331–349.
23. Munro, A. (1989). In-kind transfers, cash grants and the supply of labour. *European Economic Review, 33*, 1597–1604.
24. Omori, T. (2002, in Japanese). Public child care and economic growth. *The annual of Japan Economic Policy Association, 50*, 79–85.
25. Omori, T. (2009). Effects of public education and social security on fertility. *Journal of Population Economics, 22*, 585–601.
26. Pecchenino, R. A., & Pollard, P. S. (2002). Dependent children and aged parents: Funding education and social security in an aging economy. *Journal of Macroeconomics, 24*, 145–169.

27. Pecchenino, R. A., & Utendorf, K. R. (1999). Social security, social welfare and the aging population. *Journal of Population Economics, 12*, 607–623.
28. Razin, A., Sadka, E., & Swagel, P. (2002). The aging population and the size of the welfare state. *Journal of Political Economy, 110*, 900–918.
29. Romer, P. M. (1986). Increasing returns and long-run growth. *Journal of Political Economy, 94*, 1002–1037.
30. Samuelson, P. (1958). An exact consumption-loan model of interest with or without the social contrivance of money. *Journal of Political Economy, 66*, 467–482.
31. Tabata, K. (2003). Inverted u-shaped fertility dynamics, the poverty trap and growth. *Economics Letters, 81*, 241–248.
32. Yakita, A. (2001). Uncertain lifetime, fertility and social security. *Journal of Population Economics, 14*, 635–640.
33. Yew, S. L., & Zhang, J. (2009). Optimal social security in a dynastic model with human capital externalities, fertility and endogenous growth. *Journal of Public Economics, 93*, 605–619.
34. Wigger, B. U. (1999). Pay-as-you-go financed public pensions in a model of endogenous growth and fertility. *Journal of Population Economics, 12*, 625–640.
35. Zhang, J. (1995). Does unfunded social security also depress output growth? *Economics Letters, 49*, 307–312.
36. Zhang, J. (1995). Social security and endogenous growth. *Journal of Public Economics, 58*, 185–213.
37. Zhang, J., & Zhang, J. (1998). Social security, intergenerational transfers, and endogenous growth. *Canadian Journal of Economics, 31*, 1225–1241.
38. Zhang, J., & Zhang, J. (2003). Long-run effects of unfunded social security with earnings-dependent benefits. *Journal of Economic Dynamics and Control, 28*, 617–641.
39. Zhang, J., & Zhang, J. (2004). How does social security affect economic growth? Evidence form cross-country data. *Journal of Population Economics, 17*, 473–500.
40. Zhang, J., & Zhang, J. (2007). Optimal social security in a dynastic model with investment externalities and endogenous fertility. *Journal of Economic Dynamics and Control, 31*, 3545–3567.

Chapter 13
Environmental R&D Organization in a Differentiated Cournot Duopoly

Yasunori Ouchida

13.1 Introduction

As global warming and environmental damage caused by pollution expand, it has become increasingly necessary to reduce pollution and improve environmental quality. Since the 1980s, numerous economists have devoted their research efforts to command-and-control regulation, tradable emission permits, emission tax, and so on. Furthermore, comparative research of environmental policies has been performed to date from the viewpoint of examining the incentives of innovating environmental technology and achieving the social optimum (Requate [13, 14]).

In particular, Katsoulacos and Xepapadeas [5] derived the optimal emission tax and the optimal subsidy for the environmental policy, which are pre-committed before firms invest in pollution abatement in Cournot oligopoly with R&D spillovers. However, before the 1990s, the credibility of environmental policy had seen little challenge in previous studies of environmental economics, although it is an important issue in environmental regulation.

During the past two decades, environmental research from the viewpoint of policy's credibility has increased (see Denicolò [3], Gershbach and Glazer [4], Marsiliani and Renstrom [6], Requate [15] and others). Petrakis and Xepapadeas [9] specifically examine the timing of an emission tax for a monopolist and consider whether the emission tax should be pre-committed to or not before the firm chooses their own environmental innovative efforts. They point out that if the regulator is unable to precommit to the emission tax, then social welfare with non-precommitment tends to be less than that with pre-commitment. Actually, as the

Y. Ouchida (✉)
Department of Economics, Hiroshima University, 1-2-1 Kagamiyama, Higashi-Hiroshima city, Hiroshima 739-8525, Japan
e-mail: ouchida@hiroshima-u.ac.jp

T. Naito (ed.), *Sustainable Growth and Development in a Regional Economy*,
New Frontiers in Regional Science: Asian Perspectives 13,
DOI 10.1007/978-4-431-55294-9_13

credibility problem has come to be recognized widely, firms' unilateral actions with respect to the environment receive more attention.

Poyago-Theotoky and Teerasuwannajak [12] consider a setting in which two firms produce a differentiated good that engenders emissions. They explore the economic impacts generated by the timing of emission taxation. Their main results reveal that social welfare under a time-consistent emission tax is greater than the precommitment case when environmental R&D cost is sufficiently inefficient.

Poyago-Theotoky [11] presents examinations of whether Cournot duopolists' coordination behavior in emission-reducing R&D is socially allowable when a regulator has no precommitment capability for emissions taxes. In that study, she shows that environmental R&D cartelization is socially preferred to environmental competition when damage is slight, or if given inefficient R&D cost and severe damage.

Game-theoretic studies conducted by Poyago-Theotoky [11] and Poyago-Theotoky and Teerasuwannajak [12] represent excellent contributions presenting policy implications for environmental R&D and emissions tax policy. However, nobody knows how the degree of product differentiation affects the regulator's decision on social superiority of environmental R&D organizations: environmental R&D competition vs. environmental R&D cartelization. This chapter investigates this unanswered question. Furthermore, we examine a time-consistent negative emission tax. This chapter is regarded as an extension of the analysis conducted by Chap. 6.

This chapter proceeds as follows. Section 13.2 presents the model of a time-consistent emission tax policy developed by Poyago-Theotoky and Teerasuwannajak [12] and Poyago-Theotoky [11]. Section 13.3 presents a description of the solution procedures of the three-stage game under environmental R&D competition. Section 13.4 examines the case of environmental R&D cartelization. In Sect. 13.5, two environmental R&D regimes are compared. Section 13.6 presents policy implications derived from our theoretical investigations. In Sect. 13.7, weak aspects of Japanese competition policy are discussed. The final section summarizes the results.

13.2 Model

This chapter presents an examination of a differentiated Cournot duopoly model in a setting where the government has no precommitment ability for an emissions tax. Furthermore, we describe the regulatory circumstances under which both firms pollute with emissions and invest in environmental R&D. The analyses in this chapter assume that each firm has identical end-of-pipe type technology for emissions reduction and an identical cost structure.[1]

[1]For the case of cleaner production technology, see Chiou and Hu [1].

Throughout this chapter, we use the analytical frameworks developed respectively in work by Poyago-Theotoky and Teerasuwannajak [12] and by Poyago-Theotoky [11].

13.2.1 Market Structure and Consumers

Each firm produces a differentiated good and engages in Cournot competition. According to the analytical framework presented by Singh and Vives [16], a representative consumer's utility function is assumed to be

$$U(q_i, q_j) = a(q_i + q_j) - \frac{1}{2}(q_i^2 + 2\theta q_i q_j + q_j^2) + Z, \tag{13.1}$$

where the value of $a(> 0)$ is the parameter of market size. The value of $Z(> 0)$ captures the consumption of a numeraire good. The value of $q_i(i = 1, 2)$ denotes firm i's output level. Both goods are substitutable; the value of $\theta(\in [0, 1])$ denotes the parameter of product differentiation between both goods. When $\theta = 1(\theta = 0)$, then both goods are completely homogeneous (independent).

Utility maximization yields the following inverse demand function of good i produced by firm i:

$$p_i(q_i, q_j) = a - (q_i + \theta q_j), \tag{13.2}$$

where, $i,j = 1, 2; i \neq j$. From (13.2), the consumers' surplus CS is captured by $CS \equiv (1/2)(q_i^2 + 2\theta q_i q_j + q_j^2)$.

13.2.2 Environmental R&D and Cost

The value of each firm's emissions per-unit output is assumed to be one. Firm i's environmental R&D effort is captured by z_i. Both firms use end-of-pipe technology for pollution abatement. This chapter assumes no spillover effect of R&D activity.[2] Although this abatement technology is insufficient to reduce the figure for emissions per unit output, it mitigates emissions by cutting emissions at the end of the production process.

[2] As pointed out by De Marchi [2], many polluting firms buy the technology for pollution abatement from the outsider firm. This assumption describes such circumstances.

Firm i receives benefits (R&D fruits) only from its own environmental R&D efforts.[3] When firm i's output level is q_i, then the R&D expenditures $(\gamma/2)z_i^2$, $(\gamma > 0)$ enable firm i to abate its emissions from q_i to

$$e_i(q_i, z_i) \equiv q_i - z_i. \tag{13.3}$$

A lower value of γ means higher efficiency of the environmental R&D expenditure. No fixed costs for pollution abatement are necessary. In addition, firm i's total cost function is additively separable with respect to production costs and R&D expenditures:

$$C_i(q_i, z_i) = cq_i + (\gamma/2)z_i^2. \tag{13.4}$$

Therein, we assume that $c > 0$ and $A \equiv a - c > 0$.

13.2.3 *Environmental Externality and Social Welfare*

Firm i's net emissions, $e_i(q_i, z_i)$, depend both on the output and on environmental R&D efforts. Total emissions $E \equiv e_i(q_i, z_i) + e_j(q_j, z_j)$ cause environmental damage, as

$$D(E) \equiv dE^2/2, \tag{13.5}$$

where the value of d denotes the damage parameter. This chapter assumes that $d > \underline{d} \equiv (-1 + \sqrt{3})/2$.[4]

Social welfare function SW is defined as the sum of consumers' surplus and producer's surplus less environmental damage $D(E)$ and total R&D expenditures, as $\sum_{i=1}^{2}(\gamma/2)z_i^2$.

13.2.4 *Timing and R&D Regimes*

The government has no precommitment ability for emission tax rate t. We explore the following three-stage game under two R&D regimes: environmental R&D competition and environmental R&D cooperation. The time structure is the following.

[3]The emissions function of end-of-pipe type with R&D spillover effect is also used by Poyago-Theotoky [11] and Ouchida and Goto [8].

[4]An interior solution for environmental R&D efforts is guaranteed by the following relaxed assumption: $d > \underline{d} \equiv (-1 + \sqrt{3})/2$. In fact, two equilibrium values of R&D efforts (z_n and z_c) obtained in this chapter are both positive for all $\theta \in [0, 1]$ if $d > \underline{d}$. For details, see Ouchida and Goto [7].

(i) Environmental R&D competition.

- Stage 1: Firm i determines z_i to maximize its own profit (π_i) simultaneously and noncooperatively.
- Stage 2: The regulator determines emission tax rate (t) to maximize social welfare.
- Stage 3: Firm i determines output level (q_i) simultaneously and noncooperatively to maximize its own profit.

(ii) Environmental R&D cartelization.

- Stage 1: Firm i determines z_i to maximize joint profits ($\pi_i + \pi_j$) simultaneously and cooperatively.
- Stage 2: The regulator determines emission tax rate (t) to maximize social welfare.
- Stage 3: Firm i determines output level (q_i) simultaneously and noncooperatively to maximize its own profit.

In both regimes, the emission tax rate is set at the second stage after firms' environmental R&D. In the former regime, in the second stage, duopolists choose environmental R&D efforts simultaneously and noncooperatively. In stage 3, two firms decide their production level. The production cartel is not permitted by antitrust law.

In the time structure of the latter regime, firm i's objective function during stage 2 differs from that in the former regime. Firm i determines z_i to maximize joint profits ($\pi_i + \pi_j$) simultaneously and cooperatively in the second stage. Other points are identical to the case of environmental R&D competition.

13.3 Environmental R&D Competition

In this section, we intend to derive the SPNE outcome under environmental R&D competition. We hereby provide the solution procedures and the relevant results.

13.3.1 Production

First, we examine the final stage. In stage 3, firm i determines production level q_i simultaneously and noncooperatively to maximize its own profit as

$$\pi_i(q_i, q_j) = p_i(q_i, q_j)q_i - cq_i - t\{q_i - z_i\} - \frac{\gamma z_i^2}{2}, \tag{13.6}$$

where $i, j = 1, 2; i \neq j$.

The corresponding first-order conditions for profit-maximization are derived as

$$\frac{\partial \pi_i(q_i, q_j)}{\partial q_i} = A - t - 2q_i - \theta p_j = 0, \tag{13.7}$$

where $A \equiv a - c (> 0)$ and $i, j = 1, 2; i \neq j$.[5] From this result, it can be understood that both goods are strategic substitutes.

These conditions (Eq. 13.7) yield the symmetric equilibrium quantity level as

$$q_i(t) = \frac{A - t}{2 + \theta} \equiv q(t). \tag{13.8}$$

We obtain that $\partial q_i(t)/\partial \theta < 0$. When $\theta = 0$, then equilibrium output level is identical to the case of monopoly.

Consequently, firm i's profit is calculated as

$$\pi_i(t) = [q(t)]^2 + tz_i - \frac{\gamma z_i^2}{2}. \tag{13.9}$$

From 13.8, quantity level under *laissez-faire* (i.e., the case of $t = 0$) are derived as $A/(2+\theta)$. The emission level under *laissez-faire* is equivalent to $A/(2+\theta)$. This will be used in Sect. 13.5.7.

13.3.2 Emission Tax

In the second stage, the government determines the optimal emission tax rate t to maximize social welfare, $SW(t)$. Social welfare during the second stage is calculated as follows.

$$SW(t) = 2Aq(t) - (1+\theta)[q(t)]^2 - \frac{d}{2}\left\{2q(t) - (z_i + z_j)\right\}^2 - \sum_{i=1}^{2} \frac{\gamma z_i^2}{2}. \tag{13.10}$$

In that function, the first and the second terms respectively denote the total surplus and environmental damage. The third term presents total costs for environmental R&D.

[5] The second-order condition is satisfied.

The first-order condition for social welfare maximization is given as the following equation.

$$\frac{dSW(t)}{dt} = 2\Big(A - (1+\theta)q(t) - d(2q(t) - \{z_i + z_j\})\Big)\frac{dq(t)}{dt} = 0. \tag{13.11}$$

Therein, $dq(t)/dt = -(1/(2+\theta)) < 0$.

From the first-order condition, the optimal emission tax rate is derived as follows.[6]

$$t(z_i, z_j) = \frac{(2d-1)A - d(2+\theta)\{z_i + z_j\}}{1+\theta+2d}. \tag{13.12}$$

Therefore, we obtain that

$$\frac{\partial t(z_i, z_j)}{\partial z_i} = \frac{\partial t(z_i, z_j)}{\partial z_j} = \frac{-d(2+\theta)}{1+\theta+2d} < 0. \tag{13.13}$$

Equation (13.13) describes ratchet effect. Each firm's environmental investment level determined at the first stage affects the future emission tax rate. The emission tax rate set in the second stage decreases with larger environmental R&D efforts (see Eq. (13.13)). This ratchet effect plays a salient role between the government and firms.[7]

By substituting (13.12) into (13.8), we obtain the subgame equilibrium production level as follows.

$$q(z_i, z_j) = \frac{A + d\{z_i + z_j\}}{1+\theta+2d}. \tag{13.14}$$

This result suggests that larger environmental R&D efforts increase the production level.

Furthermore, using Eqs. (13.12) and (13.14) and the definition of E, total emissions are expressed as

$$E(z_i, z_j) = \frac{A - \{z_i + z_j\}}{(1+d)}. \tag{13.15}$$

From $\partial E/\partial z_i < 0$, one can readily find that the marginal increase of environmental R&D effort, z_i, reduces total emissions.

---

[6]The second-order condition is satisfied.

[7]For details, see the related reports presented in the Footnote 10 of Chap. 6.

Similarly, the subgame equilibrium social welfare is derived as follows.

$$SW(z_i, z_j) = 2Aq(z_i, z_j) - (1+\theta)[q(z_i, z_j)]^2$$
$$-(d/2)\{2q(z_i, z_j) - (z_i + z_j)\}^2 - \frac{\gamma}{2}z_i^2 - \frac{\gamma}{2}z_j^2. \quad (13.16)$$

Therein, $i, j = 1, 2; i \neq j$. The subgame equilibrium profit is expressed in Sect. 13.3.3 (see Eq. (13.17)).

13.3.3 Environmental R&D

In the first stage, each firm simultaneously and noncooperatively chooses a level of environmental R&D effort to maximize its own profit (π_i).

After substituting (13.12) and (13.14) into the profit function and performing some manipulation of the function, firm i's profit function in the first stage can be expressed as

$$\pi_i(z_i, z_j) = \left[q(z_i, z_j)\right]^2 + t(z_i, z_j)z_i - \frac{\gamma}{2}z_i^2, \quad (13.17)$$

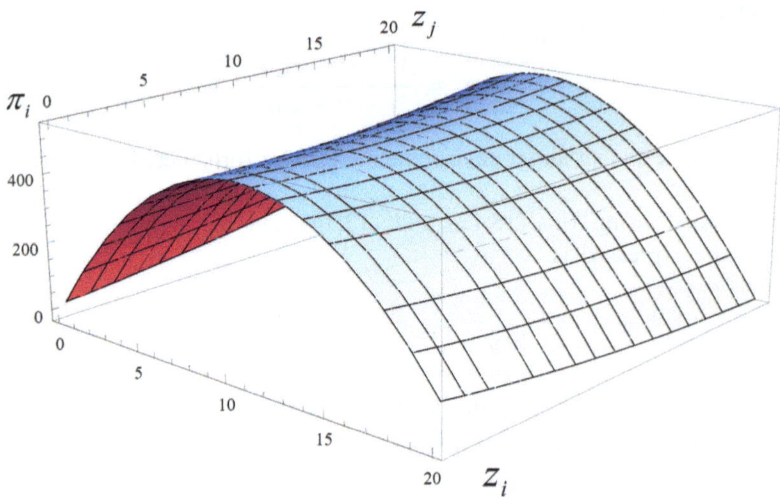

Fig. 13.1 Profit function

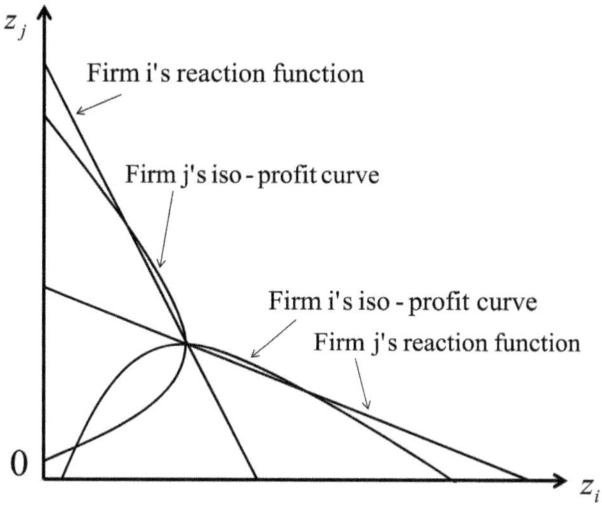

Fig. 13.2 Reaction function (i)

where $i, j = 1, 2; i \neq j$. The typical pattern of this profit function is expressed as shown in Fig. 13.1. To maximize its own profit, $\pi_i(z_i, z_j)$, firm i chooses environmental R&D effort level z_i. The first-order condition is the following.

$$\frac{\partial \pi_i(z_i, z_j)}{\partial z_i} = 2q(z_i, z_j)\frac{dq}{dt}\frac{\partial t}{\partial z_i} + z_i\frac{\partial t}{\partial z_i} + t(z_i, z_j) - \gamma z_i = 0. \tag{13.18}$$

Therein, $i, j = 1, 2; i \neq j$.

The equation above (13.18) is the firm i's reaction function. In the first stage, both firms are in the strategic interactions. Both reaction functions are linear and downward-sloping. Environmental R&D efforts are strategic substitutes.[8] In (z_i, z_j, π_i)-space, firm i's profit $\pi_i(z_i, z_j)$ presents an elliptic paraboloid or a hyperbolic paraboloid. Therefore, two typical patterns of relation exist between reaction functions and isoprofit curves (Figs. 13.2 and 13.3). Smaller γ generates the pattern depicted in Fig. 13.2. In contrast, larger γ generates the pattern depicted in Fig. 13.3.

We specifically address the symmetric equilibrium environmental R&D efforts. From the first-order condition, we obtain the equilibrium R&D effort level under environmental R&D competition as follows.[9]

$$z_{\mathrm{n}} = \frac{[(2d + 1 + \theta)(2d - 1) + 2d]A}{\Gamma}. \tag{13.19}$$

[8]Both firms' environmental R&D efforts are strategic substitutes, even if R&D spillover effects exist.

[9]The second-order condition is satisfied.

Fig. 13.3 Reaction function (ii)

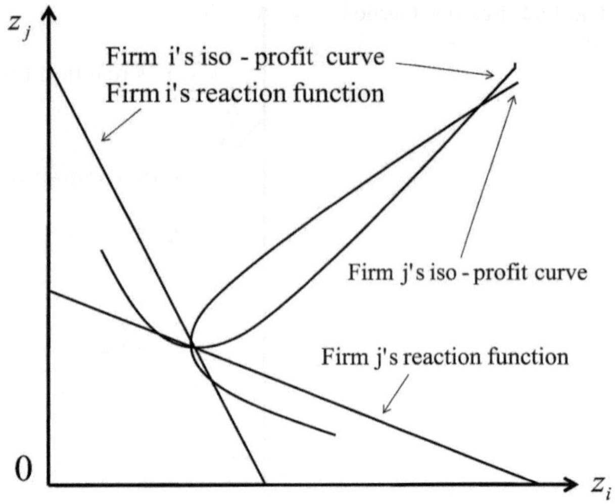

In that equation, $\Gamma \equiv \gamma(2d+1+\theta)^2 + d[3(2d+1+\theta)(2+\theta) - 4d] > 0$.[10] In Eq. (13.19), the subscript n stands for the case of environmental R&D competition. Under the assumption of $d > (-1+\sqrt{3})/2$, one can confirm that $z_n > 0$ for all $\gamma > 0$ and $\theta \in [0, 1]$.

Next, we seek SPNE outcomes for other variables. Substituting (13.19) into (13.12) and (13.14)–(13.17), one can obtain the equilibrium emission tax rate, output level, emission, profits, and social welfare.

$$t_n = \frac{[(2d-1)(1+\theta+2d)\gamma + d((2d-1)\theta - 2)]A}{\Gamma}, \tag{13.20}$$

$$q_n = \frac{[\gamma + 2d(2+2d+\gamma) + (3d+\gamma)\theta]A}{\Gamma}, \tag{13.21}$$

$$e_n = \frac{[(1+2d)(1+\gamma) + \theta(1+d+\gamma)]A}{\Gamma}, \tag{13.22}$$

$$\pi_n = q_n^2 + t_n z_n - (\gamma/2) z_n^2, \tag{13.23}$$

$$SW_n = 2Aq_n - (1+\theta)q_n^2 - 2d\{q_n - z_n\}^2 - \gamma z_n^2. \tag{13.24}$$

Therefore, one can readily confirm that $e_n > 0$ for all $\gamma > 0$, $\theta \in [0, 1]$, and that $d > \underline{d} \equiv (-1+\sqrt{3})/2$.

[10] Under the assumption of $d > \underline{d} \equiv (-1+\sqrt{3})/2$, $z_n > 0$ for all $\theta \in [0, 1]$. For details, see Section 3 of Ouchida and Goto [7].

13.4 Environmental R&D Cartelization

This section presents an exploration of the scenario of environmental R&D cartelization. In this scenario, contrary to the explanation presented in the previous section, each firm coordinates its own environmental R&D effort level to maximize joint profits.[11]

13.4.1 Production

The analysis and its results during the third stage are identical to those in the case of environmental R&D cooperation. For details, see Sect. 13.3.1. Therefore, from the first-order condition (13.7), one can derive the subgame equilibrium output level as

$$q_i(t) = \frac{A-t}{2+\theta}(= q(t)), \tag{13.25}$$

where $i, j = 1, 2; i \neq j$.

13.4.2 Emission Tax

In this scenario, the government determines the optimal emission tax rate t to maximize social welfare, $SW(t)$, during the second stage. Solution procedures and the results are identical to those in the case of environmental R&D cooperation (see Sect. 13.3.2).

As a result, the subgame equilibrium outcomes during the second stage are derived as the following.

$$t(z_i, z_j) = \frac{(2d-1)A - d(2+\theta)\{z_i + z_j\}}{1+\theta+2d}, \tag{13.26}$$

$$q(z_i, z_j) = \frac{A + d\{z_i + z_j\}}{1+\theta+2d}, \tag{13.27}$$

$$E(z_i, z_j) = \frac{A - \{z_i + z_j\}}{(1+d)}, \tag{13.28}$$

$$\pi_i(z_i, z_j) = \left[q(z_i, z_j)\right]^2 + t(z_i, z_j)z_i - \frac{\gamma}{2}z_i^2, \tag{13.29}$$

---

[11] For details of the case of pure Cournot duopoly with spillover effect, see Poyago-Theotoky [11] and Ouchida and Goto [8].

$$SW(z_i, z_j) = 2Aq(z_i, z_j) - (1+\theta)[q(z_i, z_j)]^2 \\ -(d/2)\{q(z_i, z_j) - (z_i + z_j)\}^2 - \frac{\gamma}{2}z_i^2 - \frac{\gamma}{2}z_j^2. \quad (13.30)$$

In those equations, $i, j = 1, 2; i \neq j$.

13.4.3 Environmental R&D

Next, we examine the stage of environmental R&D coordination (environmental R&D cooperation). In the first stage, each firm determines its environmental R&D efforts collusively to maximize joint profit:

$$\begin{aligned} \Pi(z_i, z_j) &\equiv \pi_i(z_i, z_j) + \pi_j(z_i, z_j) \\ &= [q(z_i, z_j)]^2 + t(z_i, z_j)z_i - \frac{\gamma}{2}z_i^2 \\ &\quad + [q(z_i, z_j)]^2 + t(z_i, z_j)z_j - \frac{\gamma}{2}z_j^2. \end{aligned} \quad (13.31)$$

The corresponding first-order condition is expressed as

$$\frac{\partial \Pi(z_i, z_j)}{\partial z_i} = 0 = \frac{\partial \Pi(z_i, z_j)}{\partial z_j}. \quad (13.32)$$

We consider here only the symmetric cooperative equilibrium. The first-order conditions (13.32) yield the equilibrium environmental R&D efforts as follows.[12]

$$z_c = \frac{[(2d+1+\theta)(2d-1) + 4d]A}{\Delta}, \quad (13.33)$$

where $\Delta \equiv \gamma(2d+1+\theta)^2 + 4d[(2d+1+\theta)(2+\theta) - 2d] > 0$. In Eq. (13.33), the subscript c stands for the case of environmental R&D cartelization. Under the assumption of $d > (-1+\sqrt{3})/2$, we can confirm that $z_c > 0$ for all $\gamma > 0$ and $\theta \in [0, 1]$.[13]

Consequently, the equilibrium emission tax rate, output level, emission, profits, and social welfare are obtained respectively as shown below:

$$t_c = \frac{[(2d-1)(1+\theta+2d)\gamma - 2d(2+\theta(2d-1))]A}{\Delta}, \quad (13.34)$$

[12]From Figs. 13.2 and 13.3, we can comfirm that both firms confront the so-called prisoner's dilemma. This chapter assumes that neither firm deviates.

[13]For details, see Section 3 of Ouchida and Goto [7].

$$q_c = \frac{[4d^2 + (1+\theta)\gamma + 2d(3+2\theta+\gamma)]A}{\Delta}, \tag{13.35}$$

$$e_c = \frac{[(1+2d)(1+\gamma) + \theta(1+2d+\gamma)]A}{\Delta}, \tag{13.36}$$

$$\pi_c = q_c^2 + t_c z_c - (\gamma/2) z_c^2, \tag{13.37}$$

$$SW_c = 2Aq_c - (1+\theta)q_c^2 - 2d\{q_c - z_c\}^2 - \gamma z_c^2. \tag{13.38}$$

Consequently, it is straightforward to confirm that $e_c > 0$ for all $\gamma > 0$, $\theta \in [0, 1]$, and $d > \underline{d} \equiv (-1 + \sqrt{3})/2$.

13.5 Comparison Between Two R&D Regimes

In this section, we compare the two R&D regimes: environmental R&D competition and environmental R&D cartelization.

13.5.1 Environmental R&D Effort

First, we provide a comparison in terms of environmental R&D effot level. The difference between z_c and z_n is obtained as

$$z_c - z_n = \frac{Ad(1+\theta+2d)^2\rho}{\Gamma\Delta} > (<)0, \tag{13.39}$$

where $\rho \equiv \theta(2d-1) - 2(1+\gamma) > (<)0$, $\Gamma \equiv \gamma(2d+1+\theta)^2 + d[3(2d+1+\theta)(2+\theta) - 4d] > 0$ and $\Delta \equiv \gamma(2d+1+\theta)^2 + 4d[(2d+1+\theta)(2+\theta) - 2d] > 0$.

The sign of $\{z_c - z_n\}$ depends on the value of ρ. The sign of ρ is positive (negative) if

$$\gamma > (<)\ \bar{\gamma} \equiv \frac{2d\theta - (2+\theta)}{2}. \tag{13.40}$$

From the definition of ρ, when $d < (2+\theta)/2\theta$, then $z_c > z_n$ for all $\gamma > 0$. If $\theta = 0$, then $\rho > 0$ for all $\gamma > 0$ and $d > \underline{d} \equiv (-1+\sqrt{3})/2$. The salient implication is that if $\theta = 0$, then $\bar{\gamma} > 0$ for all $\gamma > 0$ and $d > \underline{d} \equiv (-1+\sqrt{3})/2$. Consequently, we obtain the following theorem.

Theorem 13.1. *If $\theta = 0$, then $z_c > z_n$ for all $\gamma > 0$ and $d > \underline{d} \equiv (-1 + \sqrt{3})/2$.*

Figure 13.4 describes the results of (13.39) and (13.40). The curve $\bar{\gamma}$ (see (13.40)) is depicted in Fig. 13.4. Strictly speaking, Fig. 13.4 presents the case of $\theta = 0.75$. On the curve $\bar{\gamma}$, $z_c = z_n$. Furthermore, when parameter set $(d, \gamma; \theta)$ exists in the

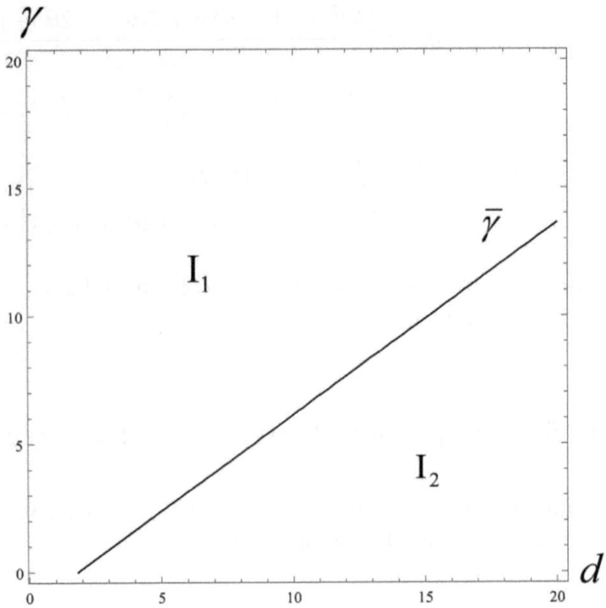

Fig. 13.4 Comparison of two R&D regimes

Region I_1, we have that $z_c > z_n$. However, when parameter set $(d, \gamma; \theta)$ exists in the Region I_2, then $z_c < z_n$.

Theorem 13.2 summarizes these results.

Theorem 13.2. *Presuming that $\theta \in (0, 1]$. Then, we have the following:*

(i) If $\underline{d} < d < (2 + \theta)/2\theta$, then $z_c > z_n$ for all $\gamma > 0$.
(ii) If $d > (2 + \theta)/2\theta$ and $\gamma > \bar{\gamma}$, then $z_c > z_n$.
(iii) If $d > (2 + \theta)/2\theta$ and $\gamma < \bar{\gamma}$, then $z_c < z_n$.

13.5.2 Production Level

Second, we carry out a comparison of equilibrium outputs: q_c and q_n. The difference between them is calculated as

$$q_c - q_n = \frac{A + 2dz_c}{1 + \theta + 2d} - \frac{A + 2dz_n}{1 + \theta + 2d} = \frac{2d\{z_c - z_n\}}{1 + \theta + 2d}. \tag{13.41}$$

The result of (13.41) implies that the sign of $\{q_c - q_n\}$ is identical to the sign of $\{z_c - z_n\}$. Consequently, the sign of $\{q_c - q_n\}$ is arbitrary. On the curve $\bar{\gamma}$ depicted in Fig. 13.4, we have that $q_c = q_n$. Furthermore, in the Region I_1 above the curve

$\bar{\gamma}$, we have that $q_c > q_n$. However, in the Region I$_2$ below the curve $\bar{\gamma}$, we have that $q_c < q_n$. These results are summarized as the following theorems.

Theorem 13.3. *If $\theta = 0$, then $q_c > q_n$ for all $\gamma > 0$ and $d > \underline{d} \equiv (-1 + \sqrt{3})/2$.*

Theorem 13.4. *Presuming that $\theta \in (0, 1)$, then we have the following:*

(i) If $\underline{d} < d < (2 + \theta)/2\theta$, then $q_c > q_n$ for all $\gamma > 0$.
(ii) If $d > (2 + \theta)/2\theta$ and $\gamma > \bar{\gamma}$, then $q_c > q_n$.
(iii) If $d > (2 + \theta)/2\theta$ and $\gamma < \bar{\gamma}$, then $q_c < q_n$.

13.5.3 Emission Tax Rate

Third, we conduct a comparison of two emission tax rates: t_c and t_n. The difference between them is yielded as

$$\begin{aligned} t_c - t_n &= \frac{(2d-1)A - 2d(1+\theta)z_c}{1+\theta+2d} - \frac{(2d-1)A - 2d(2+\theta)z_n}{1+\theta+2d} \\ &= -\frac{2d(2+\theta)\{z_c - z_n\}}{1+\theta+2d}. \end{aligned} \tag{13.42}$$

The equation above (13.42) shows that the sign of $\{t_c - t_n\}$ is completely opposite to the sign of $\{z_c - z_n\}$. Therefore, the sign of $\{t_c - t_n\}$ is arbitrary. On the curve $\bar{\gamma}$ depicted in Fig. 13.4, we have that $t_c = t_n$. Furthermore, in the Region I$_1$ above the curve $\bar{\gamma}$, we have that $t_c < t_n$. In contrast, in Region I$_2$ below the curve $\bar{\gamma}$, we have that $t_c > t_n$. The following two theorems summarize these results.

Theorem 13.5. *If $\theta = 0$, then $t_c < t_n$ for all $\gamma > 0$ and $d > \underline{d} \equiv (-1 + \sqrt{3})/2$.*

Theorem 13.6. *Presuming that $\theta \in (0, 1]$, then we have the following:*

(i) If $\underline{d} < d < (2 + \theta)/2\theta$, then $t_c < t_n$ for all $\gamma > 0$.
(ii) If $d > (2 + \theta)/2\theta$ and $\gamma > \bar{\gamma}$, then $t_c < t_n$.
(iii) If $d > (2 + \theta)/2\theta$ and $\gamma < \bar{\gamma}$, then $t_c > t_n$.

13.5.4 Total Emissions

Here, total emissions under two R&D regimes are compared. Two equilibrium values under both R&D regimes are $2e_c$ and $2e_c$. Using the result of Eq. (13.41), the difference between them is obtained as follows.

$$
\begin{aligned}
2e_c - 2e_n &= 2\{(q_c - z_n) - (z_c - z_n)\} \\
&= 2\left\{\frac{2d\{z_c - z_n\}}{1+\theta+2d} - \{z_c - z_n\}\right\} \\
&= -\frac{2(2+\theta)\{z_c - z_n\}}{1+\theta+2d}.
\end{aligned} \tag{13.43}
$$

From Eq. (13.43) above, one can confirm that the sign of $\{e_c - e_n\}$ is completely opposite to the sign of $\{z_c - z_n\}$. As a result, sign$\{e_c - e_n\}$ is arbitrary. On the curve $\bar{\gamma}$ shown in Fig. 13.4, $e_c = e_n$. Furthermore, in the Region I_1 above the curve $\bar{\gamma}$, $e_c < e_n$. In contrast, in the Region I_2 below the curve $\bar{\gamma}$, we have that $e_c > e_n$. These results are summarized as the following theorems.

Theorem 13.7. *If $\theta = 0$, then $e_c < e_n$ for all $\gamma > 0$ and $d > \underline{d} \equiv (-1+\sqrt{3})/2$.*

Theorem 13.8. *Presuming that $\theta \in (0, 1]$, we have the following:*

(i) If $\underline{d} < d < (2+\theta)/2\theta$, then $e_c < e_n$ for all $\gamma > 0$.
(ii) If $d > (2+\theta)/2\theta$ and $\gamma > \bar{\gamma}$, then $e_c < e_n$.
(iii) If $d > (2+\theta)/2\theta$ and $\gamma < \bar{\gamma}$, then $e_c > e_n$.

13.5.5 Profits

We proceed to a comparison of the firms' profits: π_c and π_n. After some manipulations, we obtain the following result.

$$
\begin{aligned}
\pi_c - \pi_n &= q_c^2 + t_c z_c - (\gamma/2) z_c^2 \\
&\quad - \{q_n^2 + t_n z_n - (\gamma/2) z_n^2\} \\
&= \frac{\Omega\{z_c - z_n\}^2 A^2}{2(1+\theta+2d)^2},
\end{aligned} \tag{13.44}
$$

Therein, $\Omega \equiv (1+\theta+2d)^2\gamma + 4d(1+\theta)(2+\theta+2d)$. We readily obtain that $\Omega > 0$ for all $\gamma > 0$, $\theta \in [0, 1]$, and $d > \underline{d} \equiv (-1+\sqrt{3})/2$.

Equation (13.44) shows that $\pi_c - \pi_n \geq 0$. As explained in Sect. 13.5.1, only when $\rho \equiv \theta(2d-1) - 2(1+\gamma) = 0$, then $z_c = z_n$.[14] Therefore, the following theorem is obtained.

[14] For details, see Eq. (13.39) in the current chapter.

Theorem 13.9. *(i) Only when* $\rho \equiv \theta(2d-1) - 2(1+\gamma) = 0$, *then* $\pi_c = \pi_n$.
(ii) If $\rho \equiv \theta(2d-1) + 2(1+\gamma) \neq 0$, *then* $\pi_c > \pi_n$.

From the part (i) of Theorem 13.9, it is apparent that $\pi_c = \pi_n$ if and only if $z_c = z_n$. Moreover, part (ii) of Theorem 13.9 suggests that both firms invariably have some incentives for environmental R&D cartelization.

13.5.6 Social Welfare

The previous section has revealed that each firm always prefers environmental R&D cartelization to environmental R&D competition. This section provides examinations of whether the government has a social incentive to allow R&D coordination in an environmental innovation area.

Hereinafter, for simplicity, our examinations proceed under the following assumption.[15]

Assumption. $\gamma = 1$.

From the SPNE outcomes under two R&D regimes, the differences between SW_c and SW_n are calculated as follows.[16]

$$\begin{aligned} SW_c - SW_n &= \{2Aq_c - (1+\theta)q_c^2 - 2d\{q_c - z_c\}^2 - \gamma z_c^2\}|_{\gamma=1} \\ &\quad -\{2Aq_n - (1+\theta)q_n^2 - 2d\{q_n - z_n\}^2 - \gamma z_n^2\}|_{\gamma=1} \\ &= \frac{\{z_c - z_n\}X}{1+2\theta+2d}, \end{aligned} \tag{13.45}$$

$$\begin{aligned} \text{Where } X &\equiv 4dA - [1+\theta+2d(2+\theta)][z_c + z_n]\} \\ &= \frac{AJ}{[\Delta|_{\gamma=1}][\Gamma|_{\gamma=1}]}. \end{aligned} \tag{13.46}$$

From examination of the sign of X, we found the following. As preliminary results, the signs of three elements in Eq. (13.46) are explored respectively. After some manipulations, we obtain the following.

$$\Gamma|_{\gamma=1} = (2d+1+\theta)^2 + d[3(2d+1+\theta)(2+\theta) - 4d] > 0, \tag{13.47}$$

$$\Delta|_{\gamma=1} = (2d+1+\theta)^2 + 4d[(2d+1+\theta)(2+\theta) - 2d] > 0, \tag{13.48}$$

$$J \equiv 4d[\Gamma|_{\gamma=1}][\Delta|_{\gamma=1}] - [1+\theta+2d(2+\theta)]$$

[15] The assumption of $\gamma = 1$ is consistent with studies produced by Petrakis and Xepapadeas [10], Wang and Wang [17], and others.

[16] See, Eqs. (13.24) and (13.38).

$$
\begin{aligned}
&\times\{[\Gamma|_{\gamma=1}][(2d+1+\theta)(2d-1)+4d]\\
&+[\Delta|_{\gamma=1}][(2d+1+\theta)(2d-1)+2d]\}\\
=\ &\theta(1+\theta)^3+(1+\theta)^2(4+\theta(19+7\theta))d\\
&+2(1+\theta)(48+\theta(105+\theta(67+12\theta)))d^2\\
&+12(1+\theta)(36+\theta(57+\theta(25+3\theta)))d^3\\
&+8(88+\theta(173+6\theta(17+3\theta)))d^4\\
&+48(2+\theta)(4+3\theta)d^5>0. \qquad (13.49)
\end{aligned}
$$

Therefore, the results of (13.47)–(13.49) prove that the sign of X is strictly positive for all $\theta \in [0, 1]$ and $d > \underline{d} \equiv (-1+\sqrt{3})/2$ (i.e., $X > 0$).

Consequently, Eq. (13.45) and the result of $X > 0$ show that the sign of $\{SW_c - SW_n\}$ depends on the sign of $\{z_c - z_n\}$. Figure 13.5 shows the graphical result of the comparison conducted by Eq. (13.45). In Fig. 13.5, curve $\hat{\theta}$ denotes the parameter set (d, θ) satisfies that $SW_c = SW_n$. If the value of d is strictly smaller than $\hat{d} = 5/2$, then we have $SW_c > SW_n$ for all $\theta \in [0, 1]$.[17] Furthermore, if $d > \hat{d}$ and $\theta < \hat{\theta}$, then $SW_c > SW_n$ (see Region II_1). In contrast, if $d > \hat{d}$ and $\theta > \hat{\theta}$, then $SW_c < SW_n$ (see Region II_2). These results are summarized as the following theorem.

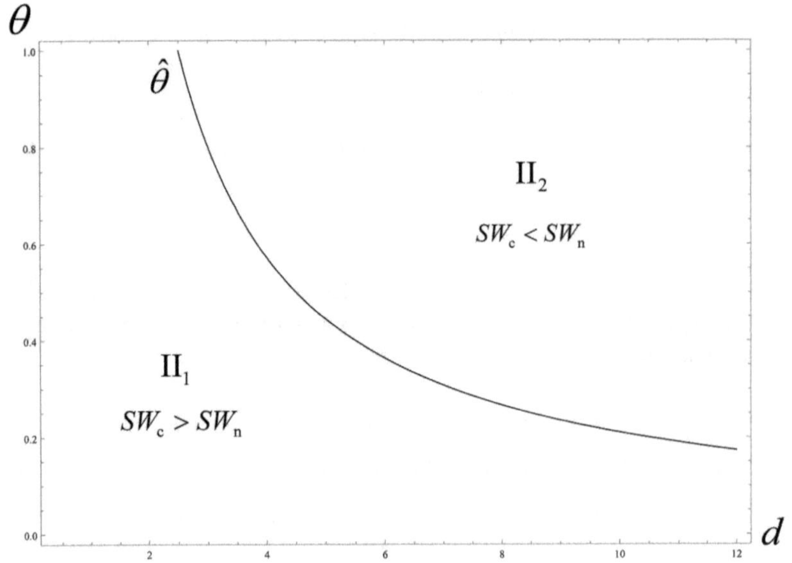

Fig. 13.5 Social welfare

[17]The value of $\hat{d}$ is derived using the definition of ρ (see Sect. 13.5.1).

Theorem 13.10. *(i) When* $\underline{d} < d < \hat{d} = 5/2$*, then* $SW_c > SW_n$ *for all* $\theta \in [0, 1]$.
(ii) When $d > \hat{d} = 5/2$ *and* $\theta < \hat{\theta} (\in [0, 1])$*, then* $SW_c > SW_n$.
(iii) When $d > \hat{d} = 5/2$ *and* $\theta > \hat{\theta} (\in [0, 1])$*, then* $SW_c < SW_n$.

From Theorems 13.9 and 13.10, we conclude that firms invariably carry out environmental R&D cartelization whenever the government allows it.

13.5.7 Sign of Emission Tax Rate

Next, we depict the sign of the equilibrium emission tax rate. Consequently, the possibility of $t_n < 0$ does not exist in Region II_2 in Fig. 13.5. Therefore, we concentrate the sign of t_c. Figure 13.6 presents the sign of t_c.

The critical value of the sign of emission tax rate is derived as

$$\theta^* \equiv \frac{4d^2 - 4d - 1}{(2d - 1)^2}. \tag{13.50}$$

On the left region of the curve θ^* (see Region II_{1A}), the government sets the negative emission tax rate ($t_c < 0$). In contrast, on the right region of the curve θ^* (see Regions ($II_{1B} + II_2$)), the government determines the positive emission tax rate ($t_c > 0$).

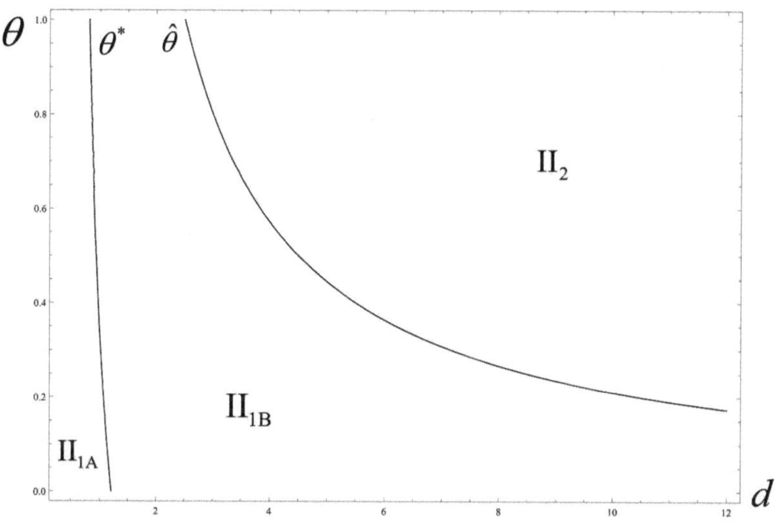

Fig. 13.6 Sign of emission tax rate

13.5.8 Emission-Reducing Effect

In the previous Sect. 13.5.7, we confirmed that the sign of t_c can be negative. We herein examine whether a time consistent-emission tax/subsidy reduce emissions under *laissez-faire*. Total emissions under *laissez-faire* are $2e_0 = 2A/(2+\theta)$ (see Sect. 13.3.1).

The difference between $2e_c$ and $2e_0$ is obtained as follows.

$$2\{e_c - e_0\} = 2\{q_c - z_c\} - \frac{2A}{3}$$
$$= \frac{2A\kappa}{3\mu}, \tag{13.51}$$

Therein, $\mu \equiv 1 + 12d + 12d^2 + \theta^2(1+4d) + 2\theta(1+8d+4d^2) > 0$ and $\kappa \equiv 5 - 12d^2 - \theta^2(1+4d) - 2\theta(-2+5d+4d^2)$.

The sign of κ is arbitrary. From the result above, it is apparent that the sign of $\{e_c - e_0\}$ depends on the sign of κ. Figure 13.7 shows the graphical result of Eq. (13.51).

In Fig. 13.7, the curve $\kappa = 0$ presents parameter set (d, θ) satisfies that $e_c = e_0$. In the left region of the curve $\kappa = 0$ (see Region $\mathrm{II}_{1A(i)}$), we have that $e_c > e_0$. In contrast, in the region between the curves $\kappa = 0$ and $\theta = \hat{\theta}$ (see Region $\mathrm{II}_{1A(ii)}$),

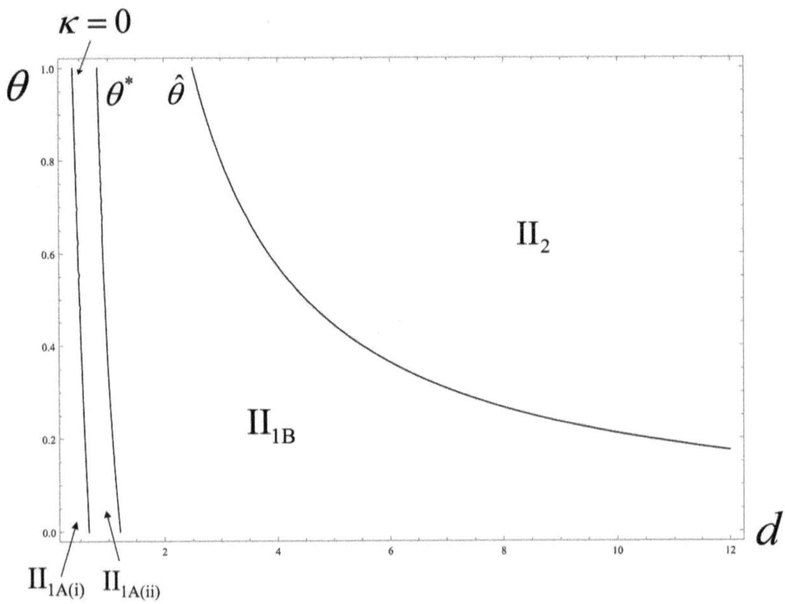

Fig. 13.7 Emission-reducing effect of time-consistent emission subsidy

we have that $e_c < e_0$. In Regions $(\mathrm{II}_{1A(i)} + \mathrm{II}_{1A(ii)})$, it is apparent that $t_c < 0$ (see Sect. 13.5.7).

Therefore, we have the following theorem.

Theorem 13.11. *(i) In Region* $\mathrm{II}_{1A(i)}$*, we have that* $t_c < 0$ *and* $e_c > e_0$.
(ii) In Region $\mathrm{II}_{1A(ii)}$*, we have that* $t_c < 0$ *and* $e_c < e_0$.
(iii) In Regions $(\mathrm{II}_{1B} + \mathrm{II}_2)$*, we have that* $t_c > 0$ *and* $e_c < e_0$.

The part (ii) of Theorem 13.11 proves the emission-reducing effect under a time-consistent emission subsidy.[18]

13.6 Policy Implications

In this section, policy implications derived from our theoretical investigations are considered. Investigations in this chapter present important implications for the policy mix of emission tax policy and competition policy. In particular, in the absence of government's precommitment ability of emission tax, this chapter specifically examines the evaluation of firms' R&D coordination in environmental area.

From Fig. 13.5 and Theorem 13.10, the following can be understood. First, in the regulatory environment of slight environmental damage, alternatively, in the large degree of product differentiation, environmental R&D cartelization is socially preferred. In contrast, in the other regulatory environments, environmental R&D competition is socially preferred. This theoretical result must contribute to design a more preferred R&D policy.

Furthermore, the part (ii) of Theorem 13.11 shows that the government can use a time-consistent emission subsidy as the policy tool for emission-reduction, if environmental damage coefficient is slight sufficient. Contrary to our expectations, emission subsidies do not always increase emissions. We should devote more attention to emission tax policy when environmental damage from a pollutant is sufficiently slight.

13.7 Policy Design and Japan's Experiences

In Japan, competition policy is actually implemented by the Japan Fair Trade Commission (JFTC).[19] The JFTC have enacted guidelines of 25 kinds since "the Act on Prohibition of Private Monopolization and Maintenance of Fair Trade (the Antimonopoly Act)" was enacted in 1947. In the field of joint recycling and

[18]Ouchida and Goto [8] first revealed this effect.

[19]For details, see the JFTC website.

research joint ventures (RJVs), the relevant guidelines have been enacted.[20] In those guidelines, important issues are whether joint activities among firms are socially allowable. Those guidelines cover firms' RJV and R&D coordination. Environmental R&D cartelization (coordination) examined in the current chapter might be regulated by such guidelines. Guidelines on RJV actually state the following.

> *"Where the risks involved or the cost of a research project are too great to be borne by a single firm, or where the firm undertaking the R&D project finds a strong need among other reasons, for joint undertaking with other firm or firms in view of the limitation of its accumulated technological resources, technological development potential and so forth, joint undertaking of the R&D project is considered necessary for the achievement of the objective of the R&D project, such undertaking is less likely to present a problem under the Antimonopoly Act. Moreover, a joint R&D project intended to address so-called external factors, such as developing an environmental or safety measure, may not in itself immediately exclude the possibility for such project to pose a problem under the Antimonopoly Act. However, taking into account cost, risk, and so forth, related to research, it may not be so easy to carry it out alone. In such a case, it is less likely to pose a problem under the Antimonopoly Act.*[21]

These are too ambiguous. No one must disagree with a joint R&D project for mitigation of environmental externality, but such cooperation must affect social welfare. When should the government allow a joint R&D project in environmental innovation area? There exists no specific standard. Why is it so ambiguous? The Japanese antitrust regulator might want strong discretionary power. However, another reason must be considered.

The economists working at the JFTC are fewer than those of other OECD countries. Many bureaucrats of the JFTC lack adequate ability necessary for the regulation designer. The current guidelines in Japanese antitrust regulation prove that the JFTC guidelines have been written by bureaucrats who might not adequately consider academic findings in the field of public health and environmental epidemiology as well as economics.

Returning to the theoretical analysis in the present chapter, the main purpose of this chapter is to examine whether the government should allow environmental R&D cartelization (coordination) in a differentiated Cournot duopoly. To proceed in our study, in line with the existing related literature, we use the quadratic damage function. However, what does the damage function describe in our real world? Many researchers in environmental economics might not have the answer. Moreover, they might have insufficient academic findings of other environmental science areas. To design efficient policies, it is strongly advised to conduct interdisciplinary discussions among bureaucrats and researchers in the areas of economics and environmental science.

---

[20]For details, see the following website.
URL:http://www.jftc.go.jp/en/legislation_gls/imonopoly_guidelines.html

[21]For details, see p.5 of "the Guidelines Concerning Joint Research and Development under the Antimonopoly Act." This guideline is appearing at the website cited in the Footnote 20.

As sketched in this model, strategic interactions exist between government and firms in our society. However, the JFTC have no adequate accumulation of economics related to academic findings. Should only bureaucrats of the JFTC be criticized? The answer is "No." To improve this problem, more economists should be employed in the public sector. Furthermore, personnel exchange among central governments and university researchers should be expanded. The key to solving that problem must be formed slowly through repeated trial-and-error.

13.8 Conclusion

This chapter extends a time-consistent emission tax model analyzed in Chap. 6. We here conducted examinations of a differentiated Cournot duopoly model in a setting in where the government has no precommitment capability for an emissions tax. Furthermore, under the assumption of end-of-pipe technology and no R&D spillover effect, we presented a comparison between two R&D regimes: environmental R&D competition and environmental R&D cartelization.

Our results obtained here show the following facts. First, if environmental damage is sufficiently slight, if and the degree of product differentiation is sufficiently great, then environmental R&D cartelization is socially more preferred. In contrast, when environmental damage is severe, and when the degree of product differentiation is sufficiently slight, environmental R&D competition is socially more preferred. Second, both firms invariably have some incentives for environmental R&D cartelization. Third, time-consistent emission subsidy might be partially justified if environmental damage is sufficiently slight. Moreover, Chap. 13 proves that the regulatory environment in which a time-consistent emission subsidy can reduce total emissions more than the case of *laissez-faire*. At the same time, we discussed weak points of Japanese competition policy.

References

1. Chiou, J. R., & Hu, J. L. (2001). Environmental research joint ventures under emission taxes. *Environmental and Resource Economics, 20*, 129–146.
2. de Marchi, V. (2012). Environmental innovation and R&D cooperation: Empirical evidence from Spanish manufacturing firms. *Research Policy, 41*(3), 614–623.
3. Denicolò, V. (1999). Pollution-reduction innovations under taxes or permits. *Oxford Economic Papers, 51*, 184–199.
4. Gersbach, H., & Glazer, A. (1999). Markets and regulatory hold-Up problem. *Journal of Environmental Economics and Management, 37*, 151–164.
5. Katsoulacos, Y., & Xepapadeas, A. (1996). Environmental R&D, spill-overs and optimal policy schemes under oligopoly. In A. Xepapadeas (Ed.), *Economic policy for the environment and natural resources* (pp. 59–79). Cheltenham: Edward Elgar.
6. Marsiliani, L., & Renstrom, T. I. (2000). Time inconsistency in environmental policy: Tax earmarking as a commitment solution. *Economic Journal, 110*, 123–138.

7. Ouchida, Y., & Goto, D. (2011). A note on environmental R&D under time-consistent emission tax. *International Journal of Business and Economics, 10*(3), 257–260.
8. Ouchida, Y., & Goto, D. (2014). Do emission subsidies reduce emission? In the context of environmental R&D organization. *Economic Modelling, 36*, 511–516.
9. Petrakis, E., & Xepapadeas, A. (1999). Does government precommitment promote environmental innovation? In E. Petrakis, E. S. Sartzetakis, & A. Xepapadeas (Eds.), *Environmental regulation and market power: Competition, time consistency and international trade* (pp. 145–161). Cheltenham: Edward Elgar.
10. Petrakis, E., & Xepapadeas, A. (2003). Location decisions of a polluting firm and the time consistency of environmental policy. *Resource and Energy Economics, 25*, 197–214.
11. Poyago-Theotoky, J. (2007). The organization of R&D and environmental policy. *Journal of Economic Behavior and Organization, 62*(1), 63–75.
12. Poyago-Theotoky, J., & Teerasuwannajak, K. (2002). The timing of environmental policy: A note on the role of product differentiation. *Journal of Regulatory Economics, 21*(3), 305–316.
13. Requate, T. (1993). Pollution control under imperfect competition: Asymmetric Bertrand duopoly with linear technologies. *Journal of Institutional and Theoretical Economics, 149*(2), 415–442.
14. Requate, T. (1993). Pollution control in a Cournot duopoly via taxes or permits. *Journal of Economics, 58*(3), 255–291.
15. Requate, T. (2005). Dynamic incentive by environmental policy instruments – A Survey. *Ecological Economics, 54*, 175–195.
16. Singh, N., & Vives, X. (1984). Price and quantity competition in a differentiated duopoly. *RAND Journal of Economics, 15*(4), 546–554.
17. Wang, L. F. S., & Wang, J. (2009). Environmental taxes in a differentiated mixed duopoly. *Economic Systems, 33*(4), 389–396.

Chapter 14
Recycling Activities and Unemployment in Economically Developing Countries

Hirofumi Fukuyama

14.1 Introduction

14.1.1 Recycling Activities and Unemployment

Environmental policies have long been discussed around the world. Among environmental problems, the disposal and recycling of wastes is as severe a problem as global warming. It is expected that waste related difficulties will be resolved quickly. Particularly, an explosive increase in waste caused by population growth in economically developing countries has become severe. Waste problems in economically developing countries exhibit the following key features in comparison with those in economically developed countries: (1) waste collection services are insufficient, (2) recovery of resources (recycling) is done almost entirely by the informal sector, and (3) environmental pollution has been generated in landfills.

Of the problems listed above, in (1), wastes are not fully collected in economically developing countries because infrastructural development is lacking and the waste collecting systems rely on unskilled labor. In addition, (2) underscores the difficulty of predicting fluctuations of recycled product pricing, preventing the participation of private companies because informal sector participants such as "scavengers" and "waste pickers" serve an important role in waste recycling in economically developing countries. According to Medina [11], about 15 million people around the world recycle (collect) waste in informal sectors. Their economic effects amount to several hundred million dollars a year. About one million people recycle (collect) wastes in informal sectors in India. Actually, 90 percent

H. Fukuyama (✉)
Faculty of Law, Economics and the Humanities, Kagoshima University, Korimoto 1-21-24, Kagoshima city, Kagoshima 8908580, Japan
e-mail: fukuyama@leh.kagoshima-u.ac.jp

T. Naito (ed.), *Sustainable Growth and Development in a Regional Economy*, New Frontiers in Regional Science: Asian Perspectives 13,
DOI 10.1007/978-4-431-55294-9_14

Table 14.1 The circumstances of wastes disposal in Asian countries (Source: Ikeguchi [10])

Countries	Level 1	Level 2	Level 3	Level 4
Bangladesh	o			
Indonesia	o	o		
Malaysia		o	o	
Philippine	o	o		
Singapore			o	
Taiwan		o	o	
Thailand		o	o	
Vietnam	o	o		
Japan				o

of the resources that enterprises recycle in Brazil is collected by the informal sectors. Therefore, the economies of developing countries are strongly influenced by informal sectors. For that reason, supporting the activities of these informal sector agents can be expected to enable sustainable development that might include employment promotion, longer useful life of landfill facilities, and a steady supply of low-cost raw materials to enterprises. Finally, (3) is caused by insufficient management of landfills, and might cause sanitary problems and fatal accidents to scavengers, as occurred with the collapse of "Smokey Mountain" in the Philippines.

Ikeguchi [10] classifies the levels of technology related to waste disposal in Asian economically developing countries into four types to illustrate the state of collecting and treating wastes as shown in Table 14.1. The level 1 indicates the technology related to waste disposal has no systematic collecting of wastes, the open dump and illegal disposal, and the collecting of resource by informal sectors. The level 2 indicates the technology has systematic collecting of wastes, but the open dump and illegal disposal. The level 3 indicates the technology has systematic collecting of wastes and hygienic landfill disposal. Japan belongs to the level 4 for separating wastes, the recovery of materials and heat, and hygienic landfill disposal. However, economically developing countries such as Bangladesh, Indonesia, the Philippines, and Vietnam belong to the level 1: waste is not systematically collected, waste is treated using the open-dump method, and are recycled only by scavengers and the waste-pickers.

Accordingly, in comparison with economically developed countries, it is difficult for economically developing countries to resolve problems of waste disposal because economically developing countries have neither the technology, the human resources, nor the funds to progress through each process of waste disposal. Moreover, people's consideration of the environment is also low in economically developing countries. Migration from rural areas to urban areas occurs through remarkable economic development, which causes more unemployment in economically developing countries. Therefore, governments of economically developing countries must devote attention to unemployment problems while pursuing environmental policies to resolve waste problem. This chapter clarifies environmental policies that can resolve waste and unemployment difficulties simultaneously.

Also, studies using the Harris and Todaro model have necessitated that a household's migration behavior be decided solely by the difference of wages between urban and rural areas. The quality of the environment between those areas does not influence the household's migration behavior to any degree. Originally, when the households decide on settling in an area, not only the wages obtained but also the level of environment in the area will be extremely important factors. For instance, bad odors and soil pollution will become apparent. Therefore, rural environments will generally be regarded as better urban areas when a waste landfill is in an urban area where the concentration of population becomes increasingly severe. However, the utility of the informal sector will be improved because they can subsist by collecting recyclable waste from the waste landfills and can sell them off to the industrial sector in urban areas when a waste landfill is located in an urban area. This study analyzes the most suitable locations of landfills, the policies of economically developing countries, and the support of economically developed countries through a comparison of landfills located in an urban area and in a rural area.

14.1.2 Related Research

The Harris and Todaro model is used (Harris and Todaro [9]).[1] Harris and Todaro [9] present mechanisms of generating unemployment in urban areas: a wage determinant mechanism that achieves full employment does not work because wages in urban areas are fixed at higher levels than those of rural areas. Consequently, people in rural areas have an incentive to migrate to urban areas seeking higher wages. Therefore, households choose urban or the rural residential areas by comparing the expected wages in the urban area and the risk of unemployment with wages in a rural area. Migration between the urban and rural areas stops when the expected wages in the urban area equal those in the rural area. Moreover, Corden and Findlay [2] consider the Harris and Todaro model, which incorporates capital flows between urban and rural areas.

In this chapter, we examine how a subsidy policy for a recycling sector and informal sectors in the urban areas affect problems of the disposal and recycling of waste and unemployment in economically developing countries using the Harris and Todaro model, which takes into account recycling activities by the recycling sector and informal sectors. Many studies have extended the Harris and Todaro model. The studies have advanced to incorporate consideration of the environmental problem in recent years. Dean and Gangopadhyay [5] assume an economy by which the production of intermediate goods (e.g. lumber) input into the industrial sector has a negative influence on the agriculture sector. They examine what influence policies such as an export tax have on an industrial sector that produces final goods. They

[1] See Chap. 3 for details of Harris and Todaro model.

assess the effects of a trade embargo of intermediate goods on an economy, showing that such a policy is effective because the trade embargo has no strong influence on unemployment. However, Chao, Kerkvliet and Yu [1] analyze the restriction of use of intermediate goods under a closed economy or open economy assuming that the production of intermediate goods input to the industrial sector has a negative influence on households. Daitoh [3] clarifies a sufficient condition for environmental policies to improve social welfare, assuming that the polluting goods input to the industrial sector have a negative influence on households. Fukuyama and Naito [8] consider the impacts that the improvement of employment promotion policy, the environmental policy, and the pollution reduction technology have on employment, the use of pollution goods, and the unemployment rate. They show that the rise of environment tax rate can improve the unemployment rate so that strengthening the environmental policy is an effective policy without reducing the unemployment rate.

Consequently, studies that address waste problems in economically developing countries are few, although some studies analyze problems related to unemployment and the environment in economically developing countries incorporating environmental problems into Harris and Todaro model in recent years. Daitoh and Yanase [4] consider the trade of recycled resources using the Harris and Todaro model and clarify that import expansion of recycled resources affects the economy in economically developing countries. However, they do not refer to the recycling activity by informal sectors. Accordingly, we devote attention to the waste management problem in economically developing countries, formalize the recycling activity by informal sectors which have been bearing the key role in recycling waste, and consider what influence a subsidy policy for a recycling sector exerts on an economy. Moreover, we analyze whether to create employment with a subsidy policy for the recycling sector by the government, or not, and whether such a subsidy policy can exert a positive impact on an economy.

Moreover, studies using the Harris and Todaro model have required that the household's migration behavior is decided only by the difference of wages between urban and rural areas, and the quality of environment between those areas doesn't influence the household's migration behavior at all. Originally, when the households decide the settlement, not only the wages obtained but also the level of environment in the areas will be an extremely important factor. For instance, a bad smell and a soil pollution will become apparent and thus the environment of rural areas will be regarded to be better than that of urban areas when there is a landfill of wastes in the urban areas where the concentration of population becomes increasingly serious. On the other hand, The utility of the informal sectors will be improved because they can subsist by collecting recyclable wastes from the landfill of wastes and sell them off to the industrial sector in the urban areas when there is a landfill of wastes in the urban areas. Therefore, we analyze the most suitable locations of landfill, the policies of economically developing countries, and the support of economically developed countries through the comparison when the landfill is located in the urban areas and when it is located in the rural areas.

The composition of this chapter is the following. In the next section, we construct a model by which waste collection activities by both the recycling sector (formal sector) in urban areas and informal sectors (unemployed workers) are added to the Harris and Todaro model. In Sect. 14.3, we derive an equilibrium condition based on the model constructed in the previous section, and perform comparative static analyses. In Sect. 14.4, we examine the effects of a subsidy policy on the recycling sector and informal sectors in the urban areas. In Sect. 14.5, we extend the model of Sect. 14.2 to the model which incorporates the best locations of landfill. In Sect. 14.6, we derive an equilibrium condition based on the model constructed in Sect. 14.5. In Sect. 14.7, we perform comparative static analyses and analyze the most suitable locations of landfill. Finally, we present a summary and remaining issues for future research.

14.2 The Model of Recycling by Informal Sectors

The economy assumed for these analyses consists of two regions: an urban area and a rural area. An agricultural sector exists in the rural area. An industrial sector and a recycling sector exist in the urban area. Households consume agricultural goods and industrial goods; they exhaust wastes associated with the consumption of industrial goods. Wastes are collected and recycled by the recycling sector. Then the recycled wastes are sold off to the industrial sector. We assume that unemployed workers in the urban area can subsist by collecting recyclable wastes from the mountain of wastes that are illegally dumped and sold off to the industrial sector.[2] Moreover, we assume a small open economy.

14.2.1 Production Sector

Agriculture Sector

The rural area has only an agriculture sector. We assume that the only production factor of agricultural goods is labor. We further assume the production output of agricultural goods to be X and assume a linear production function for labor as follows.

$$X = aL_x \tag{14.1}$$

In that equation, L_x is the labor input necessary for the production of agricultural goods; a denotes marginal production. If the price of agricultural goods is assumed to be 1, then the profit function Π_x of the agriculture sector is the following.

$$\Pi_x = aL_x - w_xL_x \tag{14.2}$$

[2] See Fukuyama [6] for details of this model.

Therein, $w_x$is the wage paid for the worker engaged in the agriculture sector. w_x equals marginal production a by the competitive condition in the labor market of the agricultural sector. Therefore, the following expressions are obtained.

$$w_x = a. \tag{14.3}$$

Industrial Sector

Industrial goods are produced using two production factors: labor and material resources. We consider only recycled resources for the simplification of analysis, although both virgin resources and recycled resources are probably used in an actual economic system. We assume the amount of labor demand in the industrial sector to be L_y; the amount of recycled resource demand is assumed to be R. We define the production function of industrial goods as follows.

$$Y = L_y^{\alpha} R^{1-\alpha} \tag{14.4}$$

Next, we assume $0 < \alpha < 1$. Wages in the urban area are assumed to be fixed as $\bar{w}$ in this minimum wage system. We assume that recycled resources are supplied from the recycling sector or the informal sector and that the price is q. Moreover, the international price of industrial goods is assumed to be p (fixed). The profit function Π_y of the industrial sector is the following.

$$\Pi_y = pL_y^{\alpha} R^{1-\alpha} - \bar{w}L_y - qR \tag{14.5}$$

The first-order condition of profit maximization is the following.

$$p\alpha \left(\frac{R}{L_y} \right)^{1-\alpha} = \bar{w} \tag{14.6}$$

$$p(1-\alpha) \left(\frac{L_y}{R} \right)^{\alpha} = q \tag{14.7}$$

We assume that the profit generated in the industrial sector is collected by the government and that it is distributed to the household in a lump sum.

Recycling Sector

Industrial goods become waste after their household consumption. The recycling sector collects, recycles the waste exhausted by the household, and supplies recycled resources to the industrial sector. It is necessary to input labor to collect wastes, recycle them, and produce recycled resources. Here, the amount of labor demand input to collect and recycle wastes is assumed to be L_r. The production function of recycled resources is the following.

$$Z = \theta(L_r)\bar{C}_y \tag{14.8}$$

$\bar{C}_y$ is assumed to be the amount of consumption (= the amount of waste) of the industrial goods by the households. C_y is an exogenous variable. We assume that $\theta(L_r)(0 < \theta < 1)$ represents the proportion of the amount of recycled wastes of $\bar{C}_r$ and assume that it rises for an increase in labor input L_r to recycle wastes. Therefore, we assume $\theta' > 0, \theta'' < 0$. The wages of the recycling sector become $\bar{w}$ because a recycling sector exists in the urban area. We assume that the economically developing country government provides a subsidy s_r for the recycling sector as an unemployment policy. Moreover, we assume that s_r is paid from the support fund by an economically advanced nation. Therefore, the profit function of the recycling sector is the following.

$$\Pi_r = q\theta(L_r)\bar{C}_y - (\bar{w} - s_r)L_r \tag{14.9}$$

The first-order condition of profit maximization is the following.

$$q\theta'(L_r)\bar{C}_y = \bar{w} - s_r \tag{14.10}$$

Here, the profit generated in the recycling sector is collected by the government. It is distributed to the households as a lump sum.

Informal Sector

Wastes are recycled mainly by informal sector actors in economically developing countries, although they are recycled by the recycling section in economically developed countries. We assume that the unemployed workers are subsisting by taking valuable resources from $(1 - \theta)\bar{C}_y$ that are not recycled by the recycling sector. They sell those resources to the industrial sector in the urban area. However, the unemployed workers might not take out valuable resources from the mountain of waste in the landfill because they do not have the expertise in the management of wastes, as might exist in the recycling sector.[3] Here, the probability of acquiring the valuable resources by the unemployed workers (effort to acquire those) is assumed

[3] We assume that the resources recycled by the recycling sector and the resources recycled by the informal sector are of the same quality for simplicity of analysis. "Recycling" in this chapter denotes the process of taking out the valuable resources of the wastes. We assume that the process of processing the valuable resources and of producing the product is done by the industrial sector.

to be $e(0 \leq e < 1)$. However, the acquisition action of the valuable resource by the informal sector is extremely risky. As described above, fires occur in the mountains of wastes in the landfill in economically developing countries. Accidents can occur in which workers die from the collapse of mountains of waste. The damage cost of an accident per unit of waste is expressed as $v(e) = \frac{b(s)}{2}e^2$ because, as effort to acquire valuable resources increases, the more accidents occur. $b(s)$ is a parameter reflecting the accident damage cost. For instance, the probability of accidents increases when landfill maintenance is insufficient; then $b(s)$ grows larger. Here, s is an amount of supporting funds for the informal sector by the economically developing country government. Presumably, when s increases (e.g. the landfill is maintained), $b(s)$ decreases ($b' < 0$). Moreover, we assume that s is paid from the support fund by the advanced country. The number of unemployed workers is assumed as L_u. Then the amount of the waste dumped to the landfill is shown as $(1-\theta)\bar{C}_y$. Therefore, when it is assumed that one unemployed worker can acquire only the valuable resource of $\frac{(1-\theta)\bar{C}_y}{L_u}$, the profit maximization problems of a representative unemployed worker are the following.

$$\max_e \left(qe - \frac{b(s)}{2}e^2\right)\frac{(1-\theta)\bar{C}_y}{L_u} \tag{14.11}$$

The first-order condition of profit maximization is the following.

$$q = b(s)e \tag{14.12}$$

14.2.2 Household

Households reside in the urban area or in the rural area. Households residing in the urban area can be engaged in the industrial sector or in the recycling sector. The households not employed in these become unemployed workers. The unemployed workers who successfully recycle wastes can obtain an income, but the others who failed cannot. However, the households residing in the rural area are employed in the agricultural sector. Therefore, households of five types will exist. Households employed in the agricultural sector are shown by subscript $i = x$. Those employed in the industrial sector are shown by $i = y$. Those employed in the recycling sector are shown by $i = r$. Those unemployed and receiving an income are denoted by $i = u1$. Those unemployed and receiving no income are shown by $i = u2$.

Here, we assume the number of households residing in the rural area to be L_x, the number residing in the urban area and employed in the industrial sector are L_y. The amount of those residing in the urban area and employed in the recycling sector are L_y. The number residing in the urban area and unemployed are L_u. The total is L. Therefore, the population constraint is given as follows.

$$L = L_x + L_y + L_r + L_u \tag{14.13}$$

Households compare the expected wage in the urban area with the wage in the rural area. They choose whether to reside in the urban area or in the rural area. Households that reside in the rural area and which are employed in the agriculture sector earn wages of w_x. Those that reside in the urban area and whom are employed in the industrial sector or in the recycling sector earn wages of $\bar{w}$. Those who reside in the urban area and who are not employed acquire valuable resources with probability of e and earn $w_u = \frac{(1-\theta)\bar{C}_y}{L_u}q$. Therefore, the equilibrium condition under which migration between the urban area and the rural area stops (so-called Harris and Todaro condition) is given as follows.

$$w_x = \frac{L_y + L_r}{L_y + L_r + L_u}\bar{w} + \frac{L_u}{L_y + L_r + L_u}ew_u \tag{14.14}$$

The revenue collected from the industrial sector and the recycling sector is distributed equally to all households. Therefore, it does not influence the Harris and Todaro condition of Eq. (14.14).

Households of each type earn wages by supplying labor for each sector used. Moreover, the revenue collected from the industrial sector and the recycling sector is distributed to the households in a lump sum. The households allot those funds to the consumption of industrial goods and agricultural goods. Therefore, the utility function of households is shown as follows.

$$U_i = \begin{cases} u\left(c_x, c_y\right) & (i = x, y, r) \\ u\left(c_x, c_y\right) - v(e) & (i = u1, u2) \end{cases} \tag{14.15}$$

In those equations, c_x, c_y stand for the consumption of agricultural goods and industrial goods. Here, it is assumed that $u(c_x, c_y)$ is a homothetic function. The prices of industrial goods and agricultural goods are shown respectively with p and 1. When the maximization problem of utility is solved under the budget constraint, the following indirect utility functions can be derived.

$$V_x = \xi(p)(w_x + T) \tag{14.16}$$

$$V_y = \xi(p)(\bar{w} + T) \tag{14.17}$$

$$V_r = \xi(p)(\bar{w} + T) \tag{14.18}$$

$$V_{u1} = \xi(p)(w_u + T) - v(e) \tag{14.19}$$

$$V_{u2} = \xi(p)T - v(e) \tag{14.20}$$

Therein, T represents the amount of distributed revenues collected from the industrial sector and the recycling sector per household. Moreover, $\xi'(p) < 0$ holds. When households consume industrial goods, they exhaust the same amount of wastes. We assume the amount of consumption of industrial goods by each household derived from the maximization problem of utility as $c_y^x(p), c_y^y(p), c_y^r(p), c_y^{u1}(p)$. Then the total amount of wastes of the whole economy C_y is the following.

$$\bar{C}_y = L_x c_y^x(p) + L_y c_y^y(p) + L_r c_y^r(p) + eL_u c_y^{u1}(p) \tag{14.21}$$

14.3 Market Equilibrium on Recycling by Informal Sectors

We have modeled the behavior of each sector and household in the previous section. We next seek to derive the market equilibrium $(w_x^*, q^*, e^*, R^*, L_x^*, L_y^*, L_r^*, L_u^*)$. First, we derive the equilibrium wages w_x^* in the agriculture sector and the equilibrium price q^* of recycled resources. w_x^* is determined as equal to the marginal production of agricultural goods: $w_x^* = a$. The equilibrium price q^* of recycled resources is given as follows from Eqs. (14.6) and (14.7), which respectively show two demands of production factors in the industrial sector because, under a small country assumption, the relative price p and the wage $\bar{w}$ in the urban area are given exogenously.

$$q^* = p(1-\alpha)\left(\frac{p\alpha}{\bar{w}}\right)^{\frac{\alpha}{1-\alpha}} \tag{14.22}$$

Here, the effort level e^* necessary for the informal sector to acquire recyclable resources is shown as follows by substitution of (14.22) for (14.12).

$$e^* = \frac{q^*}{b(s)} \tag{14.23}$$

From (14.23), the more supporting funds s for the informal sector rise, the more that effort level e^* increases as follows.

$$\frac{de^*}{ds} = -\frac{q^* b'(s)}{b^2(s)} > 0 \tag{14.24}$$

Second, we derive the equilibrium for labor input in each sector as $(L_x^*, L_y^*, L_r^*, L_u^*)$. Also, (14.10) derives the equilibrium on labor input of the recycling sector L_r^*. The following equation is obtained using the implicit function theorem for (14.10).

$$\frac{dL_r^*}{ds_r} = -\frac{1}{q\theta''(L_r)\bar{C}_y} > 0 \tag{14.25}$$

Equation (14.25) means that the labor demand for the recycling sector increases because the labor input cost decreases by the increase of the subsidy rate for the recycling sector.

Demand R for the industrial sector is expected to become equal to the sum of the supply $\frac{(1-\theta)\bar{C}_y}{L_u} \times eL_u$ for the informal sector and the supply $\theta(L_r)\bar{C}_y$ for recycling sector as follows in the market for recycled resources.

$$R = \theta(L_r)\bar{C}_y + (1-\theta(L_r))\bar{C}_y e \tag{14.26}$$

By substituting L_r^* obtained from (14.10) and e^* obtained from (14.23)–(14.26), the equilibrium demand R^* for recycled resources in the recycling sector is the following.

$$R^* = \theta(L_r^*)\bar{C}_y + (1-\theta(L_r^*))\bar{C}_y e^* \tag{14.27}$$

By substituting (14.27)–(14.6) representing the labor demand in the industrial sector and transforming it, the following equilibrium labor input L_y^* the industrial sector can be obtained.

$$L_y^* = \left(\frac{p\alpha}{\bar{w}}\right)^{\frac{1}{1-\alpha}} \bar{C}_y\left[\theta(L_r^*) + (1-\theta(L_r^*))e^*\right] \tag{14.28}$$

Differentiating (14.28) by s_r, the following equation holds from (14.25).

$$\frac{dL_y^*}{ds_r} = \left(\frac{p\alpha}{\bar{w}}\right)^{\frac{1}{1-\alpha}} \bar{C}_y\theta'\frac{dL_r^*}{ds_r}(1-e^*) > 0 \tag{14.29}$$

Therefore, the labor demand in the industrial sector increases because the labor demand in the recycling sector increases and the supply for recycled resources increases by the rise of the subsidy rate s_r to the recycling sector. Next, differentiating (14.28) by s, the following equation holds from (14.24).

$$\frac{dL_y^*}{ds} = \left(\frac{p\alpha}{\bar{w}}\right)^{\frac{1}{1-\alpha}} \bar{C}_y(1-\theta)\frac{de^*}{ds} > 0 \tag{14.30}$$

Therefore, the labor demand in the industrial sector increases because the level of effort to acquire the recyclable resource by the informal sector increases and the supply of recycled resources increases by the rise of supporting funds s for the informal sector.

The Harris and Todaro condition of (14.14) is rewritten as follows by substituting the equilibrium solution $L_y^*, L_r^*, and\ e^*$ obtained above as (14.14).

$$a = \frac{L_y^* + L_r^*}{L_y^* + L_r^* + L_u}\bar{w} + \frac{e^{*2}b(s)(1-\theta(L_r^*))\bar{C}_y}{L_y^* + L_r^* + L_u} \tag{14.31}$$

From (14.31), the equilibrium number of unemployed workers L_u^* is the following.

$$L_u^* = \frac{(\bar{w}-a)(L_y^* + L_r^*) + e^{*2}b(s)(1-\theta(L_r^*))\bar{C}_y}{a} \tag{14.32}$$

Differentiating (14.32) by s_r, the following equation holds from (14.25) and (14.29).

$$\frac{dL_u^*}{ds_r} = \frac{\bar{w} - a}{a}\left(\frac{dL_y^*}{ds_r} + \frac{dL_r^*}{ds_r}\right) - \frac{e^{*2}b(s)\theta'\bar{C}_y}{a}\frac{dL_r^*}{ds_r} \tag{14.33}$$

Equation (14.33) has two effects. The increasing subsidy rate s_r for the recycling sector enhances the incentive to migrate to the urban area to raise the labor demand for the industrial sector and the recycling sector and to improve the probability that the households can get a job in the urban area. Therefore, clause 1 of (14.33) is an effect of increasing the number of unemployed workers by the rise of s_r. Clause 2 of (14.33) is an effect of decreasing the number of unemployed workers to increase the amount of waste recycled by the recycling sector, to decrease the amount of waste to be recycled by informal sectors, and to decrease the profit for informal sectors by the rise of s_r. The sign of (14.33) is determined depending on which effect is greater. For instance, the rise of subsidy rate s_r for the recycling sector decreases unemployment if the marginal production of the agriculture sector a is sufficiently large, which suggests the importance of improving agricultural productivity while supplementing the subsidy for the recycling sector to decrease unemployment.

Theorem 14.1. *A rising subsidy rate for the recycling sector decreases unemployment if the marginal productivity of the agriculture sector is sufficiently high.*

Next, differentiating (14.32) by s, the following equation holds from (14.24) and (14.30).

$$\begin{aligned}\frac{dL_u^*}{ds} &= \frac{\bar{w} - a}{a}\frac{dL_y^*}{ds} + \frac{2eb(s)(1-\theta)\bar{C}_y}{a}\frac{de^*}{ds} + \frac{e^{*2}b'(1-\theta)\bar{C}_y}{a} \\ &= \frac{\bar{w} - a}{a}\frac{dL_y^*}{ds} - \frac{e^{*2}(1-\theta)\bar{C}_y b'}{a} > 0\end{aligned} \tag{14.34}$$

Equation (14.34) presents two effects. The increase of supporting funds s for the informal sector enhances the incentive for migration to the urban area to raise the labor demand for the industrial sector and to improve the probability that the households can get a job in the urban area. That has the effect of increasing the number of unemployed workers. Moreover, that has the effect of increasing the number of unemployed workers to raise the probability that they can acquire the recyclable resources.

Theorem 14.2. *Raising of supporting funds for the informal sector increases unemployment.*

Finally, the equilibrium labor demand for the agriculture sector L_x^* is the following from the population constraint equation of (14.13).

$$L_x^* = L - L_y^* - L_r^* - L_u^* \tag{14.35}$$

Differentiating (14.35) by s_r and s, the following equations hold.

$$\frac{dL_x^*}{ds_r} = -\frac{dL_y^*}{ds_r} - \frac{dL_r^*}{ds_r} - \frac{dL_u^*}{ds_r} \tag{14.36}$$

$$\frac{dL_x^*}{ds} = -\frac{dL_y^*}{ds} - \frac{dL_u^*}{ds} < 0 \tag{14.37}$$

From (14.37), the increase of supporting funds s for the informal sector decreases labor demand for the agricultural sector to increase that for the informal sector and the industrial sector. However, from (14.36), because the increase of subsidy rate s_r for the recycling sector does not determine the effect on unemployment, it does not determine an effect on labor demand for the agriculture sector either.

14.4 Welfare Analysis on Recycling by Informal Sectors

The influence of subsidy rate s_r on the recycling sector and the supporting funds s of the informal sector effects on social welfare are examined next. Here, the social welfare function is shown as follows as the sum of an indirect utility of all households in the entire economy.

$$W = L_x^* V_x + L_y^* V_y + L_r^* V_r + e^* L_u^* V_{u1} + (1 - e^*) L_u^* V_{u2} \tag{14.38}$$

By substituting (14.16)–(14.20), (14.35)–(14.38) and transforming it, the social welfare function can be formulated as follows.

$$\begin{aligned} W &= L_x^* \xi(p) a + L_y^* \xi(p) \bar{w} + L_r^* \xi(p) \bar{w} + L_u^* \xi(p) e^* w_u \\ &\quad - \frac{b(s)}{2} e^{*2} (1 - \theta(L_r^*)) \bar{C}_y + L\xi(p) T \\ &= L\xi(p) a + \xi(p)(\bar{w} - a)(L_y^* + L_r^*) - L_u^* \xi(p) a \\ &\quad + \left[b(s) e^{*2} \xi(p) - \frac{b(s)}{2} e^{*2} \right] (1 - \theta(L_r^*)) \bar{C}_y + L\xi(p) T \end{aligned} \tag{14.39}$$

Therein, L_y^* and L_r^*, L_u^* are the function of the subsidy rate s_r for the industrial sector, so the social welfare function W is also the function of s_r. Differentiating (14.39) by s_r, the following equation is obtained.

$$\frac{dW}{ds_r} = \xi(p)(\bar{w} - a)\left(\frac{dL_y^*}{ds_r} + \frac{dL_r^*}{ds_r}\right) - \xi(p) a \frac{dL_u^*}{ds_r} - (2\xi(p) - 1)\frac{b(s)}{2} e^{*2} \bar{C}_y \theta' \frac{dL_r^*}{ds_r} \tag{14.40}$$

the Clause 1 of (14.40) shows a positive effect by which the rising of s_r increases the wages of households and improves the indirect utility to increase the number of those who are employed not in the agriculture sector but in the industrial sector and in the recycling sector. Clause 2 presents a negative effect by which the rising of s_r decreases the wages of households and reduces the indirect utility of increasing the number of those who migrated from the rural area to the urban area and became unemployed workers. Clause 3 presents a negative effect by which the rising of s_r decreases the recyclable resources to be acquired by informal sectors and reduces their indirect expected utility because it decreases the amount of waste dumped into the landfill to increase the labor demand for the recycling sector. Moreover, by substituting (14.29) and (14.33)–(14.40) and transforming it, the rising of s_r raises social welfare as shown below.

$$\frac{dW}{ds_r} = \frac{b(s)}{2} e^{*2} \theta' \bar{C}_y \frac{dL_r^*}{ds_r} > 0 \tag{14.41}$$

Therefore, the following Theorem 14.3 holds.

Theorem 14.3. *A rising subsidy rate for the recycling sector improves social welfare.*

Next, L_y^* and L_u^*, e^* are function of the supporting funds s for the informal sector, so the social welfare function W is also a function of s. Differentiating (14.39) by s, the following equation holds.

$$\begin{aligned}\frac{dW}{ds} &= \xi(p)(\bar{w} - a)\frac{dL_y^*}{ds} - \xi(p)a\frac{dL_u^*}{ds} + b(s)e^*(2\xi(p) - 1)\frac{de^*}{ds}(1-\theta)\bar{C}_y \\ &\quad + (\xi(p) - \frac{1}{2})b' e^{*2}(1-\theta)\bar{C}_y\end{aligned} \tag{14.42}$$

Clause 1 of (14.42) shows a positive effect by which the rising of s increases the wages of households and improves the indirect utility to increase the number of those who are employed not in the agricultural sector but in the industrial sector. Clause 2 shows a negative effect by which rising of s decreases the wages of households and reduces the indirect utility to increase the number of those who migrated from the rural area to the urban area and became unemployed workers. Clauses 3 and 4 represent positive effects by which the rising of s increases the expected wage of the informal sector and increases the indirect expected utility to raise the possibility of acquiring the recyclable resources and a negative effect by which the rising of s raises the probability of injury by accident of recycling activities to increase the number of unemployed workers. Moreover, by substituting (14.24) and (14.34)–(14.42) and transforming it, the rising of s degrades social welfare as shown below.

$$\frac{dW}{ds} = \frac{e^{*2}}{2}(1-\theta)\bar{C}_y b' < 0 \tag{14.43}$$

Raising of supporting funds for the informal sector increases the expected wage for the informal sector to raise the possibility of acquiring the recyclable resources. However, the raising of supporting funds degrades the social welfare by increasing the probability of injury by accident through recycling activities. It also decreases the amount of acquiring recyclable resources per unit of unemployed workers by increasing those. Therefore, the following Theorem 14.4 holds.

Theorem 14.4. *Raising of supporting funds for the informal sector degrades social welfare.*

14.5 The Model of Landfill Location

In the model of this section as well as that of Sect. 14.2, the economy assumed for these analyses consists of two regions: an urban area and a rural area. An intermediate goods sector exists in a rural area. A final goods sector and a waste collection sector exist in an urban area. We presume that fixed wage levels that are higher in urban areas than in rural areas might cause migration from rural areas to urban areas and might therefore increase unemployment in urban areas as described by Harris and Todaro [9]. We assume that unemployed workers (informal sector) in an urban area can subsist by collecting recyclable waste from the mountain of waste (waste landfills) as described in Sect. 14.2. These waste recycling activities conducted by the informal sector account for most of the mass of recycled waste in economically developing countries. They are important activities that cannot be ignored. Unemployed workers can earn an income by engaging in recycling activities when the waste landfills are in urban areas, but they cannot engage in recycling activities because no waste is near when the waste landfills are in rural areas.[4] We will formulate the activities of the sectors as follows.

14.5.1 Intermediate Goods Sector

A rural area has only an intermediate goods sector. The intermediate goods assumed here are the wood resources, etc. We assume that the only production factor of intermediate goods is labor. The production output of intermediate goods is X. Therefore, the linear production function for labor is the following.

$$X = bL_x \tag{14.44}$$

[4]See Fukuyama [7] for details of this model.

In that equation, L_x represents the labor input necessary for the production of intermediate goods; b denotes marginal production. If the price of intermediate goods is assumed to be q, then the profit function Π_x of the intermediate goods sector is the following.

$$\Pi_x = qbL_x - w_xL_x \tag{14.45}$$

Therein, w_x is the wage paid for the worker engaged in the intermediate goods sector. w_x is obtained as follows by the competitive condition in the labor market of the intermediate goods sector. Therefore, the following expressions are obtained.

$$w_x = qb. \tag{14.46}$$

14.5.2 Final Goods Sector

Final goods are produced using two production factors: labor and material resources. The resources input as production factors include intermediate goods resources supplied by the intermediate goods sector in a rural area, intermediate goods resources imported from abroad, and recycled resources supplied by the recycling activities of the informal sector in a case in which the waste landfill is in an urban area. The prices of the three resources equals the price q of intermediate goods because these resources are homogeneous. Moreover, price q is the international price of intermediate goods. It is fixed because we assume a small open economy for intermediate goods. The profit function of the final goods sector is the following when the labor demand for final goods sector is represented as L_y and the demand for resources is represented as M.

$$Y = L_y^{\alpha}M^{1-\alpha} \tag{14.47}$$

Presumably, $0 < \alpha < 1$. Wages in an urban area are assumed to be fixed as $\bar{w}$ in the minimum wage system as posited also in Sect. 14.2. The price of final goods is shown as p. The profit function Π_y of the final goods sector is the following.

$$\Pi_y = pL_y^{\alpha}M^{1-\alpha} - \bar{w}L_y - (q+t)M \tag{14.48}$$

In that equation, t is the tax rate for using the resources. Then we assume that the tax revenue would be used for the cost of the collection and transportation of waste. The first-order conditions of profit maximization are the following.

$$p\alpha\left(\frac{M}{L_y}\right)^{1-\alpha} = \bar{w} \tag{14.49}$$

$$p(1-\alpha)\left(\frac{L_y}{M}\right)^{\alpha} = q + t \tag{14.50}$$

14.5.3 Waste Collection Sector

After the final goods are consumed by households, they become waste. Because the resources M input to produce the final goods would become waste after the final goods are consumed, the amount of waste is denoted by M.

The waste collection sector collects the waste discharged by the households and transports it to the landfill. It is necessary to input the labor to collect and transport the waste. An amount of labor necessary to collect and transport one unit of waste is assumed to be $\bar{l}_r$. Actually, $\bar{l}_r$ represents the technology level of waste collection in economically developing countries. The wage in the waste collection sector is $\bar{w}$ because the waste collection sector is in an urban area. Therefore, the total cost of the waste collection and transportation is shown as $\bar{w}M\bar{l}_r$.

When the waste collection sector is the public sector, and it is necessary to finance the cost of collecting and transporting the waste by the tax revenue, the equality of balance in the economically developing countries government can be shown as

$$\bar{w}M\bar{l}_r = tM \Leftrightarrow \bar{w}\bar{l}_r = t. \tag{14.51}$$

The right side shows revenue by resources use taxation imposed the final goods sector in economically developing countries.

14.5.4 Household

Households reside in an urban area or in a rural area. Households that reside in a rural area and which are employed in the intermediate goods sector earn wages of w_x. However, households residing in an urban area can be engaged in the final goods sector or in the waste collection sector and can earn wages of $\bar{w}$, but the households not employed in these become unemployed workers. The unemployed workers can earn an income by selling the recyclable resources to the final goods sector if they have acquired those resources from the waste landfills when a landfill exists in an urban area. However, the unemployed workers cannot acquire the recyclable resources and cannot earn an income because there is no the landfill in their residence when a landfill exists in a rural area.

Therefore, households of four types will exist. Households employed in the intermediate goods sector are denoted by subscript $i = x$. Those employed in the final goods sector are denoted by $i = y$. Those employed in the waste collection sector are denoted by $i = r$. Unemployed households are denoted by $i = u$. Moreover, we assume that the number of households residing in a rural area are L_x, the number residing in an urban area and employed in the final goods sector are L_y.

The numbers of those residing in an urban area and employed in the waste collection sector are $L_r = M\bar{l}r$. The number residing in an urban area and unemployed workers are L_u. The total is L. Therefore, the population constraint is given as follows.

$$L = L_x + L_y + M\bar{l}_r + L_u \tag{14.52}$$

Here, we assume that the utility function of a representative household is the following.

$$U(y, e) = ay - v(e) = ay - \frac{c}{2}e^2 \tag{14.53}$$

In this equation, y stands for the consumption of final goods, $e(0 \leq e < 1)$ stands for the level of effort to acquire the recyclable resources from waste landfills by the unemployed workers (probability of acquiring them), and $v(e) = \frac{c}{2}e^2$ stands for the disutility associated with the effort to acquire the recyclable resources. Because the households use all the wages to consume the final goods, the utility function of a representative household of (14.53) can be rewritten as

$$U(w_i, e) = a\frac{w_i}{p} - \frac{c}{2}e^2, \tag{14.54}$$

where $w_i(i = x, y, r, u)$ stands for the wages of households i.

14.5.5 Recycling Activities by Informal Sector

Waste is recycled mainly by the informal sector in economically developing countries. In this subsection, we present consideration of the recycling activities by the informal sector. Unemployed workers cannot geographically perform recycling activities because there is no mountain of waste when the landfill is in a rural area. However, they can earn income by selling the recyclable resources to the final goods sector if they have succeeded in the acquisition of those resources from a mountain of waste when the landfill is in an urban area. In this subsection, we describe the formulation of the recycling activities by the informal sector in the case in which a landfill exists in an urban area.

The unemployed workers in an urban area can earn income by selling recyclable resources to the final goods sector by acquiring those resources from the mountain of waste (amount of the waste M). However, the unemployed workers might not take out the recyclable resources from the mountain of waste in the landfill because they have no expertise in the management of waste. The resources demanded by the final goods sector consist of the intermediate goods (virgin resources) supplied by the intermediate goods sector and the resources imported from abroad in addition to the recyclable resources supplied by the unemployed workers (the informal sector). These resources are all assumed to be homogeneous. The properties between the recycled resources and the virgin resources are generally different. Therefore, it is necessary to introduce the parameter of heterogeneity. However, introduction of the parameter of heterogeneity does not strongly influence the result. Therefore, we assume these resources to be homogeneous.

As noted previously, the level of effort necessary to acquire recyclable resources from the waste landfills by unemployed workers (probability of acquiring those) is shown by $e(0 \leq e < 1)$. The acquisition activities of the recyclable resources by the informal sector are dangerous because accidents that might even cause the death of a worker often occurs because of fires that can occur on the mountain of waste and by the collapse of waste piles in economically developing countries. Therefore, the greater the acquisition effort of recyclable resources rises, the more accidents can be expected to occur. Therefore, disutility by the acquisition activities of the recyclable resources are shown as $v(e) = \frac{c}{2}e^2$. Therein, c stands for the parameter on disutility.

A representative unemployed worker determines the level of effort necessary to acquire the recyclable resources e to maximize the indirect utility of Eq. (14.54). Presumably, even if unemployed workers succeed in acquiring the recyclable resources, one unemployed worker obtains only the recyclable resources of one unit at most. There, the indirect utility maximization problem of a representative unemployed worker is the following.

$$\max_{e} \; a\frac{w_u}{p} - \frac{c}{2}e^2 = a\frac{eq}{p} - \frac{c}{2}e^2 \tag{14.55}$$

The first-order condition of the indirect utility maximization is the following from Eq. (14.55).

$$e = \frac{aq}{pc} \tag{14.56}$$

In this section, the range of the parameter of which $aq < pc$ holds is assumed.

14.6 Market Equilibrium on Landfill Location

14.6.1 Market Equilibrium in the Case in Which the Landfill Is in a Rural Area

In this subsection, we present consideration of the market equilibrium in the case in which the landfill is in a rural area. It is noteworthy that the unemployed workers in an urban area cannot conduct recycling activities when a landfill is located in a rural area.

First, the equilibrium wages of the intermediate goods sector w_x^* are determined to be $w_x^* = qb$ because the price of intermediate goods q is given exogenously by the small country assumption from Eq. (14.46). The equilibrium tax rate for using the resources t^* becomes $t^* = \bar{w}\bar{l}_r$ to equal the collection cost per unit of waste from Eq. (14.51). The price of intermediate goods q and the wages in an urban area $\bar{w}$ are given exogenously. Therefore, the equilibrium price of the final goods p^* is the following from Eqs. (14.49)–(14.51).

$$p^* = \left(\frac{q + \bar{w}\bar{l}_r}{1-\alpha}\right)^{1-\alpha}\left(\frac{\bar{w}}{\alpha}\right) \tag{14.57}$$

A landfill exists in a rural area. Therefore, the level of effort for acquiring the recyclable resources by the informal sector becomes 0 ($e^* = 0$).

Second, all final goods are produced in the domestic final goods sector and are consumed domestically. Therefore, the supply–demand equation on the final goods holds as

$$L_x\frac{qb}{p} + (L_y + M\bar{l}_r)\frac{\bar{w}}{p} = L_y^{\alpha}M^{1-\alpha} \tag{14.58}$$

The left side is an aggregate amount of final goods consumed by the households. The right side is an aggregate amount produced by the final goods sector. Actually, the unemployed workers have no wages. Therefore, their amount of consumption of final goods is 0.

Third, households choose the urban or the rural residential areas by comparing the expected wages considering the risk of unemployment in an urban area with the wages in a rural area. If the households migrate to a rural area, then they are employed by the intermediate goods sector and obtain the wages $w_x^* = qb$. Consequently, the indirect utility is the following from Eq. (14.54).

$$U(qb, 0) = a\frac{qb}{p} \tag{14.59}$$

If the households migrate to an urban area, then they obtain wages $\bar{w}$ when they are employed by the final goods sector or the waste collection sector. However, they are unable to obtain the wages when they become unemployed. Then they are unable to acquire the recyclable resources ($e = 0$) because no landfill exists in an urban area. Therefore, the indirect utility is the following from Eq. (14.54).

$$\frac{L_y + M\bar{l}_r}{L_y + M\bar{l}_r + L_u}U(\bar{w}, 0) + \frac{L_u}{L_y + M\bar{l}_r + L_u}U(0, 0) = \frac{L_y + M\bar{l}_r}{L_y + M\bar{l}_r + L_u}a\frac{\bar{w}}{p} \tag{14.60}$$

The Harris and Todaro condition is the following from Eqs. (14.59) and (14.60).

$$qb = \frac{L_y + M\bar{l}_r}{L_y + M\bar{l}_r + L_u}\bar{w} \tag{14.61}$$

As noted, $qb < \bar{w}$ must hold to establish the Harris and Todaro condition. Here, by transforming (14.49) into the equation of M and substituting it for Eqs. (14.52), (14.58), and (14.61), Eqs. (14.52), (14.58), and (14.61) are as follows.

$$L = L_x + \left(1 + \bar{l}_r\left(\frac{\bar{w}}{p^*\alpha}\right)^{\frac{1}{1-\alpha}}\right)L_y + L_u \tag{14.62}$$

$$L_x qb + \left(1 + \bar{l}_r\left(\frac{\bar{w}}{p^*\alpha}\right)^{\frac{1}{1-\alpha}}\right)L_y\bar{w} = \frac{\bar{w}}{\alpha}L_y \tag{14.63}$$

$$qb = \frac{L_y\left(1 + \bar{l}_r\left(\frac{\bar{w}}{p^*\alpha}\right)^{\frac{1}{1-\alpha}}\right)}{L_y\left(1 + \bar{l}_r\left(\frac{\bar{w}}{p^*\alpha}\right)^{\frac{1}{1-\alpha}}\right)+L_u}\bar{w} \tag{14.64}$$

It is possible to obtain (L_x, L_y, L_u) as follows from three Eqs. (14.62)–(14.64).

$$L_x^* = L\left(1 - \frac{\alpha(1 + \bar{l}_r(\bar{w}/p^*\alpha)^{\frac{1}{1-\alpha}})}{\bar{w}}\right) \tag{14.65}$$

$$L_y^* = \frac{qbL}{\bar{w}^2} \tag{14.66}$$

$$L_u^* = L\left(\frac{1 + \bar{l}_r(\bar{w}/p^*\alpha)^{\frac{1}{1-\alpha}}}{\bar{w}}\right)\left(\alpha - \frac{qb}{\bar{w}}\right) \tag{14.67}$$

By substituting Eq. (14.66) for Eq. (14.49), M standing for the equilibrium amount of resources input (= amount of waste) is the following.

$$M^* = \left(\frac{\bar{w}}{p^*\alpha}\right)^{\frac{1}{1-\alpha}}\frac{qb}{\bar{w}^2}L \tag{14.68}$$

Effects of Intermediate Goods Prices

We will carry out comparative static analysis of the market equilibrium $(t^*, p^*, L_x^*, L_y^*, L_u^*, M^*)$ using the policies parameter $(q, \bar{l}_r)$ when a landfill exists in a rural area.

First, we will carry out comparative static analysis by the international price of intermediate goods q. Economically developing country governments can control the domestic price of intermediate goods indirectly by imposing a tariff on the imported resources. Therefore, it is important to consider the effects on the market equilibrium by increasing the price q of intermediate goods.

From Eq. (14.57), increasing the price q of intermediate goods raises the price p^* of final goods. Therefore, some of the intermediate goods are attributable to the price of final goods. They raise the price of final goods when the prices of intermediate goods that are the productive factors of final goods increase.

From Eq. (14.65), the increase of the price q of intermediate goods raises the labor demand L_x^* of the intermediate goods sector. Therefore, the labor demand rises because of the increasing of the price of intermediate goods.

From Eq. (14.66), the increase of the price q of intermediate goods raises the labor demand L_y^* of the final goods sector. Therefore, the price of final goods rises by the increasing of the price of intermediate goods. Therefore, the final goods sector raises the labor input.

From Eq. (14.68), the increase of the price q of intermediate goods decreases the resources input M^*. Therefore, the amount of resources input decreases so that the increasing of the price of intermediate goods might raise the resource input cost.

From Eq. (14.67), the increase of the price q of intermediate goods decreases the unemployed workers L_u^*. Therefore, the unemployed workers decrease so that the labor demand for the intermediate goods sector and the final goods sector rise by the increase of the price of intermediate goods.

Theorem 14.5. *The increase of the price of intermediate goods raises the labor demand for the intermediate goods sector and raises the price of final goods. Therefore, it raises the labor demand for the final goods sector and decreases the number of unemployed workers.*

Effects of Waste Collection Technology

Second, we will carry out comparative static analysis of waste collection technology $\bar{l}_r$. There is a technology supply for waste collection in economically developing countries as one support of economically developed countries to economically developing countries. We will consider how the waste collection technology in economically developing countries affects the labor demand for each sector.

From Eq. (14.51), waste collection technology improvement (in other words, decreasing of $\bar{l}_r$) decreases the tax rate t^* of using resources. Therefore, unemployed workers decrease so that the labor demand for the intermediate goods sector and the final goods sector rise by the increase of the price of intermediate goods. Therefore, the wage in the waste collection sector is financed by the revenue from taxes of using resources. Therefore, the tax rate of using resources decreases when the waste collection cost of one unit decreases.

From Eq. (14.57), waste collection technology improvement decreases the price p^* of final goods. Therefore, the waste collection technology is improved and the tax rate of using resources decreases. Therefore, the cost of intermediate goods input decreases. The price of final goods decreases too.

From Eq. (14.68), waste collection technology improvement raises the amount of resource input (amount of waste) M^*. Therefore, if waste collection technology is improved, then the input cost of intermediate goods that are productive factors of the final goods decrease. Therefore, the amount of resource input (amount of waste) increases. Moreover, one cannot ascertain whether the improvement of the technology of waste raises or decreases the labor demand $\bar{l}_r M^*$ in the waste collection sector collection. Consequently, when waste collection technology is improved, the amount of resources input (amount of waste) increases and the labor demand increases. However, the amount of labor necessary for waste collection decreases.

From Eq. (14.66), waste collection technology improvement does not affect the labor demand L_y^* in the final goods sector. Therefore, the improvement effect of waste collection technology affects only the labor demand in waste collection.

From Eq. (14.65), the waste collection technology improvement raises or decreases the labor demand L_x^* in the intermediate goods sector, which means the following. The improvement of technology of the waste collection does not affect the labor demand in the final goods sector. Therefore, if the number of workers employed in the waste collection sector increases by improving the waste collection technology, then the employment rate in an urban area increases, a population influx occurs in an urban area, and the intermediate goods sector labor demand in a rural area decreases. However, if the number of workers employed in the waste collection sector decreases by improving the waste collection technology, then the employment rate in an urban area decreases, a population influx occurs in a rural area, and the intermediate goods sector labor demand in a rural area increases.

From Eq. (14.67), the waste collection technology improvement raises or decreases the number of unemployed workers L_u^*, which means the following. If the number of workers employed in the waste collection sector increases by improvement of the waste collection technology, then the employment rate in an urban area increases, a population influx occurs in an urban area, and the unemployed workers increase. However, if the number of workers employed in the waste collection sector decreases because of improved waste collection technology, then the employment rate in an urban area decreases, a population influx occurs in a rural area, and the unemployed workers decrease.

Theorem 14.6. *Waste collection technology improvement does not affect the labor demand in the final goods sector. However, it affects the waste collection sector labor demand: (1) if it raises the waste collection sector labor demand, then the intermediate goods sector labor demand decreases and the unemployed workers increase; (2) if it decreases the waste collection sector labor demand, then the intermediate goods sector labor demand increases and the unemployed workers decrease.*

14.6.2 Market Equilibrium for the Case in Which the Landfill Is in an Urban Area

In this subsection, we will present consideration of the market equilibrium in the case in which the landfill is in urban area. The first difference from the case in which a landfill exists in a rural area is that the possibility exists that the informal sector seeks recyclable resources from the landfill (mountain of waste) and obtains the wage by selling the recyclable resources to the final goods sector. The second difference is that locating the landfill in an urban area degrades the urban environment by odor and the soil contamination and reduces the utility of the households in an urban area.

First, by substituting (14.57) for (14.56), the level of effort to acquire the recyclable resources e^* by the representative informal sector is the following.

$$e^* = \frac{aq}{p^*c} \tag{14.69}$$

From Eq. (14.69), the level of effort to acquire the recyclable resources e^* increases for the rise of the price q of intermediate goods and decreases for the rise of the price p^* of final goods. Therefore, the rise of q raises the revenue by acquiring the recyclable resources. It raises the incentive to make an effort to acquire the recyclable resources. However, the rise of p decreases the amount of consumption of final goods and decreases the indirect utility. Therefore, it decreases the incentive to make an effort to acquire the recyclable resources.

Second, we assume that the indirect utility of households living in an urban area decreases by $\lambda (0 < \lambda < 1)$ times, causing the deterioration of urban environment from setting the landfill in an urban area. Comparing life in an urban area with that in a rural area, unemployed workers of the informal sector can seek the recyclable resources from the landfill and obtain the wage by selling the recyclable resources. Therefore, the indirect utility rises while the deterioration of the urban environment from setting the landfill in an urban area decreases the indirect utility of households. Therefore, when a landfill exists in an urban area, Eq. (14.64) of the Harris and Todaro condition is shown as follows by substituting (14.69) for (14.64).

$$qb = \frac{L_y\left(1 + \bar{l}_r\left(\frac{\bar{w}}{p^*\alpha}\right)^{\frac{1}{1-\alpha}}\right)}{L_y\left(1 + \bar{l}_r\left(\frac{\bar{w}}{p^*\alpha}\right)^{\frac{1}{1-\alpha}}\right)+L_u}\bar{w}\lambda + \frac{L_u}{L_y\left(1 + \bar{l}_r\left(\frac{\bar{w}}{p^*\alpha}\right)^{\frac{1}{1-\alpha}}\right)+L_u}\frac{aq^2}{2cp^*}\lambda \tag{14.70}$$

The left side of (14.70) is the indirect utility of households when they migrate to a rural area. Clause 1 of right side shows the indirect utility employed by the final goods sector or the waste collection sector when they migrate to an urban area. Clause 2 of the right side is the expected indirect utility of unemployed workers when they migrate to an urban area. The differences from Eq. (14.64) are adding clause 2 to the right side and multiplying the indirect utility of the right side by the urban environmental parameter λ.

Third, the unemployed workers can consume the final goods by obtaining the wage if a landfill exists in an urban area. Therefore, Eq. (14.63) is rewritten as follows by substituting (14.69) for (14.63).

$$L_x qb + \left(1 + \bar{l}_r\left(\frac{\bar{w}}{p^*\alpha}\right)^{\frac{1}{1-\alpha}}\right)L_y\bar{w} + L_u\frac{aq^2}{p^*c} = \frac{\bar{w}}{\alpha}L_y \tag{14.71}$$

The left side of (14.71) stands for the amount of consumption of final goods: clause 3 is added to Eq. (14.63).

Consequently, when a landfill exists in an urban area, the market equilibrium $(L_x^{**}, L_y^{**}, L_u^{**}, M^{**})$ is obtained as follows from Eqs. (14.49), (14.52), (14.70), and (14.71).

$$L_u^{**} = \frac{qbL}{qb - \frac{aq^2}{p^*c}\lambda - \left((qb-1)\Omega + \frac{\bar{w}}{\alpha}\right)\Omega\left(\frac{qb - q^2\lambda/2cp^*}{qb - \bar{w}\lambda}\right)} \tag{14.72}$$

$$L_y^{**} = \Omega\frac{qb - \frac{aq^2}{2cp^*}\lambda}{\bar{w}\lambda - qb}L_u^{**} \tag{14.73}$$

$$L_x^{**} = L - \Omega L_y^{**} - L_u^{**} \tag{14.74}$$

$$M^{**} = \left(\frac{\bar{w}}{p^*\alpha}\right)^{\frac{1}{1-\alpha}} L_y^{**} \tag{14.75}$$

$$\textit{where } \Omega \equiv 1 + \bar{l}_r\left(\frac{\bar{w}}{p^*\alpha}\right)^{\frac{1}{1-\alpha}}.$$

Effects of Urban Environment Improvement

We next consider how the urban environment parameter λ affects the market equilibrium $L_x^{**}, L_y^{**}, L_u^{**}, M^{**}$ when a landfill exists in an urban area. It is important to maintain the urban environment in economically developing countries for improving the utility of households residing in an urban area as support by economically developed countries.

First, partially differentiating Eq. (14.72) by the urban environment parameter λ, the following holds because $\bar{w}$ is sufficiently large.

$$\frac{\partial L_u^{**}}{\partial \lambda} = \frac{(qb)^2 L\left(\bar{w} - \frac{q^2}{2cp^*}\right)}{\left(qb - \frac{aq^2}{p^*c}\lambda - \left((qb-1)\Omega + \frac{\bar{w}}{\alpha}\right)\Omega\left(\frac{qb - q^2\lambda/2cp^*}{qb - \bar{w}\lambda}\right)\right)^2} > 0 \tag{14.76}$$

The number of unemployed workers increases by urban environment improvement (the rise of λ) because the population influx to an urban area results from urban environment improvement.

Second, we consider the manner in which the urban environment parameter λ affects L_x^{**}, L_y^{**}. By substituting (14.51) for (14.52) and transforming for L_u and by substituting it for L_u of Eqs. (14.70) and (14.71) and solving it for L_y, the following holds.

$$L_y = \frac{(L - L_x)\left(\frac{qb}{\lambda} - \frac{aq^2}{2cp^*}\right)}{\left(1 + \bar{l}_r\left(\frac{\bar{w}}{p^*\alpha}\right)^{\frac{1}{1-\alpha}}\right)\left(\bar{w} - \frac{aq}{2cp^*}\right)} \tag{14.77}$$

$$L_y = \frac{\left(qb - \frac{qq^2}{p^*c}\left(1 - \frac{aq - aq/2cp^*}{\bar{w} - aq/2cp^*}\right)\right)L_x + \frac{aq^2}{p^*c}L\left(1 - \frac{aq - aq/2cp^*}{\bar{w} - aq/2cp^*}\right)}{\frac{\bar{w}}{\alpha} - \left(1 + \bar{l}_r\left(\frac{\bar{w}}{p^*\alpha}\right)^{\frac{1}{1-\alpha}}\right)} \tag{14.78}$$

Figure 14.1 shows that L_x^{**}, L_y^{**} are obtained as an intersection of Eqs. (14.77) and (14.78). We analyze the effect of the urban environment parameter λ on the labor demand L_x^{**} for the intermediate goods sector and the labor demand L_x^{**} for the final goods sector using Fig. 14.1. Here, we assume L_x^{**}, L_y^{**} after the rise of λ to be $L_x^{**'}, L_y^{**'}$.

It is apparent from Fig. 14.1 that improvement of the urban environment decreases the labor demand L_x^{**} for the intermediate goods sector and the labor demand L_x^{**} for the final goods sector respectively. Moreover, one can readily

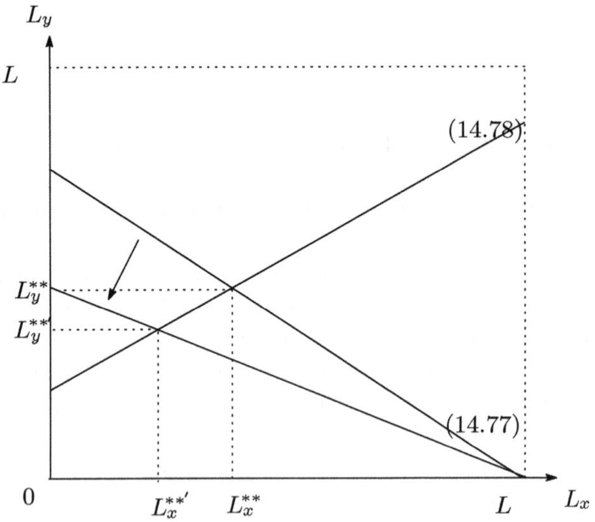

Fig. 14.1 Effects of urban environment improvement

confirm that the improvement of urban environment decreases the labor demand $\bar{l}_r M^{**}$ for the intermediate goods sector from Eq. (14.75).

In summary, improvement of the urban environment causes a population influx to an urban area. Therefore, it decreases the labor demand for the intermediate goods sector and increases the number of unemployed workers. However, if the number of unemployed workers increases, i.e., the ratio of the population with low wage increases, then the amount of supply of final goods decreases because of the reduction of final goods. Therefore, if the urban environment is improved, then the labor demand for the final goods sector and the intermediate goods sector decreases.

Theorem 14.7. *Improvement of the urban environment causes the population influx to an urban area and increases the number of unemployed workers. However, it decreases the labor demand for the final goods sector, the intermediate goods sector, and the waste collection sector.*

14.7 Comparative Analysis for Cases Where a Landfill Exists in an Urban Area or in a Rural Area

This section presents a policy implication related to the measures undertaken by the economically developing country government and support by the economically developed countries for the unemployment problems and the urban environmental problems caused by setting the landfill in an urban area through the comparative analysis of the market equilibrium under cases in which there are, respectively a landfill in an urban area and in a rural area.

Figure 14.2 presents equilibria obtained in cases in which a landfill exists in a rural area and in a rural area. Figure 14.2 portrays the addition of two straight lines of Eqs. (14.79) and (14.80) standing for the equilibrium in the case a landfill exists in a rural area to Fig. 14.1 standing for the equilibrium in the case a landfill exists in an urban area. Equations (14.79) and (14.80) are obtained by solving (14.62) for L_u and substituting it for Eqs. (14.63) and (14.64).

$$L_y = \frac{(L - L_x)qb}{\left(1 + \bar{l}_r\left(\frac{\bar{w}}{p^*\alpha}\right)^{\frac{1}{1-\alpha}}\right)\bar{w}} \tag{14.79}$$

$$L_y = \frac{qb}{\frac{\bar{w}}{\alpha} - \left(1 + \bar{l}_r\left(\frac{\bar{w}}{p^*\alpha}\right)^{\frac{1}{1-\alpha}}\right)} L_x \tag{14.80}$$

The positions of two straight lines of (14.77) and (14.79) depend on the size of urban environmental parameter λ. By comparing Eq. (14.77) with Eq. (14.79), the left side of Fig. 14.2 holds if λ is sufficiently large, whereas the right side of Fig. 14.2 holds if λ is sufficiently small: the following holds.

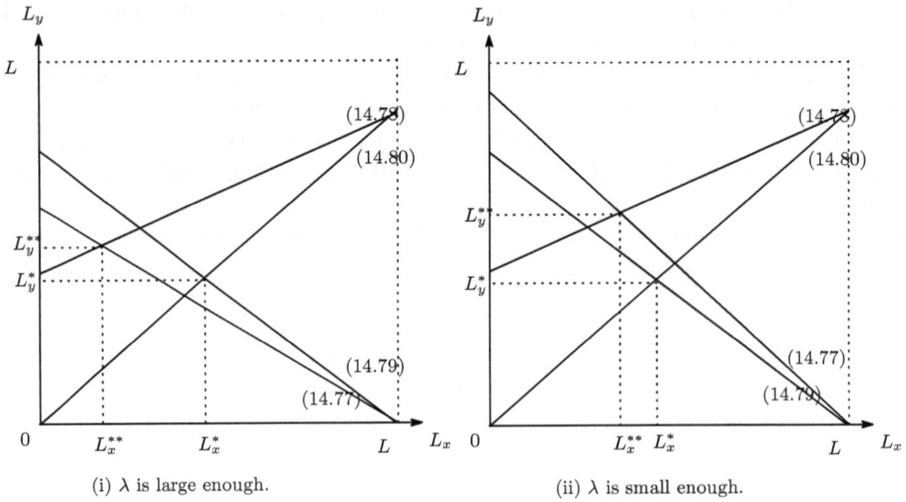

Fig. 14.2 Comparative analysis of cases in which a landfill exists in an urban area or in a rural area

$$\lambda > \frac{\bar{w}qb}{\bar{w}qb + (\bar{w} - qb)\frac{aq}{2cp^*}} \Rightarrow \textit{The left side of Fig. 14.2}$$

$$\lambda < \frac{\bar{w}qb}{\bar{w}qb + (\bar{w} - qb)\frac{aq}{2cp^*}} \Rightarrow \textit{The right side of Fig. 14.2}$$

From Fig. 14.2, one can confirm that $L_x^* > L_x^{**}, L_y^* < L_y^{**}$ irrespective of the size of λ: the labor demand for the intermediate goods sector in the case in which a landfill exists in a rural area is larger than that in the case in which a landfill exists in an urban area, whereas the labor demand for the final goods sector in the case in which a landfill exists in an urban area is greater than that in the case in which a landfill exists in a rural area. Moreover, $L_y^* < L_y^{**}$ holds. Therefore, $M^* < M^{**}$ holds from Eq. (14.49) and $L_r^* = \bar{l}_r M^* < L_r^{**} = \bar{l}_r M^{**}$ holds: the labor demand for the waste collection sector in the case in which a landfill exists in an urban area is greater than that in the case in which a landfill exists in a rural area. The large/small relation of the number of unemployed workers is not clear comparing Eq. (14.67) with Eq. (14.72), but from Eq. (14.76), the number of unemployed workers in the case in which a landfill exists in an urban area increases when λ grows. Therefore, the size relation of $L_u^* < L_u^{**}$ might hold: the number of unemployed workers in the case in which a landfill exists in an urban area might be larger than that in the case in which a landfill exists in a rural area if the urban environment is improved.

Theorem 14.8. *Labor demands for the final goods sector and the waste collection sector in the case in which a landfill exists in an urban area is greater than that in the case in which a landfill exists in a rural area: the labor demand for the* *intermediate goods sector shows an opposite relation. Moreover, the number of unemployed workers in the case in which a landfill exists in an urban area is larger than that in the case in which a landfill exists in a rural area if the urban environment is improved.*

Therefore, policy implications are the following. The unemployed workers increase the indirect utility by obtaining income from the recycling activities when a landfill exists in an urban area. Therefore, labor demand for the final goods sector and the waste collection sector and the number of unemployed workers increases because the charm of an urban area increases and the population influx to an urban area occurs when a landfill exists in an urban area. However, if the policy to improve the urban environment is conducted, then the charm of an urban area increases and the population influx to an urban area occurs, but the number of unemployed workers increases because the wages in urban area are fixed at higher levels and the number of workers employed in the final goods sector and the waste collection sector is limited when a landfill exists in an urban area. The demand for final goods decreases as the number of unemployment workers with the low wage increases. Therefore, labor demands for the final goods sector and the waste collection sector decrease conversely. When a landfill exists in an urban area, improving the urban environment decreases the number of workers in the final goods sector and in the waste collection sector who obtain the higher wage and who have higher indirect utility. It increases the number of unemployed workers who obtain the lower wage and has the lower indirect utility. Therefore, it decreases social welfare. Results show that the economically developing country government does not improve the urban environment but must raise the price of the intermediate goods and the final goods and increase the labor demand for the final goods sector when a landfill exists in an urban area.

14.8 Concluding Remarks

In this chapter, we considered both the problems of recycling wastes and unemployment in economically developing countries using the Harris and Todaro model, incorporating the recycling activities by actors in the recycling sector and informal sectors. We clarified how the subsidy policy for the recycling sector and supporting funds for informal sectors affected the level of social welfare in economically developing countries.

Results show that the raising of subsidy rates for the recycling sector improved the level of social welfare, whereas the rising of supporting funds for informal sector deteriorated. Therefore, raising subsidies for the recycling sector and economically developing them improves social welfare in economically developing countries. Supporting informal sectors has been playing an important role in recycling activities in economically developing countries. Therefore, the results presented herein can suggest policy implications for determining support for economically developing countries.

We considered the policies of economically developing countries and the support of economically developed countries through a comparison of outcomes obtained when the landfill is located in an urban area and when it is located in a rural area.

Results show that the labor demand for the final goods sector and the waste collection sector in the case in which a landfill in an urban area is greater than that in the case in which a landfill exists in a rural area, although the labor demand for the intermediate goods sector shows an opposite relation. However, the number of unemployed workers in the case in which a landfill exists in an urban area is greater than that in the case in which a landfill exists in a rural area if the urban environment is improved. Therefore, the economically developing country government must raise the price of intermediate goods and increase the labor demand for the final goods sector when a landfill exists in an urban area.

However, some points should be revisited in future analyses. First, we have argued this point under the assumption of an open economy. It is necessary to compare the results of analyses under the assumption of an open economy with those obtained under the assumption of a closed economy. Second, we have examined a subsidy for the recycling sector and supporting funds for the informal sector exogenously. Therefore, these were fixed parameters. Future research must necessarily an derive optimal subsidy rate and an optimal level of supporting funds given the budget constraint for the government of an economically developing country. Third, it is necessary to consider the imports of recyclable resources from other countries, as explained by Daitoh and Yanase [4]. These points remain as future tasks for our research. Fourth, we have examined intermediate goods (virgin resources) and the recyclable resources to be homogeneous. We should conduct analyses considering heterogeneity between the intermediate goods (virgin resources) and recyclable resources.

References

1. Chao, C., Kervliet, J. R., & Yu, E. S. H. (2000). Environmental preservation, sectoral unemployment, and trade in resources. *Review of Development Economics, 4*, 39–50.
2. Corden, W. M., & Findlay, R. (1975). Urban unemployment, intersectoral capital mobility and development policy. *Economica, 42*(165), 59–78.
3. Daitoh, I. (2003). Environmental protection and urban unemployment: Environmental policy reform in a polluted dualistic economy. *Review of Development Economics, 7*, 496–509.
4. Daitoh, I., & Yanase, A. (2009). Waste recycling and international trade in a dualistic economy. Spring Meeting of Japan Association for Applied Economics, Mimeo.
5. Dean, J. M., & Gangopadhyay, S. (1997). Export bans, environmental protection, and unemployment. *Review of Development Economics, 1*, 324–336.
6. Fukuyama, H. (2010). Recycling business and unemployment of developing country in the Harris-Todaro model. *Keizaigaku-Ronshu, 74*, 59–71.
7. Fukuyama, H. (2010). An economic analysis on the optimal location of waste processing facilities and recycling in developing country. *Keizaigaku-Ronshu, 75*, 27–40.

8. Fukuyama, H., & Naito, T. (2007). Unemployment, trans-boundary pollution, and environmental policy in a dualistic economy. *Review of Urban and Regional Development Studies, 19*(2), 154–172.
9. Harris, J. R., & Todaro, M. P. (1970). Migration, unemployment and development: A two-sector analysis. *American Economic Review, 60*(1), 126–142.
10. Ikeguchi, T. (2006). Disposal of wastes in developing countries: Current status and issues, solutions. Presentation Material of 2006 Special Speech of Center for Environmental Science in Saitama, Mimeo
11. Medina, M. (2007). 3R and sustainable consumption and production in developing countries: Activities through Informal sector. Presentation Material of 2006 International Symposium of Kansai Research Centre of Institute for Global Environmental Strategies, Mimeo

Further Reading

1. Fujita, M. (1989). *Urban economic theory: Land use and city size*. Cambridge: Cambridge University Press.
2. Fujita, M., Krugman, P. R., & Venables, A. (2001). *The spatial economy: Cities, regions, and international trade*. Cambridge: MIT.
3. Kolstad, C. (1999). *Environmental economics*. New York: Oxford University Press.
4. Ohno, T., Kawasaki, A., & Naito, T. (2015). Optimal pollution tax and mixed oligopoly in closed versus integrated economy. *Bangladesh Journal of Regional Science*, 2(1), 1–12.

T. Naito (ed.), *Sustainable Growth and Development in a Regional Economy*,
New Frontiers in Regional Science: Asian Perspectives 13,
DOI 10.1007/978-4-431-55294-9

Index

T. Naito (ed.), *Sustainable Growth and Development in a Regional Economy*,
New Frontiers in Regional Science: Asian Perspectives 13,
DOI 10.1007/978-4-431-55294-9

MIX
Papier aus verantwortungsvollen Quellen
Paper from responsible sources
FSC® C105338

FSC
www.fsc.org

If you have any concerns about our products,
you can contact us on
ProductSafety@springernature.com

In case Publisher is established outside the EU,
the EU authorized representative is:
Springer Nature Customer Service Center GmbH
Europaplatz 3, 69115 Heidelberg, Germany

Printed by Libri Plureos GmbH
in Hamburg, Germany